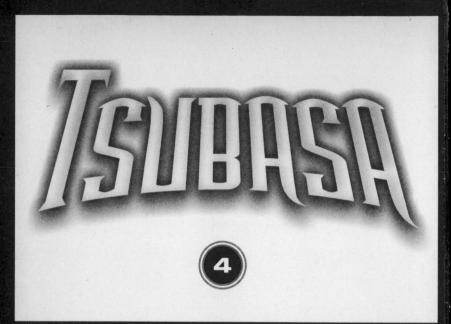

TSUBASA

4

CLAMP

TRANSLATED AND ADAPTED BY
William Flanagan

LETTERED BY
Dana Hayward

BALLANTINE BOOKS • NEW YORK

Tsubasa crosses over with *xxxHOLiC*. Although it isn't necessary to read *xxxHOLiC* to understand the events in *Tsubasa*, you'll get to see the same events from different perspectives if you read both!

Tsubasa, Volume 4 is a work of fiction. Names, characters, places, and incidents are the products of the author's imagination or are used fictitiously. Any resemblance to actual events, locales, or persons, living or dead, is entirely coincidental.

2005 Del Rey Books Trade Paperback Edition

Published in the United States by Del Rey Books, an imprint of The Random House Publishing Group, a division of Random House, Inc., New York.

Del Rey is a registered trademark and the Del Rey colophon is a trademark of Random House, Inc.

First published in serialization and subsequently published in book form by Kodansha Ltd. Tokyo in 2004.

ISBN 0-345-47791-X

Printed in the United States of America

Del Rey Books website address: www.delreymanga.com

9 8 7 6

Lettered by Dana Hayward

Contents

Honorifics

Throughout the Del Rey Manga books, you will find Japanese honorifics left intact in the translations. For those not familiar with how the Japanese use honorifics, and more important, how they differ from American honorifics, we present this brief overview.

Politeness has always been a critical facet of Japanese culture. Ever since the feudal era, when Japan was a highly stratified society, use of honorifics — which can be defined as polite speech that indicates relationship or status — has played an essential role in the Japanese language. When addressing someone in Japanese, an honorific usually takes the form of a suffix attached to one's name (example: "Asuna-san"), or as a title at the end of one's name or in place of the name itself (example: "Negi-sensei," or simply "Sensei!").

Honorifics can be expressions of respect or endearment. In the context of manga and anime, honorifics give insight into the nature of the relationship between characters. Many translations into English leave out these important honorifics, and therefore distort the "feel" of the original Japanese. Because Japanese honorifics contain nuances that English honorifics lack, it is our policy at Del Rey not to translate them. Here, instead, is a guide to some of the honorifics you may encounter in Del Rey Manga.

-san: This is the most common honorific, and is equivalent to Mr., Miss, Ms., Mrs., etc. It is the all-purpose honorific and can be used in any situation where politeness is required.

-sama: This is one level higher than "-san." It is used to confer great respect.

-dono: This comes from the word "tono," which means "lord." It is an even higher level than "-sama," and confers utmost respect.

-kun: This suffix is used at the end of boys' names to express familiarity or endearment. It is also sometimes used by men among friends, or when addressing someone younger or of a lower station.

-chan: This is used to express endearment, mostly toward girls. It is also used for little boys, pets, and even among lovers. It gives a sense of childish cuteness.

Bozu: This is an informal way to refer to a boy, similar to the English term "kid" or "squirt."

Sempai: This title suggests that the addressee is one's "senior" in a group or organization. It is most often used in a school setting, where underclassmen refer to their upperclassmen as "sempai." It can also be used in the workplace, such as when a newer employee addresses an employee who has seniority in the company.

Kohai: This is the opposite of "sempai," and is used toward underclassmen in school or newcomers in the workplace. It connotes that the addressee is of lower station.

Sensei: Literally meaning "one who has come before," this title is used for teachers, doctors, or masters of any profession or art.

-[blank]: Usually forgotten in these lists, but perhaps the most significant difference between Japanese and English. The lack of honorific means that the speaker has permission to address the person in a very intimate way. Usually, only family, spouses, or very close friends have this kind of permission. Known as *yobisute*, it can be gratifying when someone who has earned the intimacy starts to call one by one's name without an honorific. But when that intimacy hasn't been earned, it can also be very insulting.

Previously in *Tsubasa* . . .

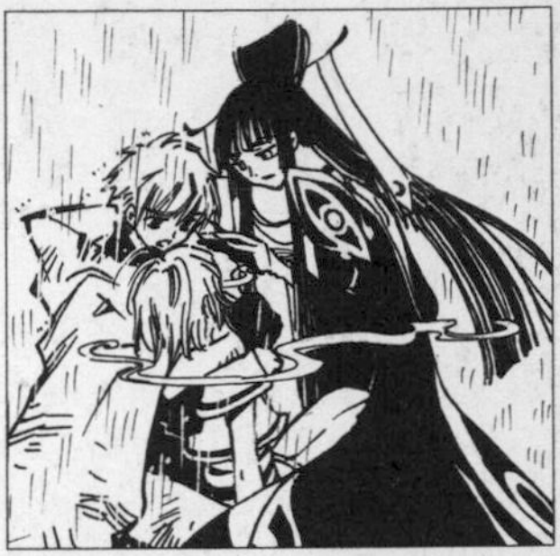

Brought together by Yûko, the Space-Time Witch, Fai, Kurogane, and Syaoran travel from world to world. While each has his own reasons for being on the journey, they follow Syaoran in his quest to locate and retrieve the lost pieces of Sakura's soul. Each piece takes the form of a feather, and as they return them to Sakura, she regains a bit of her strength and memory. Lost forever, however, is her memory of Syaoran, her one true love. For this was the price Syaoran had to pay to make the journey to save Sakura—that Sakura lose all memory of him and their time together.

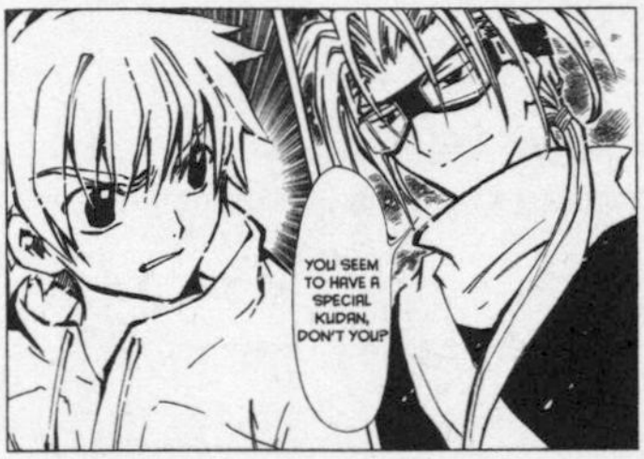
YOU SEEM TO HAVE A SPECIAL KUDAN, DON'T YOU?

Mokona travels with them as well, to guide them from world to world, and find the lost feathers.

Their first stop brought them to the Hanshin Republic, where Syaoran gained the strange power of his Kudan. Here they encountered Sorata and Arashi, who gave them food and shelter. Finding and returning this world's feather to Sakura enabled her to wake from her coma.

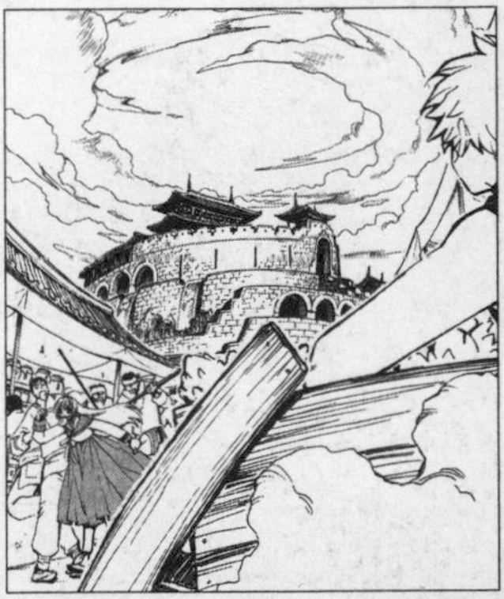

Mokona next brought Syaoran and friends to the town of Ryonfi in the land of Koryo, ruled by the ruthless Ryanban (actually a term referring to corrupt leaders of sixteenth-century Korea). Here they met Chu'nyan, daughter of the town's Shinban (a kind of wizard). They helped Chu'nyan defend the town against the Ryanban and his son, then realized that the Ryanban held one of Sakura's feathers. Together, Syaoran, Fai, and Kurogane attacked the castle to retrieve the feather, but Syaoran became separated from Fai and Kurogane . . .

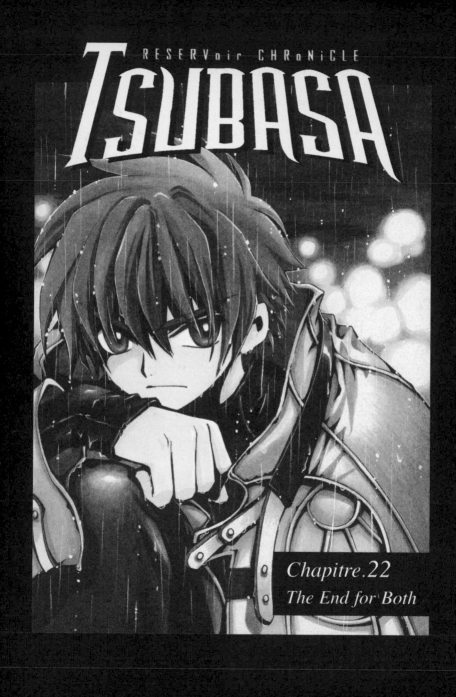

RESERVoir CHRoNiCLE

TSUBASA

Chapitre.22
The End for Both

ツバサ
RESERVoir CHRoNiCLE

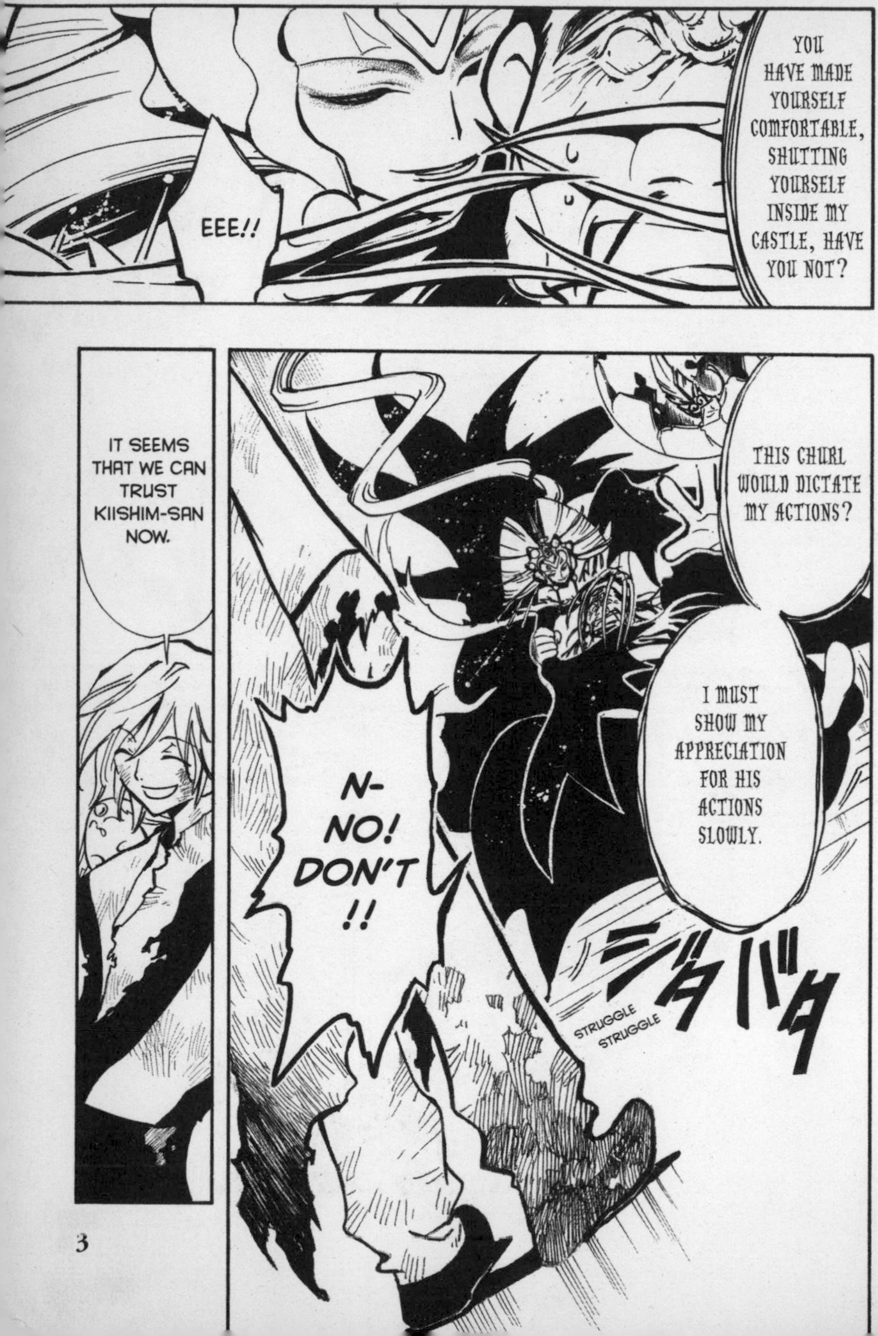
YOU HAVE MADE YOURSELF COMFORTABLE, SHUTTING YOURSELF INSIDE MY CASTLE, HAVE YOU NOT?
EEE!!
THIS CHURL WOULD DICTATE MY ACTIONS?
I MUST SHOW MY APPRECIATION FOR HIS ACTIONS SLOWLY.
N-NO! DON'T!!
STRUGGLE STRUGGLE
IT SEEMS THAT WE CAN TRUST KIISHIM-SAN NOW.

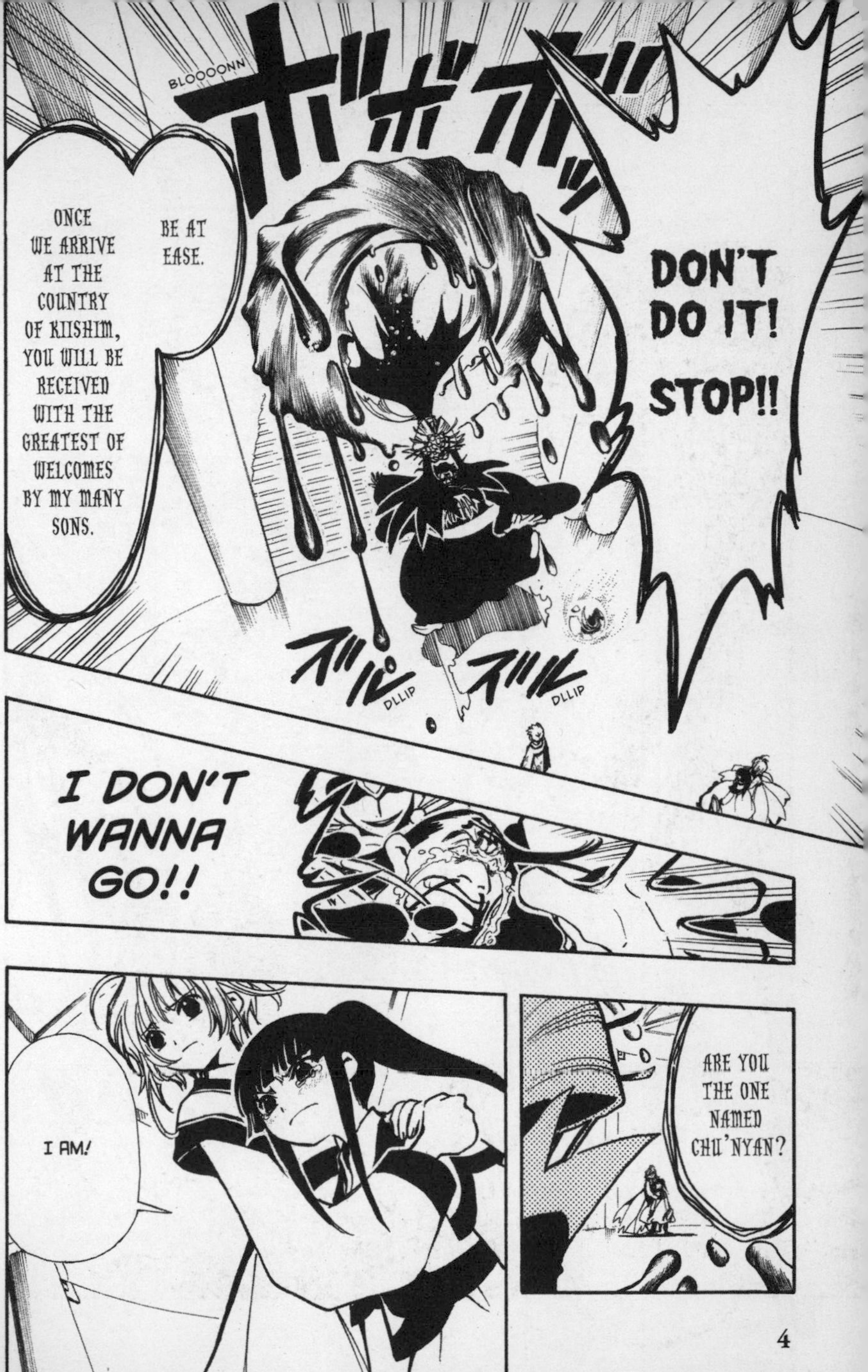
BLOOOONN
DON'T DO IT! STOP!!
BE AT EASE.
ONCE WE ARRIVE AT THE COUNTRY OF KIISHIM, YOU WILL BE RECEIVED WITH THE GREATEST OF WELCOMES BY MY MANY SONS.
DLLIP
DLLIP
I DON'T WANNA GO!!
ARE YOU THE ONE NAMED CHU'NYAN?
I AM!

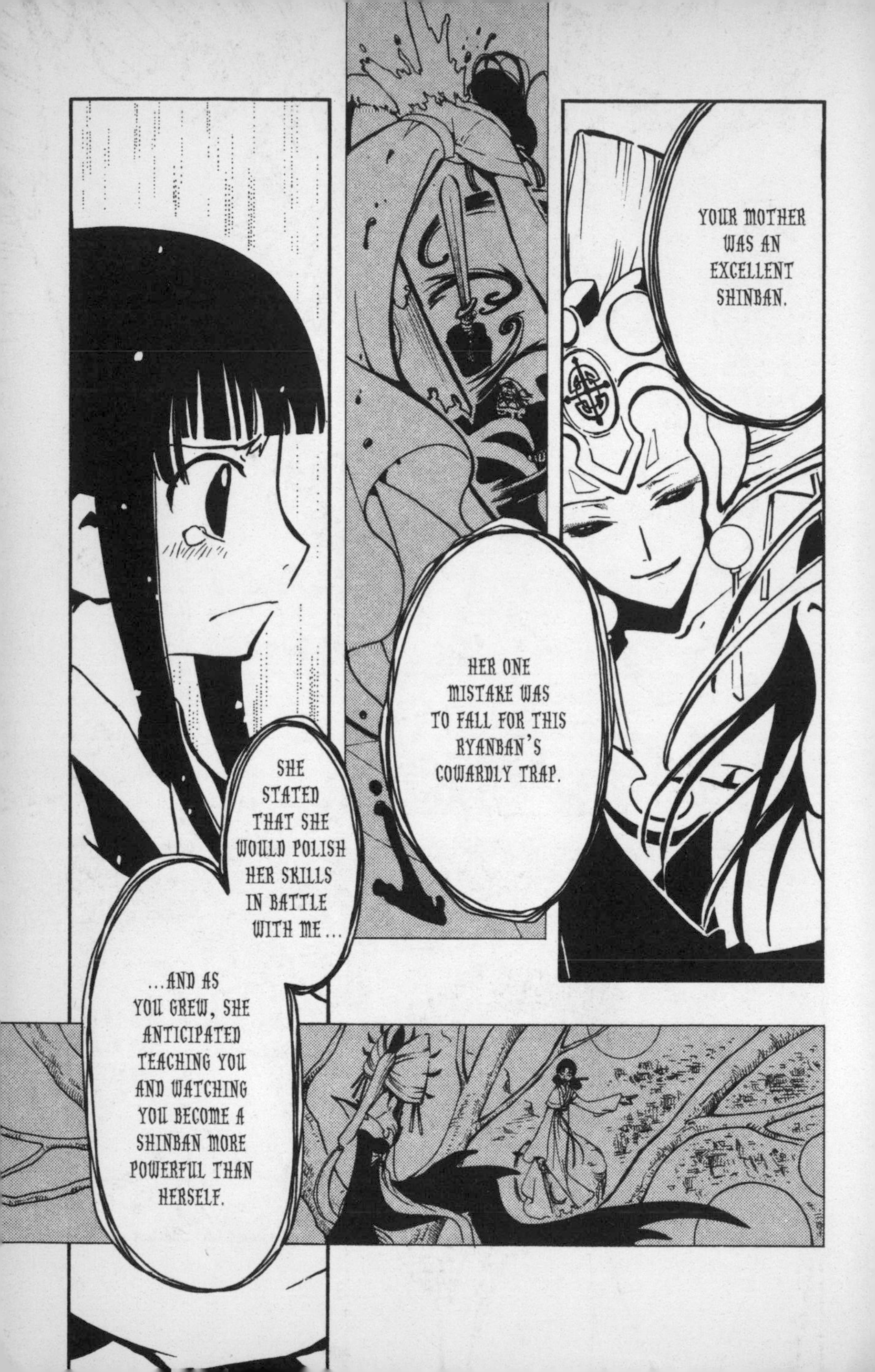
YOUR MOTHER WAS AN EXCELLENT SHINBAN.
HER ONE MISTAKE WAS TO FALL FOR THIS RYANBAN'S COWARDLY TRAP.
SHE STATED THAT SHE WOULD POLISH HER SKILLS IN BATTLE WITH ME...
...AND AS YOU GREW, SHE ANTICIPATED TEACHING YOU AND WATCHING YOU BECOME A SHINBAN MORE POWERFUL THAN HERSELF.

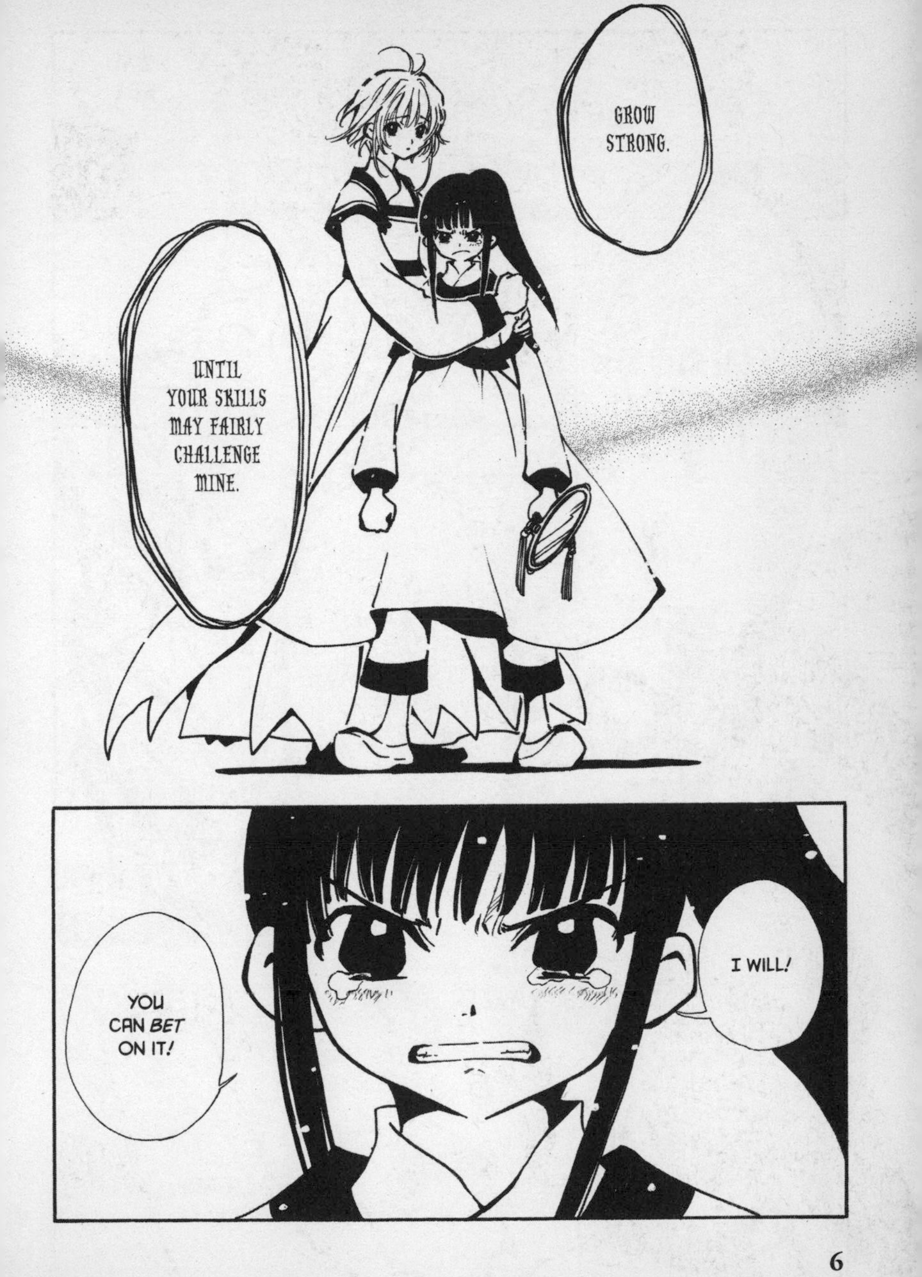
GROW STRONG.
UNTIL YOUR SKILLS MAY FAIRLY CHALLENGE MINE.
I WILL!
YOU CAN *BET* ON IT!

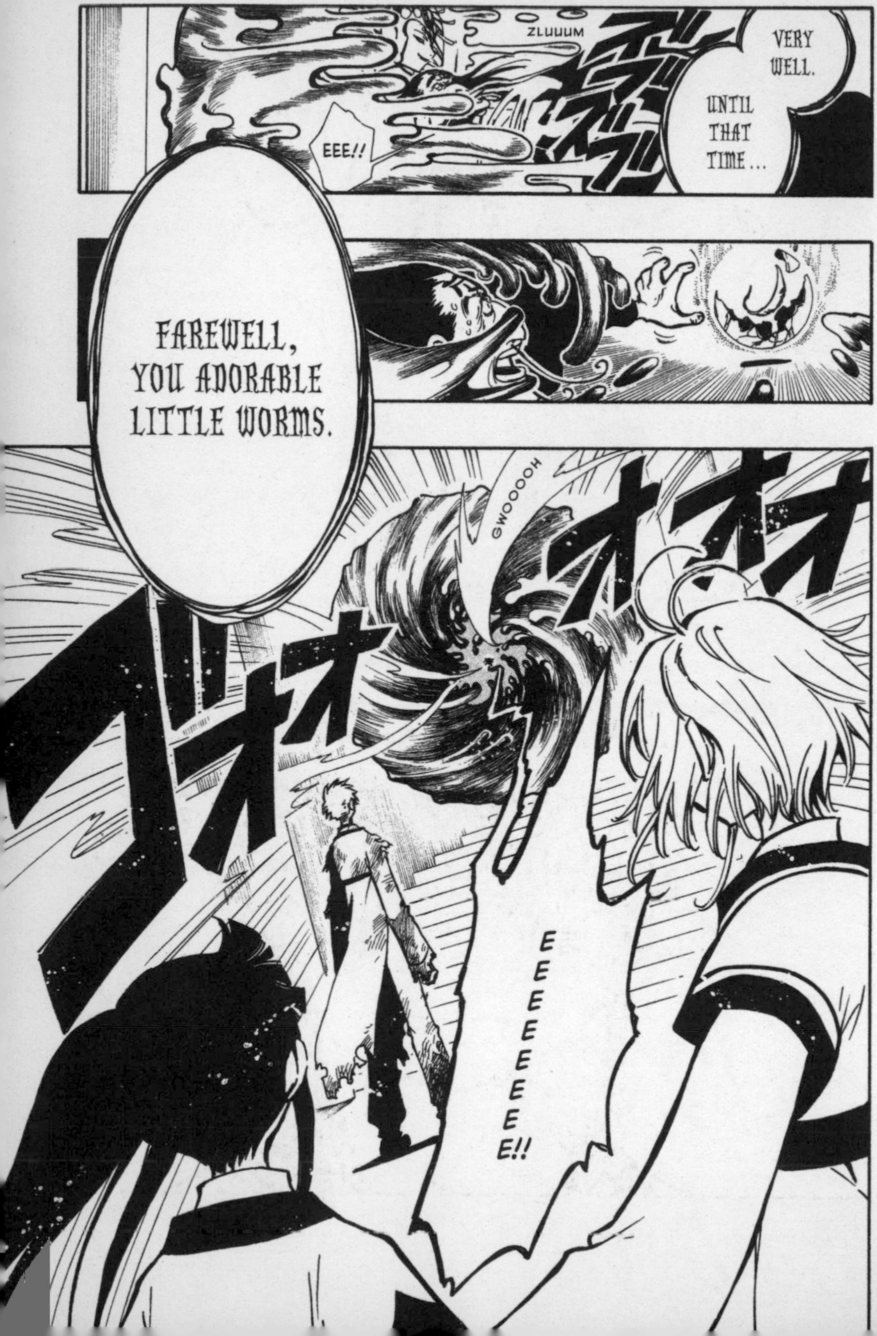
VERY WELL.
UNTIL THAT TIME...
ZLUUUM
EEE!!
FAREWELL, YOU ADORABLE LITTLE WORMS.
GWOOOOH
EEEEEEEEEE!!

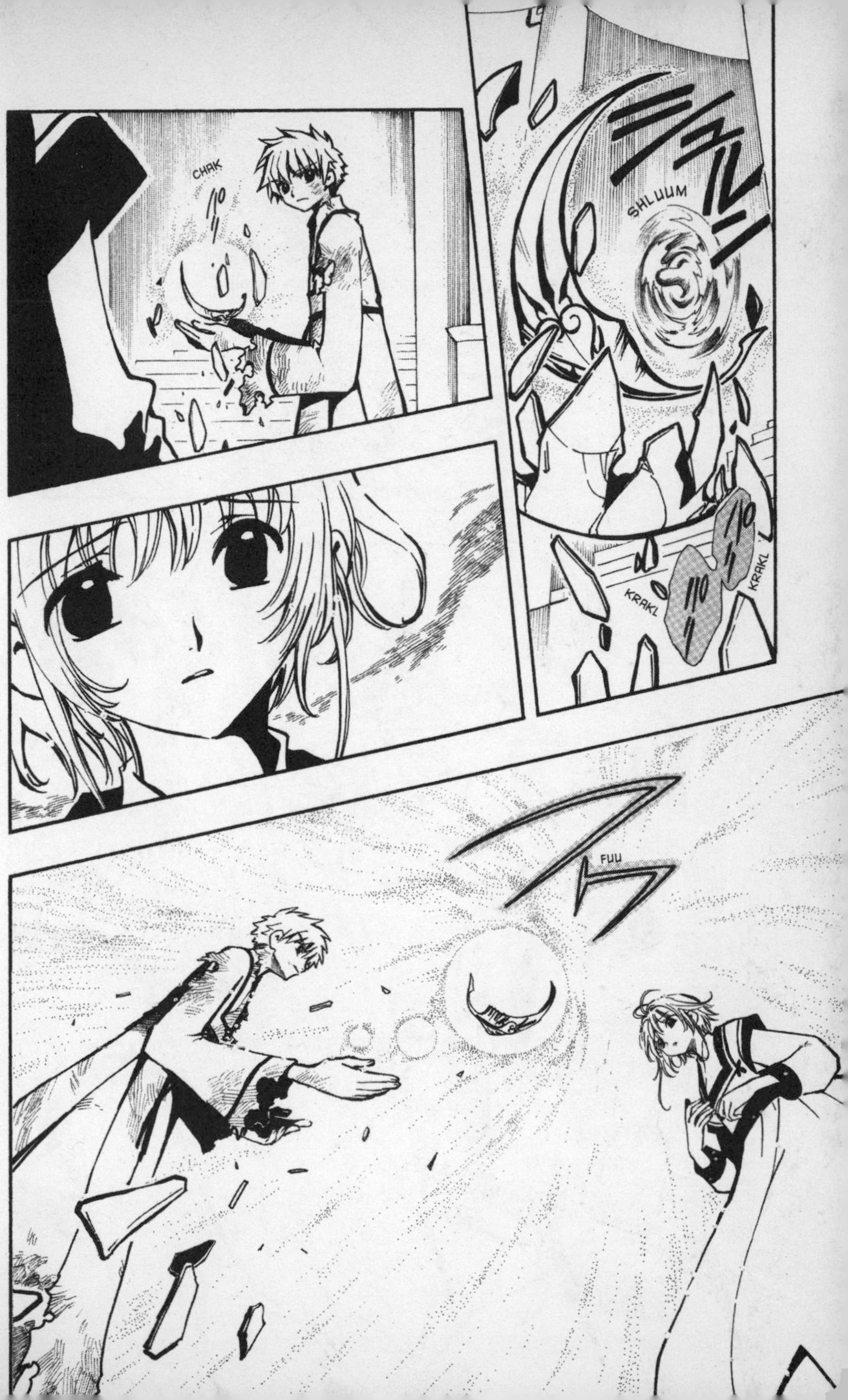
SHLUUM
KRAKL
KRAKL
CHAK
FUU

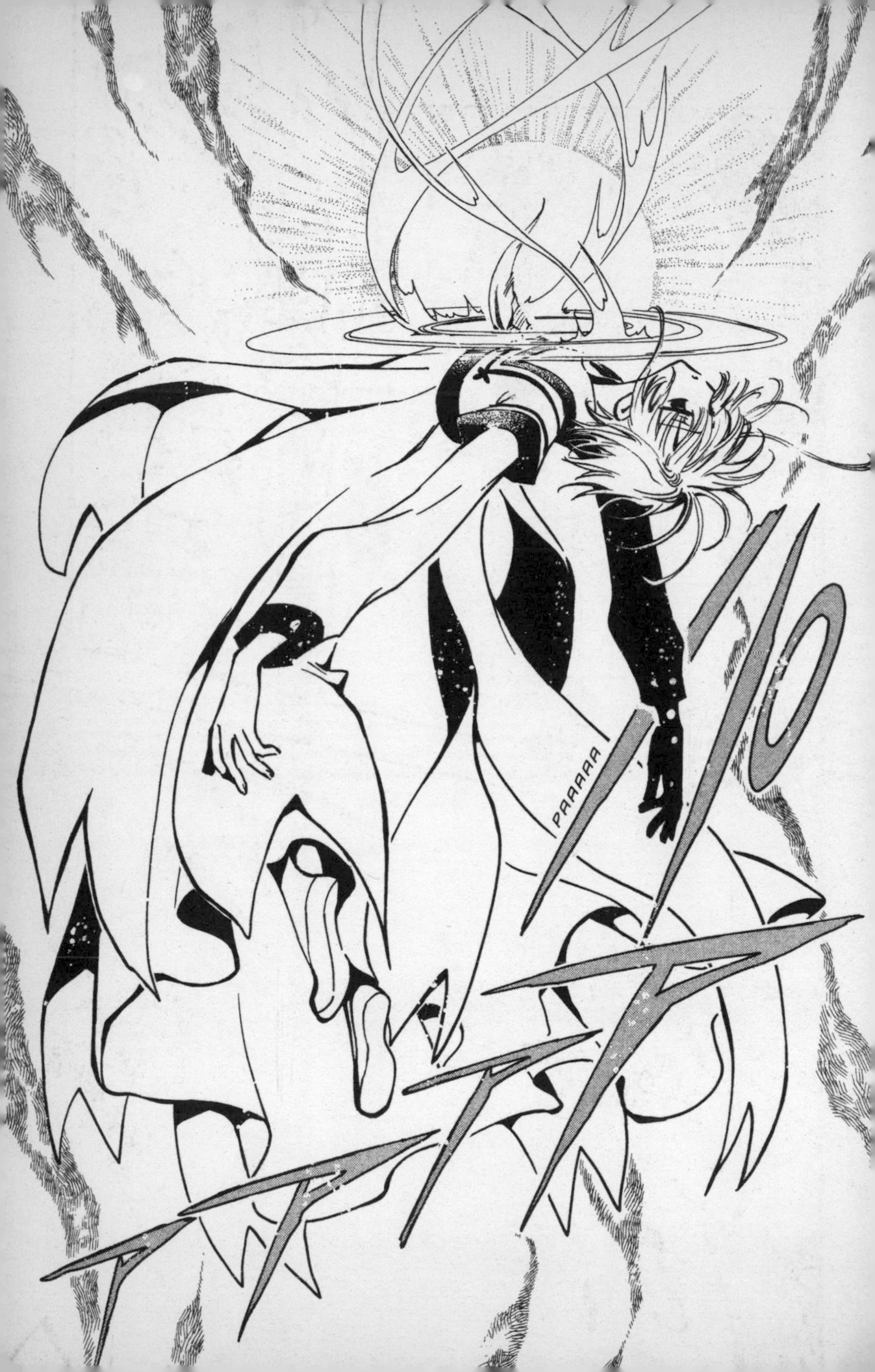
PAAAAA

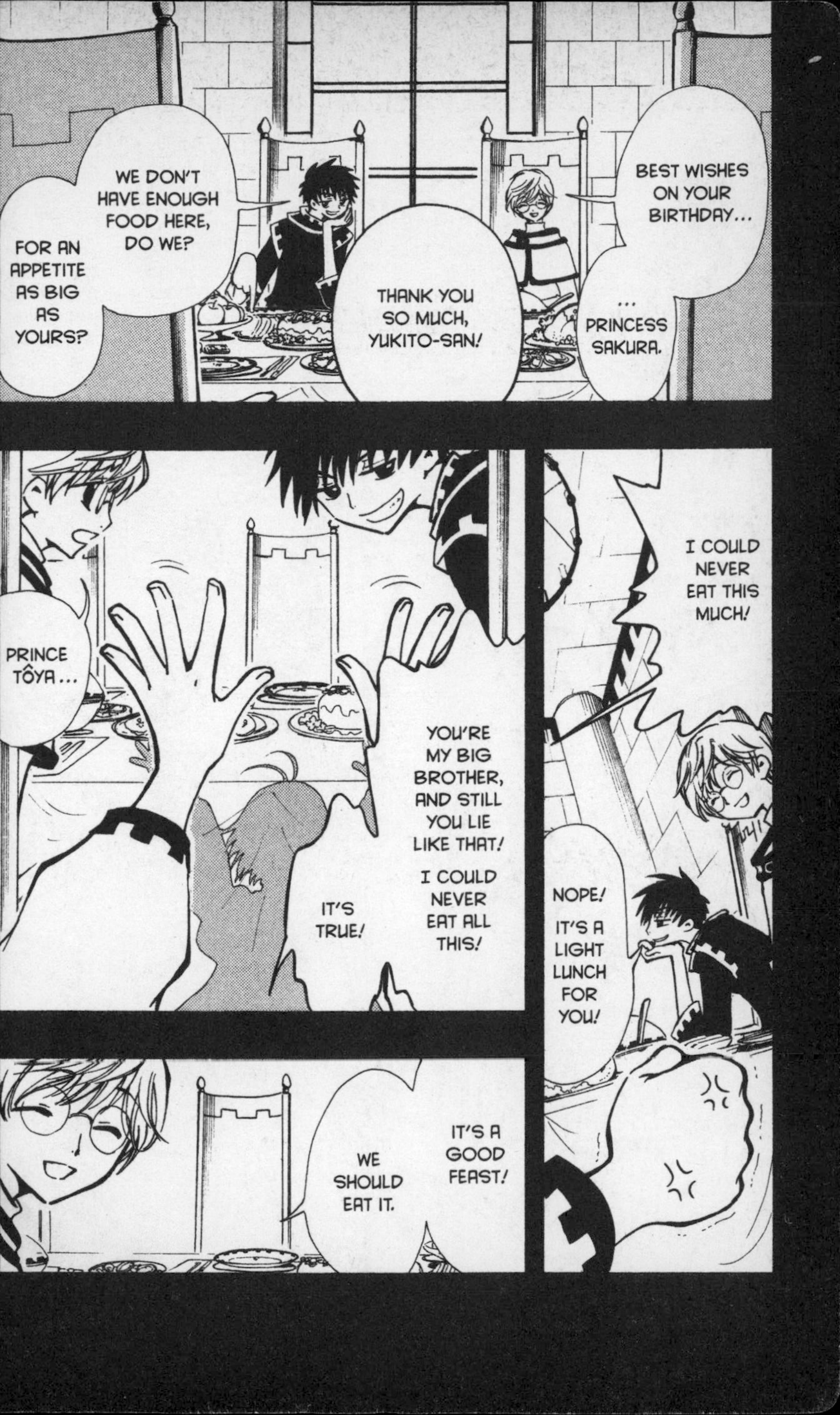
BEST WISHES ON YOUR BIRTHDAY...
...PRINCESS SAKURA.
THANK YOU SO MUCH, YUKITO-SAN!
WE DON'T HAVE ENOUGH FOOD HERE, DO WE?
FOR AN APPETITE AS BIG AS YOURS?
I COULD NEVER EAT THIS MUCH!
NOPE!
IT'S A LIGHT LUNCH FOR YOU!
YOU'RE MY BIG BROTHER, AND STILL YOU LIE LIKE THAT!
I COULD NEVER EAT ALL THIS!
IT'S TRUE!
PRINCE TÔYA...
IT'S A GOOD FEAST!
WE SHOULD EAT IT.

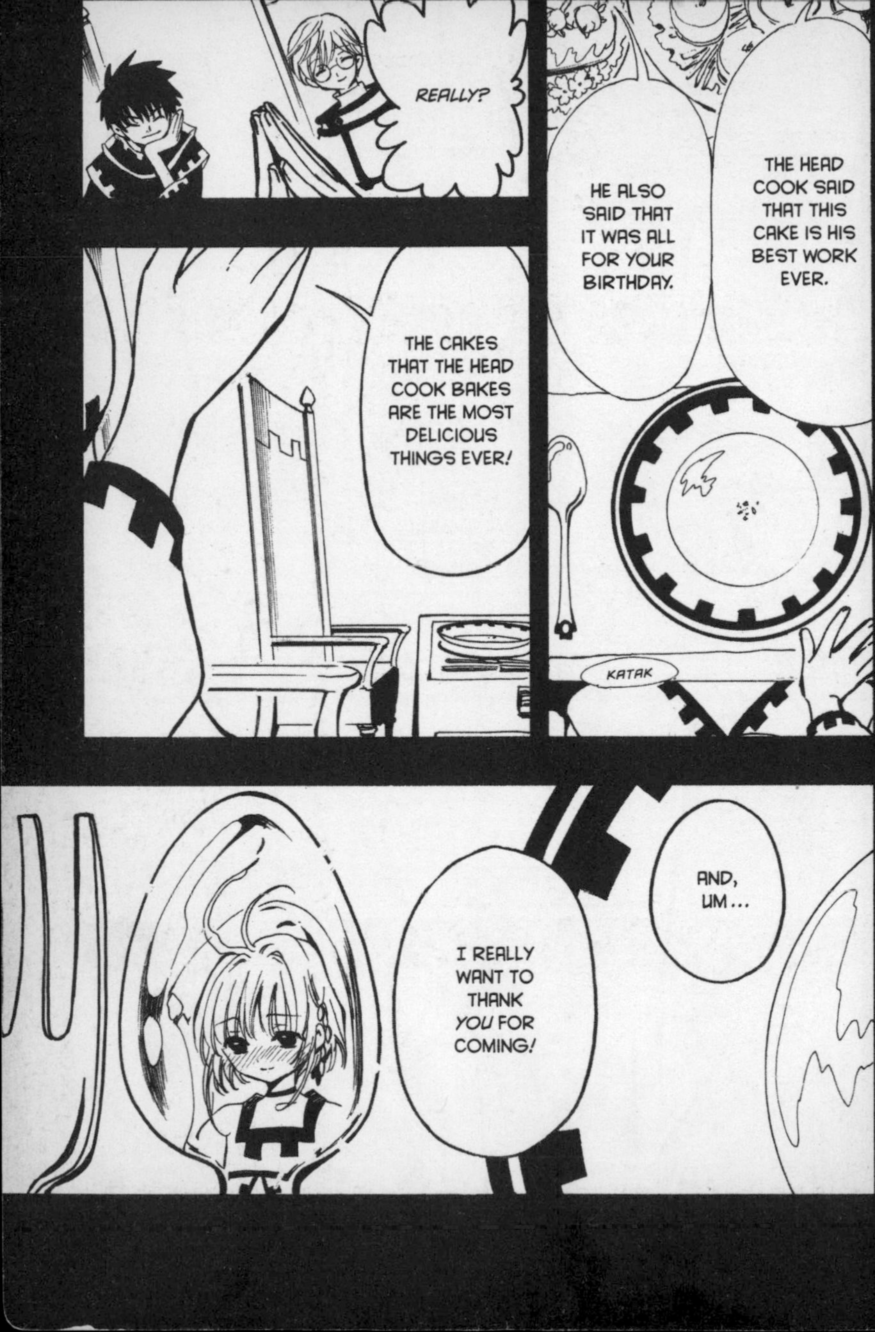
THE HEAD COOK SAID THAT THIS CAKE IS HIS BEST WORK EVER.
HE ALSO SAID THAT IT WAS ALL FOR YOUR BIRTHDAY.
KATAK
REALLY?
THE CAKES THAT THE HEAD COOK BAKES ARE THE MOST DELICIOUS THINGS EVER!
AND, UM...
I REALLY WANT TO THANK *YOU* FOR COMING!

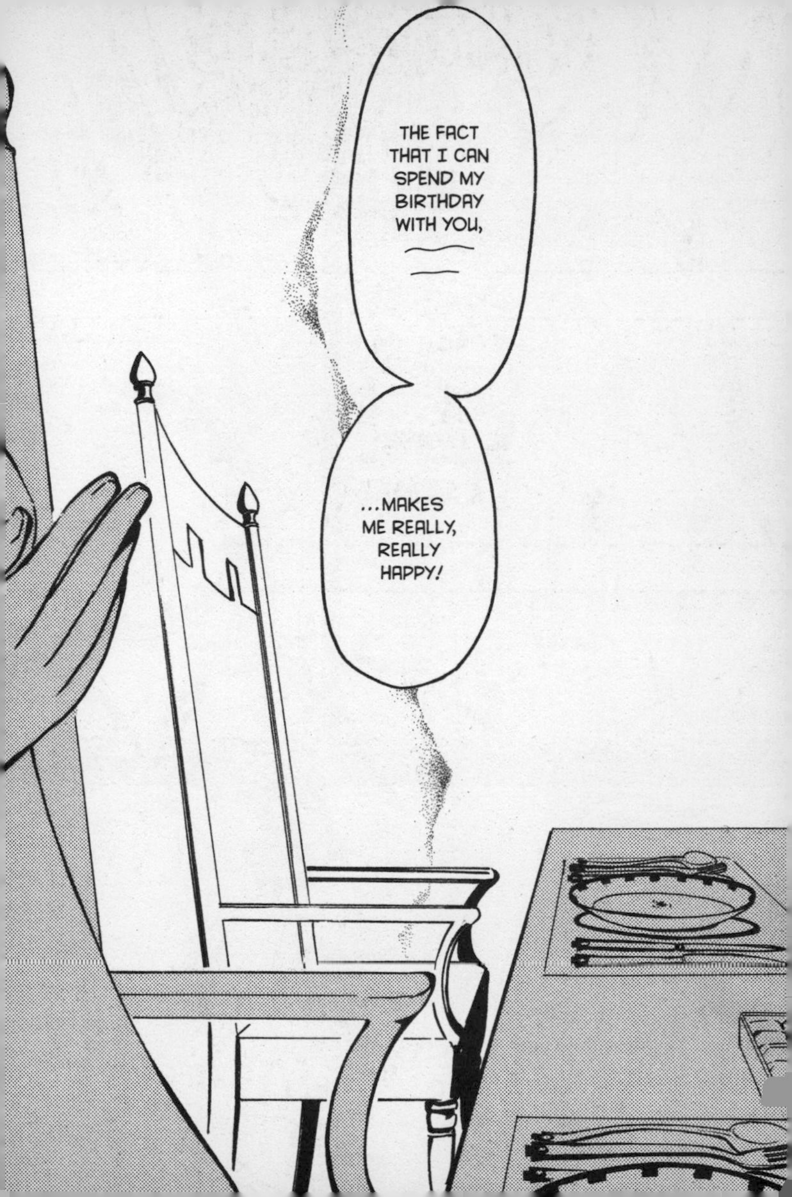
THE FACT THAT I CAN SPEND MY BIRTHDAY WITH YOU,
...MAKES ME REALLY, REALLY HAPPY!

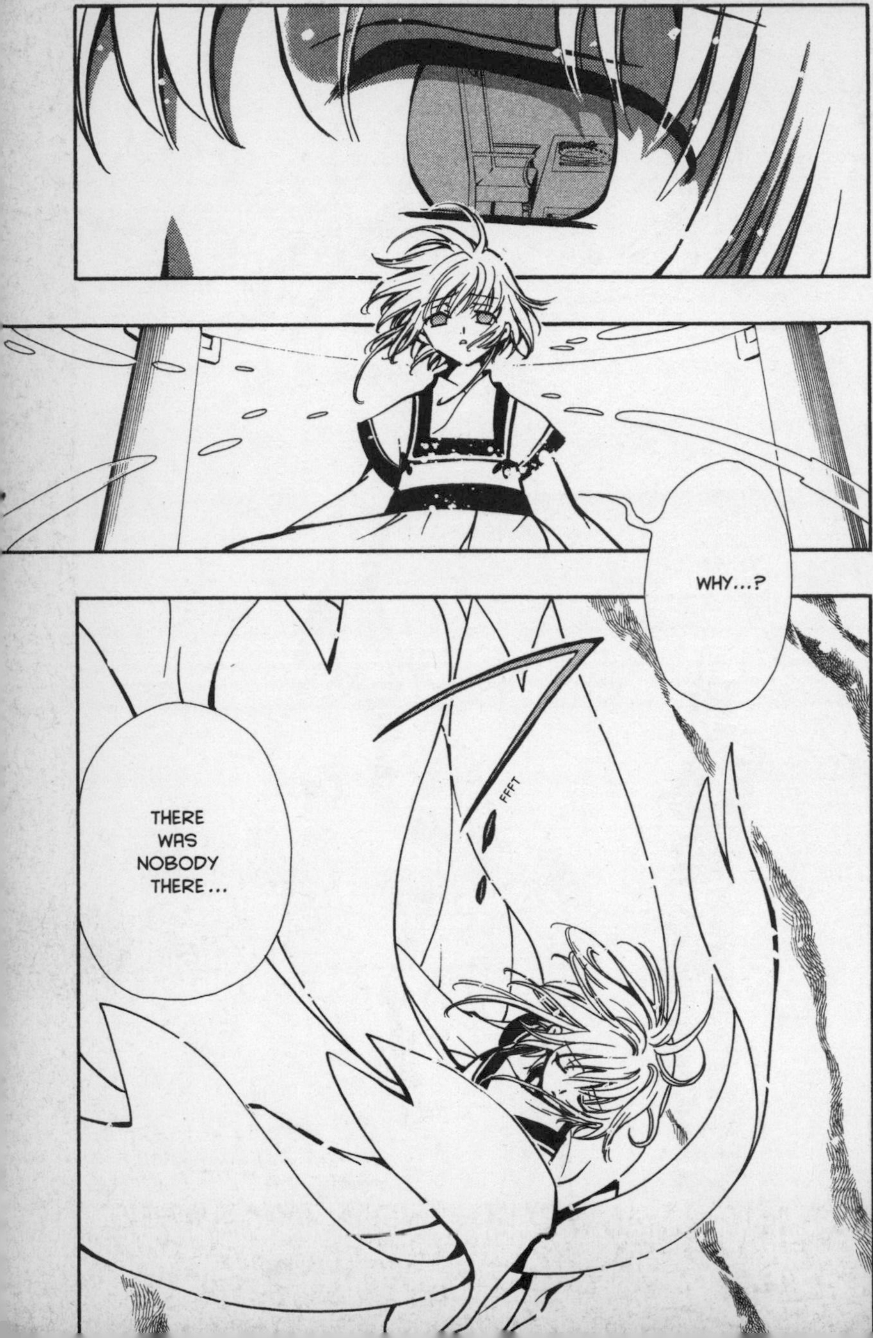
WHY...?
FFFT
THERE WAS NOBODY THERE...

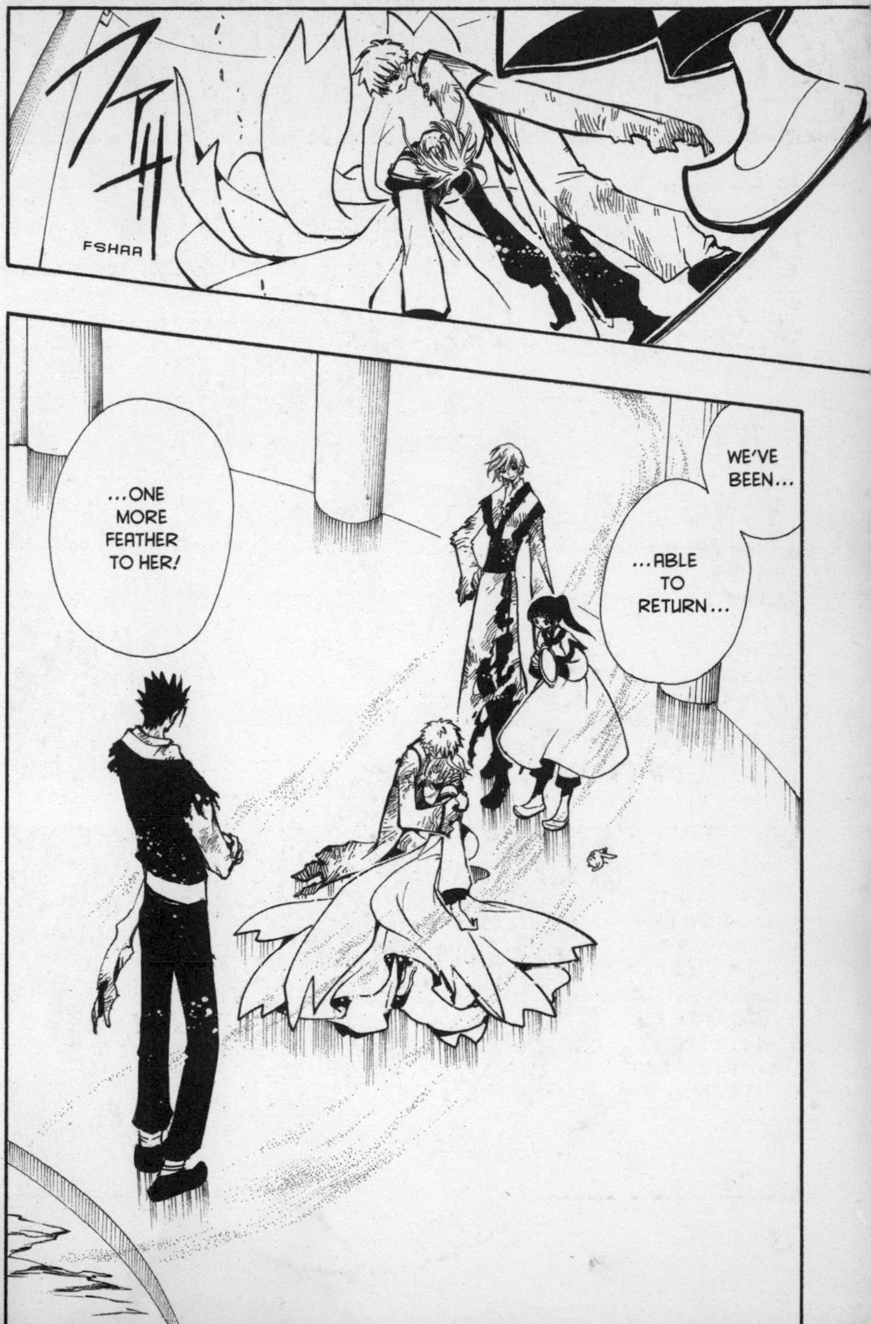
FSHAA
WE'VE BEEN...
...ABLE TO RETURN...
...ONE MORE FEATHER TO HER!

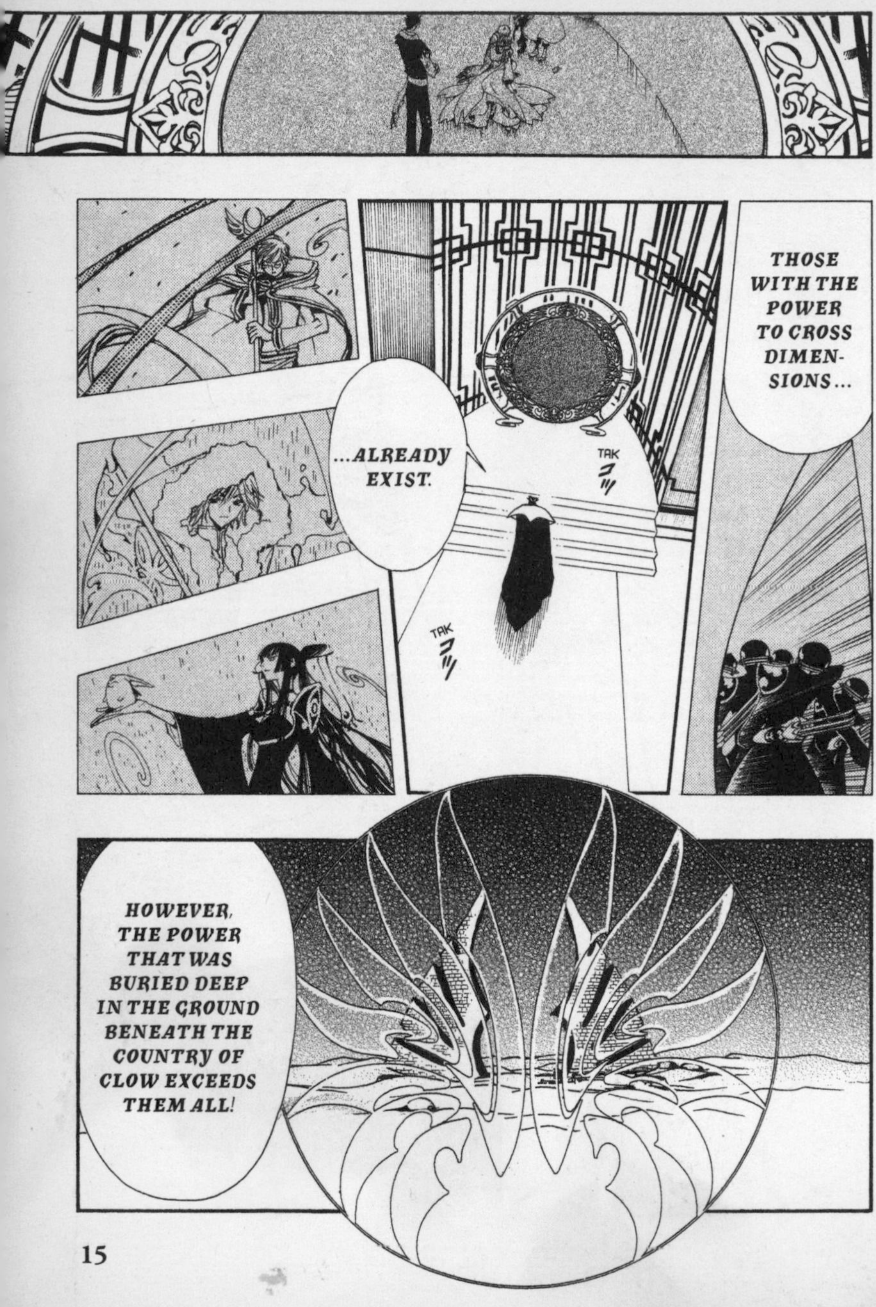
THOSE WITH THE POWER TO CROSS DIMEN-SIONS...
...ALREADY EXIST.
TAK
TAK
HOWEVER, THE POWER THAT WAS BURIED DEEP IN THE GROUND BENEATH THE COUNTRY OF CLOW EXCEEDS THEM ALL!

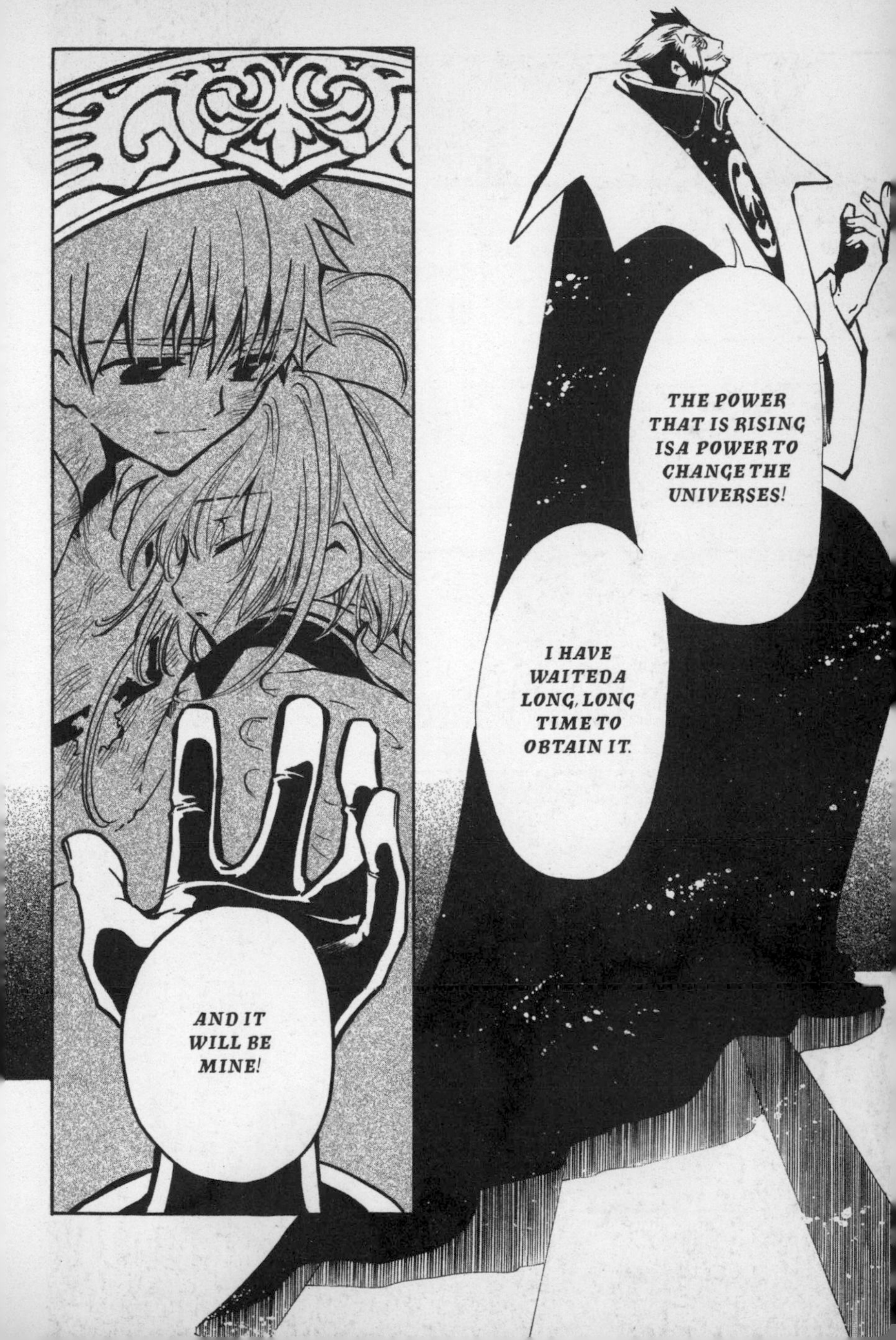
THE POWER THAT IS RISING ISA POWER TO CHANGE THE UNIVERSES!
I HAVE WAITEDA LONG, LONG TIME TO OBTAIN IT.
AND IT WILL BE MINE!

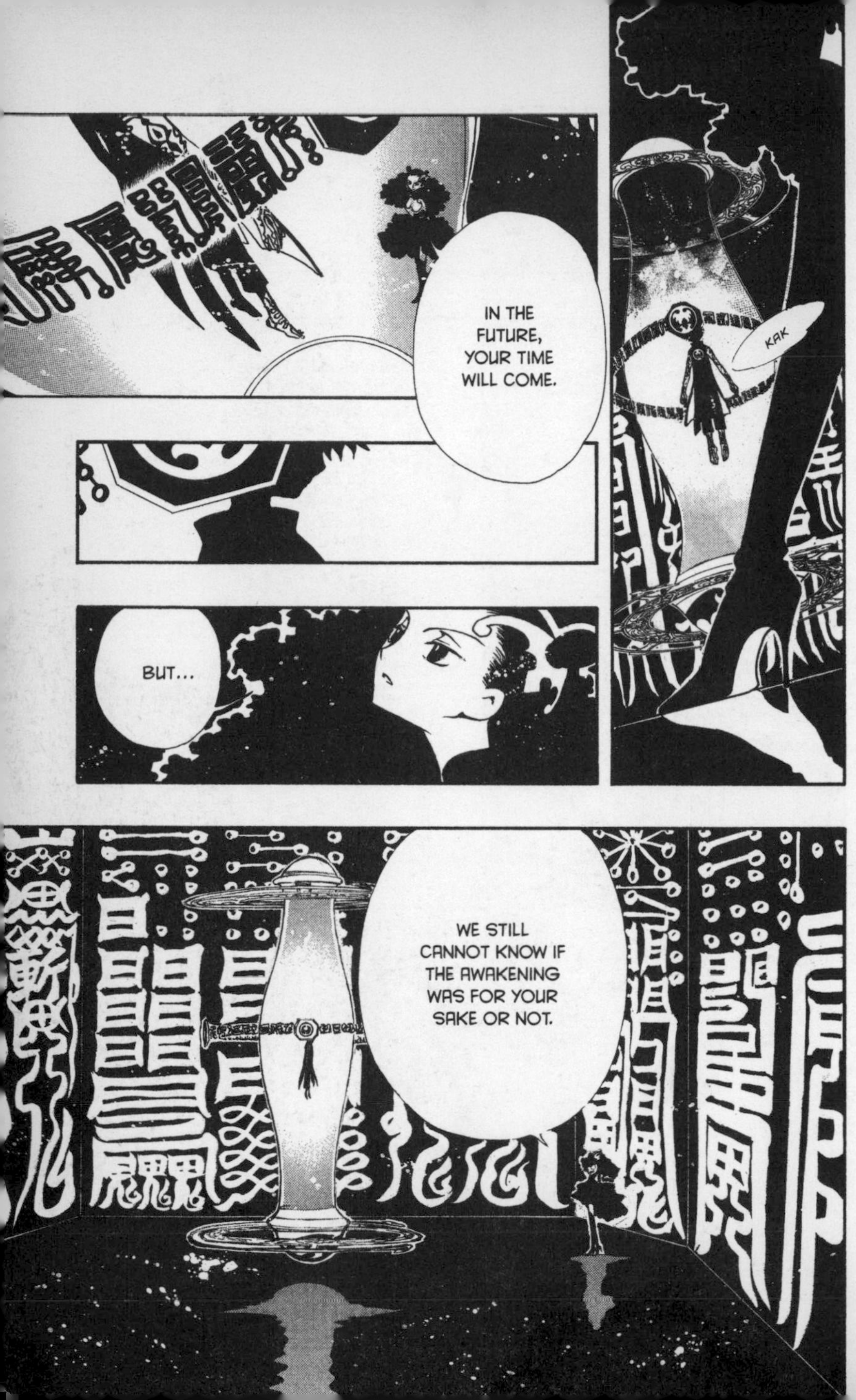
KAK
IN THE FUTURE, YOUR TIME WILL COME.
BUT...
WE STILL CANNOT KNOW IF THE AWAKENING WAS FOR YOUR SAKE OR NOT.

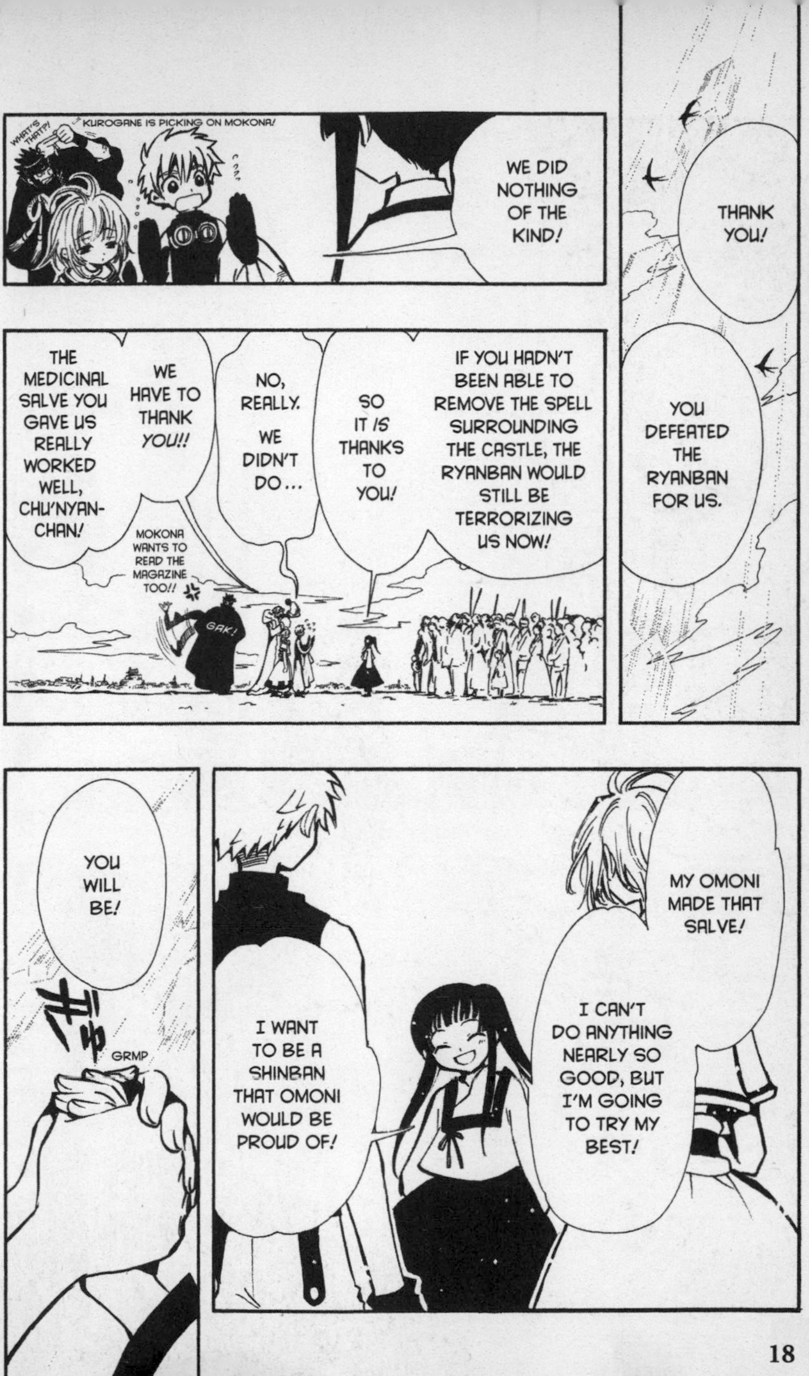
THANK YOU!
YOU DEFEATED THE RYANBAN FOR US.
WE DID NOTHING OF THE KIND!
KUROGANE IS PICKING ON MOKONA!
WHAT'S THAT?!
IF YOU HADN'T BEEN ABLE TO REMOVE THE SPELL SURROUNDING THE CASTLE, THE RYANBAN WOULD STILL BE TERRORIZING US NOW!
SO IT *IS* THANKS TO YOU!
NO, REALLY. WE DIDN'T DO...
WE HAVE TO THANK *YOU!!*
THE MEDICINAL SALVE YOU GAVE US REALLY WORKED WELL, CHU'NYAN-CHAN!
MOKONA WANTS TO READ THE MAGAZINE TOO!!
GAK!
MY OMONI MADE THAT SALVE!
I CAN'T DO ANYTHING NEARLY SO GOOD, BUT I'M GOING TO TRY MY BEST!
I WANT TO BE A SHINBAN THAT OMONI WOULD BE PROUD OF!
YOU WILL BE!
GRMP

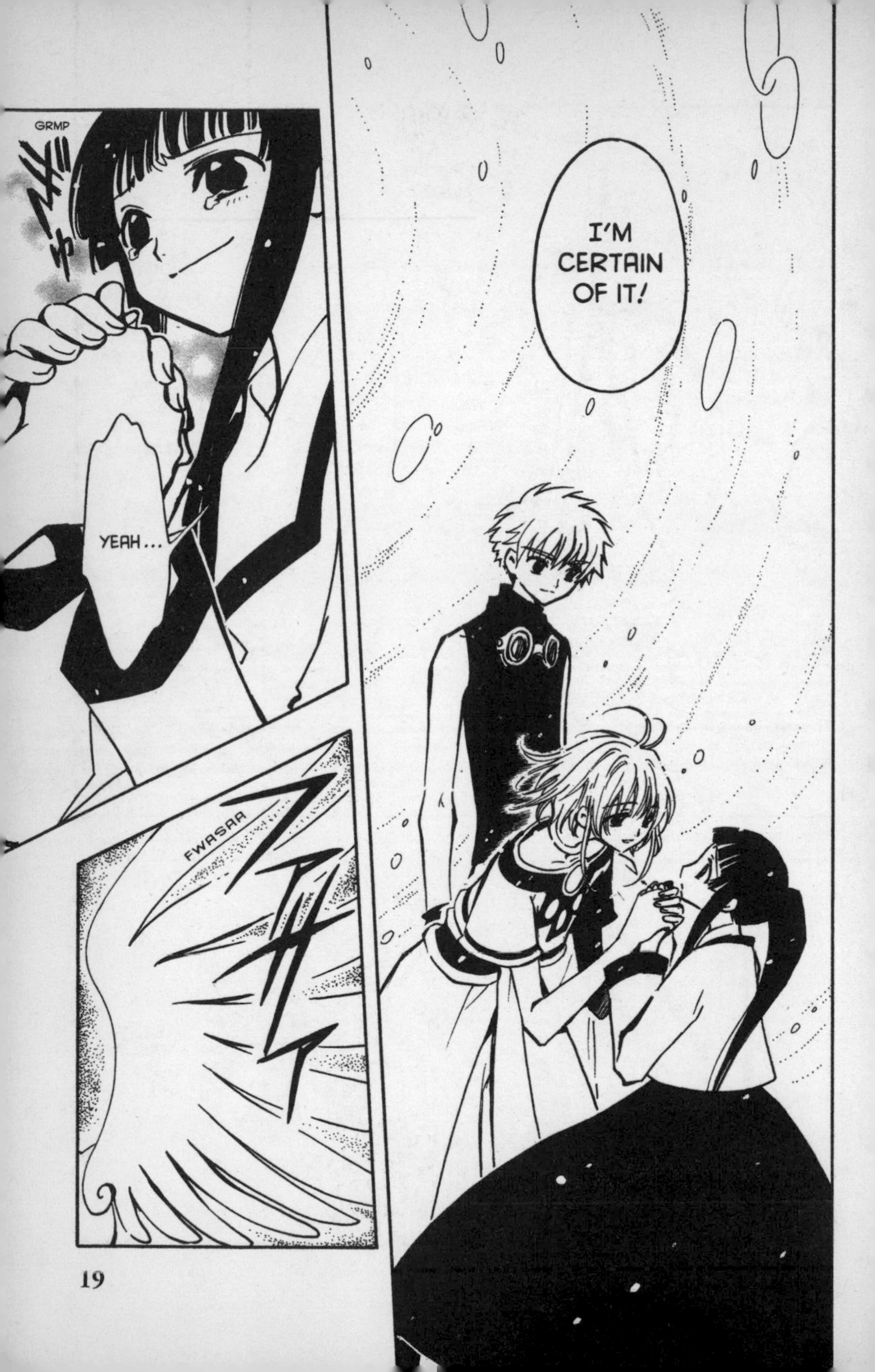
I'M CERTAIN OF IT!
GRMP
YEAH...
FWASAA

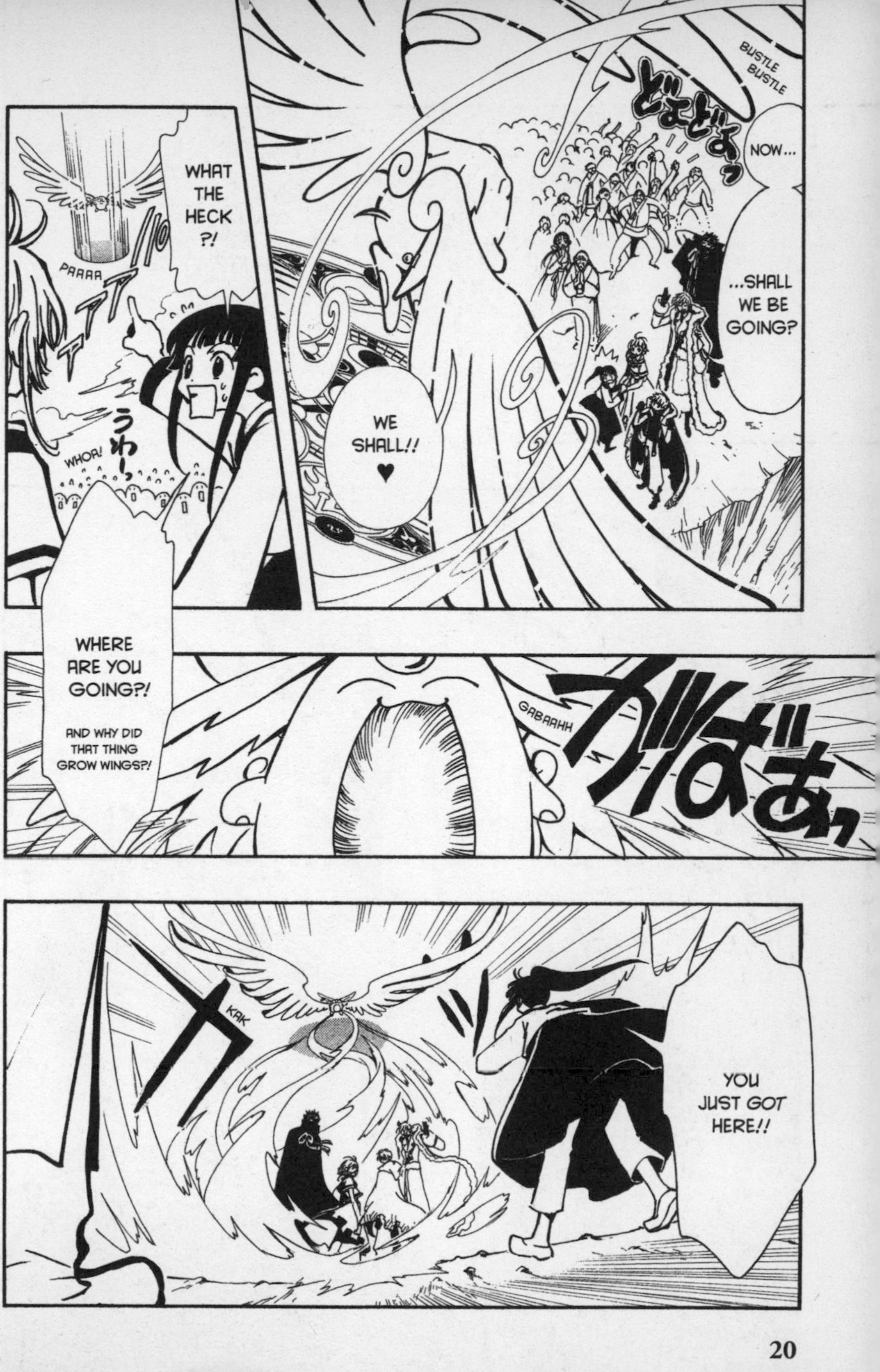
BUSTLE BUSTLE
どよどよっ
NOW...
...SHALL WE BE GOING?
WE SHALL!! ♥
PAAAA
WHAT THE HECK ?!
うわーっ
WHOA!
WHERE ARE YOU GOING?!
AND WHY DID THAT THING GROW WINGS?!
GABAAHH
KAK
YOU JUST GOT HERE!!

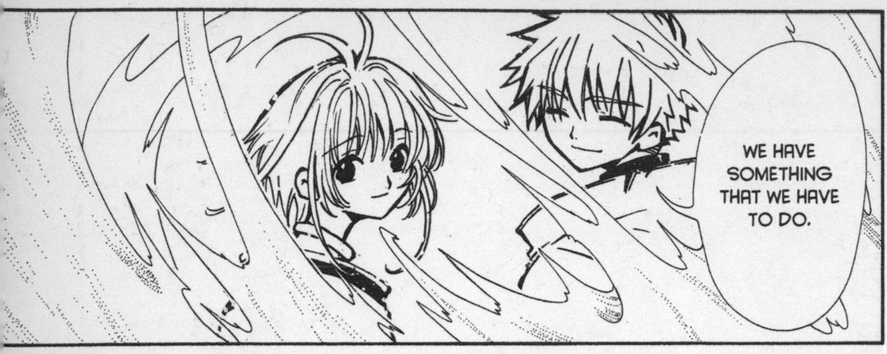
WE HAVE SOMETHING THAT WE HAVE TO DO.

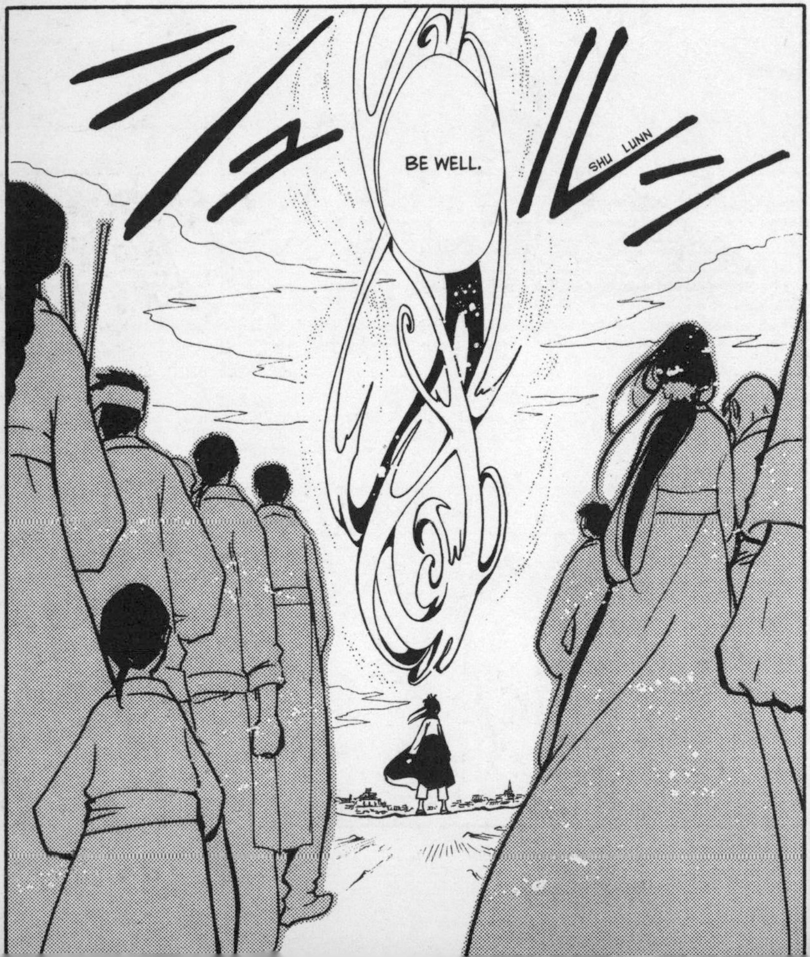
BE WELL.
SHU LUNN

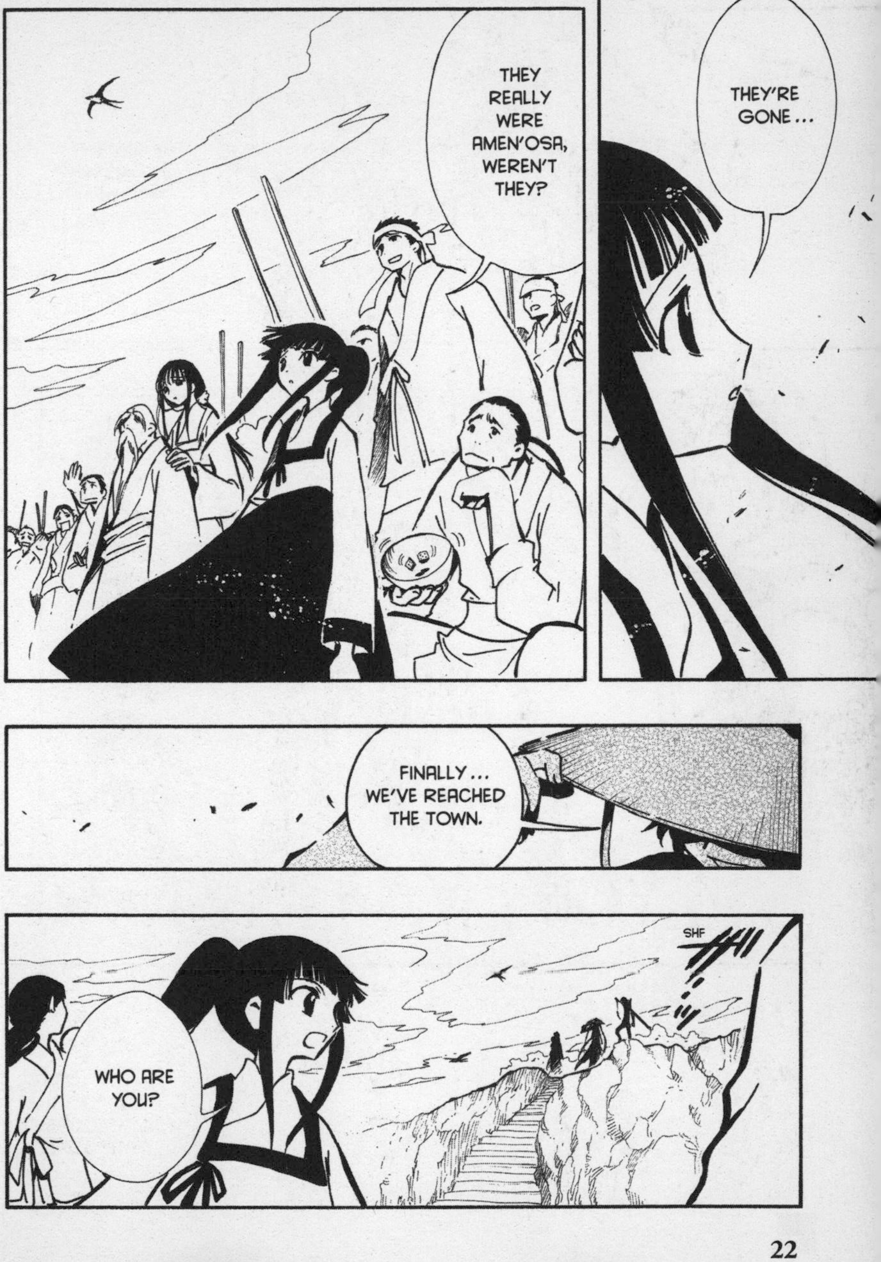
THEY'RE GONE...
THEY REALLY WERE AMEN'OSA, WEREN'T THEY?
FINALLY... WE'VE REACHED THE TOWN.
SHF
WHO ARE YOU?

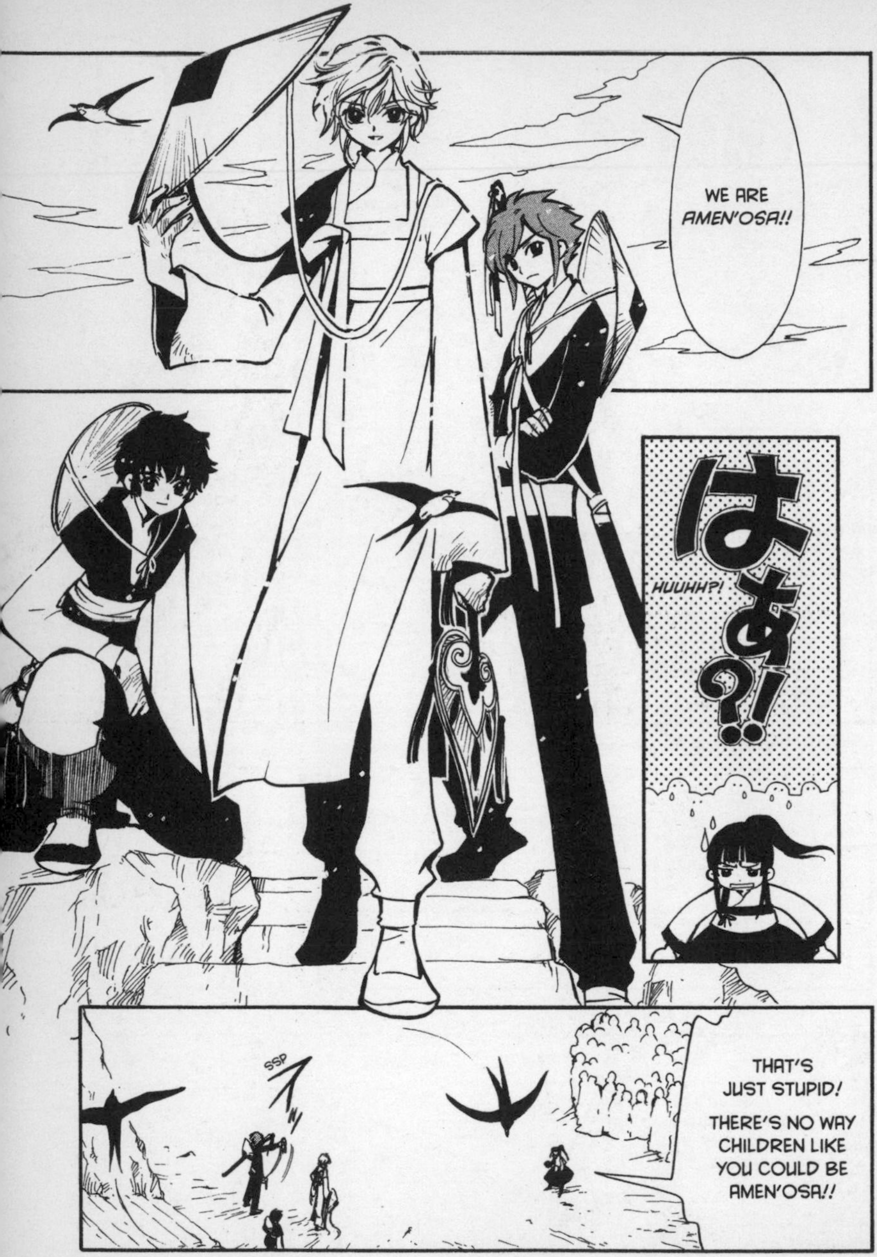
WE ARE AMEN'OSA!!
はぁ?!
HUUHH?!
THAT'S JUST STUPID!
THERE'S NO WAY CHILDREN LIKE YOU COULD BE AMEN'OSA!!
SSP

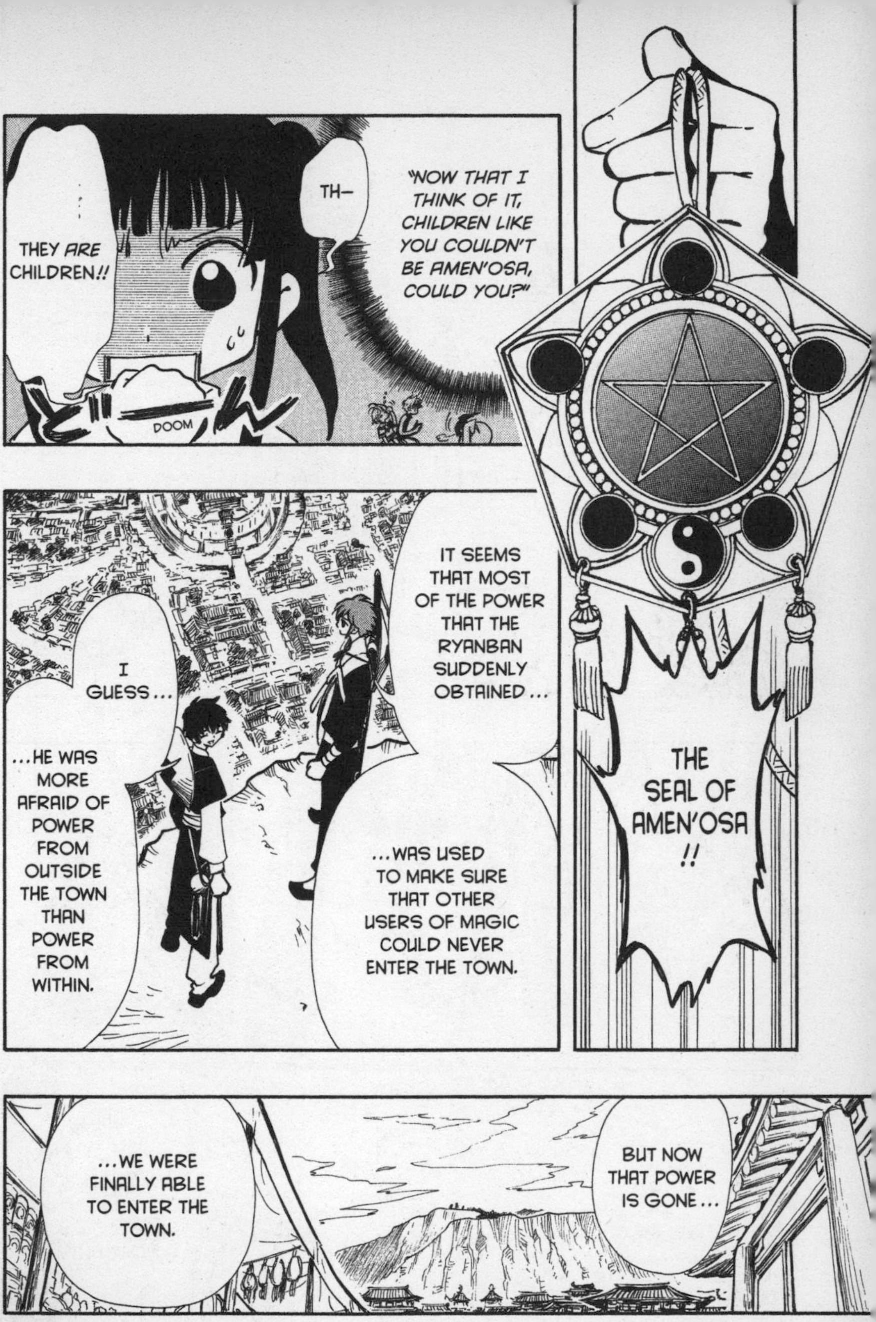

THE SEAL OF AMEN'OSA !!
"NOW THAT I THINK OF IT, CHILDREN LIKE YOU COULDN'T BE AMEN'OSA, COULD YOU?"
TH—
THEY ARE CHILDREN!!
DOOM
IT SEEMS THAT MOST OF THE POWER THAT THE RYANBAN SUDDENLY OBTAINED...
...WAS USED TO MAKE SURE THAT OTHER USERS OF MAGIC COULD NEVER ENTER THE TOWN.
I GUESS...
...HE WAS MORE AFRAID OF POWER FROM OUTSIDE THE TOWN THAN POWER FROM WITHIN.
BUT NOW THAT POWER IS GONE...
...WE WERE FINALLY ABLE TO ENTER THE TOWN.

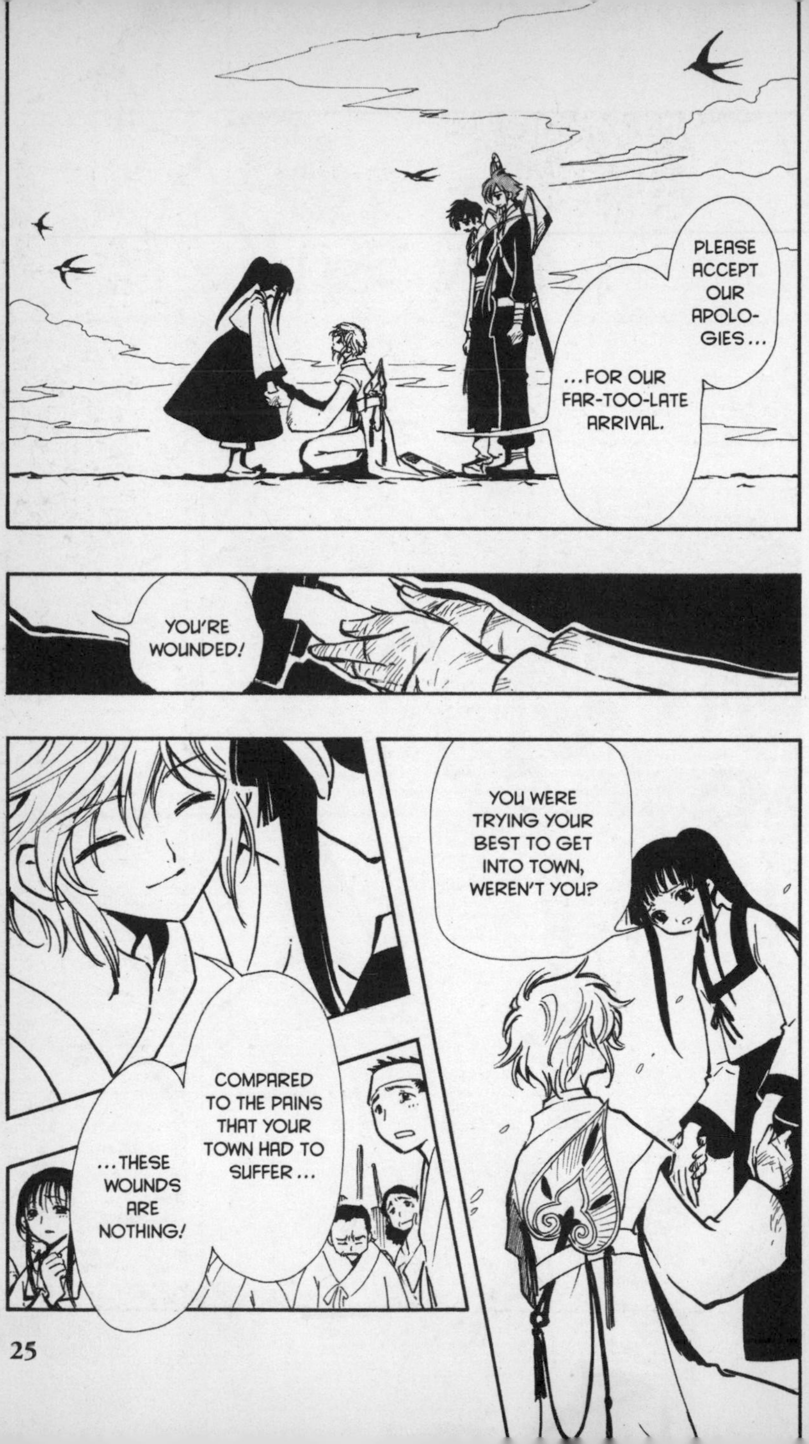
PLEASE ACCEPT OUR APOLOGIES...
...FOR OUR FAR-TOO-LATE ARRIVAL.
YOU'RE WOUNDED!
YOU WERE TRYING YOUR BEST TO GET INTO TOWN, WEREN'T YOU?
COMPARED TO THE PAINS THAT YOUR TOWN HAD TO SUFFER...
...THESE WOUNDS ARE NOTHING!

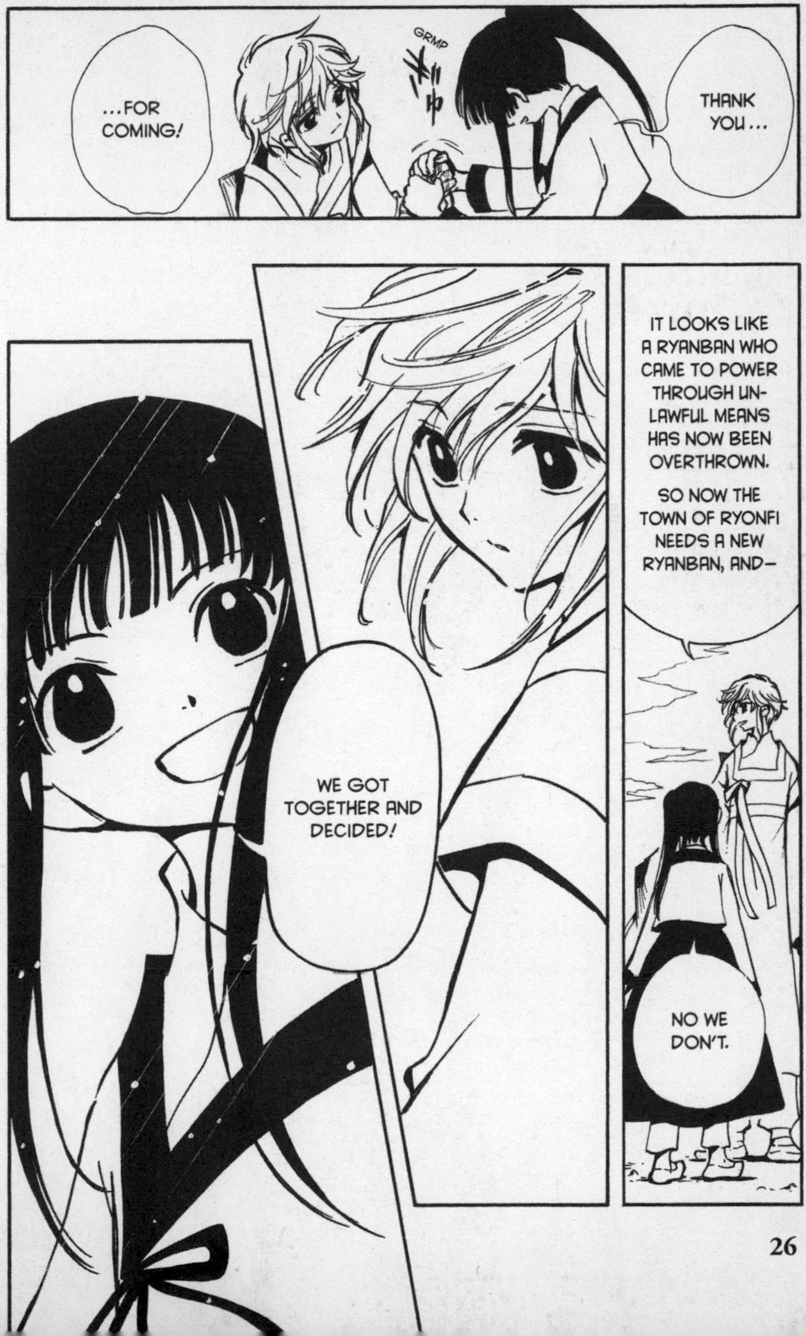
THANK YOU...
GRMP
...FOR COMING!
IT LOOKS LIKE A RYANBAN WHO CAME TO POWER THROUGH UN-LAWFUL MEANS HAS NOW BEEN OVERTHROWN.
SO NOW THE TOWN OF RYONFI NEEDS A NEW RYANBAN, AND—
NO WE DON'T.
WE GOT TOGETHER AND DECIDED!

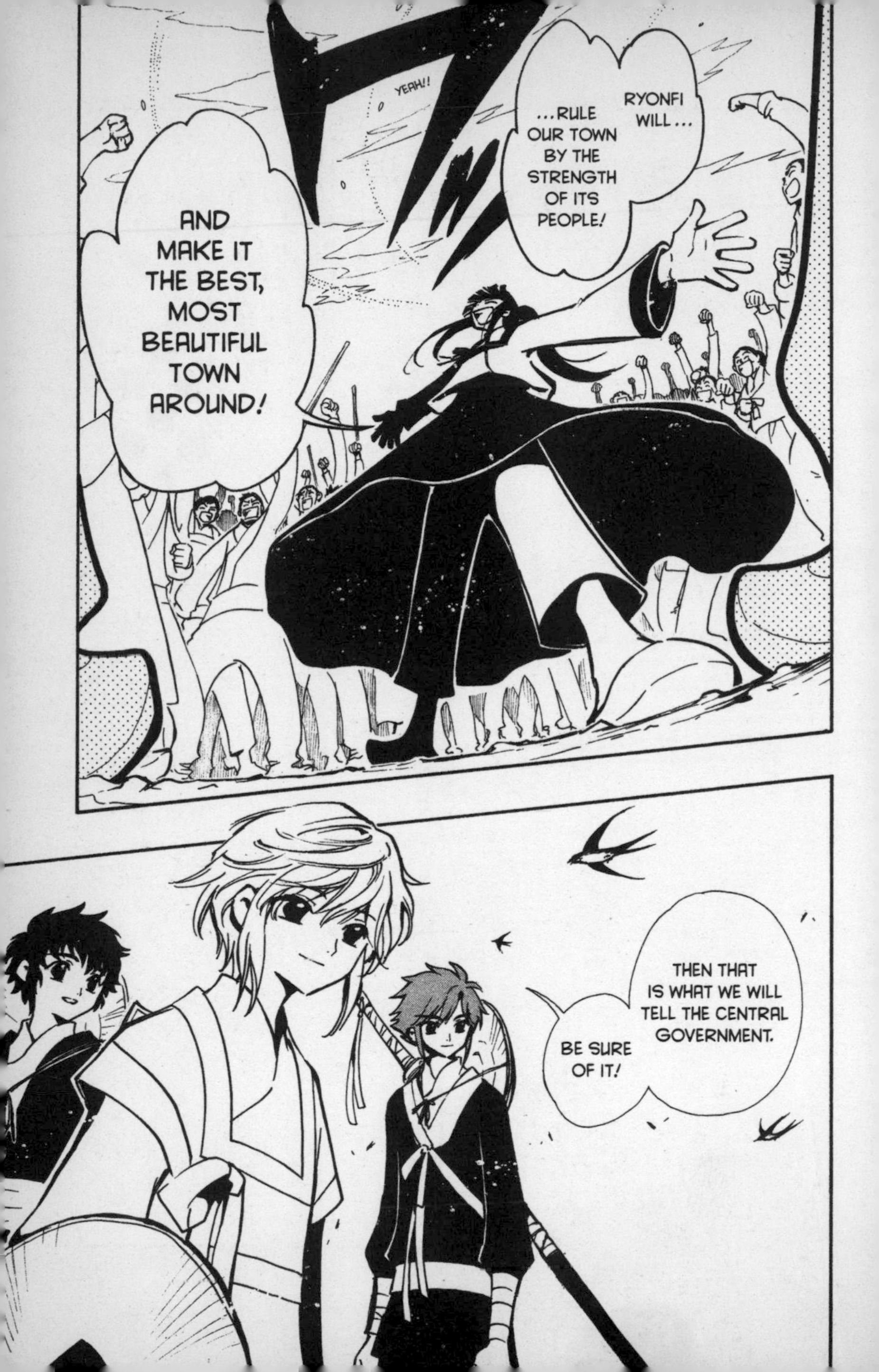
RYONFI WILL... ...RULE OUR TOWN BY THE STRENGTH OF ITS PEOPLE!
YEAH!!
AND MAKE IT THE BEST, MOST BEAUTIFUL TOWN AROUND!
THEN THAT IS WHAT WE WILL TELL THE CENTRAL GOVERNMENT.
BE SURE OF IT!

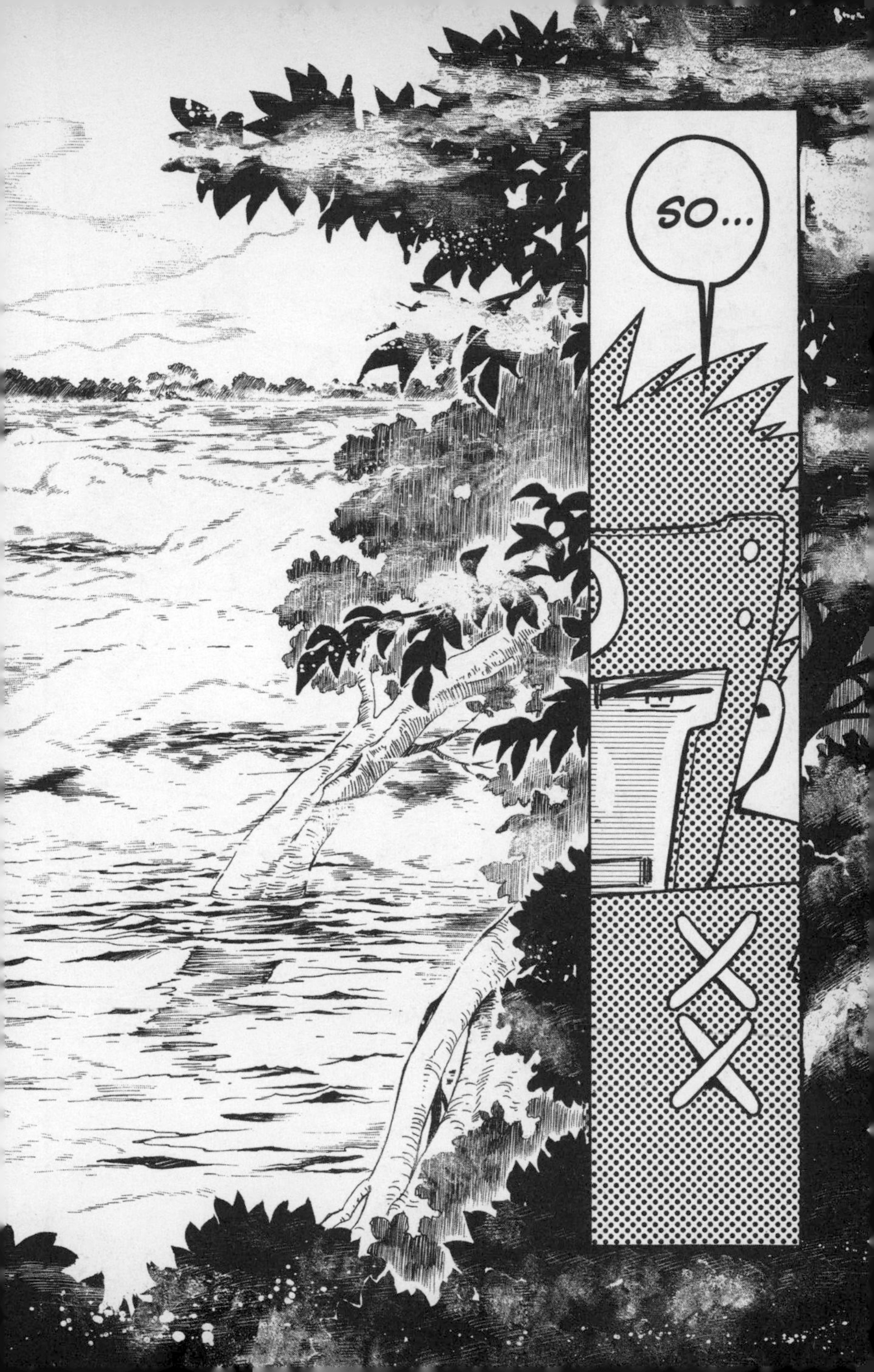
SO...

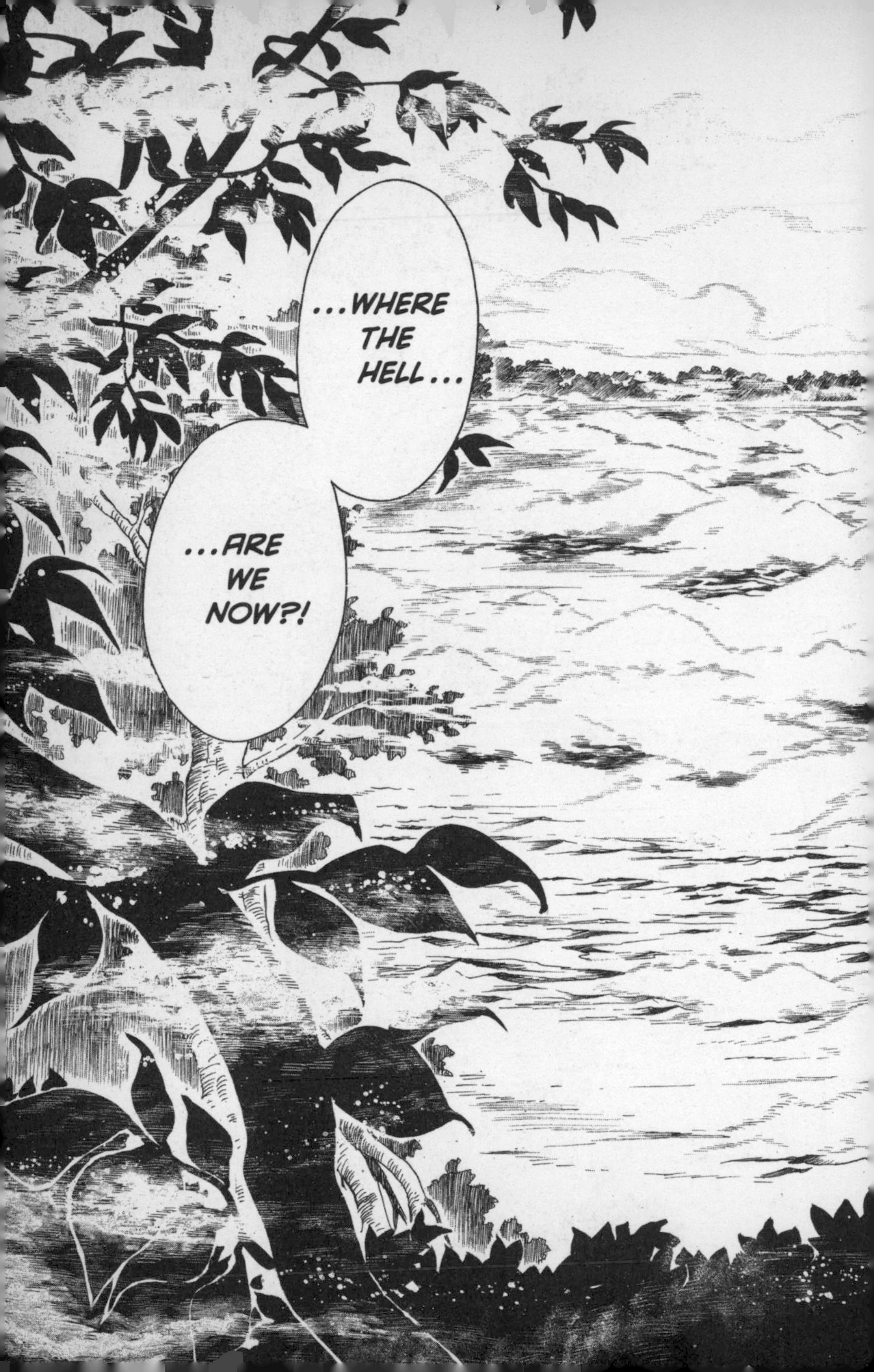
...WHERE THE HELL...
...ARE WE NOW?!

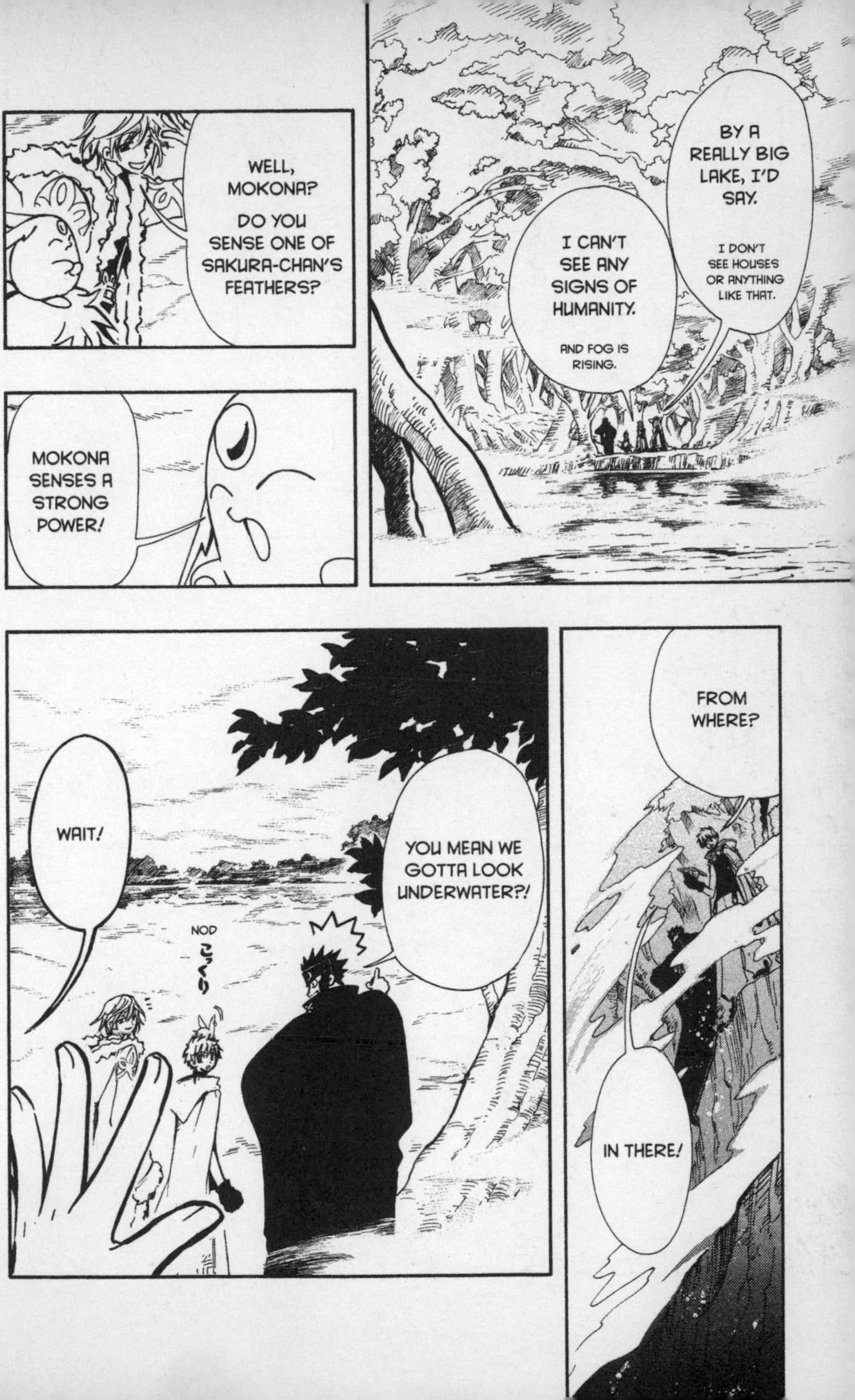
BY A REALLY BIG LAKE, I'D SAY.
I DON'T SEE HOUSES OR ANYTHING LIKE THAT.
I CAN'T SEE ANY SIGNS OF HUMANITY.
AND FOG IS RISING.
WELL, MOKONA?
DO YOU SENSE ONE OF SAKURA-CHAN'S FEATHERS?
MOKONA SENSES A STRONG POWER!
FROM WHERE?
IN THERE!
YOU MEAN WE GOTTA LOOK UNDERWATER?!
WAIT!
NOD
こっくり

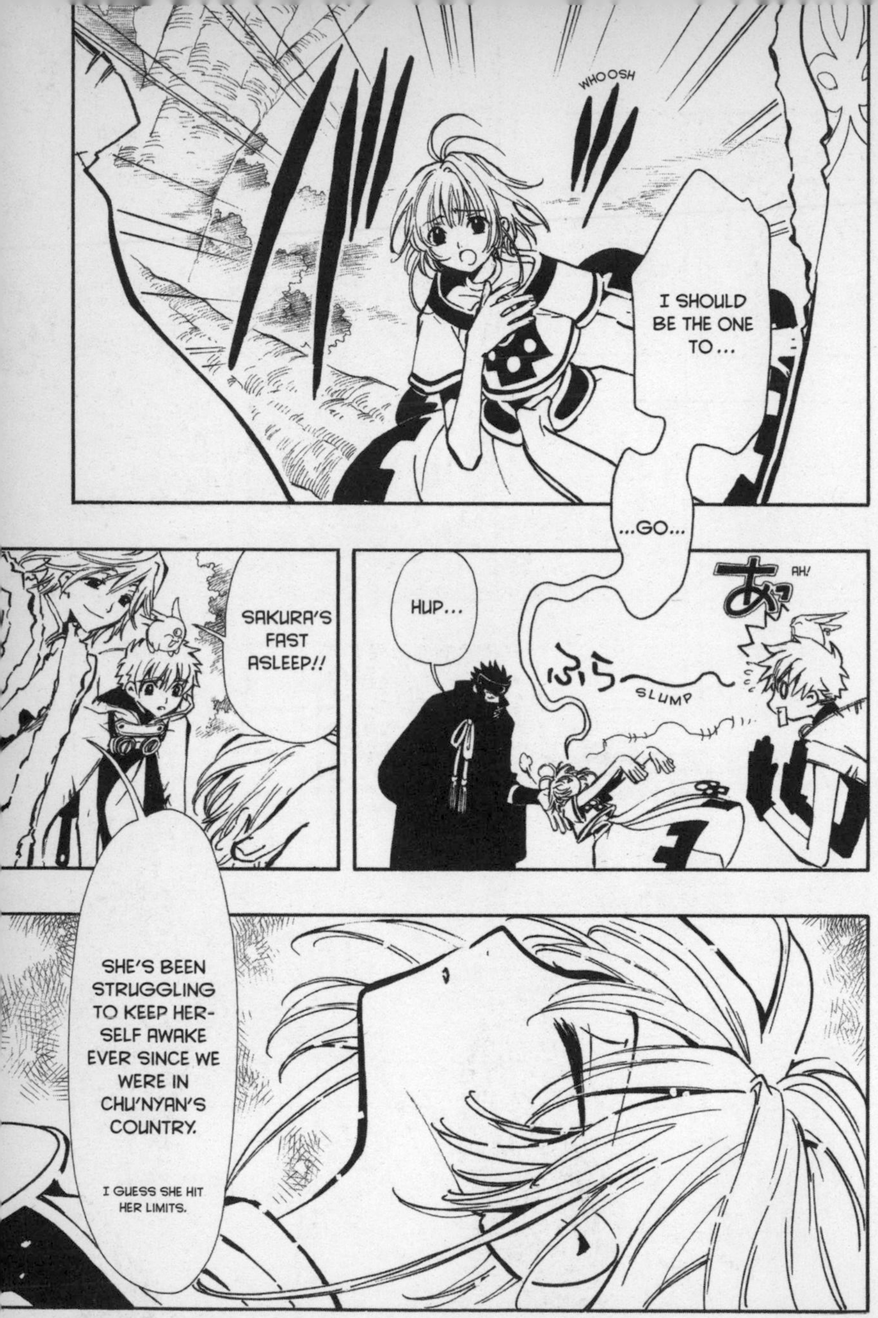
WHOOSH
I SHOULD BE THE ONE TO...
...GO...
あ AH!
ふら SLUMP
HUP...
SAKURA'S FAST ASLEEP!!
SHE'S BEEN STRUGGLING TO KEEP HER-SELF AWAKE EVER SINCE WE WERE IN CHU'NYAN'S COUNTRY.
I GUESS SHE HIT HER LIMITS.

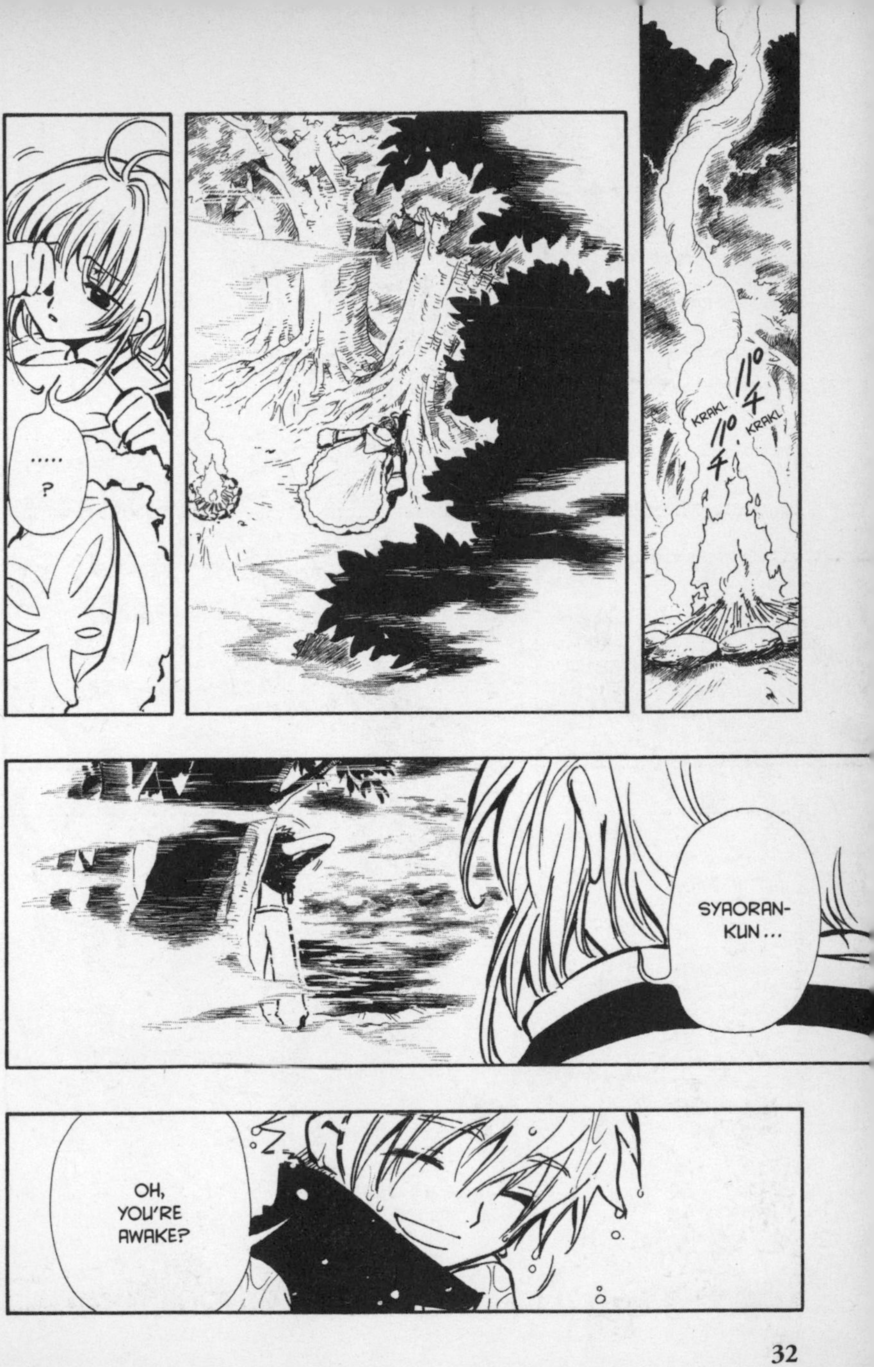
KRAKL KRAKL
.....?
SYAORAN-KUN...
OH, YOU'RE AWAKE?

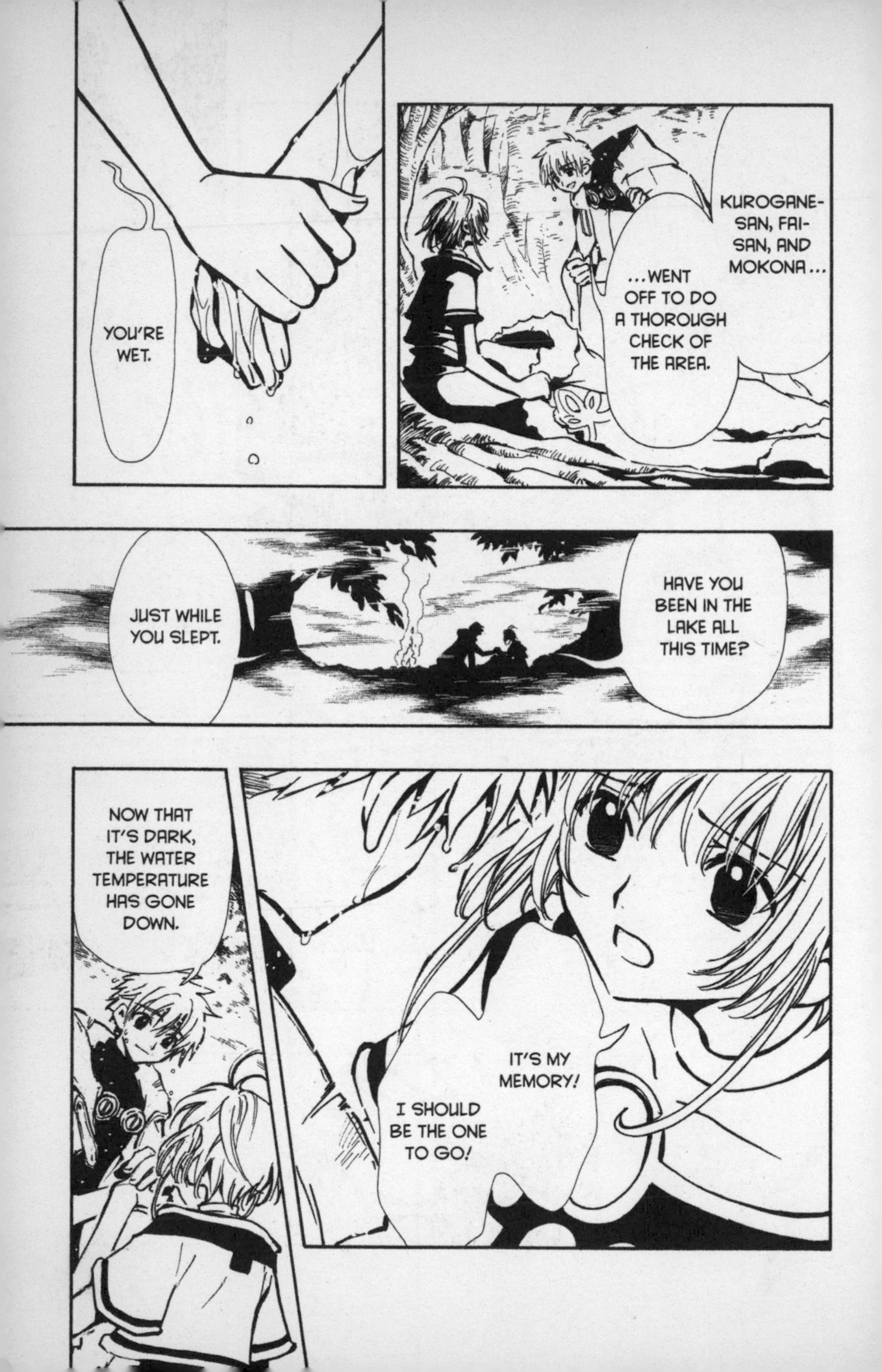
KUROGANE-SAN, FAI-SAN, AND MOKONA...
...WENT OFF TO DO A THOROUGH CHECK OF THE AREA.
YOU'RE WET.
HAVE YOU BEEN IN THE LAKE ALL THIS TIME?
JUST WHILE YOU SLEPT.
IT'S MY MEMORY!
I SHOULD BE THE ONE TO GO!
NOW THAT IT'S DARK, THE WATER TEMPERATURE HAS GONE DOWN.

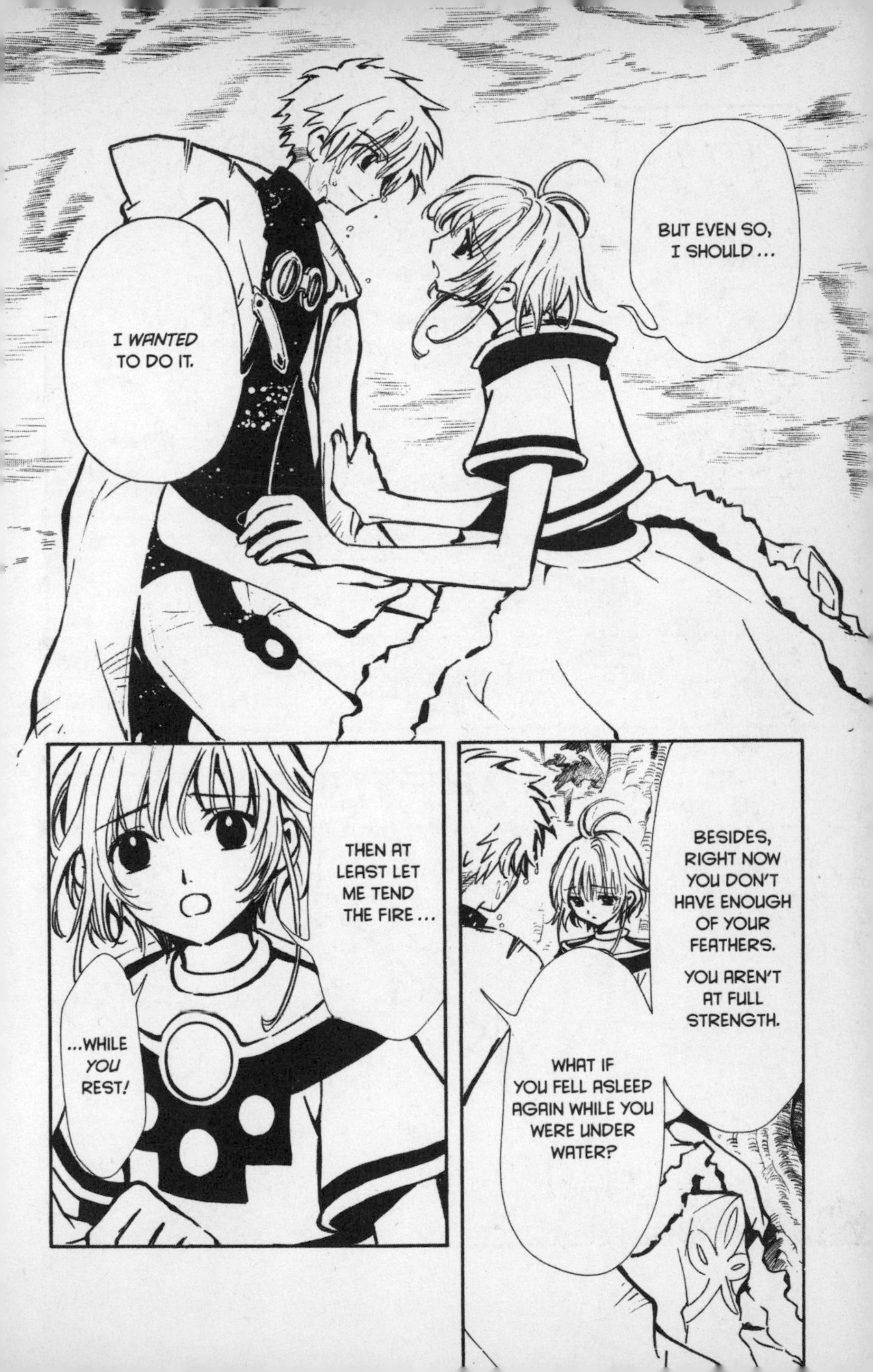
BUT EVEN SO, I SHOULD...
I *WANTED* TO DO IT.
BESIDES, RIGHT NOW YOU DON'T HAVE ENOUGH OF YOUR FEATHERS.
YOU AREN'T AT FULL STRENGTH.
WHAT IF YOU FELL ASLEEP AGAIN WHILE YOU WERE UNDER WATER?
THEN AT LEAST LET ME TEND THE FIRE...
...WHILE *YOU* REST!

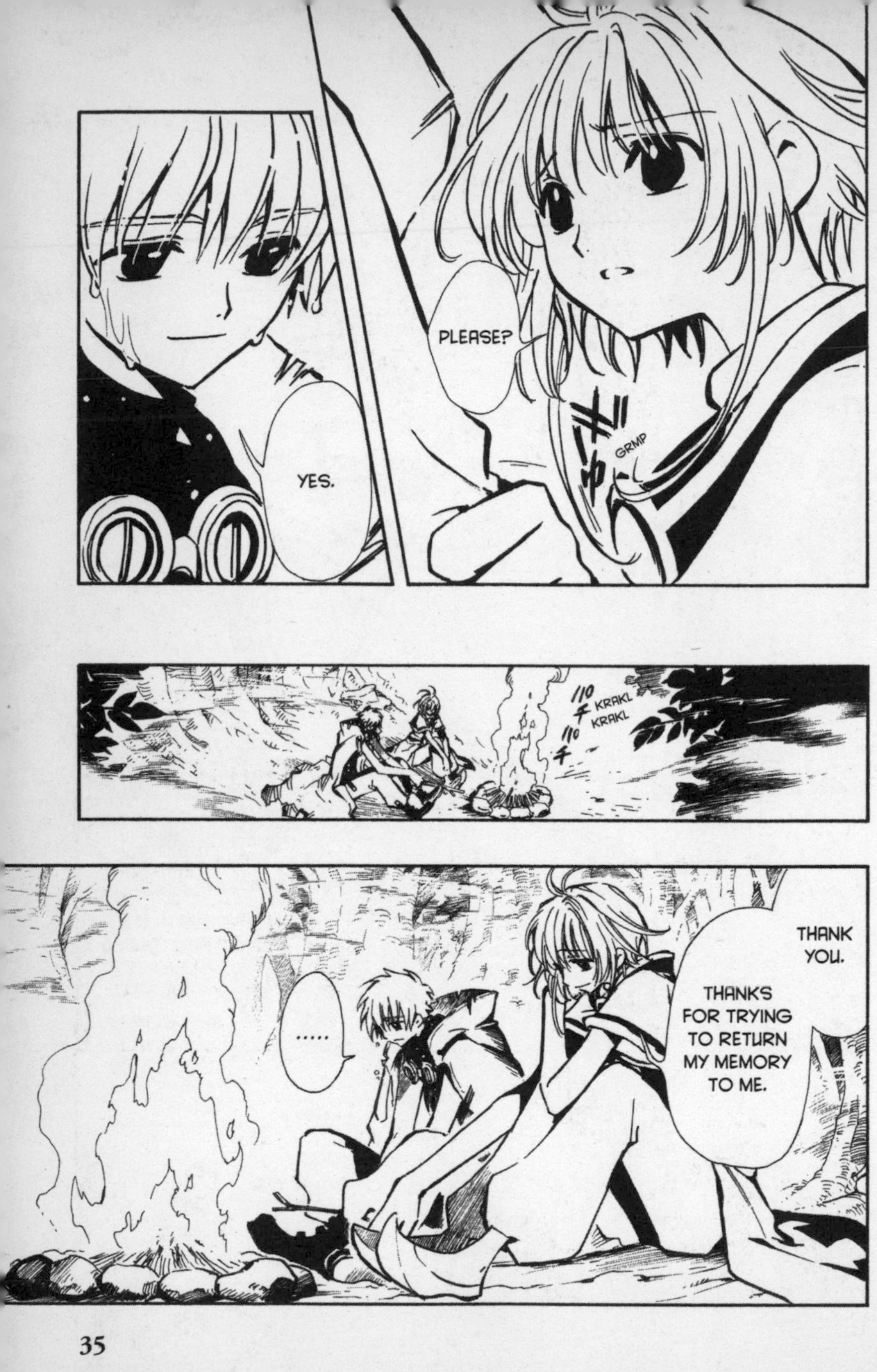
PLEASE?
GRMP
YES.
KRAKL
KRAKL
THANK YOU.
THANKS FOR TRYING TO RETURN MY MEMORY TO ME.
......

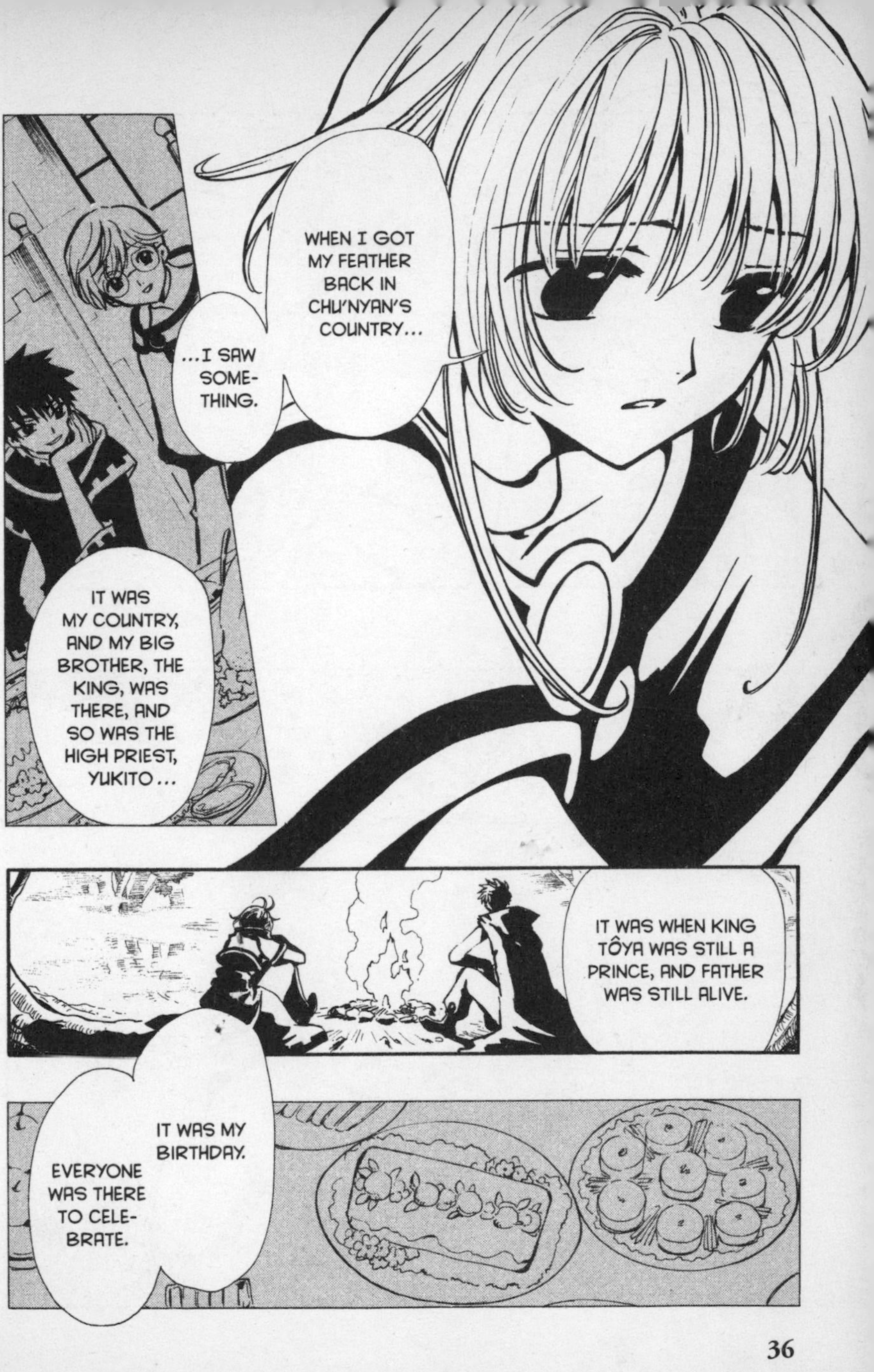
WHEN I GOT MY FEATHER BACK IN CHU'NYAN'S COUNTRY...
...I SAW SOME-THING.
IT WAS MY COUNTRY, AND MY BIG BROTHER, THE KING, WAS THERE, AND SO WAS THE HIGH PRIEST, YUKITO...
IT WAS WHEN KING TÔYA WAS STILL A PRINCE, AND FATHER WAS STILL ALIVE.
IT WAS MY BIRTHDAY.
EVERYONE WAS THERE TO CELE-BRATE.

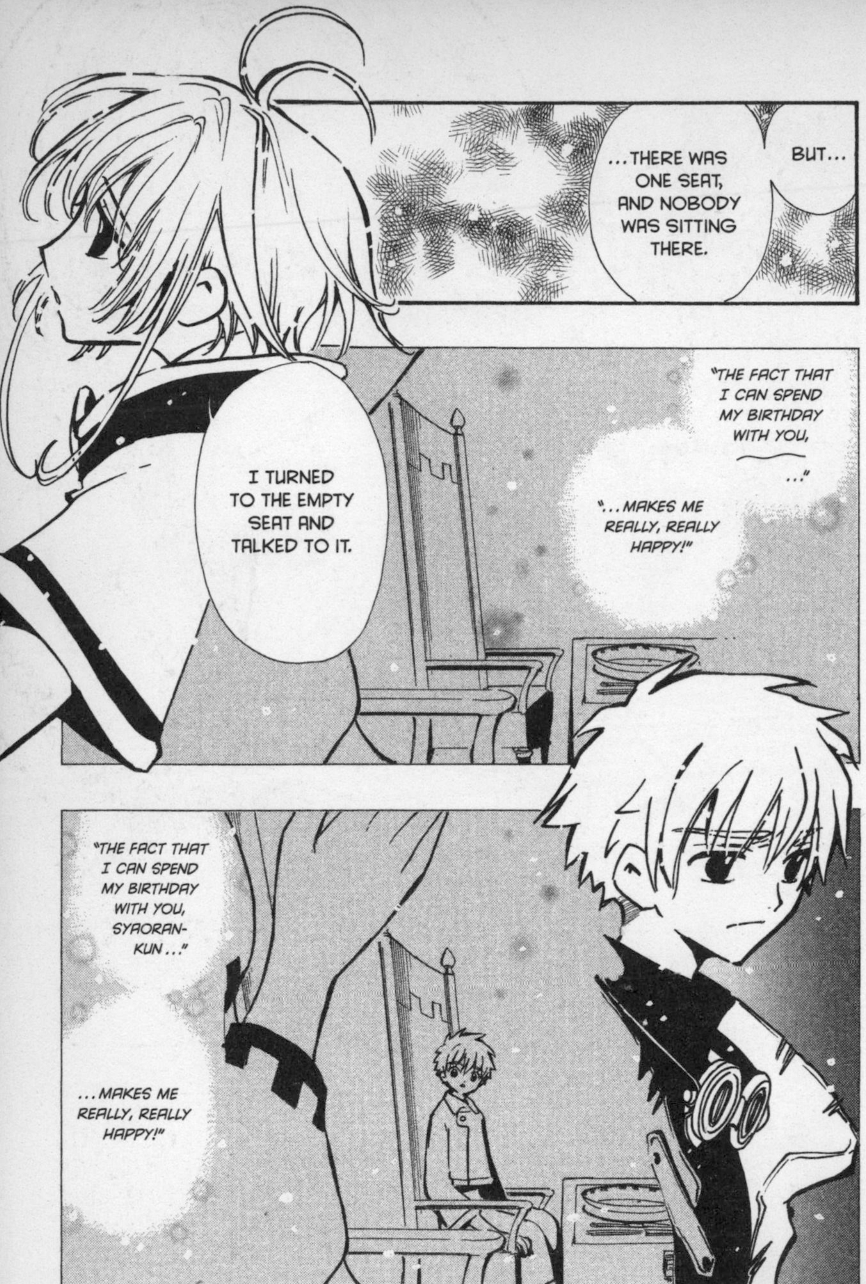
BUT...
...THERE WAS ONE SEAT, AND NOBODY WAS SITTING THERE.
"THE FACT THAT I CAN SPEND MY BIRTHDAY WITH YOU,
..."
"...MAKES ME REALLY, REALLY HAPPY!"
I TURNED TO THE EMPTY SEAT AND TALKED TO IT.
"THE FACT THAT I CAN SPEND MY BIRTHDAY WITH YOU, SYAORAN-KUN..."
...MAKES ME REALLY, REALLY HAPPY!"

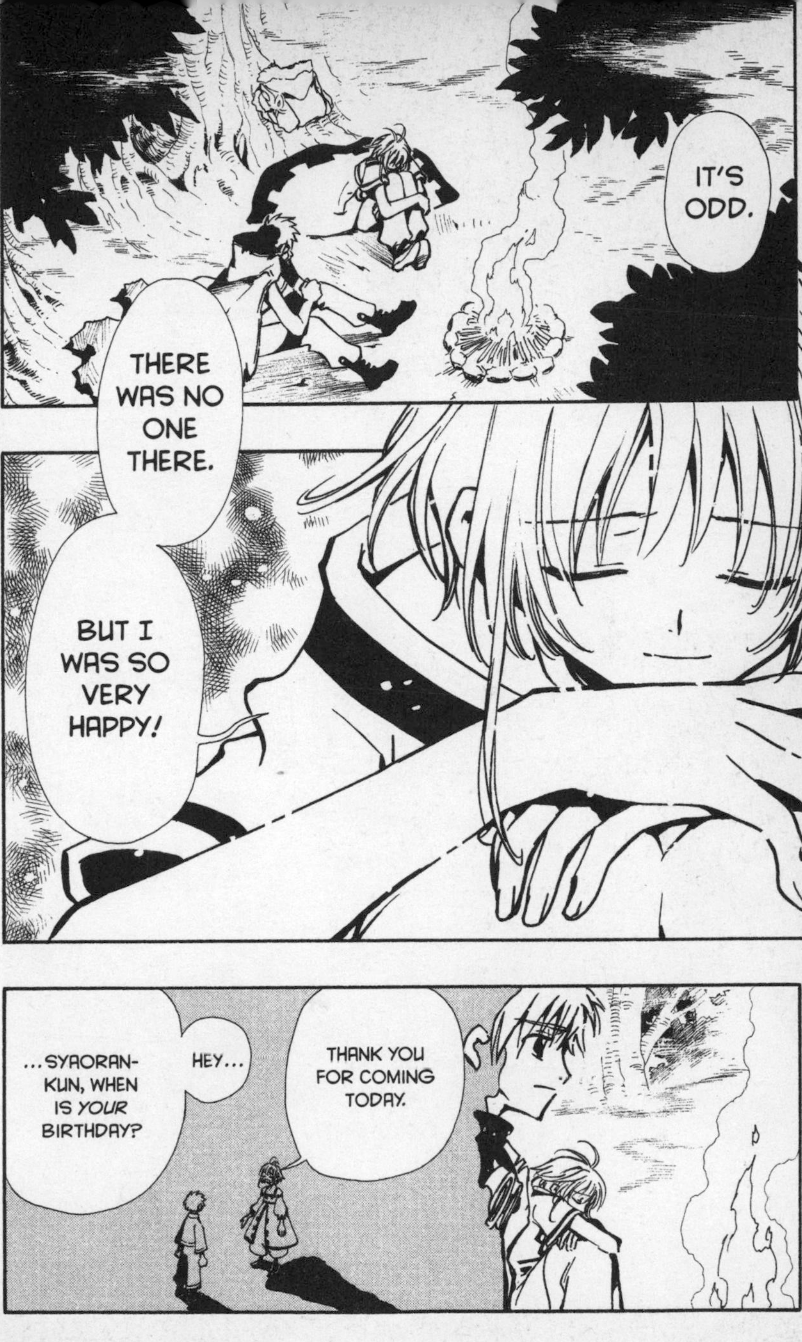
IT'S ODD.
THERE WAS NO ONE THERE.
BUT I WAS SO VERY HAPPY!
THANK YOU FOR COMING TODAY.
HEY...
...SYAORAN-KUN, WHEN IS *YOUR* BIRTHDAY?

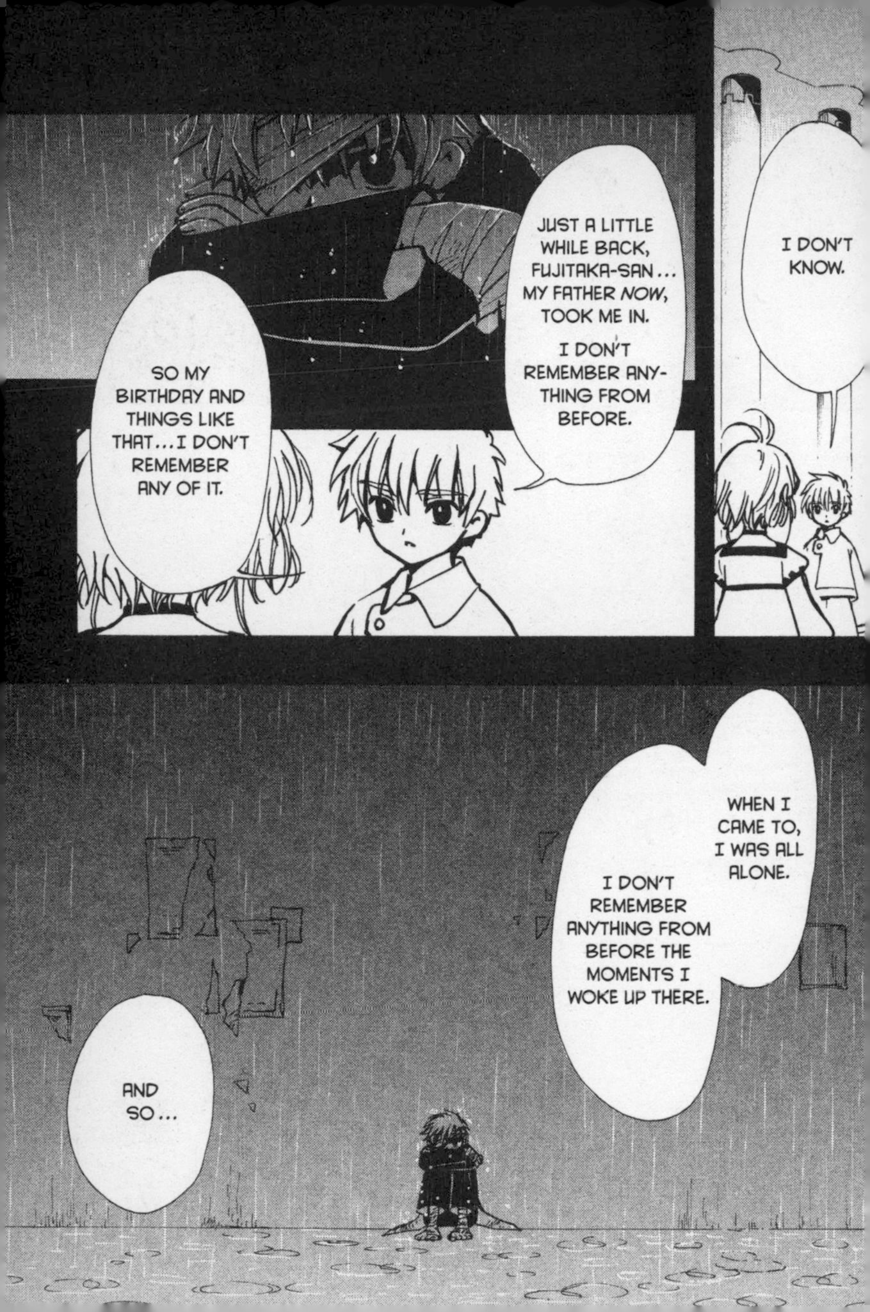

I DON'T KNOW.
JUST A LITTLE WHILE BACK, FUJITAKA-SAN... MY FATHER *NOW*, TOOK ME IN.
I DON'T REMEMBER ANY-THING FROM BEFORE.
SO MY BIRTHDAY AND THINGS LIKE THAT... I DON'T REMEMBER ANY OF IT.
WHEN I CAME TO, I WAS ALL ALONE.
I DON'T REMEMBER ANYTHING FROM BEFORE THE MOMENTS I WOKE UP THERE.
AND SO...

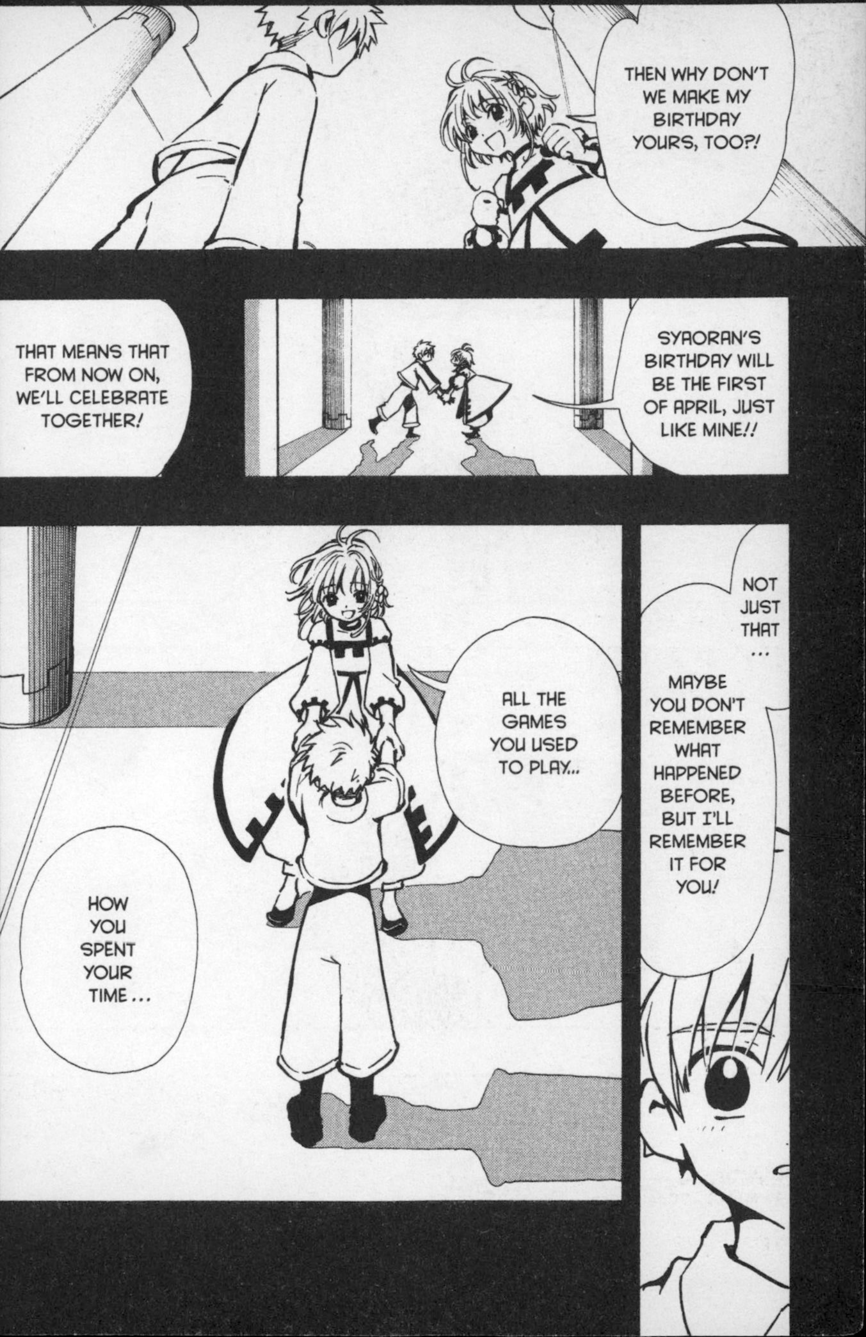
THEN WHY DON'T WE MAKE MY BIRTHDAY YOURS, TOO?!
SYAORAN'S BIRTHDAY WILL BE THE FIRST OF APRIL, JUST LIKE MINE!!
THAT MEANS THAT FROM NOW ON, WE'LL CELEBRATE TOGETHER!
NOT JUST THAT...
MAYBE YOU DON'T REMEMBER WHAT HAPPENED BEFORE, BUT I'LL REMEMBER IT FOR YOU!
ALL THE GAMES YOU USED TO PLAY...
HOW YOU SPENT YOUR TIME...

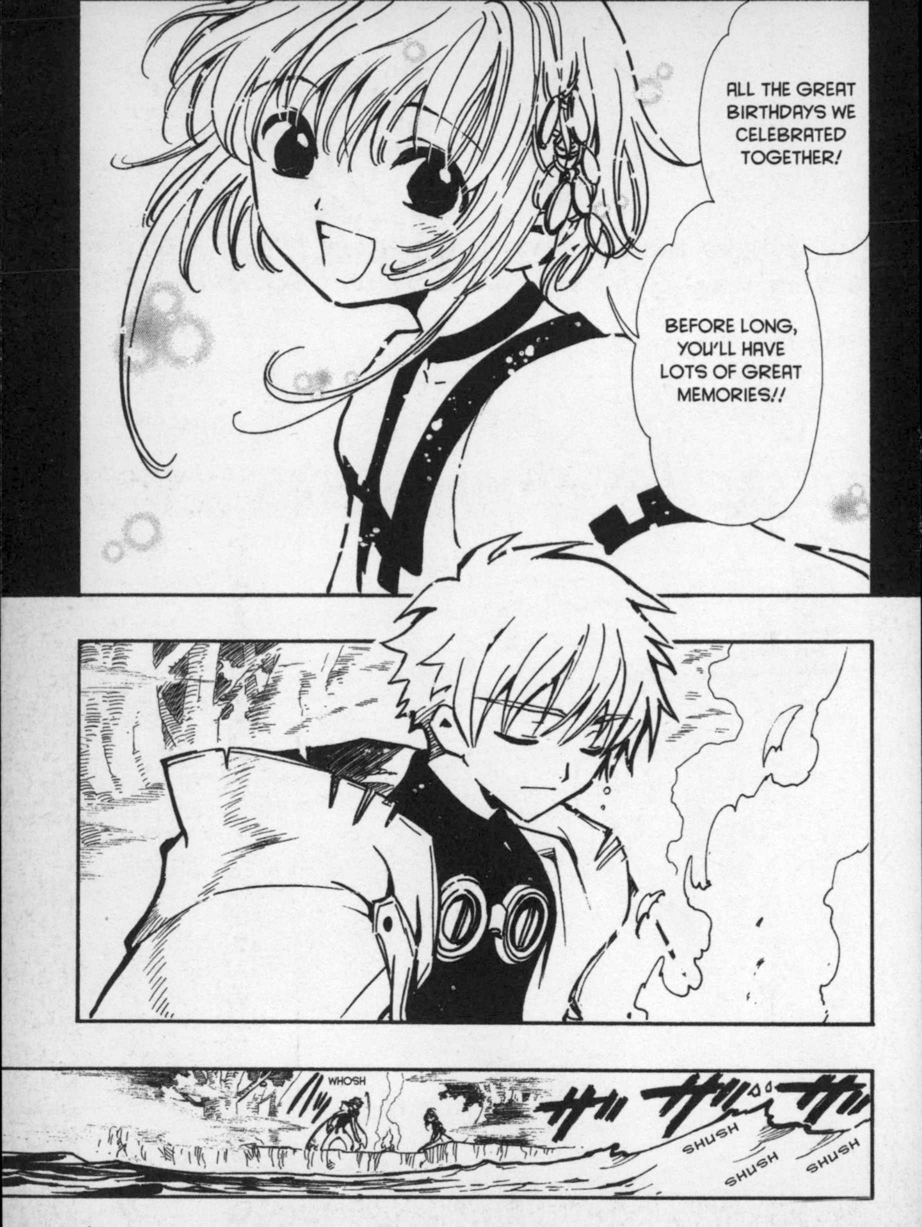
ALL THE GREAT BIRTHDAYS WE CELEBRATED TOGETHER!
BEFORE LONG, YOU'LL HAVE LOTS OF GREAT MEMORIES!!
WHOSH
SHUSH
SHUSH
SHUSH

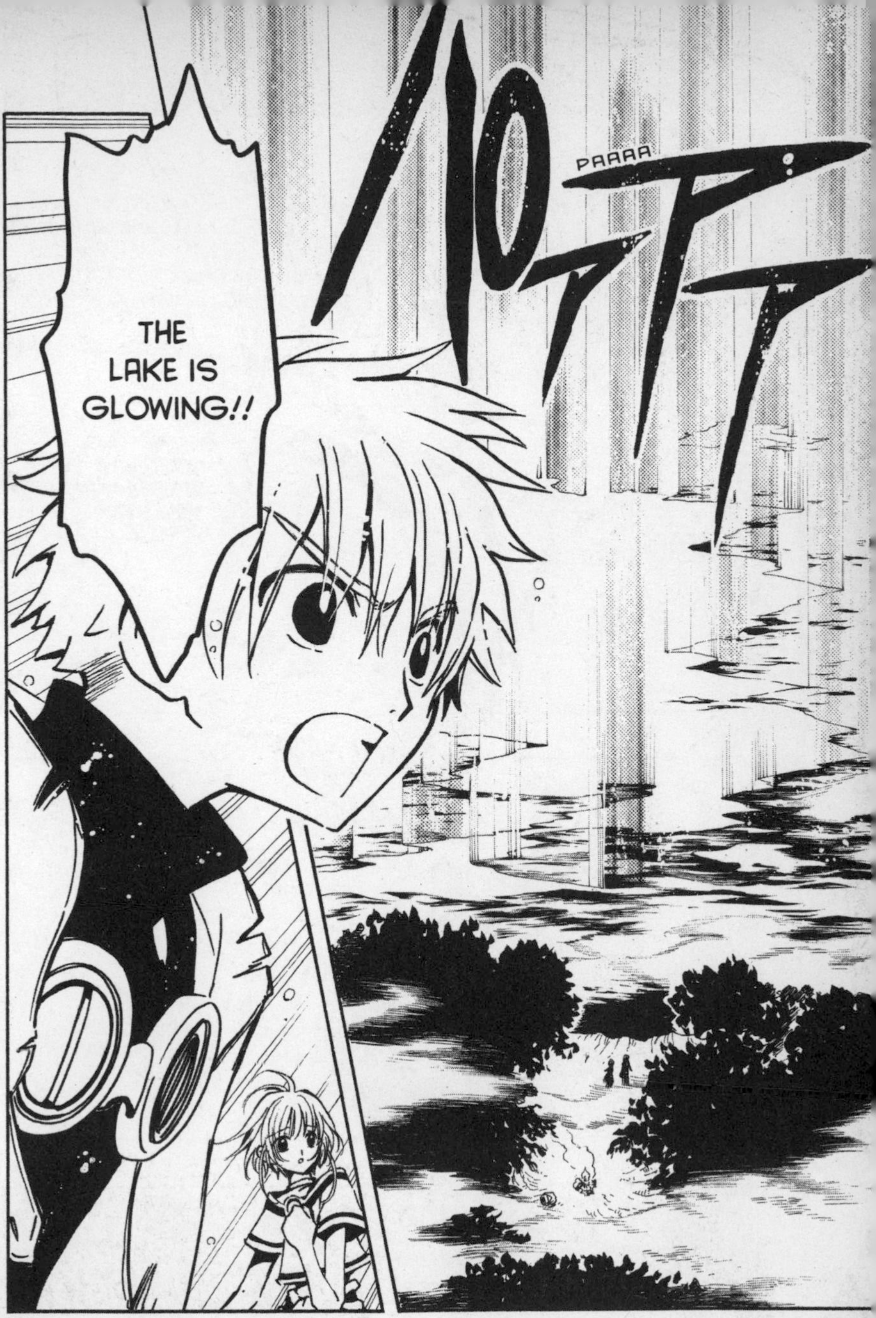
PAAAA
ハアア
THE LAKE IS GLOWING!!

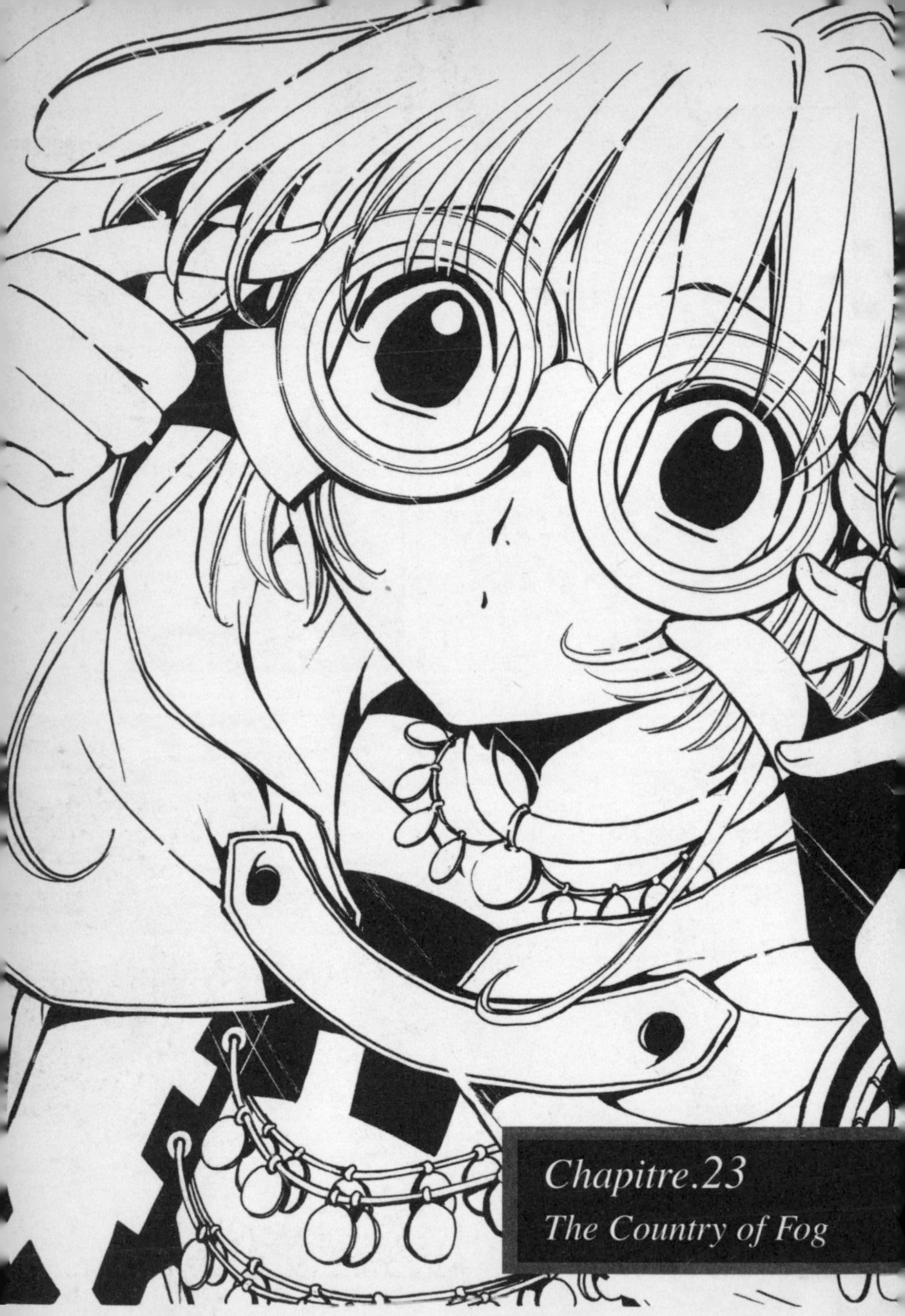
Chapitre.23
The Country of Fog

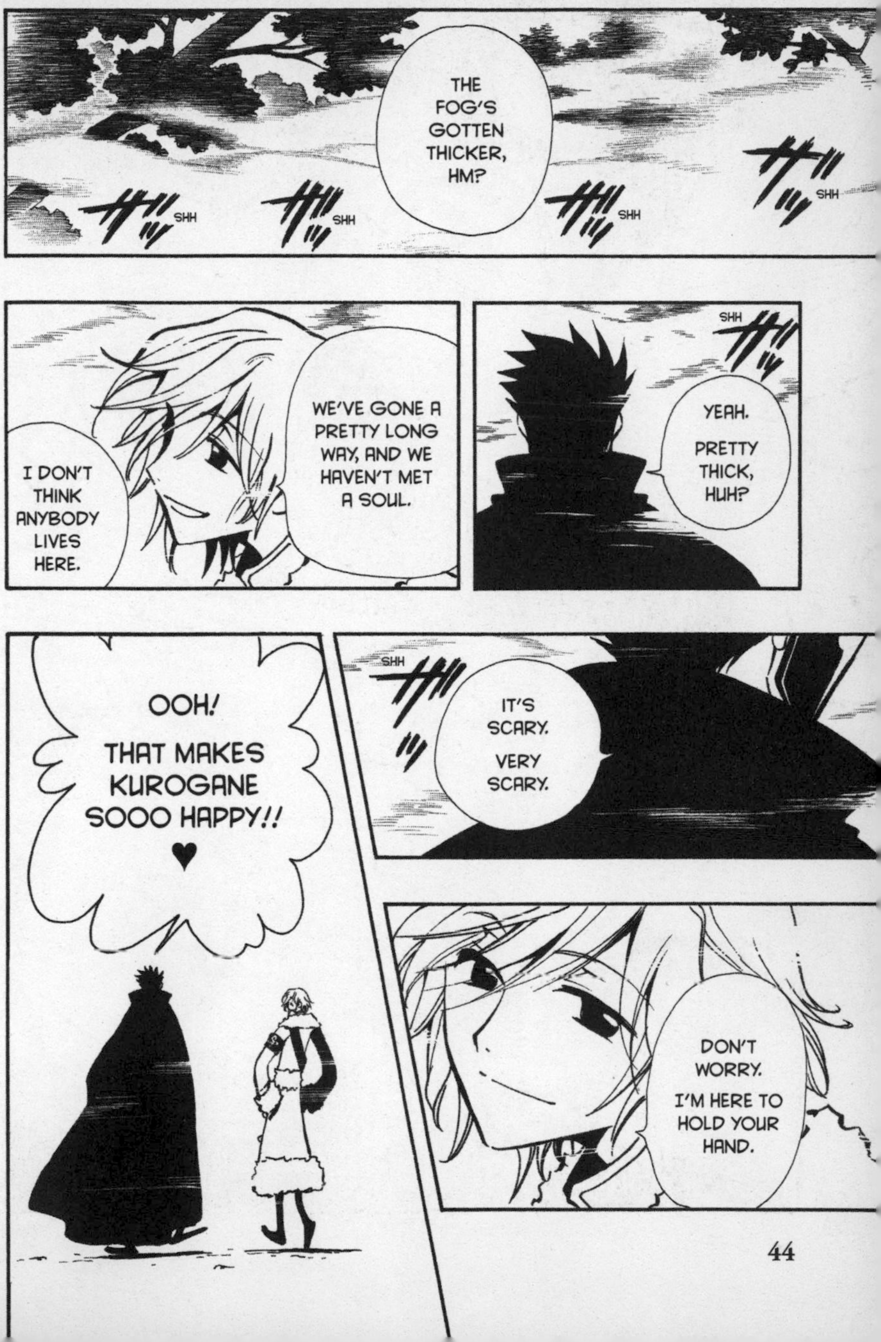
THE FOG'S GOTTEN THICKER, HM?
SHH
SHH
SHH
SHH
SHH
YEAH. PRETTY THICK, HUH?
WE'VE GONE A PRETTY LONG WAY, AND WE HAVEN'T MET A SOUL.
I DON'T THINK ANYBODY LIVES HERE.
SHH
IT'S SCARY. VERY SCARY.
DON'T WORRY. I'M HERE TO HOLD YOUR HAND.
OOH! THAT MAKES KUROGANE SOOO HAPPY!! ♥

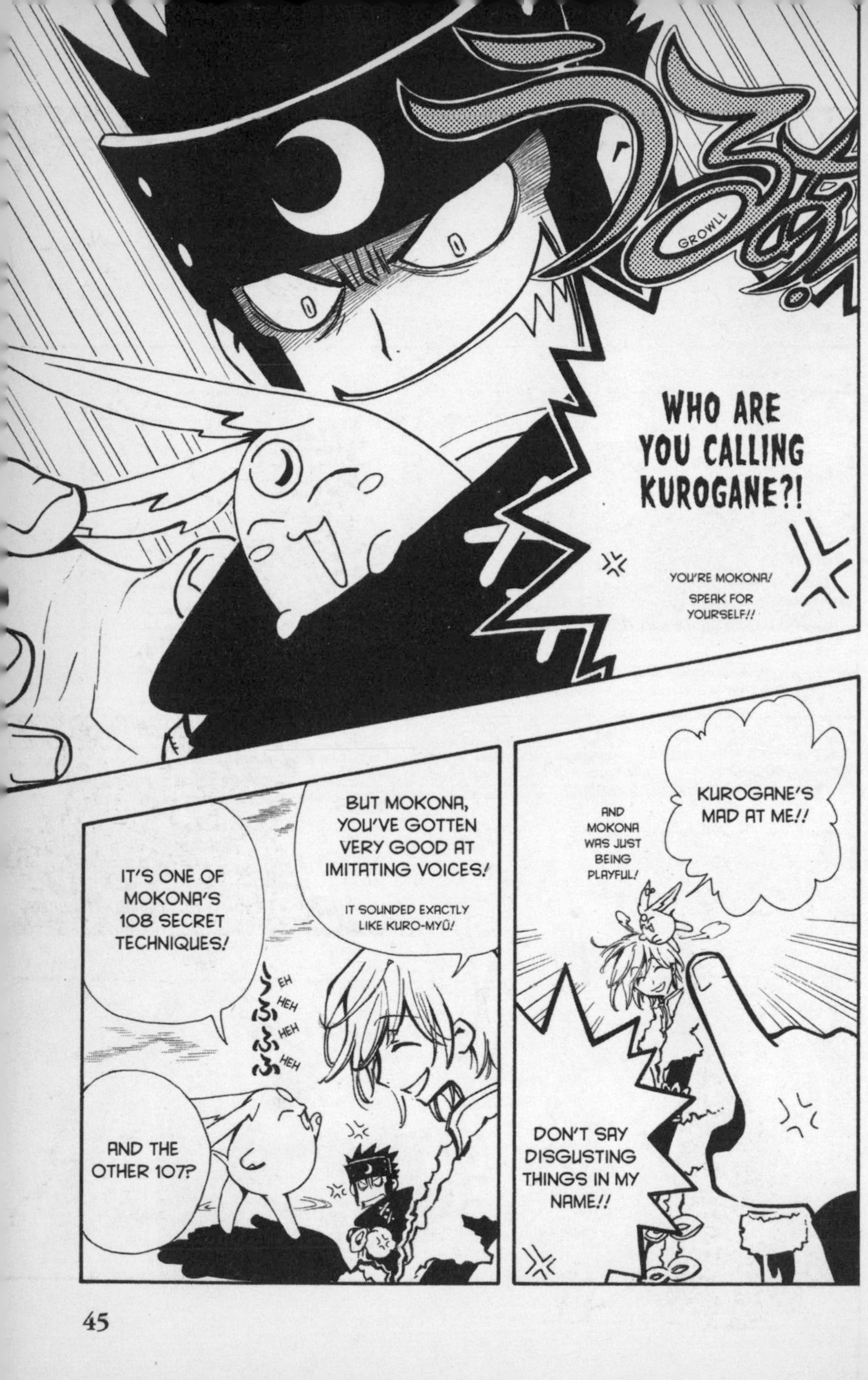
GROWLL
WHO ARE YOU CALLING KUROGANE?!
YOU'RE MOKONA! SPEAK FOR YOURSELF!!
KUROGANE'S MAD AT ME!!
AND MOKONA WAS JUST BEING PLAYFUL!
DON'T SAY DISGUSTING THINGS IN MY NAME!!
BUT MOKONA, YOU'VE GOTTEN VERY GOOD AT IMITATING VOICES!
IT SOUNDED EXACTLY LIKE KURO-MYÛ!
IT'S ONE OF MOKONA'S 108 SECRET TECHNIQUES!
うふふふ
EH HEH HEH HEH
AND THE OTHER 107?

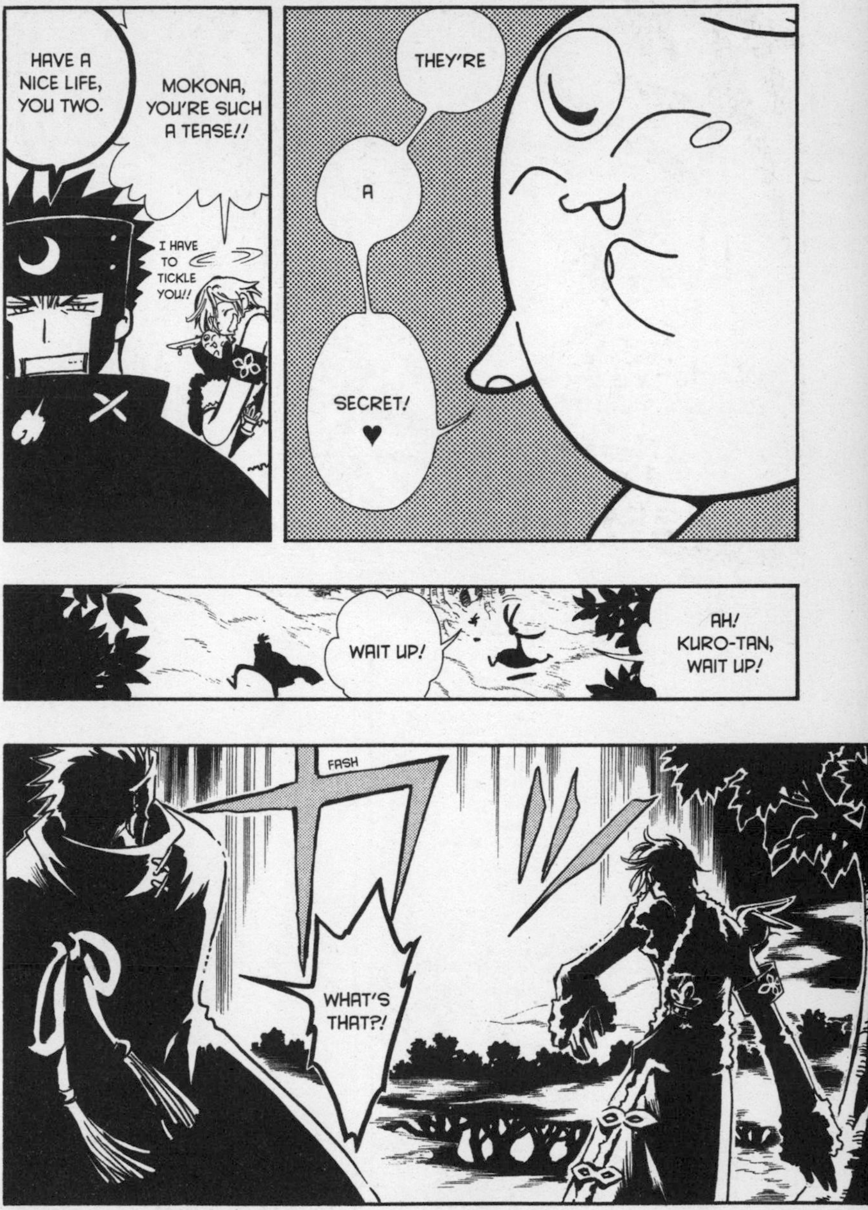
THEY'RE
A
SECRET! ♥
HAVE A NICE LIFE, YOU TWO.
MOKONA, YOU'RE SUCH A TEASE!!
I HAVE TO TICKLE YOU!!
AH! KURO-TAN, WAIT UP!
WAIT UP!
FASH
WHAT'S THAT?!

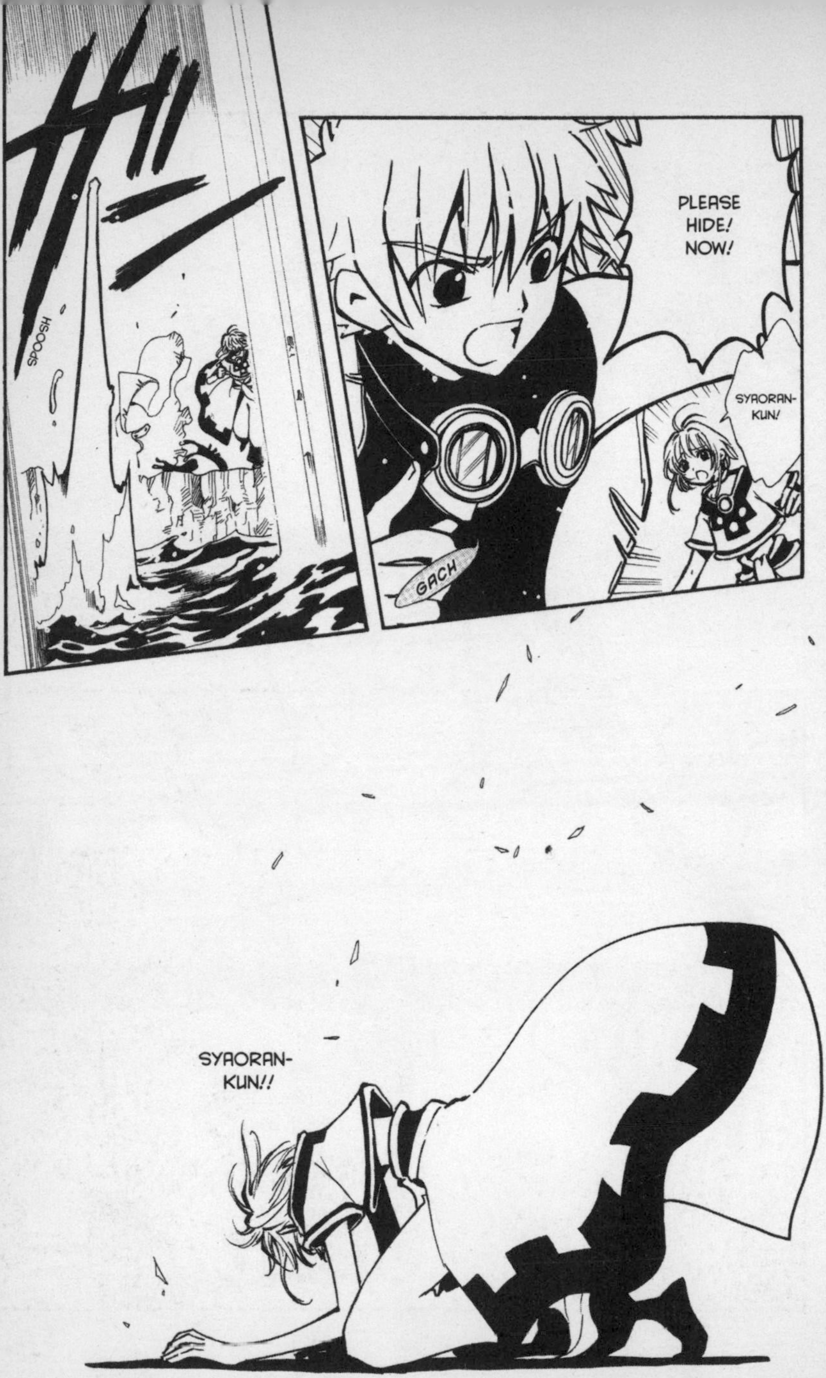
PLEASE HIDE! NOW!
SYAORAN-KUN!
GACH
SPOOSH
SYAORAN-KUN!!

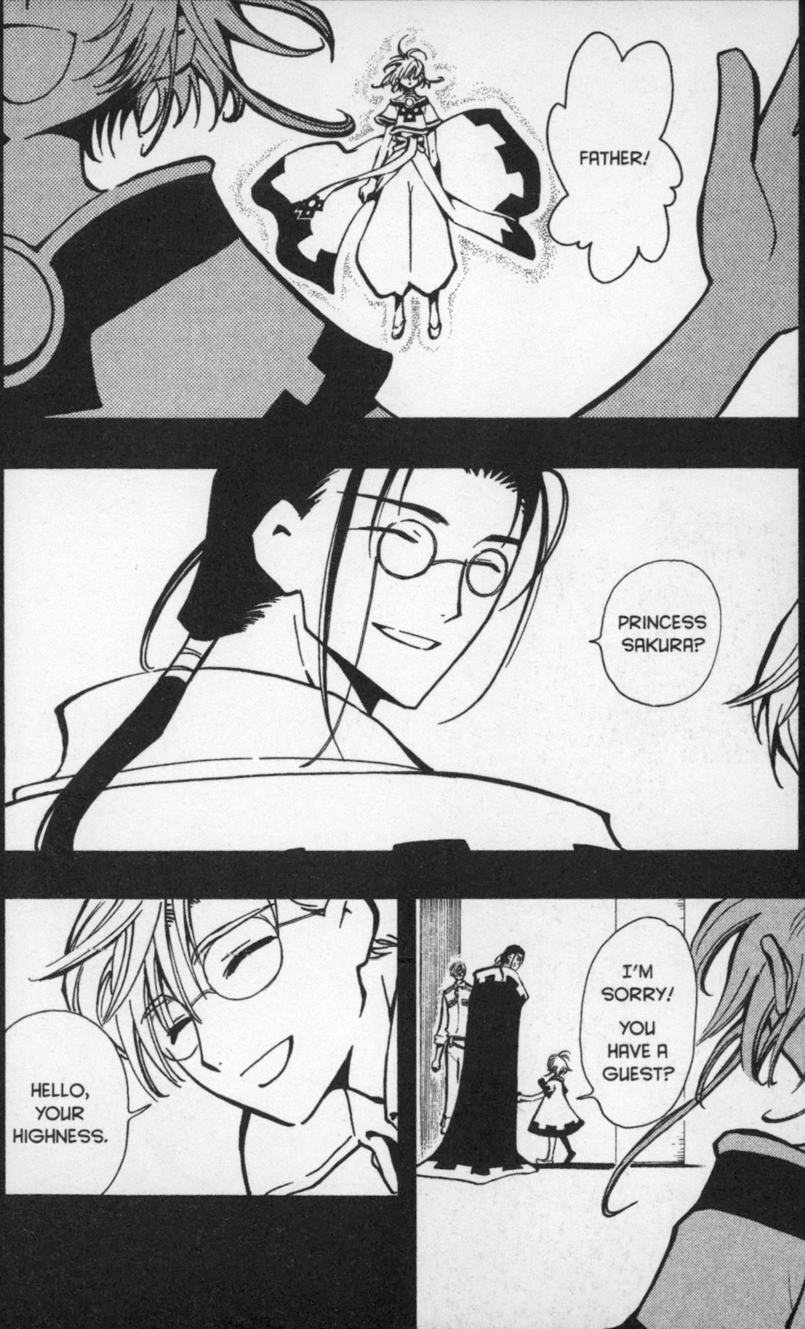
FATHER!
PRINCESS SAKURA?
I'M SORRY!
YOU HAVE A GUEST?
HELLO, YOUR HIGHNESS.

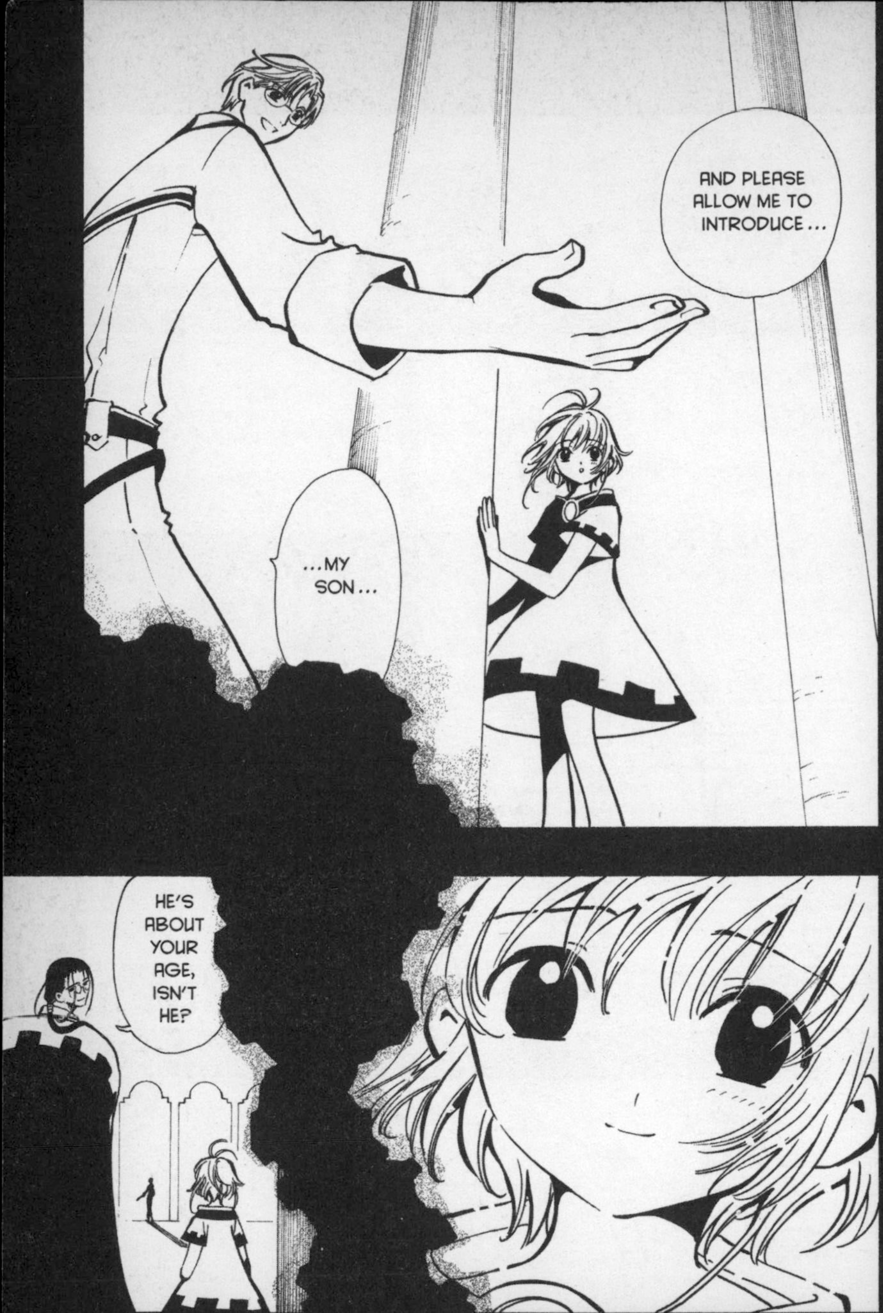
AND PLEASE ALLOW ME TO INTRODUCE...
...MY SON...
HE'S ABOUT YOUR AGE, ISN'T HE?

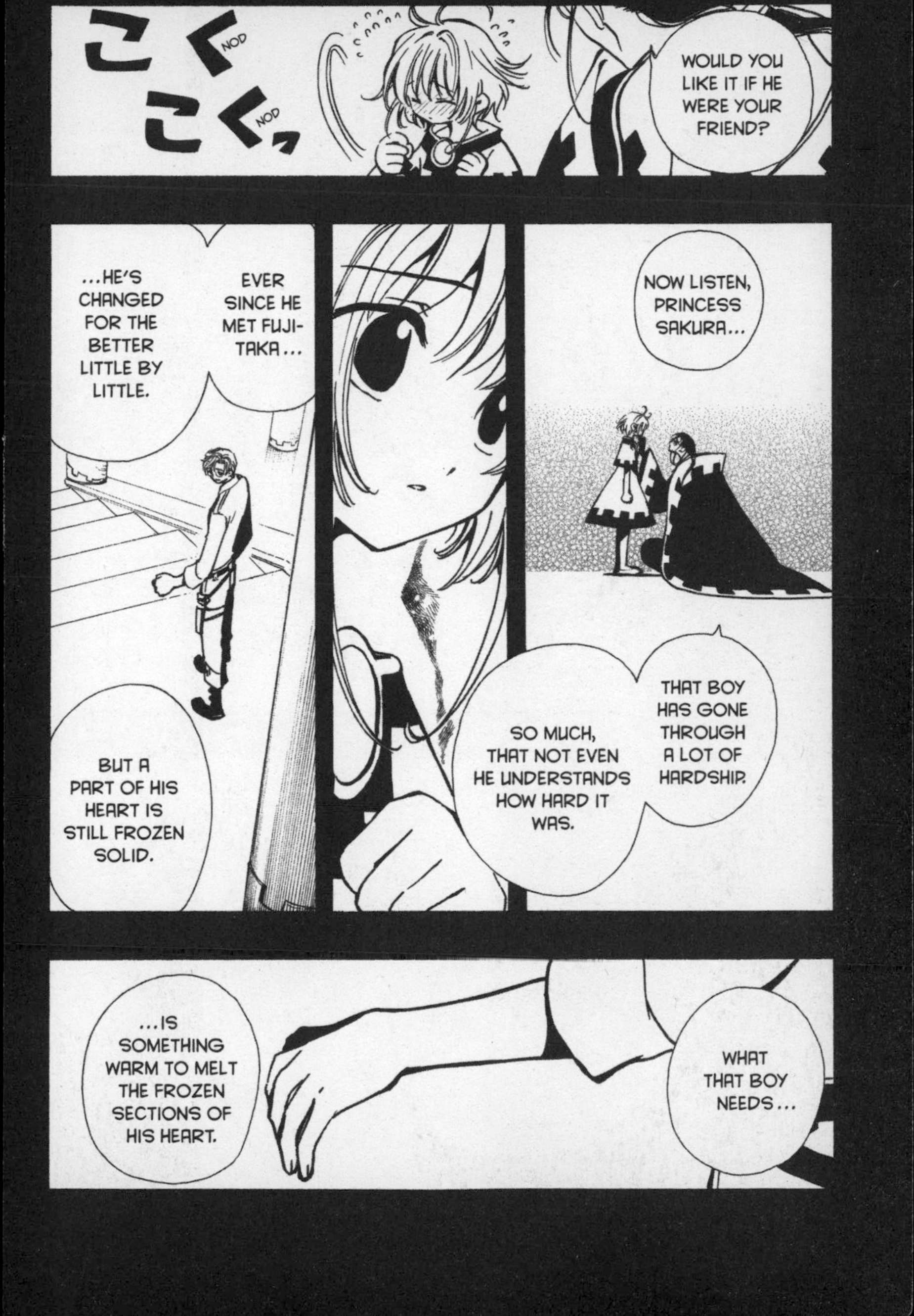
WOULD YOU LIKE IT IF HE WERE YOUR FRIEND?
こく NOD
こくっ NOD
NOW LISTEN, PRINCESS SAKURA...
THAT BOY HAS GONE THROUGH A LOT OF HARDSHIP.
SO MUCH, THAT NOT EVEN HE UNDERSTANDS HOW HARD IT WAS.
EVER SINCE HE MET FUJI-TAKA...
...HE'S CHANGED FOR THE BETTER LITTLE BY LITTLE.
BUT A PART OF HIS HEART IS STILL FROZEN SOLID.
WHAT THAT BOY NEEDS...
...IS SOMETHING WARM TO MELT THE FROZEN SECTIONS OF HIS HEART.

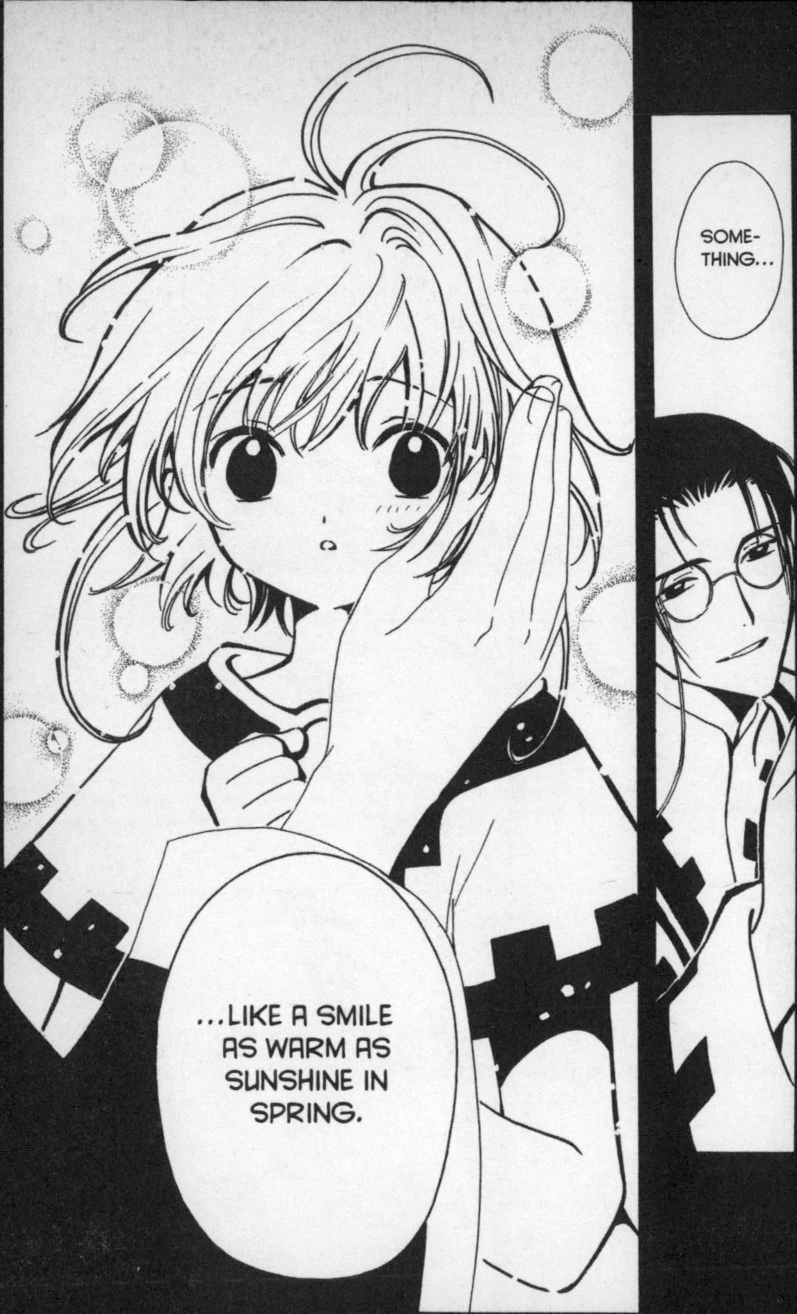
SOME-
THING...
...LIKE A SMILE
AS WARM AS
SUNSHINE IN
SPRING.

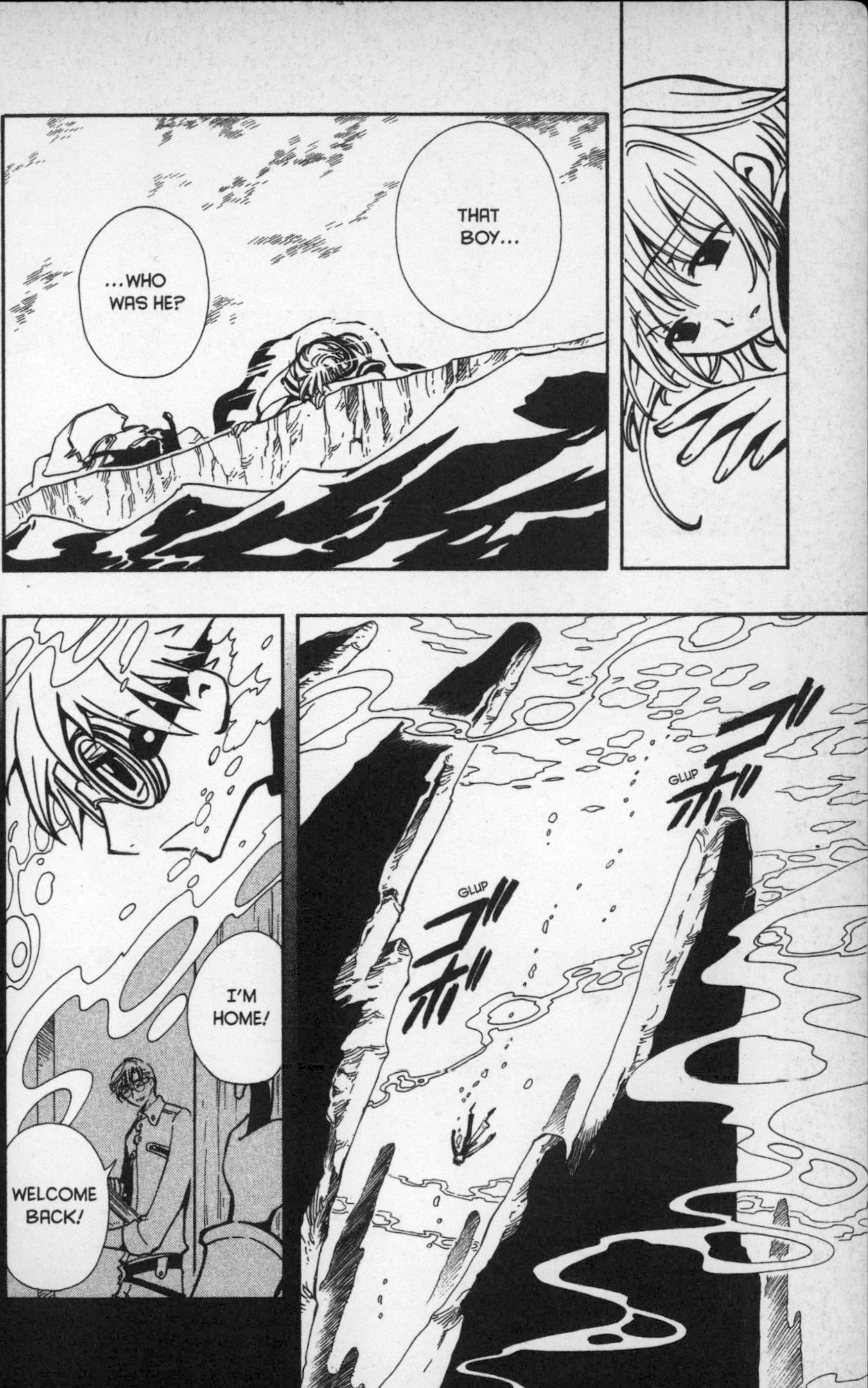
THAT BOY...
...WHO WAS HE?
GLUP
GLUP
I'M HOME!
WELCOME BACK!

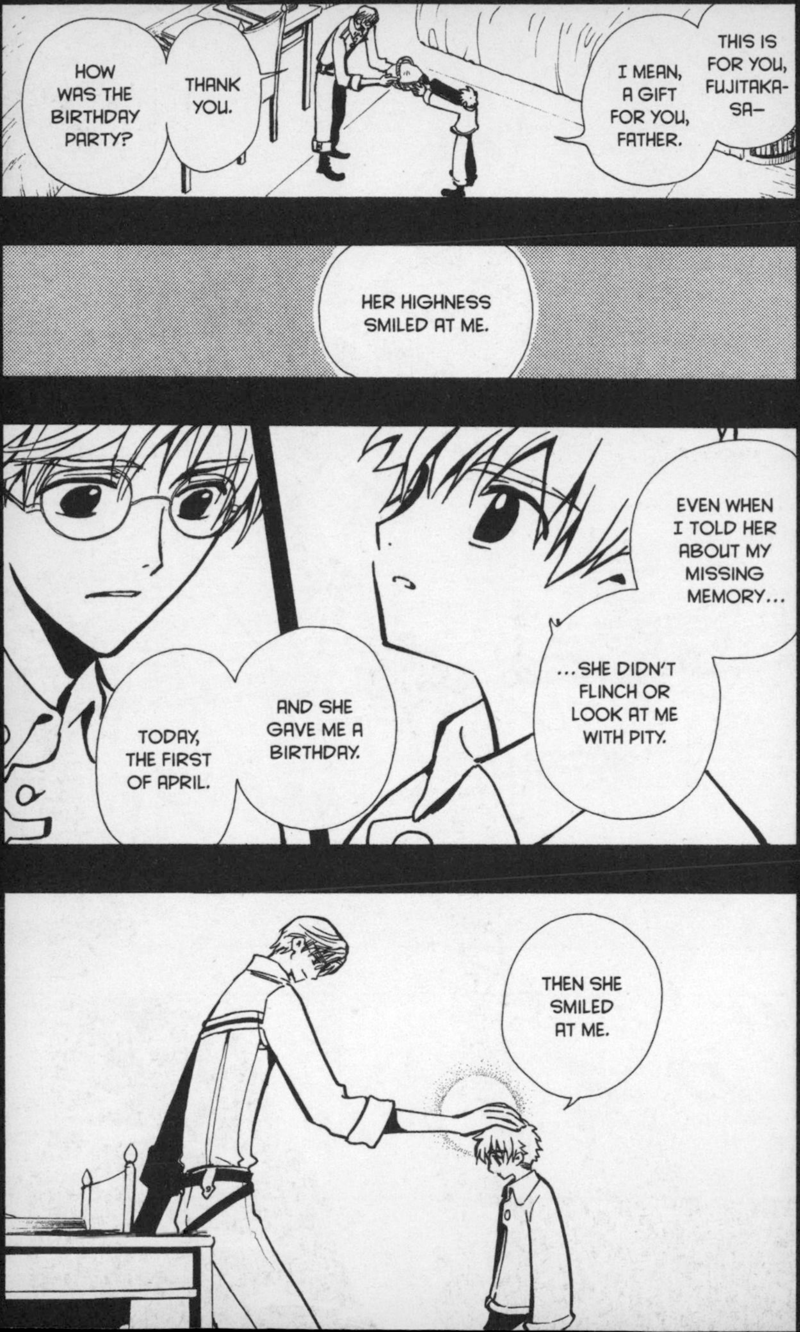
THIS IS FOR YOU, FUJITAKA-SA—
I MEAN, A GIFT FOR YOU, FATHER.
THANK YOU.
HOW WAS THE BIRTHDAY PARTY?
HER HIGHNESS SMILED AT ME.
EVEN WHEN I TOLD HER ABOUT MY MISSING MEMORY...
...SHE DIDN'T FLINCH OR LOOK AT ME WITH PITY.
AND SHE GAVE ME A BIRTHDAY.
TODAY, THE FIRST OF APRIL.
THEN SHE SMILED AT ME.

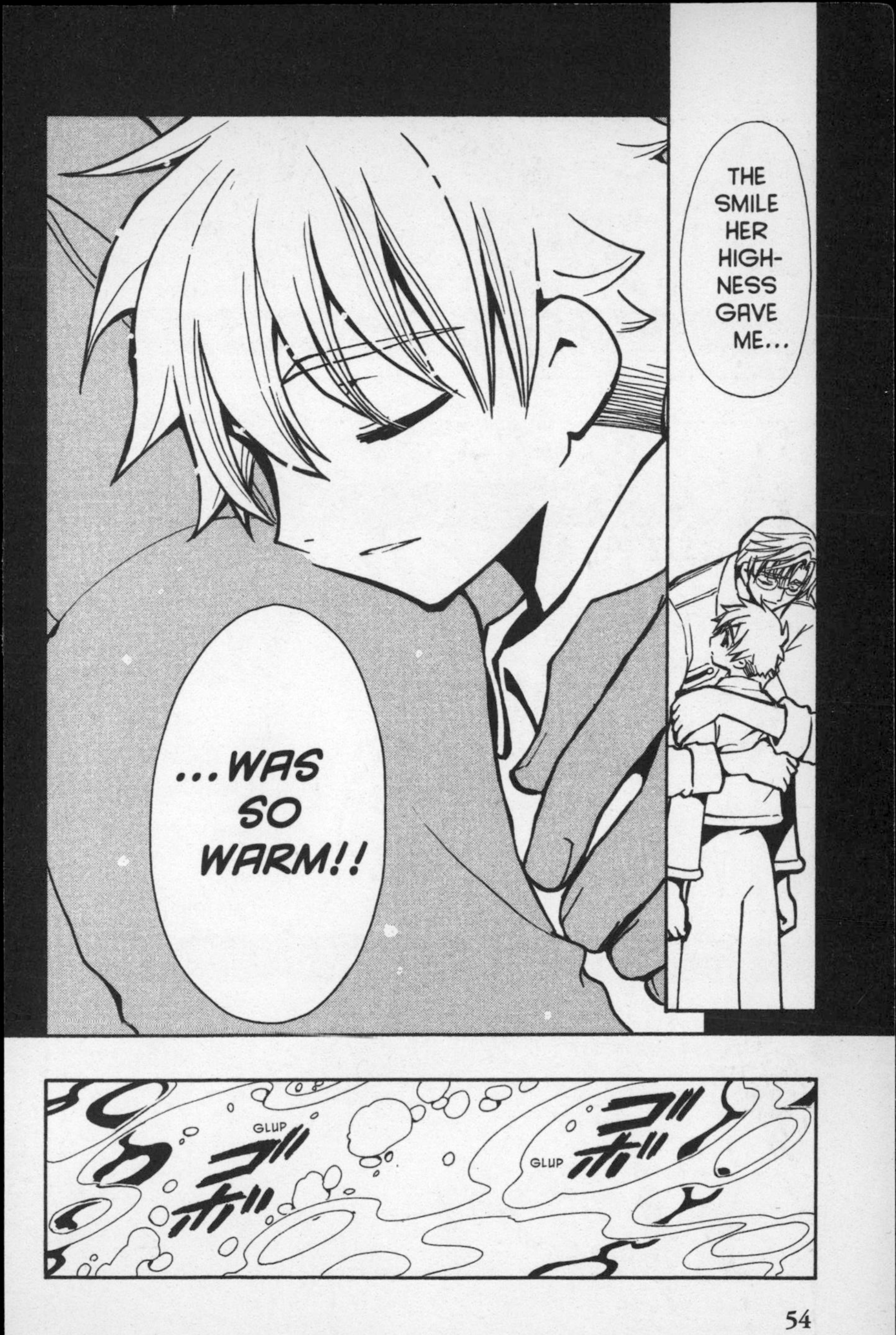
THE SMILE HER HIGHNESS GAVE ME...
...WAS SO WARM!!
GLUP
GLUP

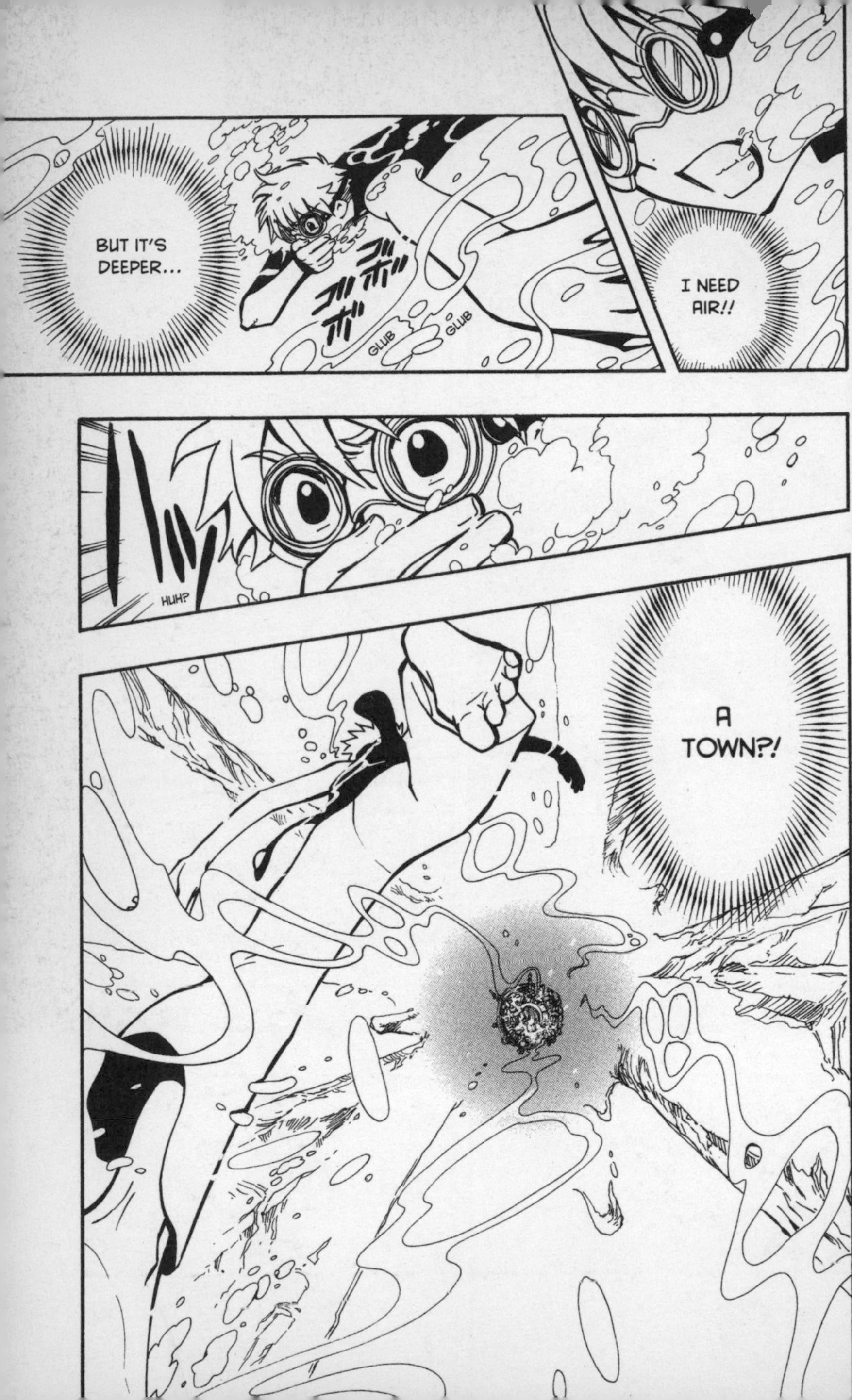
I NEED AIR!!
BUT IT'S DEEPER...
GLUB GLUB
HUH?
A TOWN?!

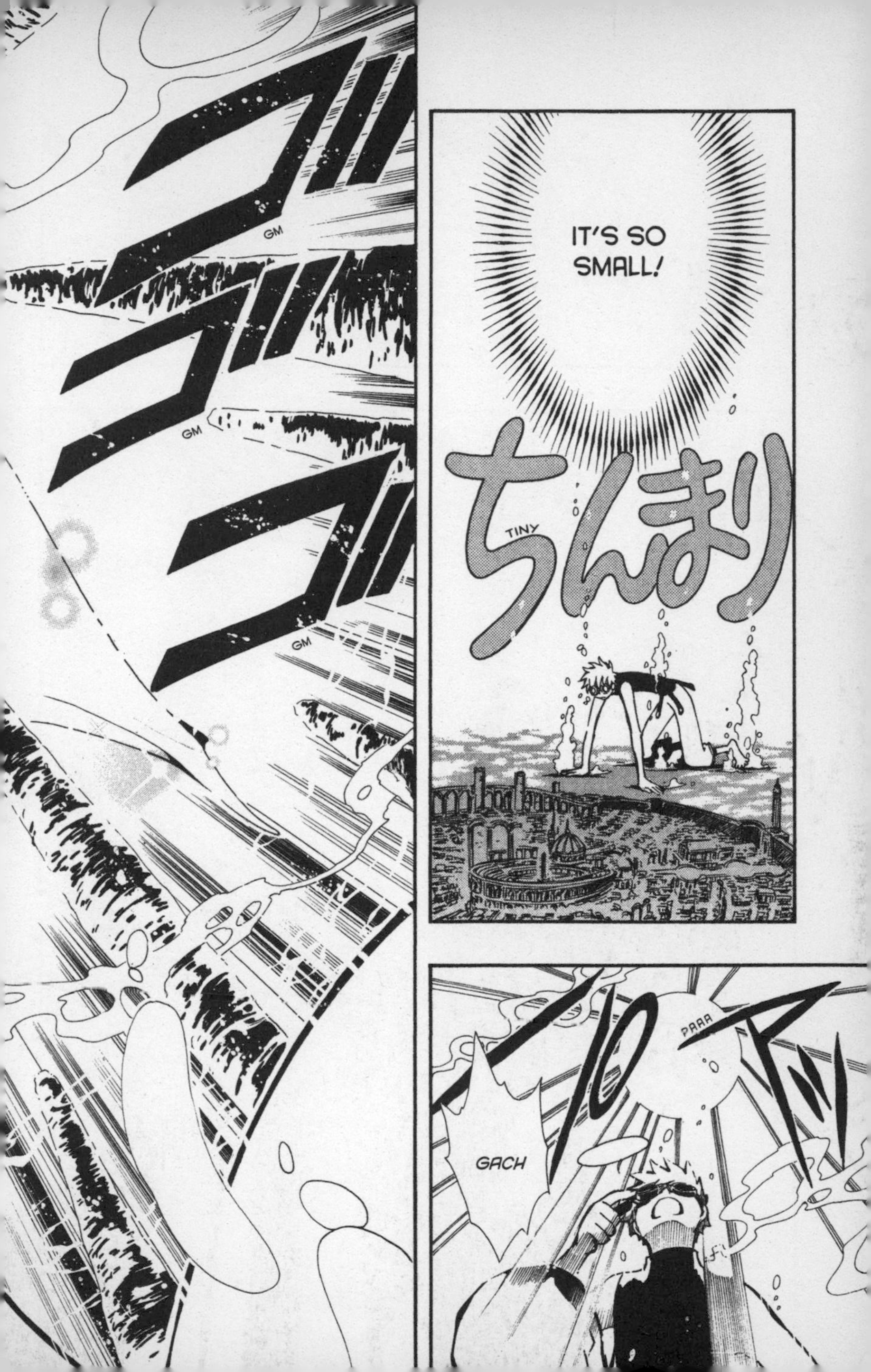
IT'S SO SMALL!
TINY
ちんまり
PAAA
GACH
GM
GM
GM

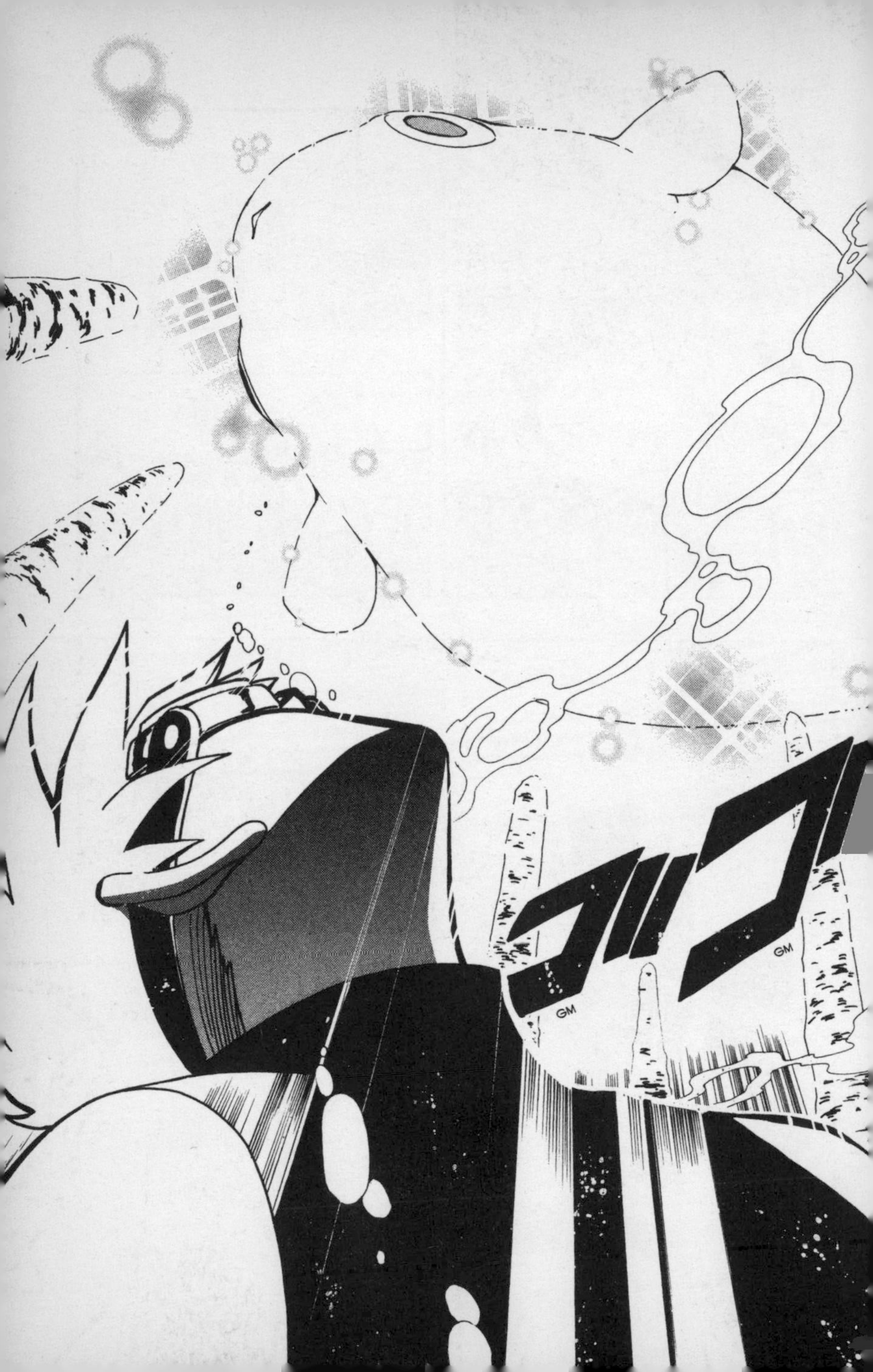
GM
GM

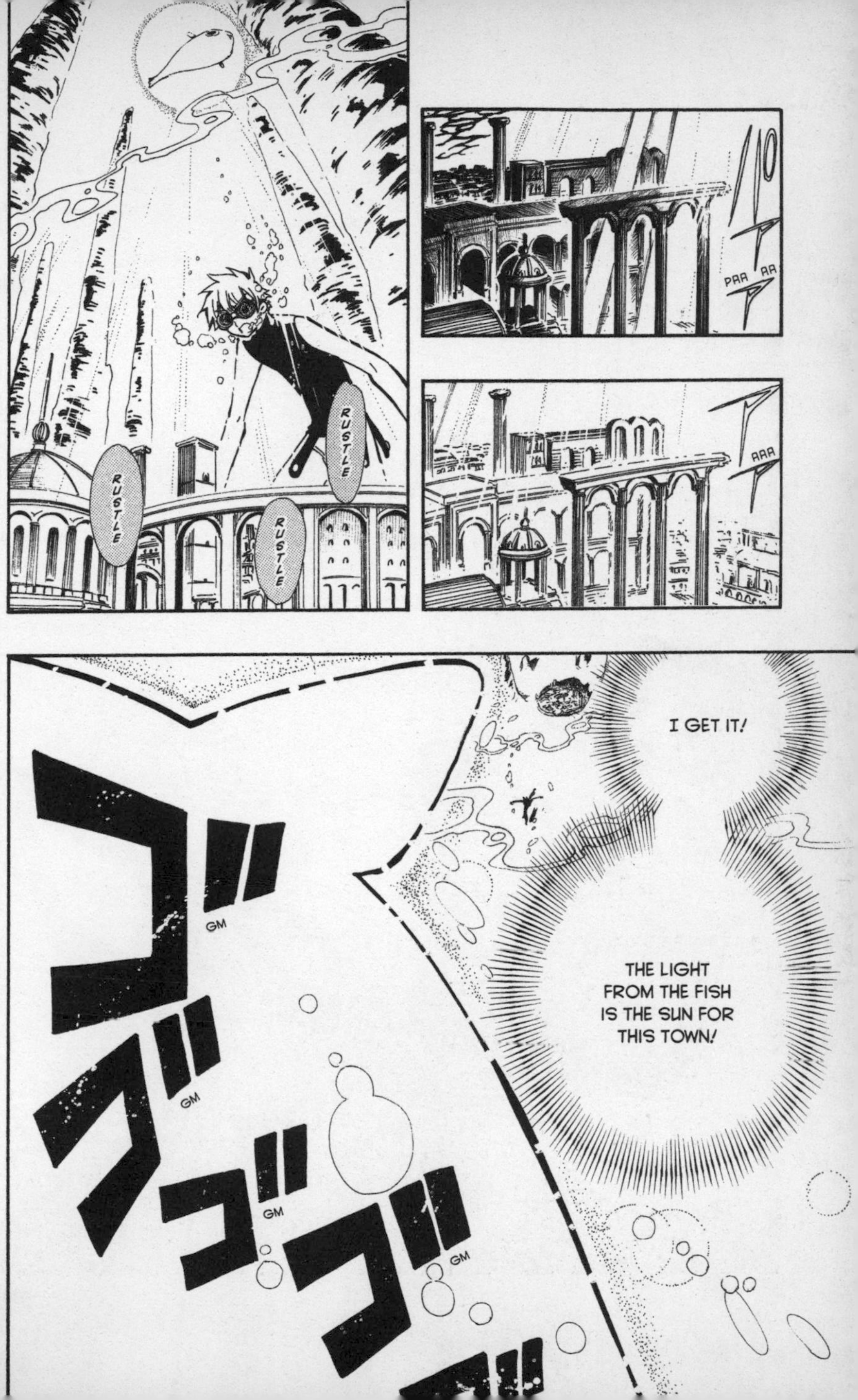
PAA AA
AAA
RUSTLE
RUSTLE
RUSTLE
I GET IT!
THE LIGHT FROM THE FISH IS THE SUN FOR THIS TOWN!
GM
GM
GM
GM

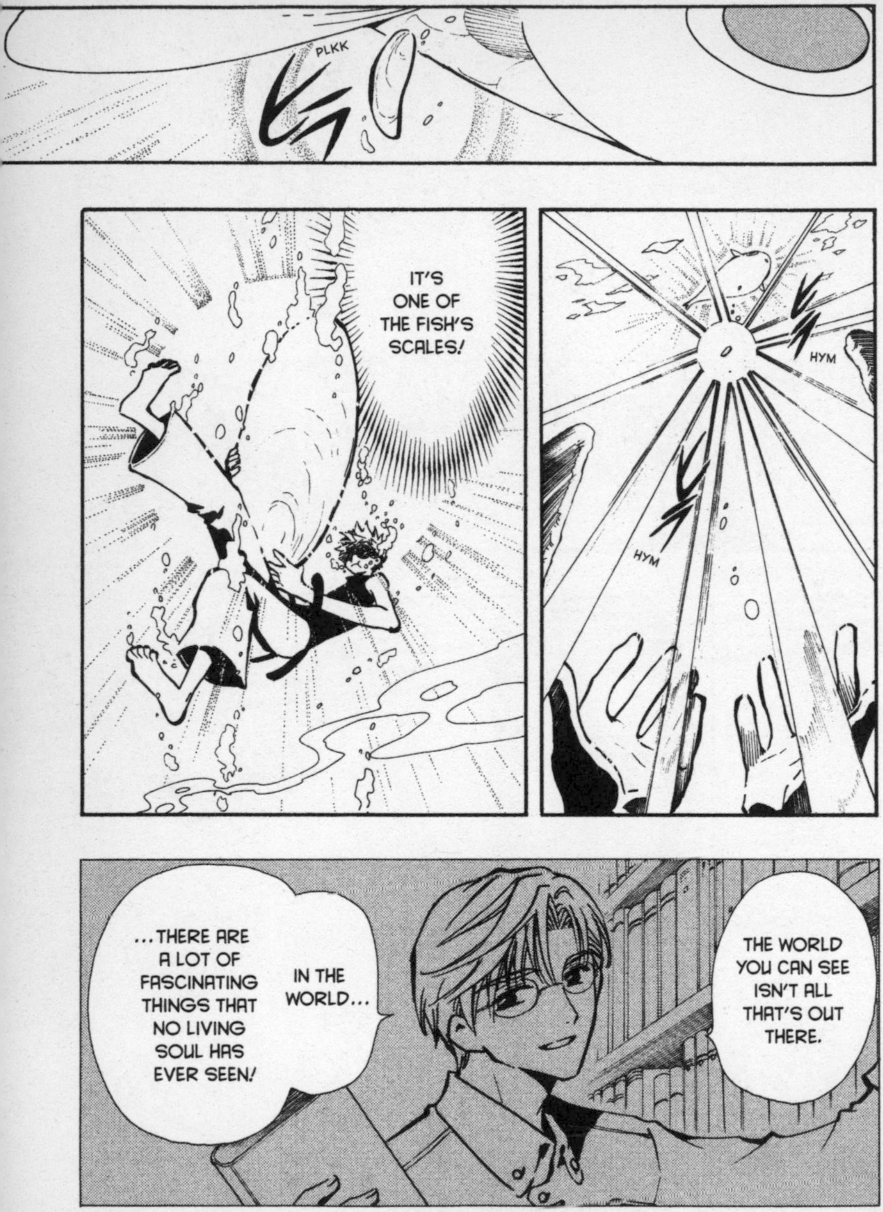
PLKK
HYM
HYM
IT'S ONE OF THE FISH'S SCALES!
THE WORLD YOU CAN SEE ISN'T ALL THAT'S OUT THERE.
IN THE WORLD...
...THERE ARE A LOT OF FASCINATING THINGS THAT NO LIVING SOUL HAS EVER SEEN!

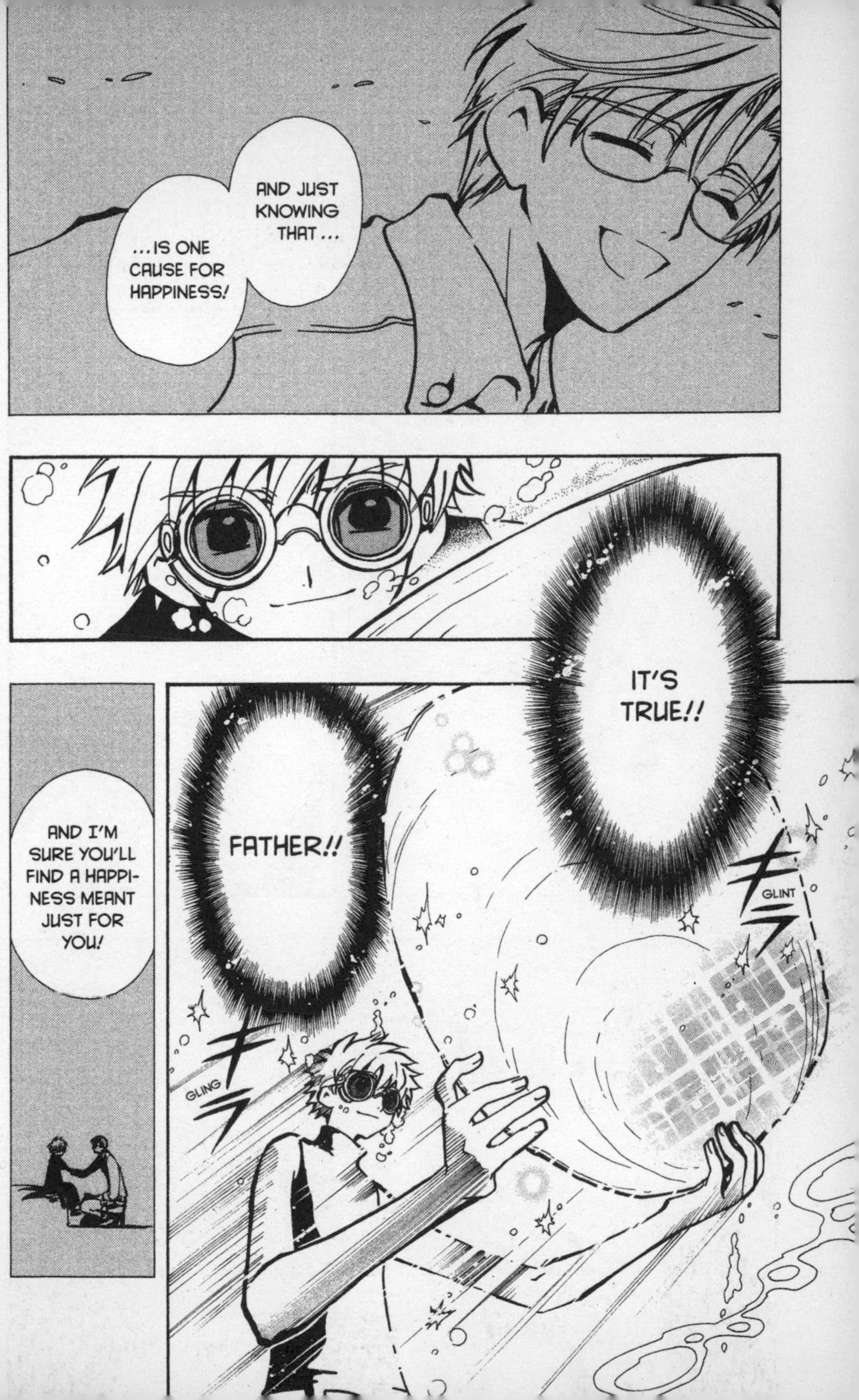
AND JUST KNOWING THAT...
...IS ONE CAUSE FOR HAPPINESS!
IT'S TRUE!!
FATHER!!
GLINT
GLING
AND I'M SURE YOU'LL FIND A HAPPINESS MEANT JUST FOR YOU!

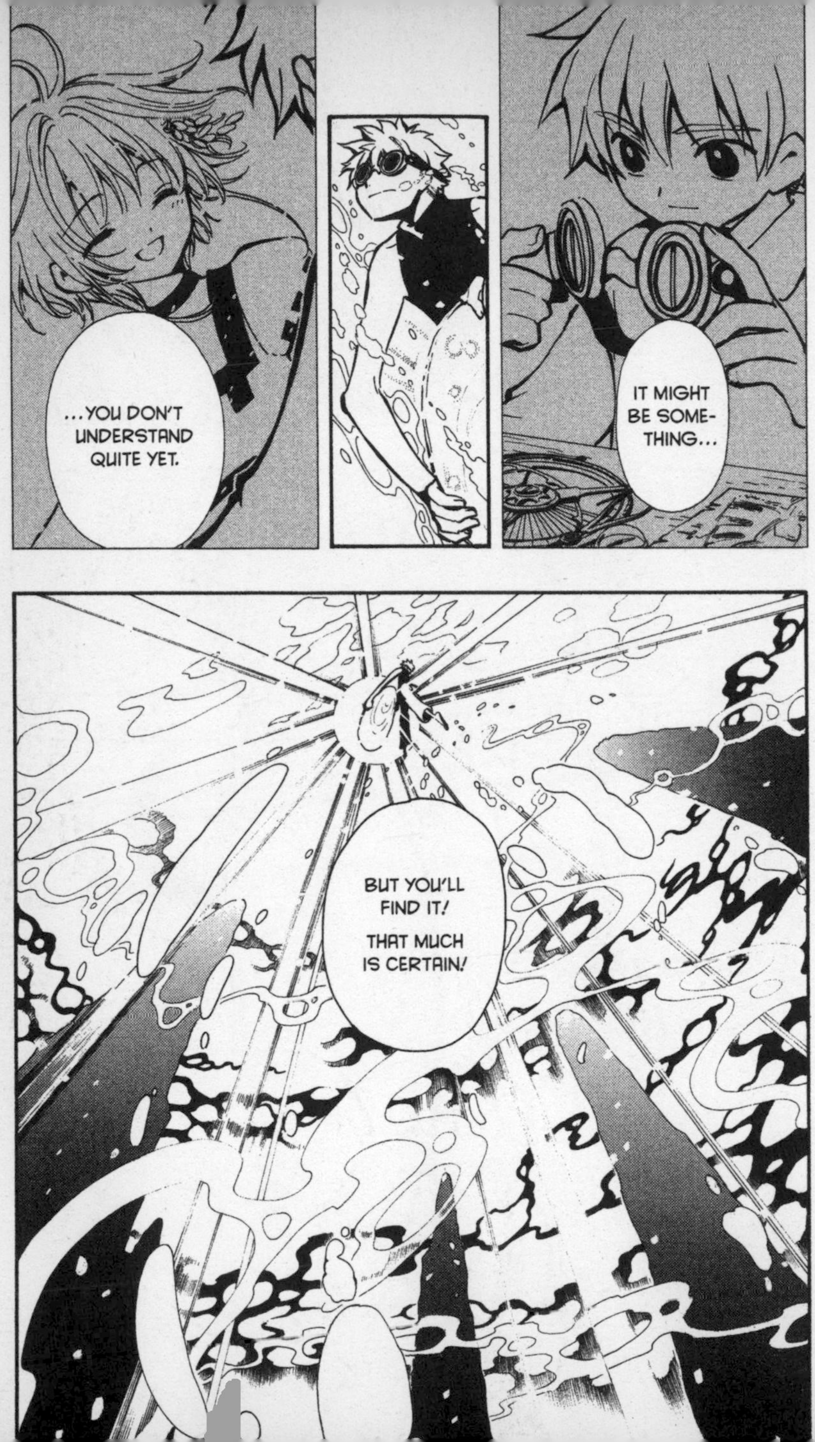
IT MIGHT BE SOME-THING...
...YOU DON'T UNDERSTAND QUITE YET.
BUT YOU'LL FIND IT!
THAT MUCH IS CERTAIN!

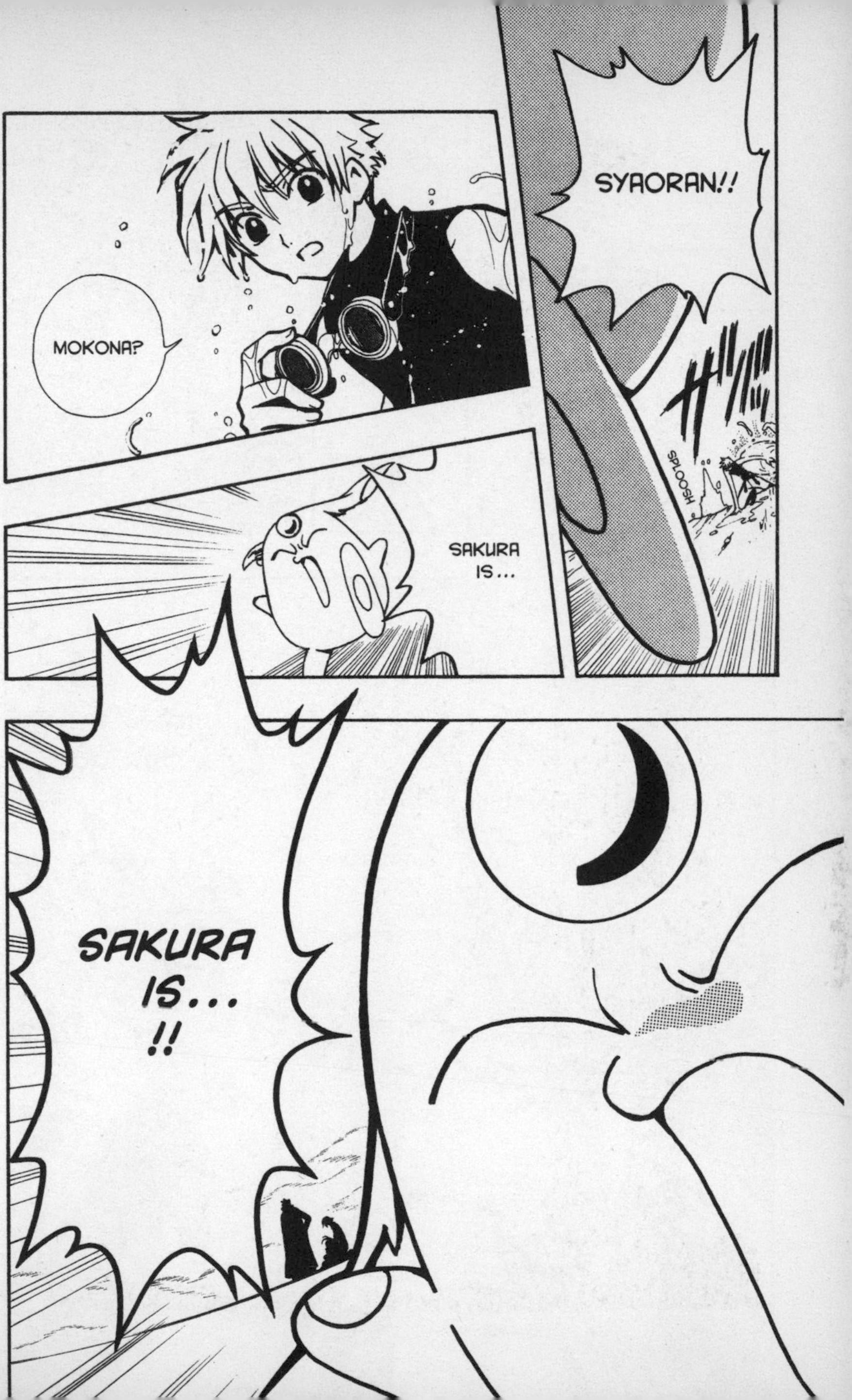
SYAORAN!!
SPLOOSH
MOKONA?
SAKURA IS...
SAKURA IS... !!

Chapitre.24
Where the Smile Went

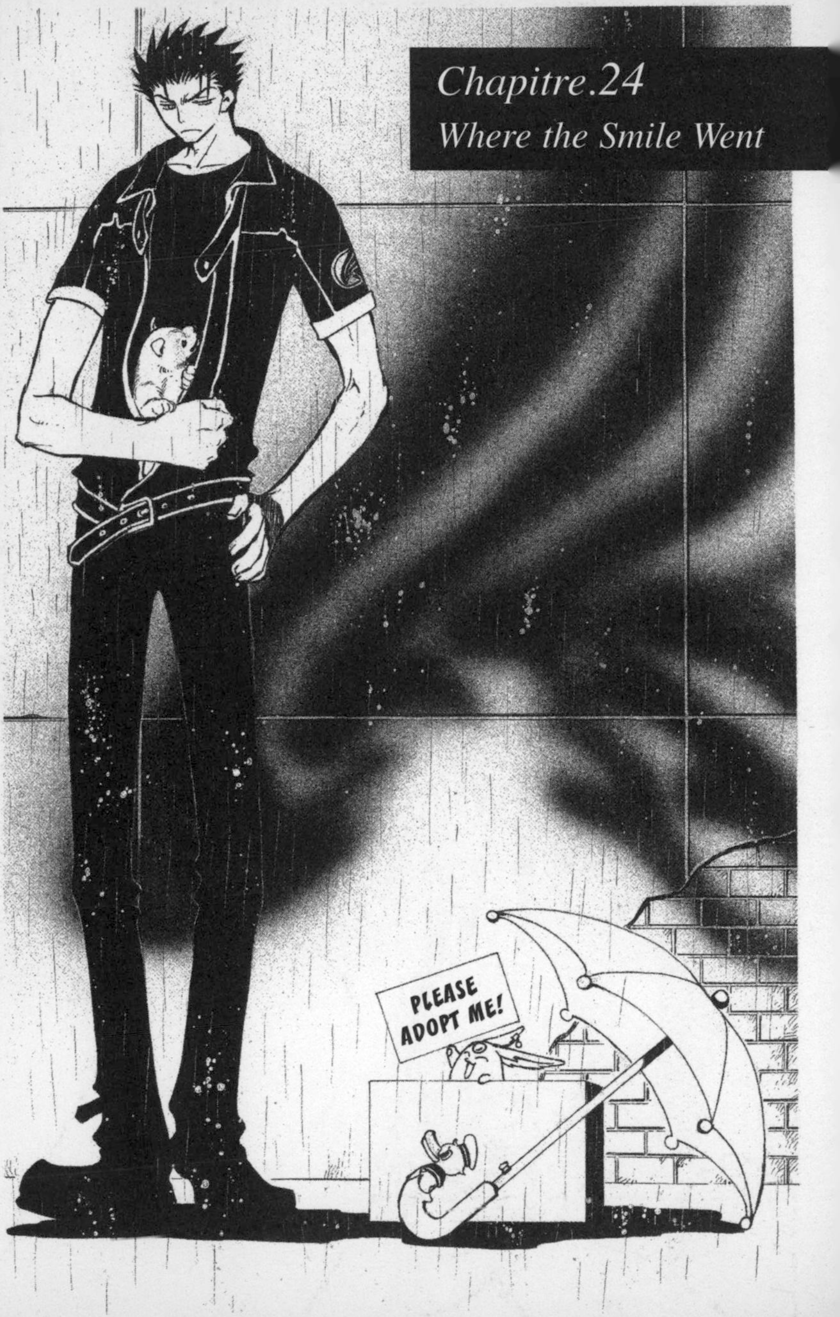
PLEASE
ADOPT ME!

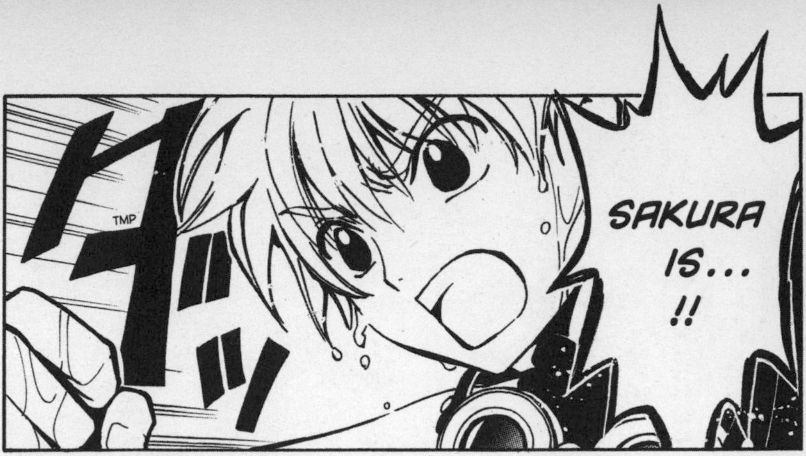
SAKURA IS... !!
TMP
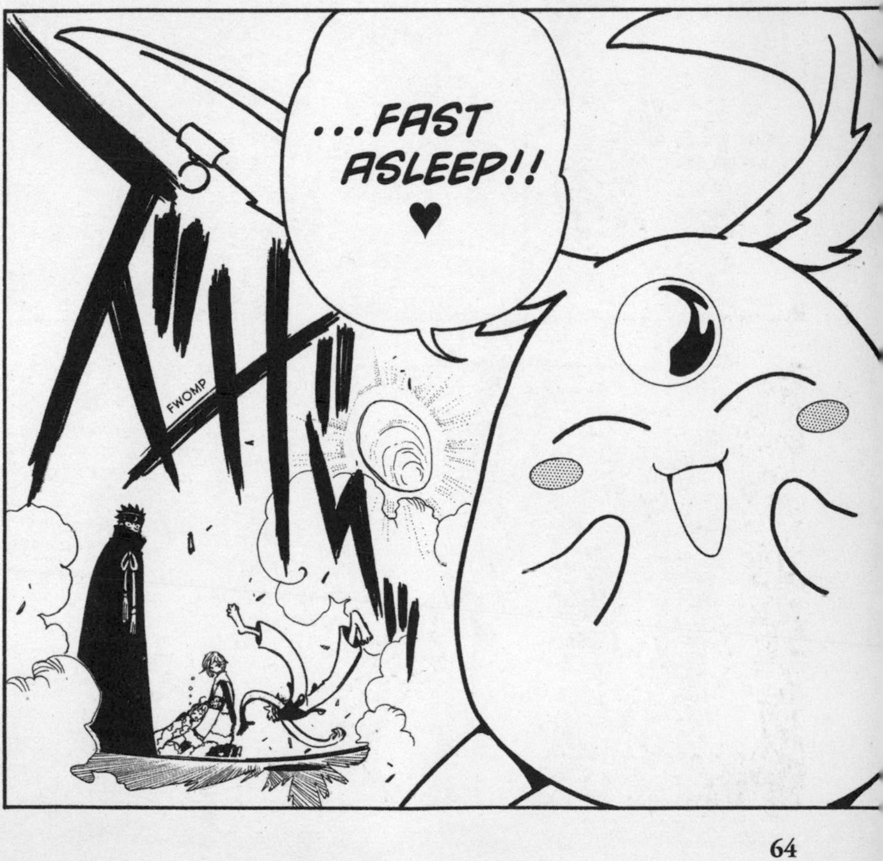
...FAST ASLEEP!! ♥
FWOMP

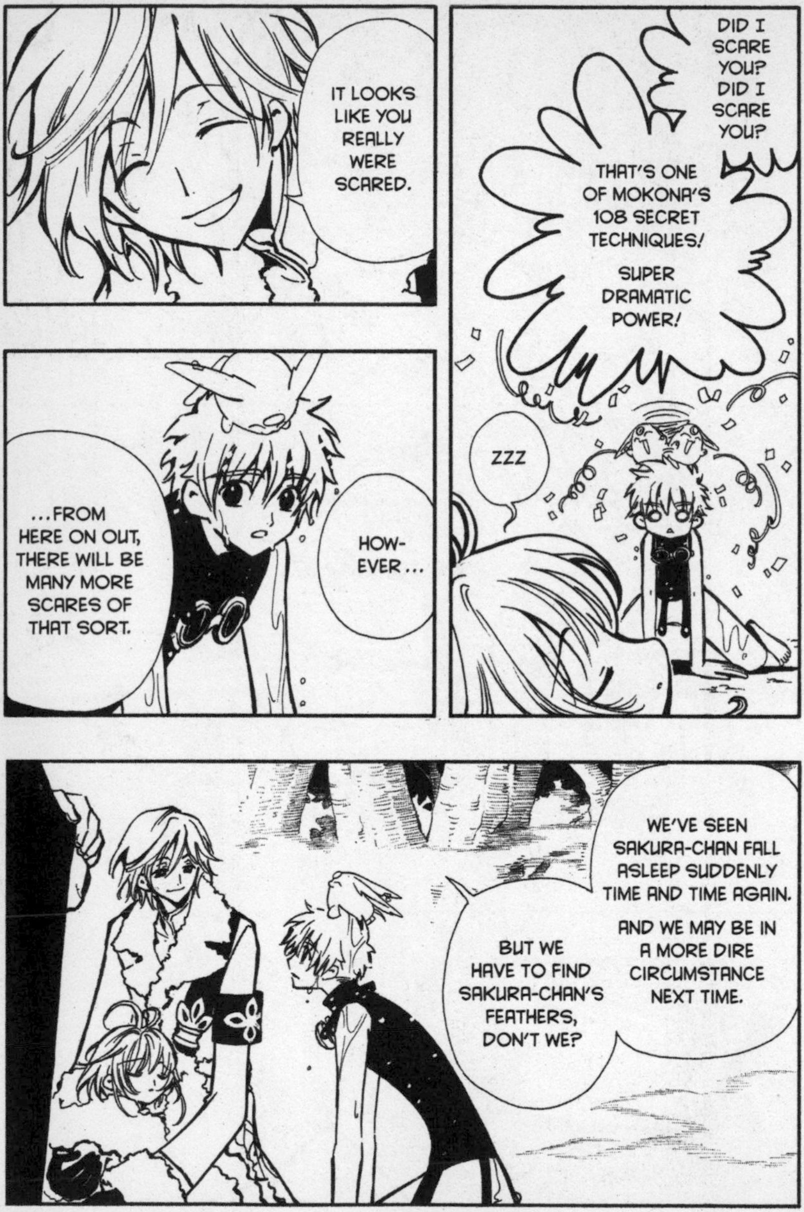
DID I SCARE YOU? DID I SCARE YOU?
THAT'S ONE OF MOKONA'S 108 SECRET TECHNIQUES!
SUPER DRAMATIC POWER!
ZZZ
IT LOOKS LIKE YOU REALLY WERE SCARED.
HOW-EVER...
...FROM HERE ON OUT, THERE WILL BE MANY MORE SCARES OF THAT SORT.
WE'VE SEEN SAKURA-CHAN FALL ASLEEP SUDDENLY TIME AND TIME AGAIN.
AND WE MAY BE IN A MORE DIRE CIRCUMSTANCE NEXT TIME.
BUT WE HAVE TO FIND SAKURA-CHAN'S FEATHERS, DON'T WE?

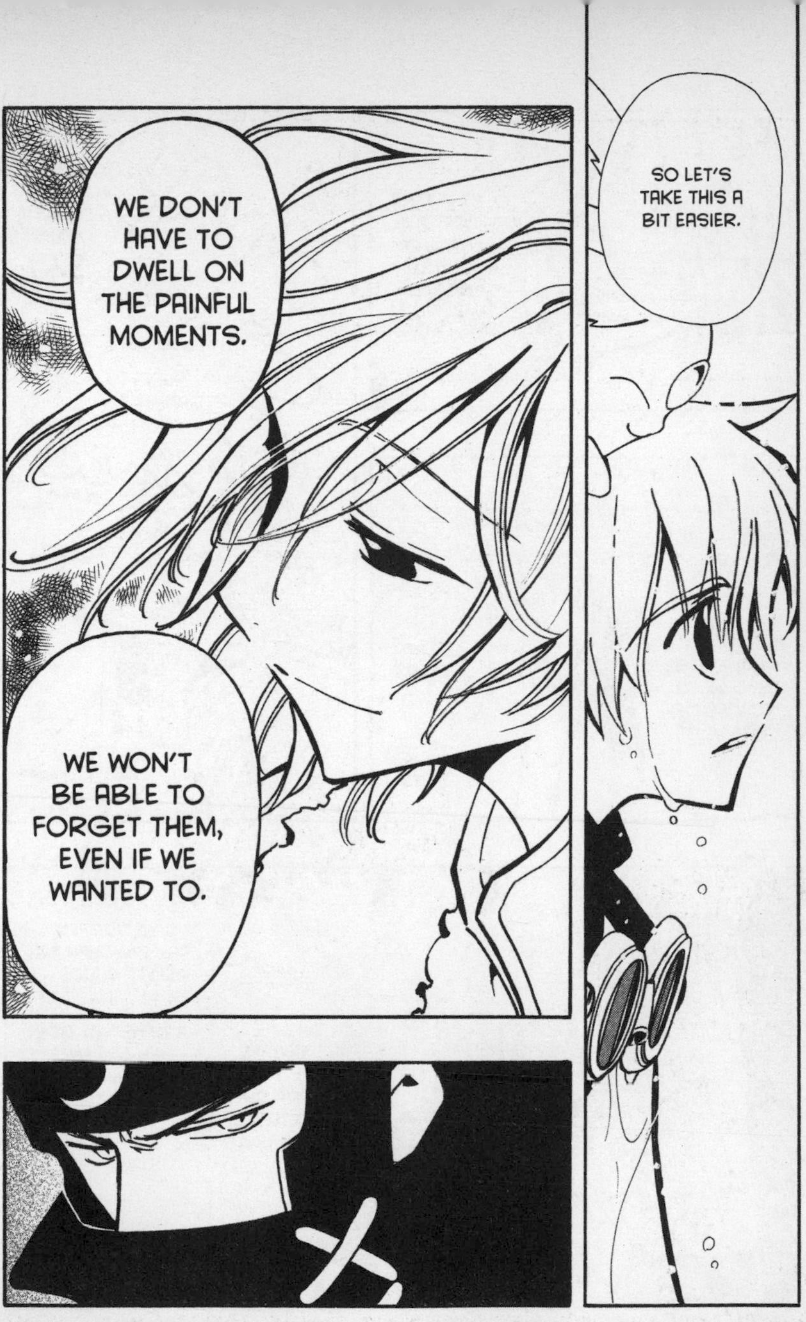
WE DON'T HAVE TO DWELL ON THE PAINFUL MOMENTS.
WE WON'T BE ABLE TO FORGET THEM, EVEN IF WE WANTED TO.
SO LET'S TAKE THIS A BIT EASIER.

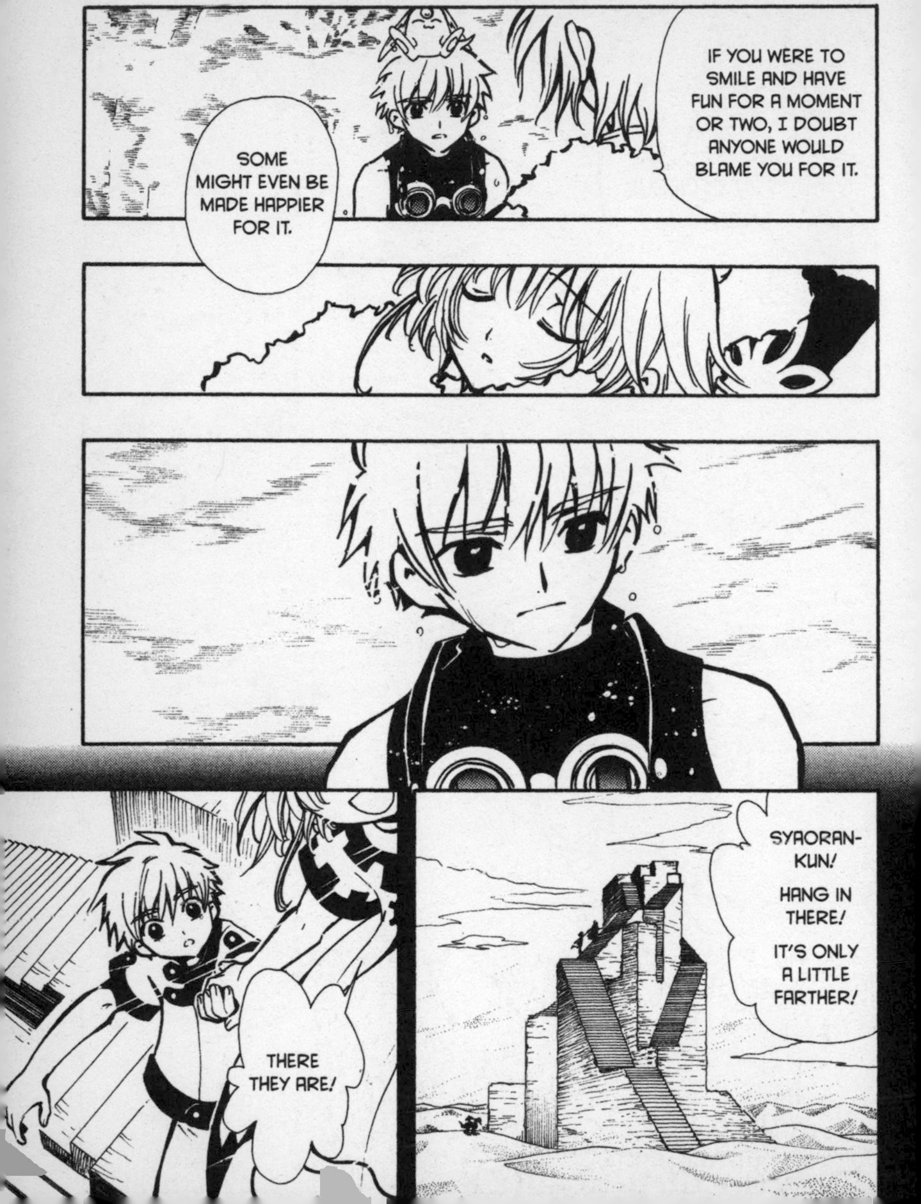
IF YOU WERE TO SMILE AND HAVE FUN FOR A MOMENT OR TWO, I DOUBT ANYONE WOULD BLAME YOU FOR IT.
SOME MIGHT EVEN BE MADE HAPPIER FOR IT.
SYAORAN-KUN!
HANG IN THERE!
IT'S ONLY A LITTLE FARTHER!
THERE THEY ARE!

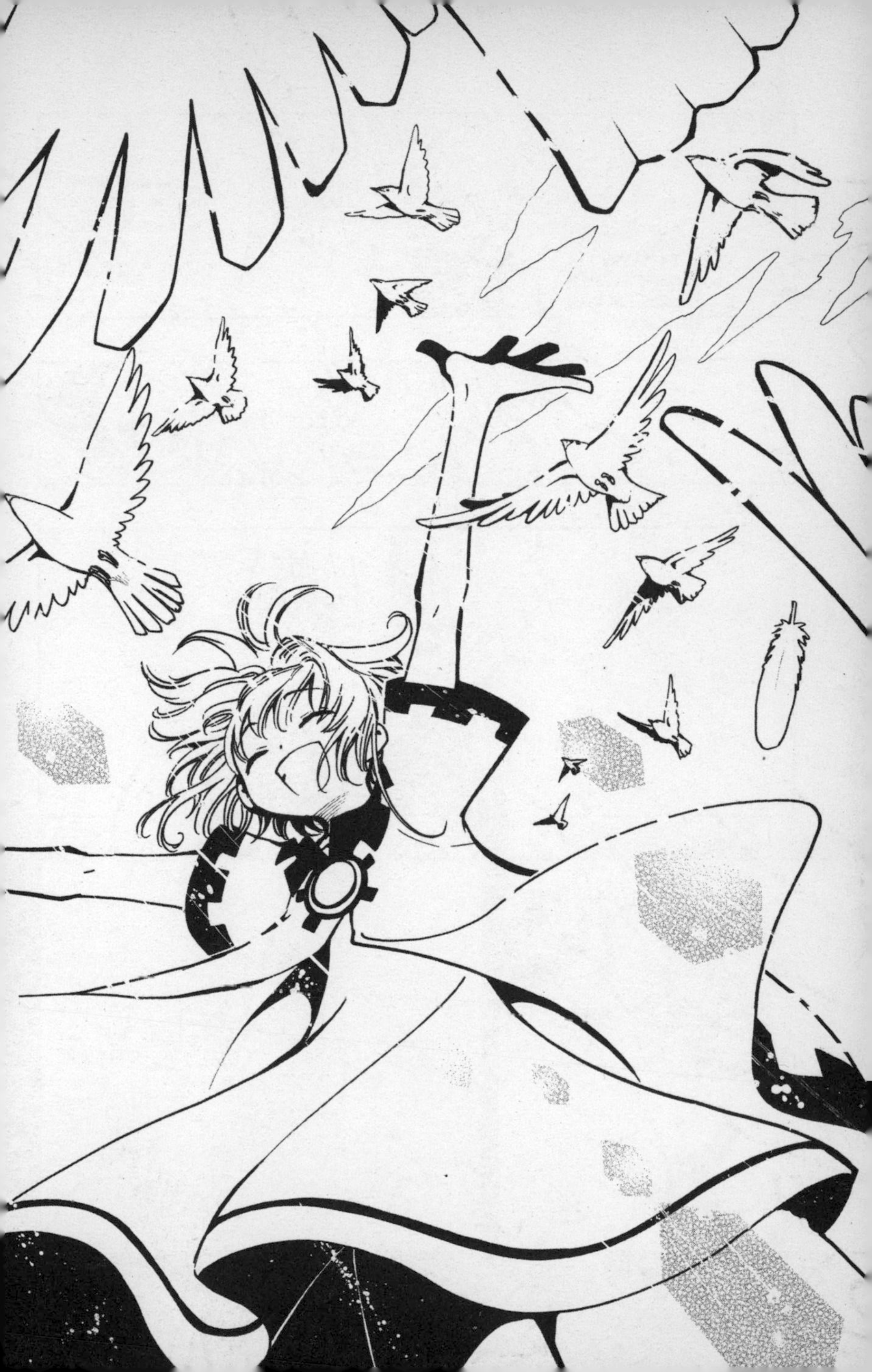

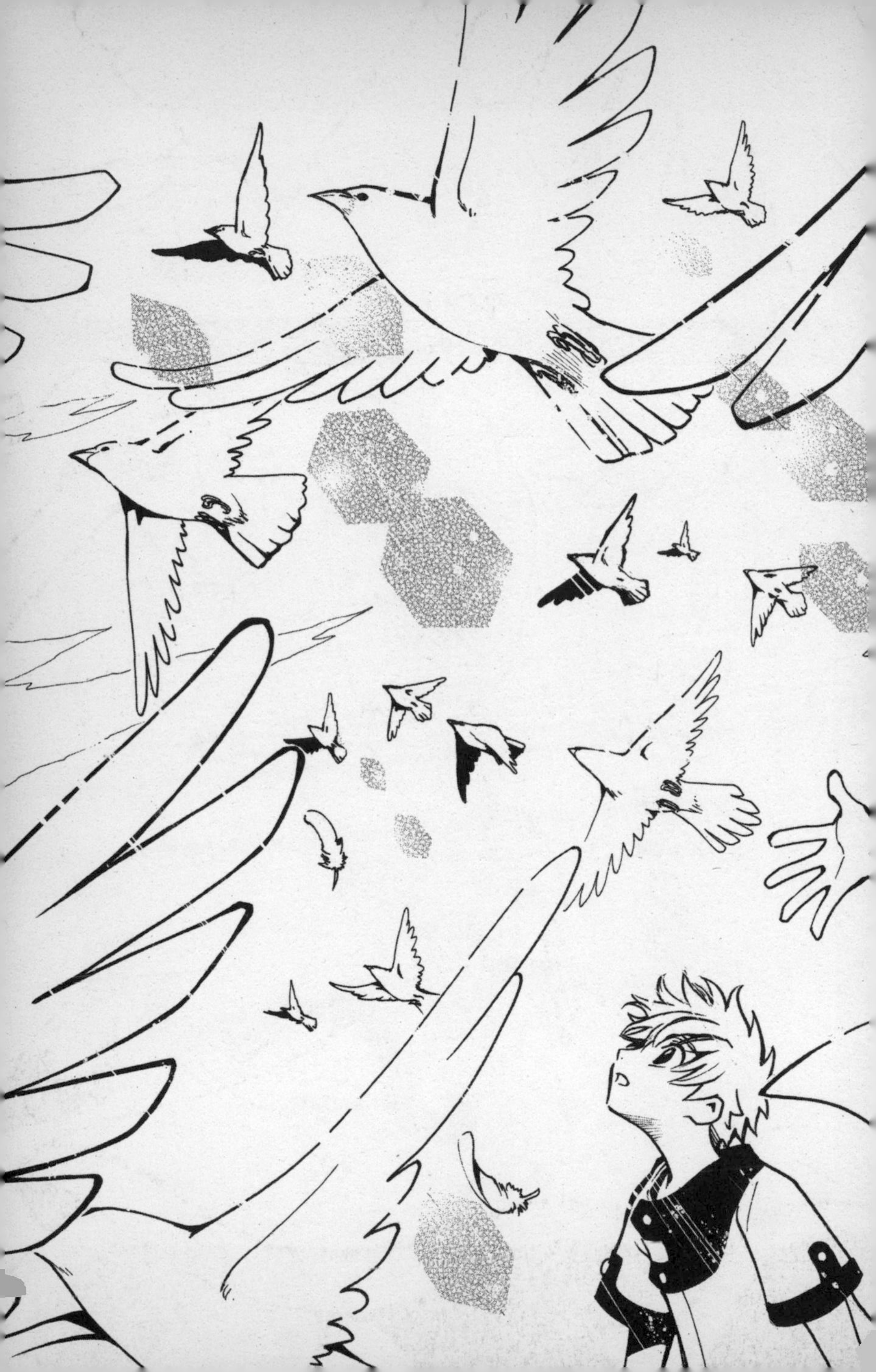

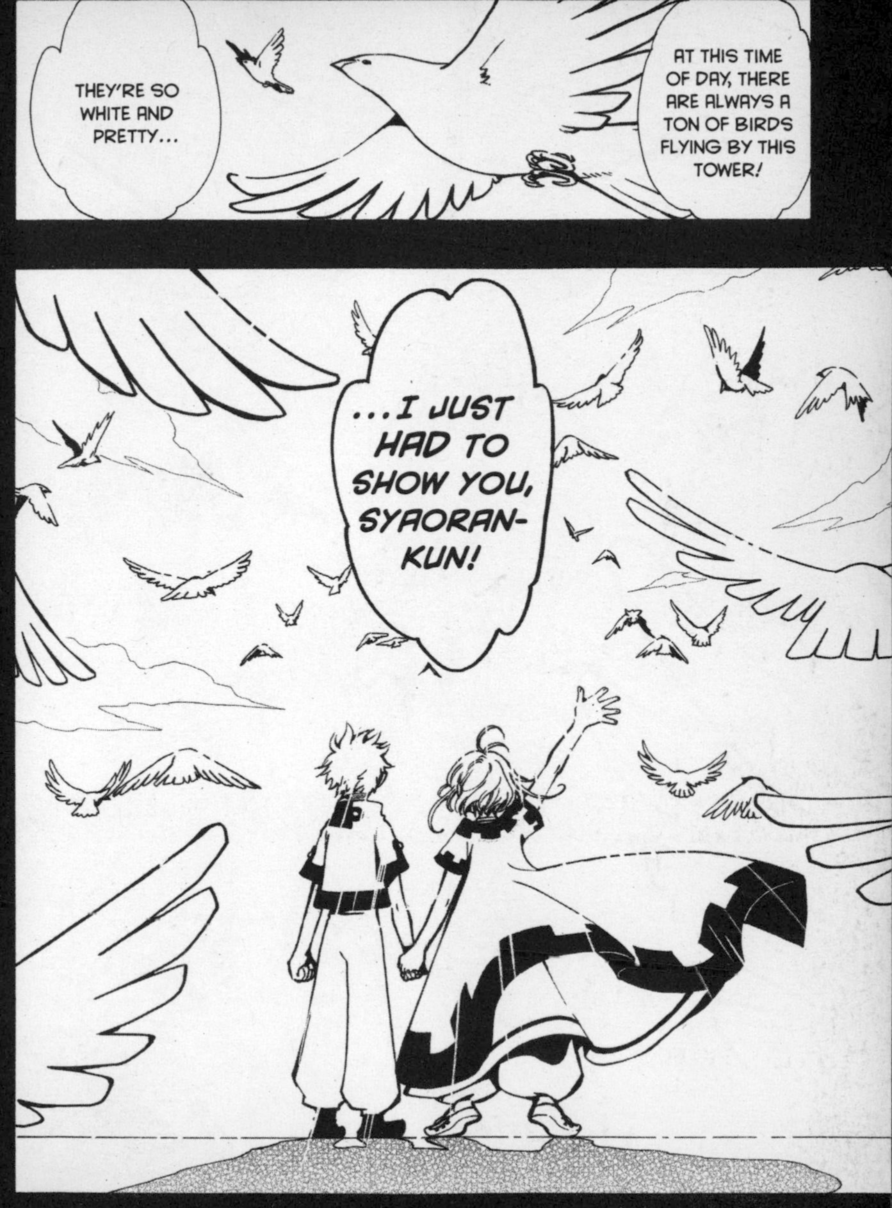
AT THIS TIME OF DAY, THERE ARE ALWAYS A TON OF BIRDS FLYING BY THIS TOWER!
THEY'RE SO WHITE AND PRETTY...
...I JUST HAD TO SHOW YOU, SYAORAN-KUN!

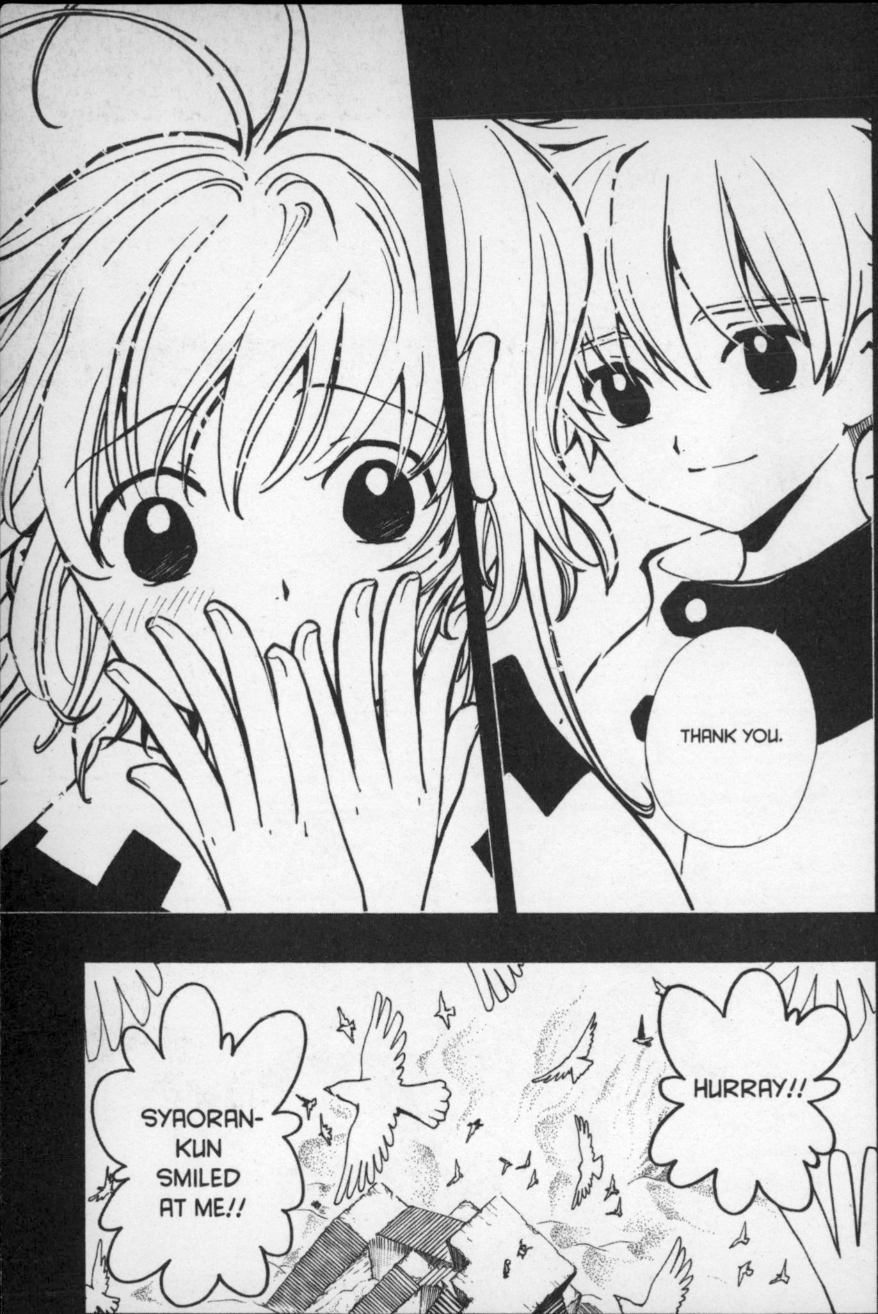
THANK YOU.
HURRAY!!
SYAORAN-KUN SMILED AT ME!!

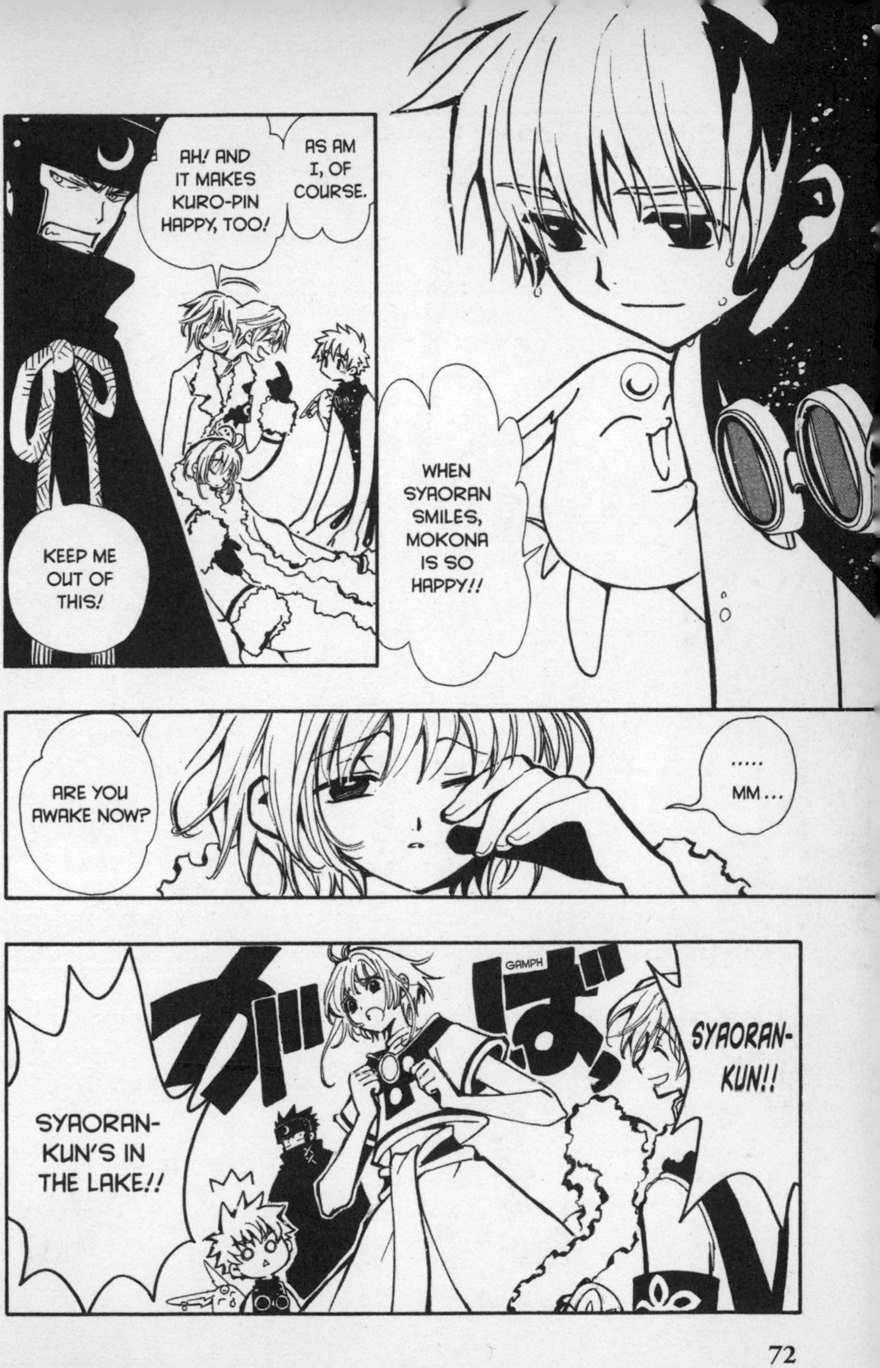
WHEN SYAORAN SMILES, MOKONA IS SO HAPPY!!
AS AM I, OF COURSE.
AH! AND IT MAKES KURO-PIN HAPPY, TOO!
KEEP ME OUT OF THIS!
..... MM...
ARE YOU AWAKE NOW?
GAMPH
SYAORAN-KUN!!
SYAORAN-KUN'S IN THE LAKE!!

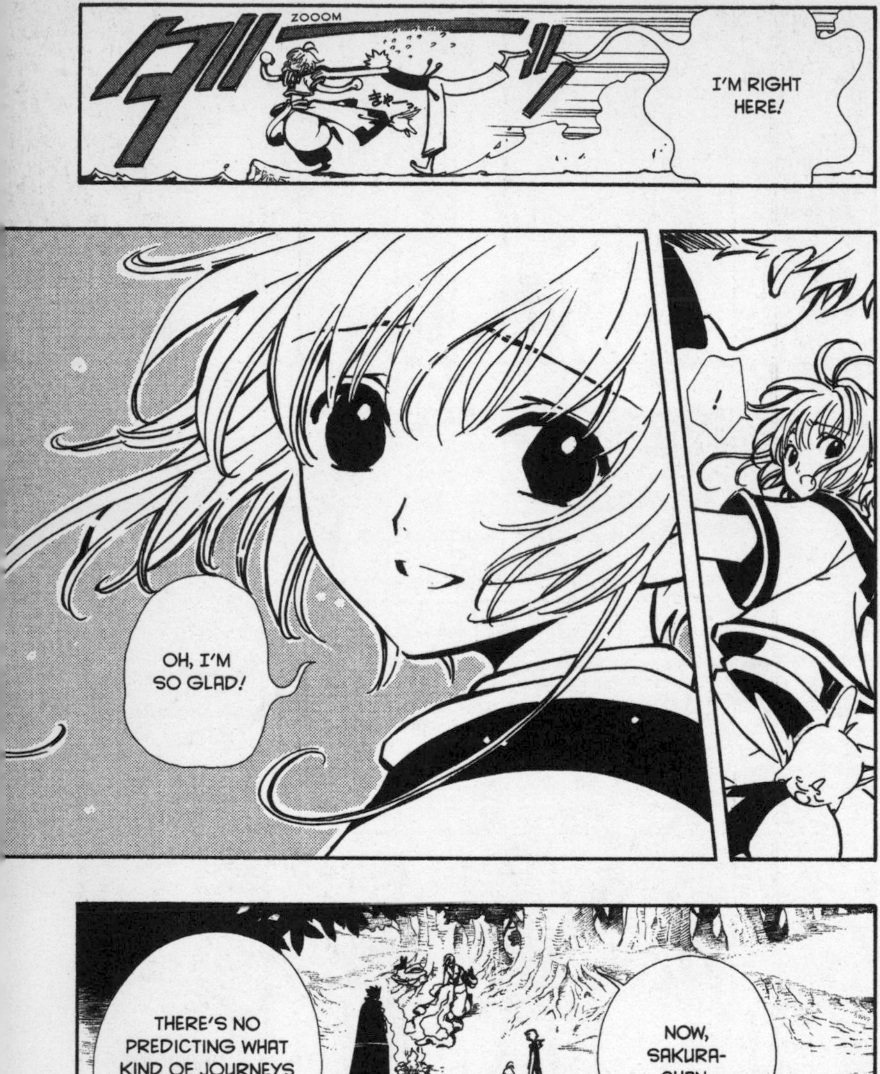
ZOOOM
I'M RIGHT HERE!
!
OH, I'M SO GLAD!
NOW, SAKURA-CHAN...
THERE'S NO PREDICTING WHAT KIND OF JOURNEYS WE'LL BE TAKING FROM NOW ON.

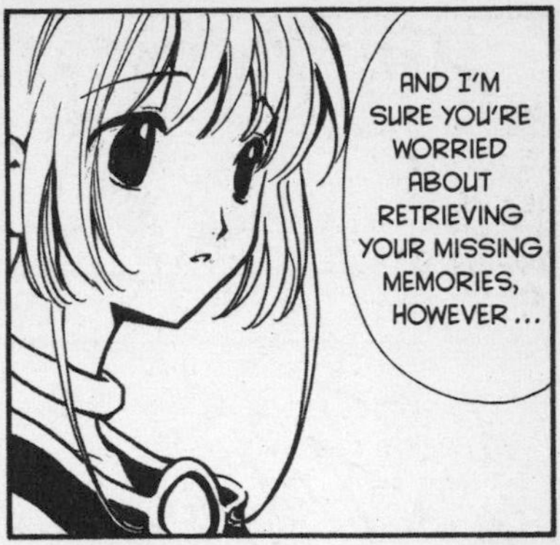
AND I'M SURE YOU'RE WORRIED ABOUT RETRIEVING YOUR MISSING MEMORIES, HOWEVER ...

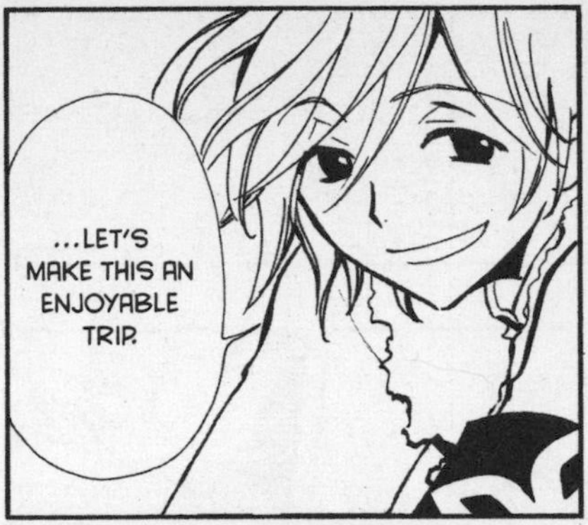
...LET'S MAKE THIS AN ENJOYABLE TRIP.

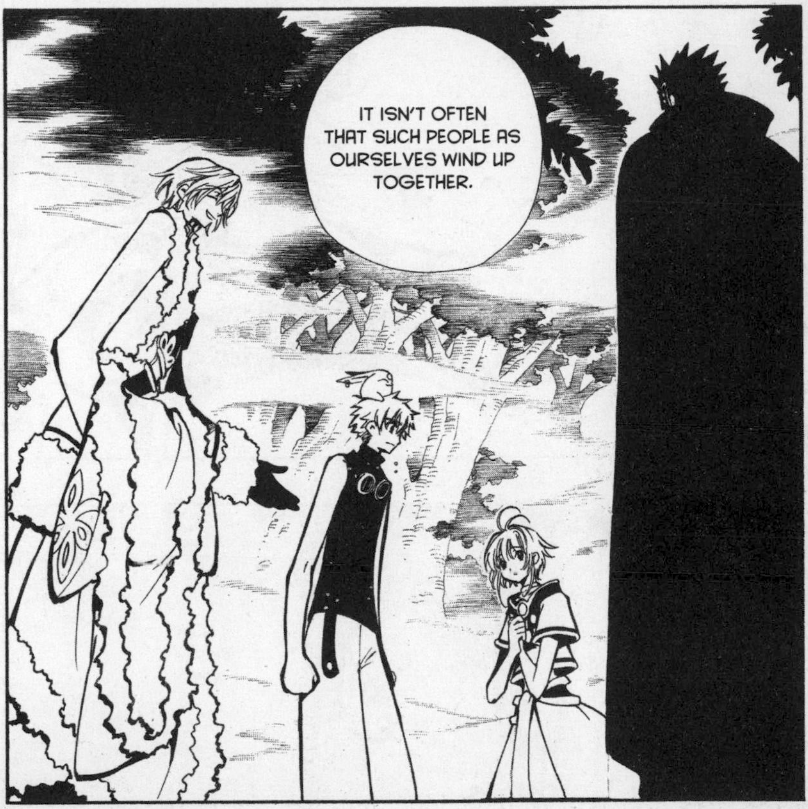
IT ISN'T OFTEN THAT SUCH PEOPLE AS OURSELVES WIND UP TOGETHER.

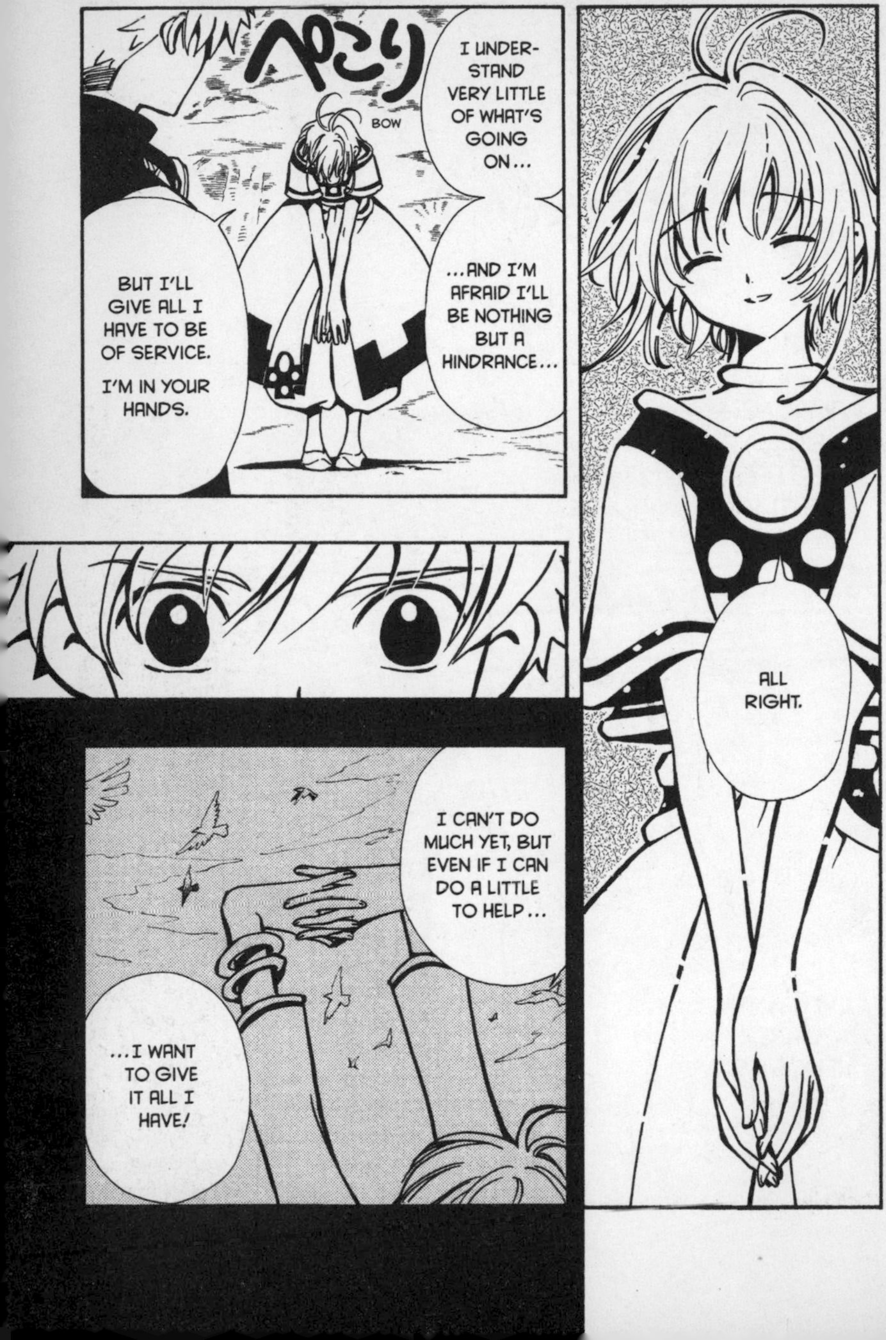
ALL RIGHT.
I UNDERSTAND VERY LITTLE OF WHAT'S GOING ON...
BOW
...AND I'M AFRAID I'LL BE NOTHING BUT A HINDRANCE...
BUT I'LL GIVE ALL I HAVE TO BE OF SERVICE.
I'M IN YOUR HANDS.
I CAN'T DO MUCH YET, BUT EVEN IF I CAN DO A LITTLE TO HELP...
...I WANT TO GIVE IT ALL I HAVE!

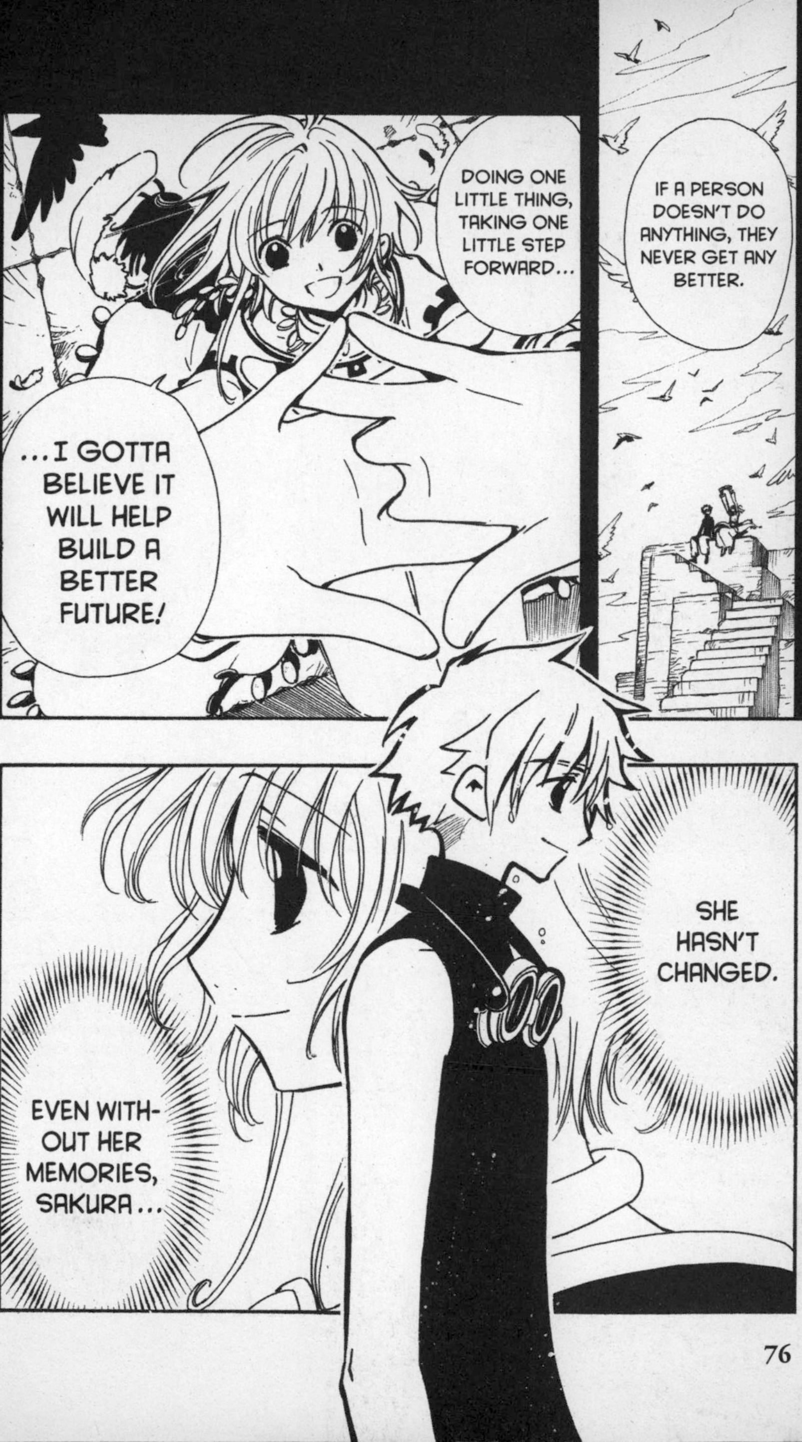
IF A PERSON DOESN'T DO ANYTHING, THEY NEVER GET ANY BETTER.
DOING ONE LITTLE THING, TAKING ONE LITTLE STEP FORWARD...
...I GOTTA BELIEVE IT WILL HELP BUILD A BETTER FUTURE!
SHE HASN'T CHANGED.
EVEN WITH-OUT HER MEMORIES, SAKURA...

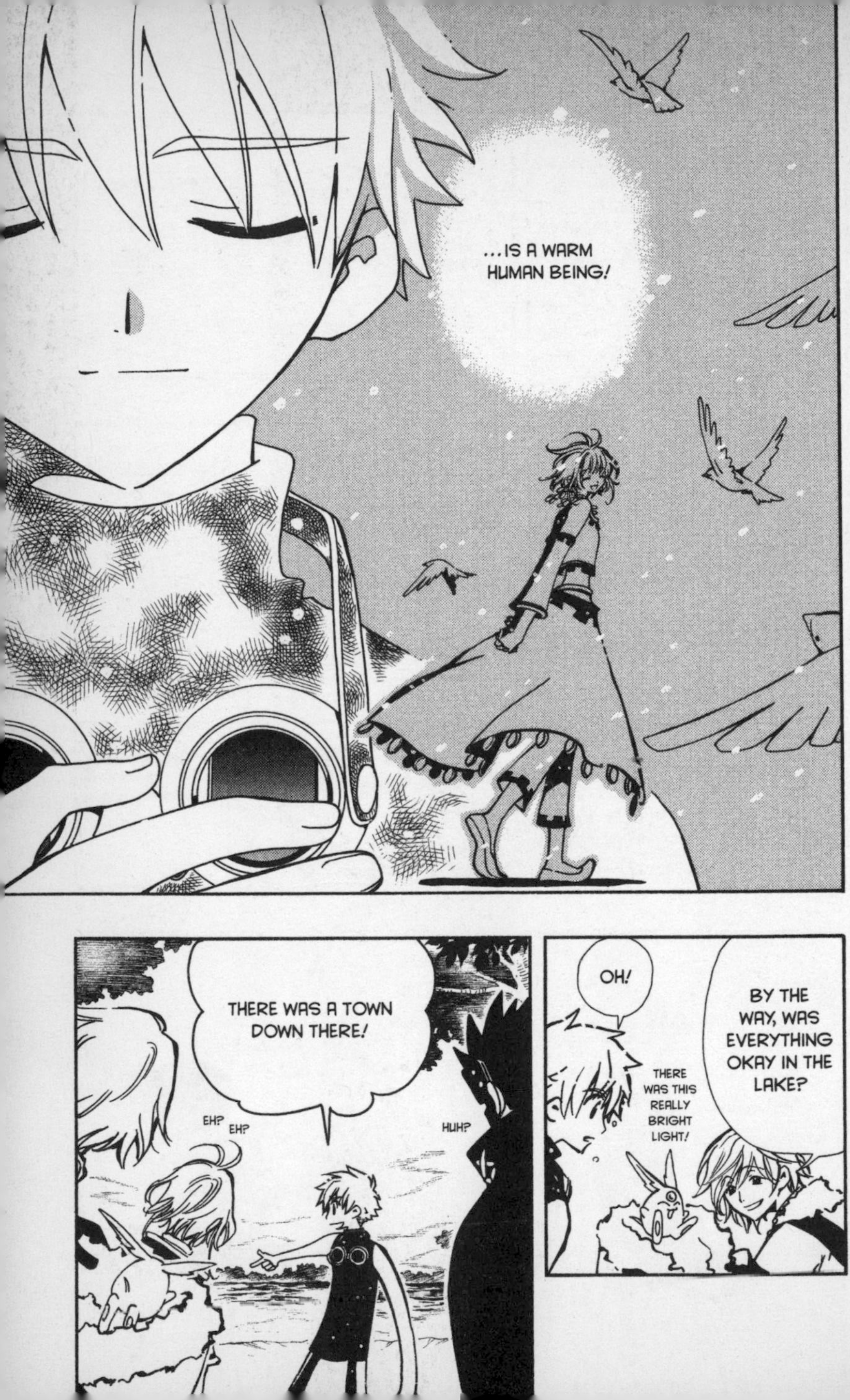
...IS A WARM HUMAN BEING!
BY THE WAY, WAS EVERYTHING OKAY IN THE LAKE?
OH!
THERE WAS THIS REALLY BRIGHT LIGHT!
THERE WAS A TOWN DOWN THERE!
HUH?
EH? EH?

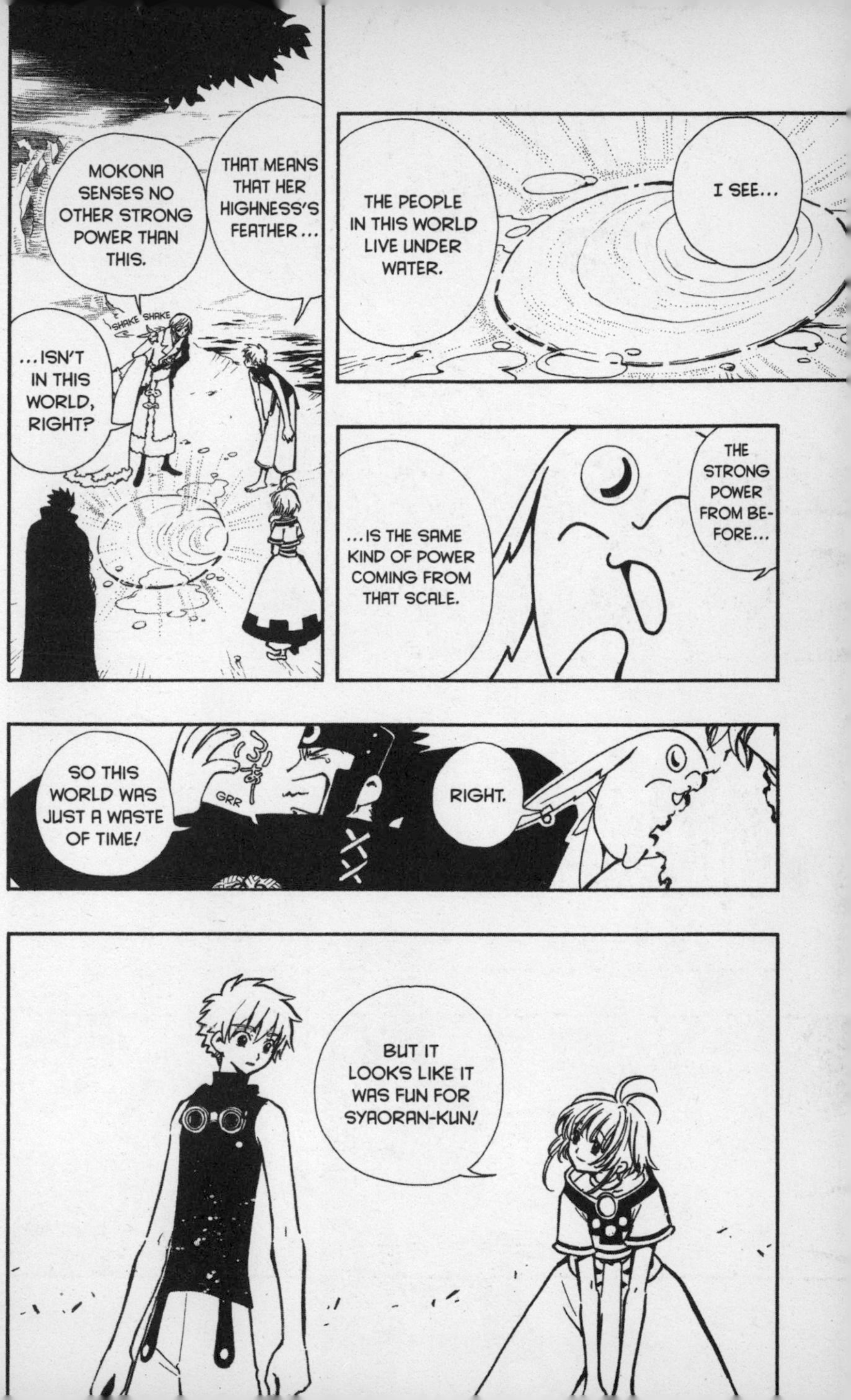
I SEE...
THE PEOPLE IN THIS WORLD LIVE UNDER WATER.
THE STRONG POWER FROM BEFORE...
...IS THE SAME KIND OF POWER COMING FROM THAT SCALE.
THAT MEANS THAT HER HIGHNESS'S FEATHER...
MOKONA SENSES NO OTHER STRONG POWER THAN THIS.
SHAKE SHAKE
...ISN'T IN THIS WORLD, RIGHT?
RIGHT.
GRR
SO THIS WORLD WAS JUST A WASTE OF TIME!
BUT IT LOOKS LIKE IT WAS FUN FOR SYAORAN-KUN!

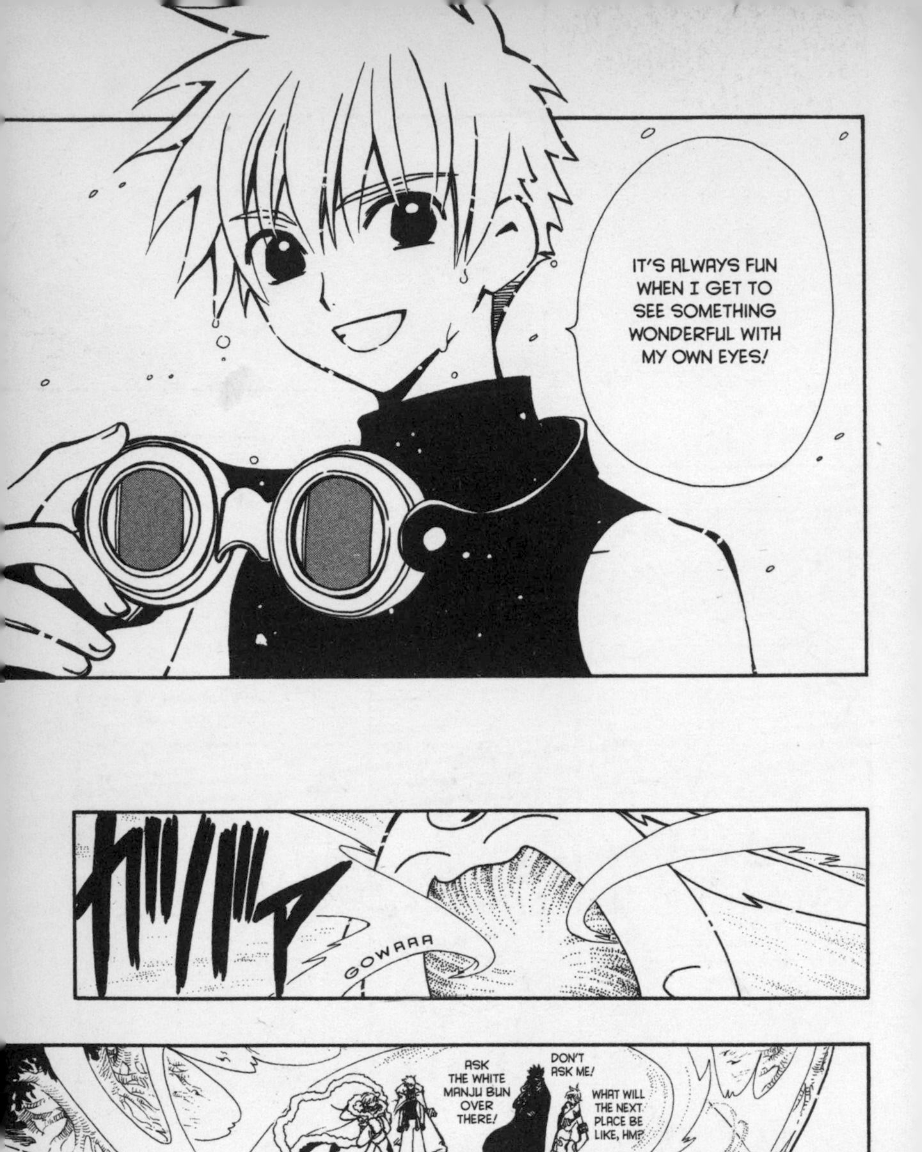
IT'S ALWAYS FUN WHEN I GET TO SEE SOMETHING WONDERFUL WITH MY OWN EYES!
GOWAAA
WHAT WILL THE NEXT PLACE BE LIKE, HM?
DON'T ASK ME!
ASK THE WHITE MANJU BUN OVER THERE!

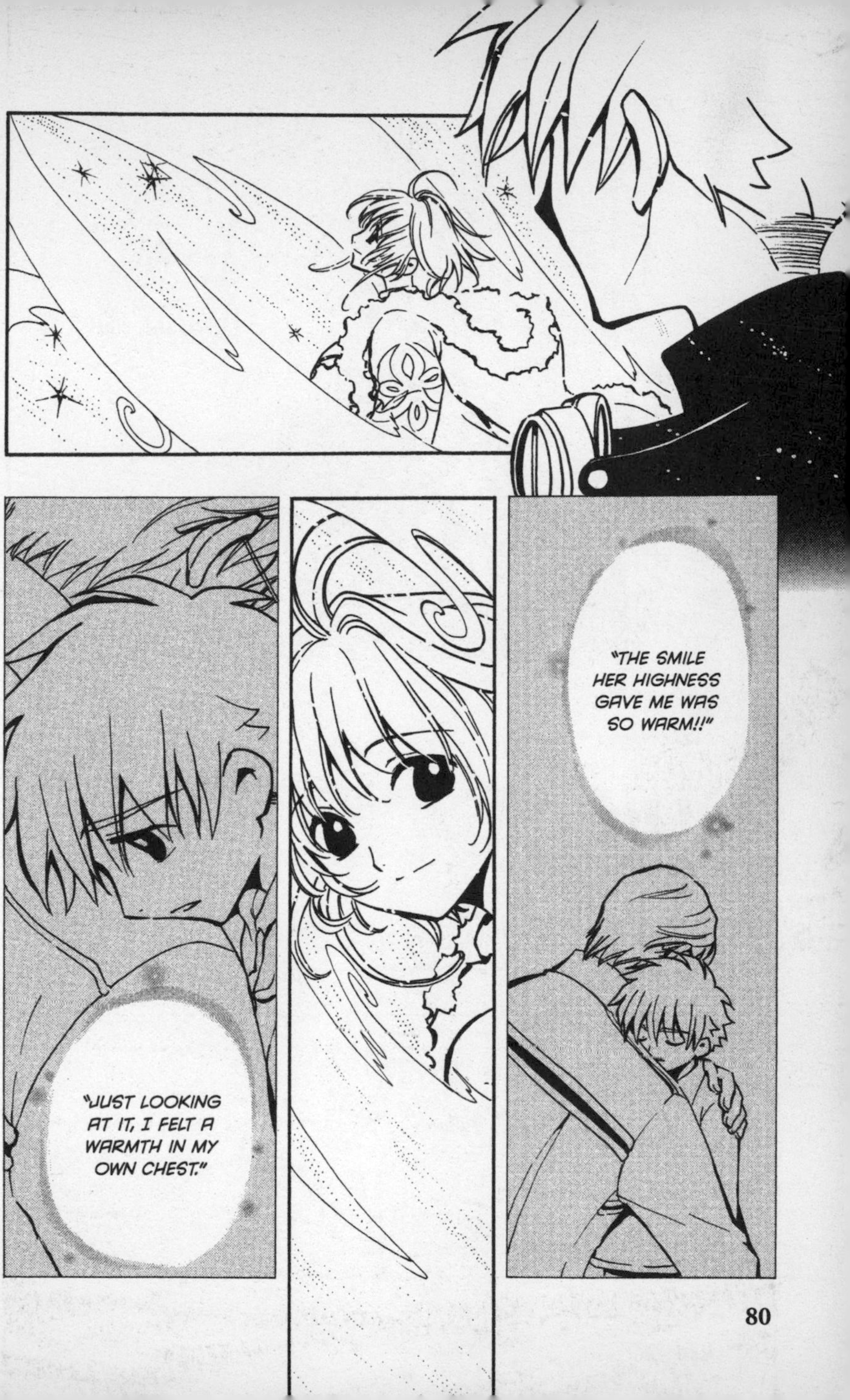
"THE SMILE HER HIGHNESS GAVE ME WAS SO WARM!!"
"JUST LOOKING AT IT, I FELT A WARMTH IN MY OWN CHEST."

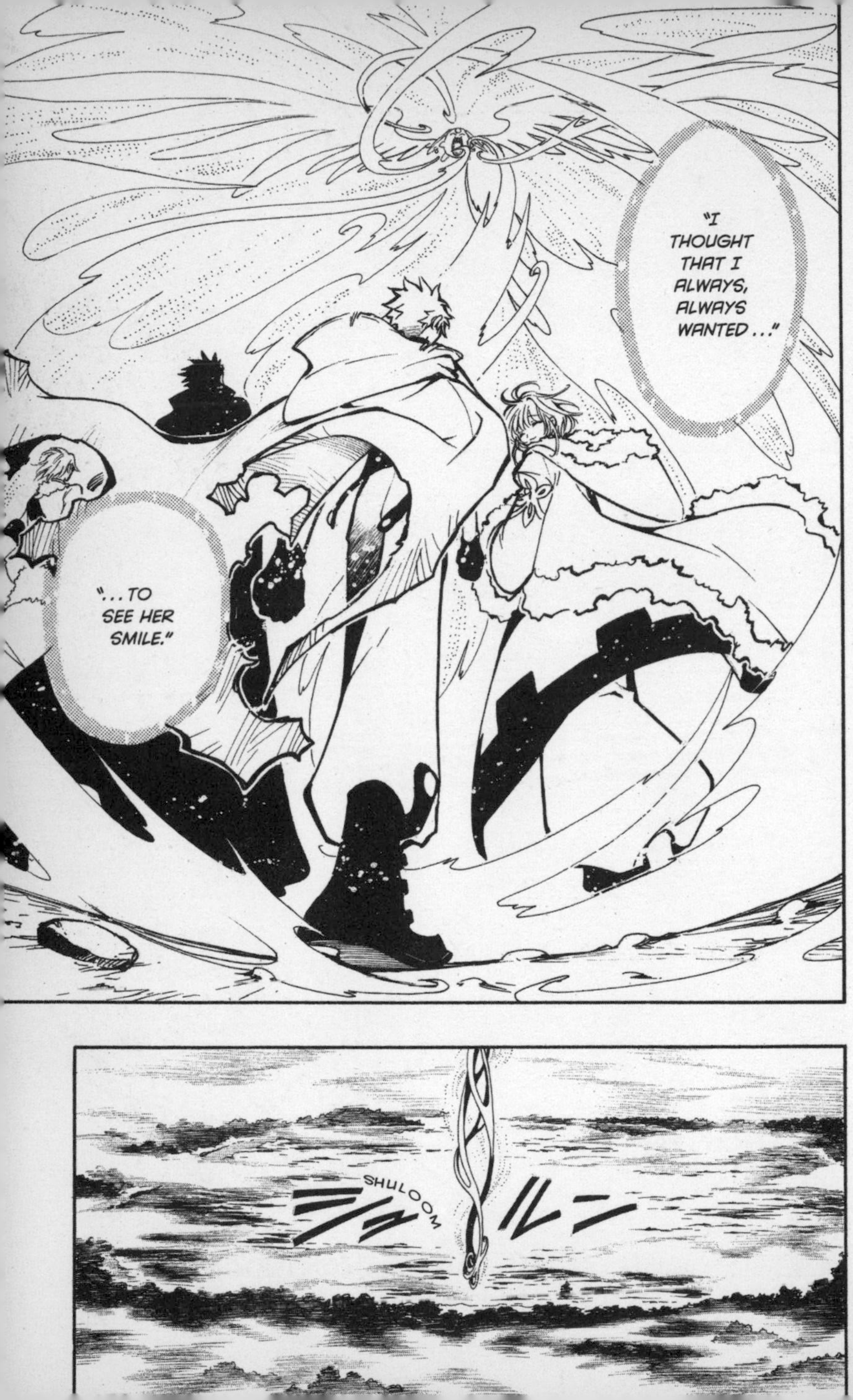
"I THOUGHT THAT I ALWAYS, ALWAYS WANTED..."
"...TO SEE HER SMILE."
SHULOOM

ツバサ

RESERVoir CHRoNiCLE

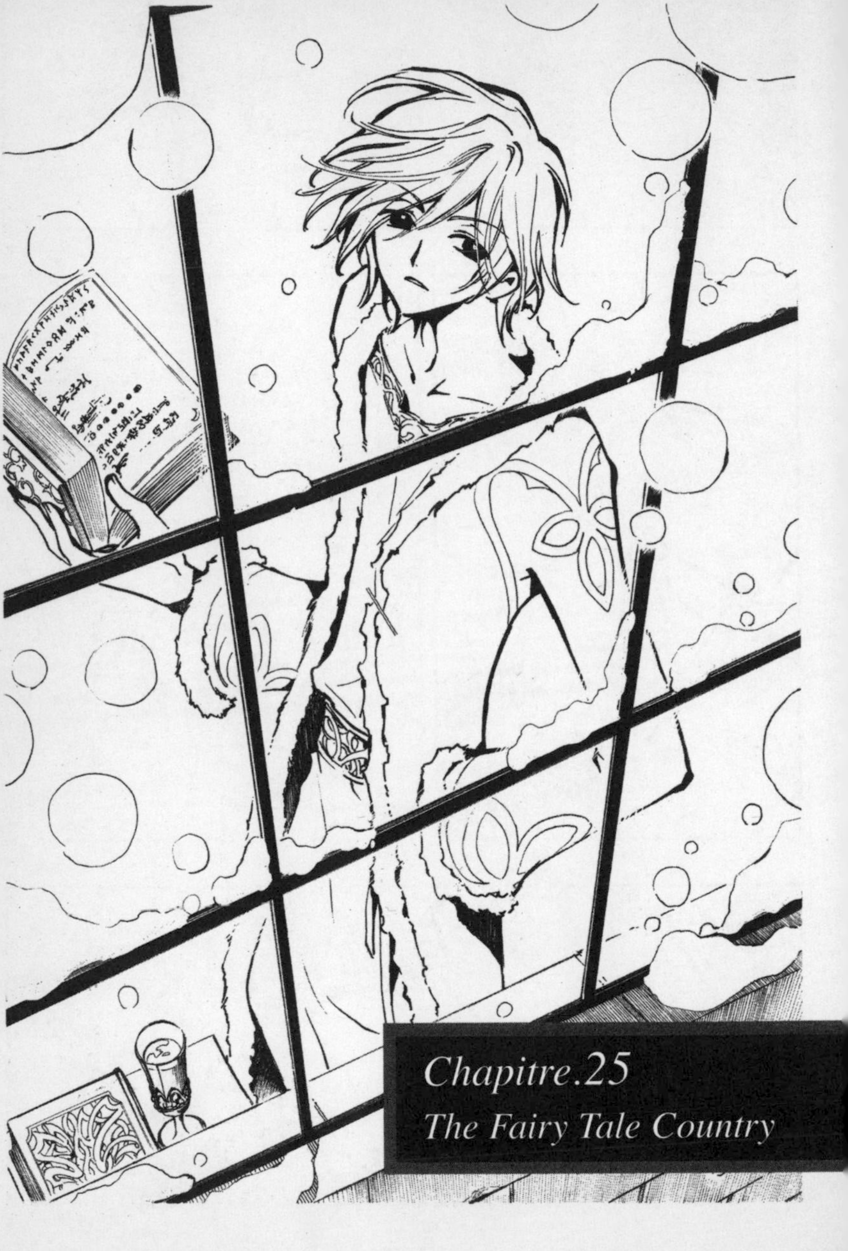

Chapitre.25

The Fairy Tale Country

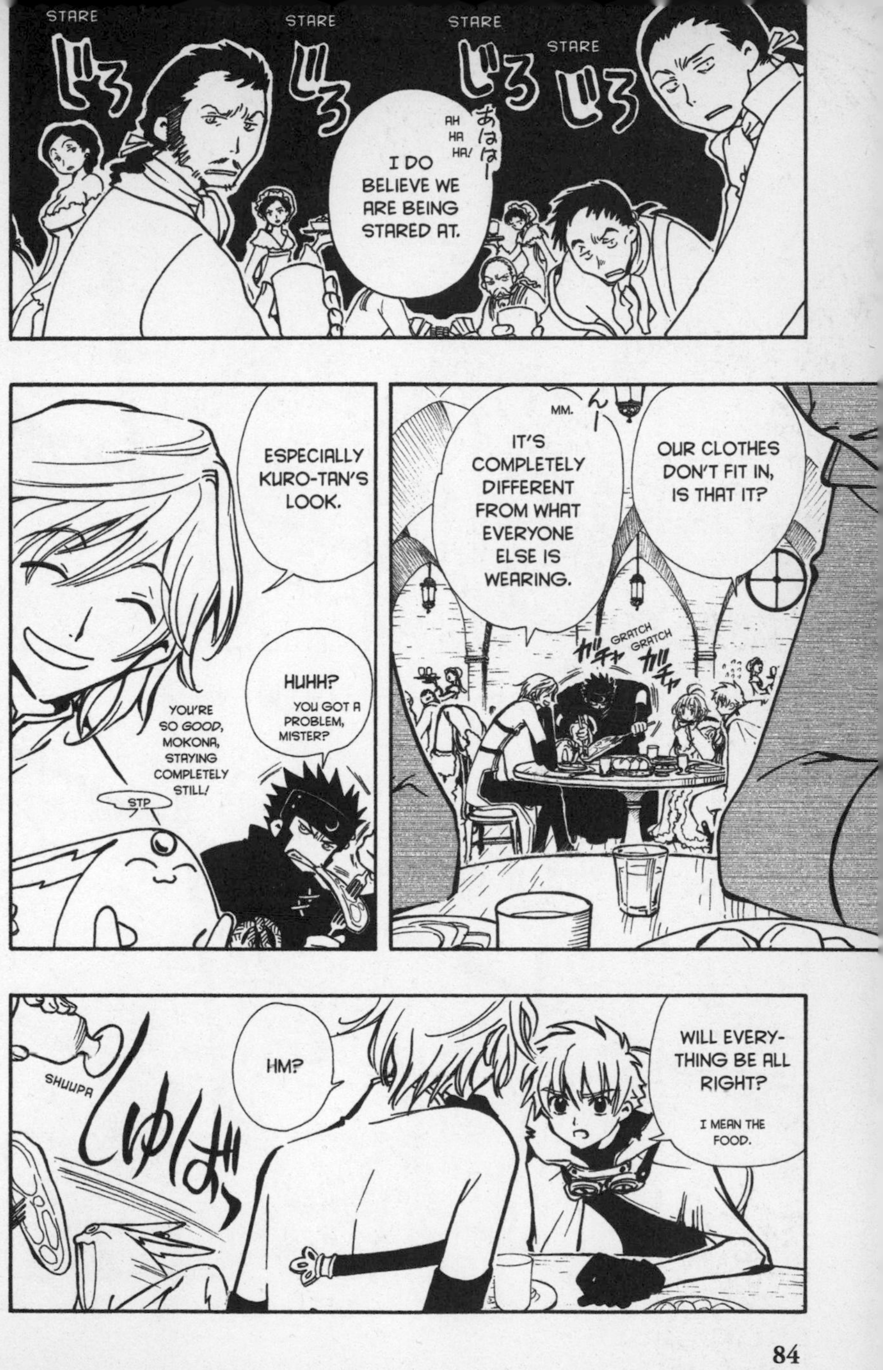
STARE
じろ
STARE
じろ
STARE
じろ
STARE
じろ
AH HA HA!
あはは—
I DO BELIEVE WE ARE BEING STARED AT.
OUR CLOTHES DON'T FIT IN, IS THAT IT?
MM.
んー
IT'S COMPLETELY DIFFERENT FROM WHAT EVERYONE ELSE IS WEARING.
GRATCH GRATCH
ガチャガチャ
ESPECIALLY KURO-TAN'S LOOK.
HUHH?
YOU GOT A PROBLEM, MISTER?
YOU'RE SO GOOD, MOKONA, STAYING COMPLETELY STILL!
STP
WILL EVERY-THING BE ALL RIGHT?
I MEAN THE FOOD.
HM?
SHUUPA
しゅぱっ

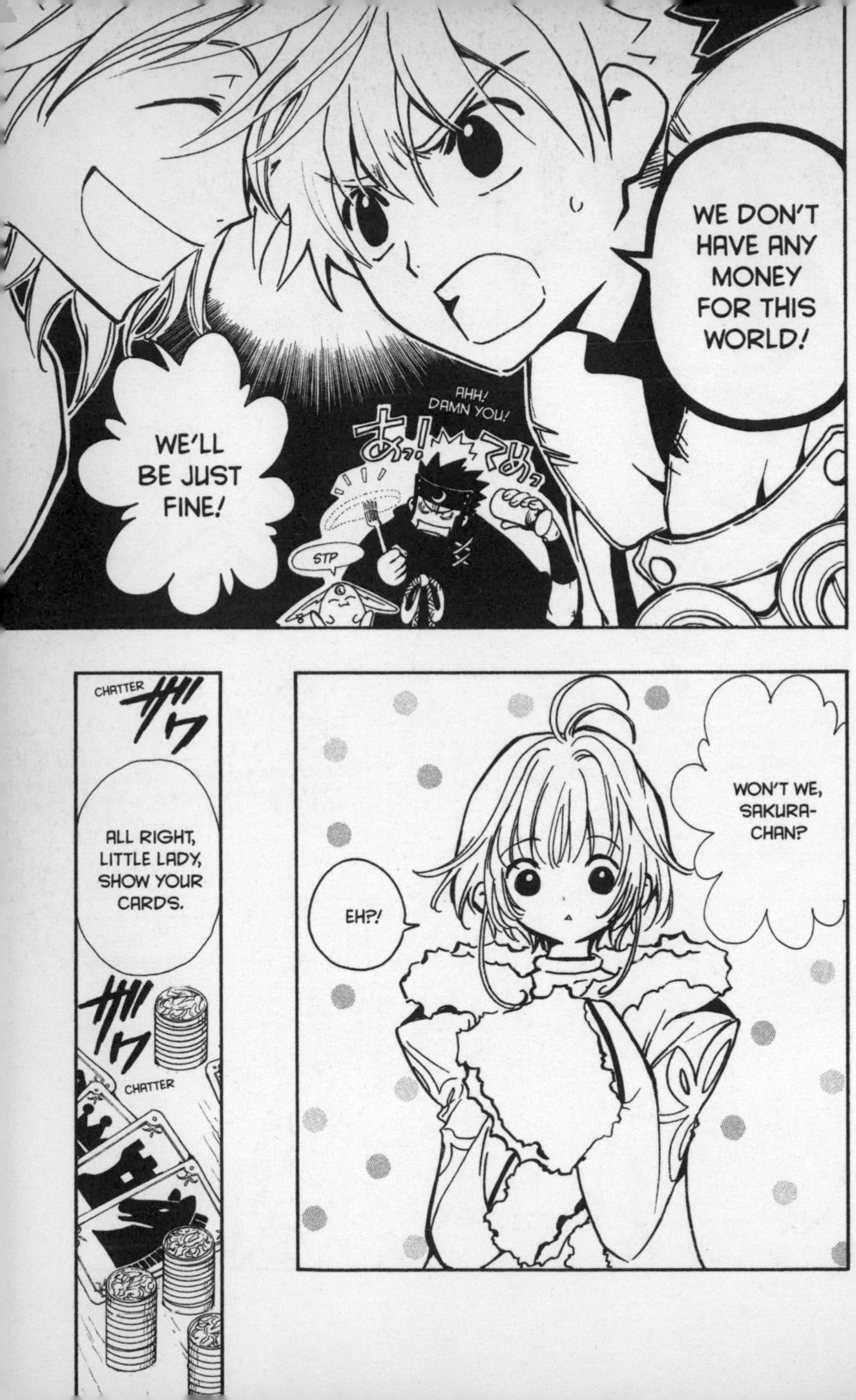
WE DON'T HAVE ANY MONEY FOR THIS WORLD!
AHH! DAMN YOU!
あっ! てめっ
STP
WE'LL BE JUST FINE!
WON'T WE, SAKURA-CHAN?
EH?!
CHATTER
ザワ
ALL RIGHT, LITTLE LADY, SHOW YOUR CARDS.
ザワ
CHATTER

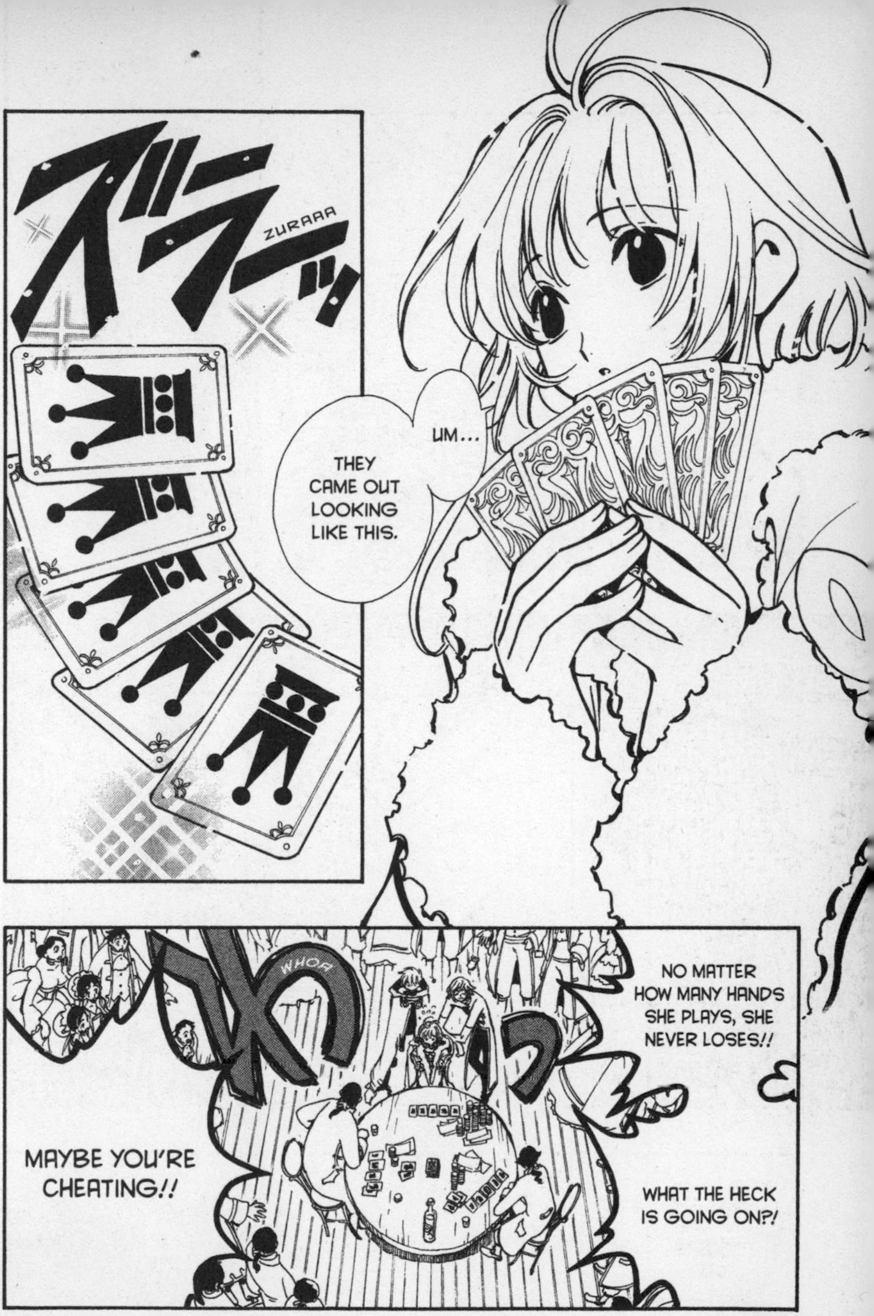
UM...
THEY CAME OUT LOOKING LIKE THIS.
ZURAAA
WHOA
NO MATTER HOW MANY HANDS SHE PLAYS, SHE NEVER LOSES!!
WHAT THE HECK IS GOING ON?!
MAYBE YOU'RE CHEATING!!

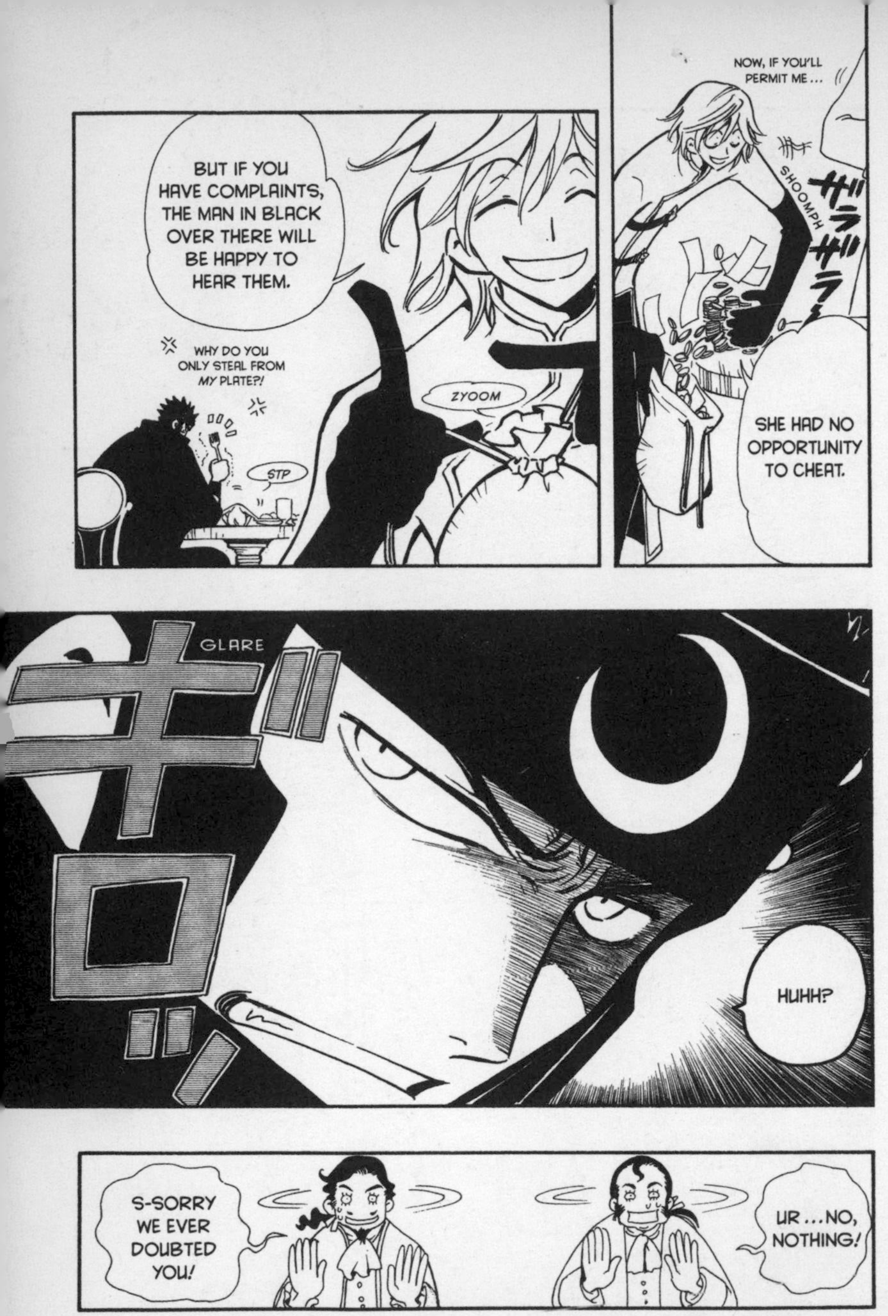
NOW, IF YOU'LL PERMIT ME ...
SHOOMPH
SHE HAD NO OPPORTUNITY TO CHEAT.
BUT IF YOU HAVE COMPLAINTS, THE MAN IN BLACK OVER THERE WILL BE HAPPY TO HEAR THEM.
ZYOOM
WHY DO YOU ONLY STEAL FROM *MY PLATE*?!
STP
GLARE
HUHH?
UR ... NO, NOTHING!
S-SORRY WE EVER DOUBTED YOU!

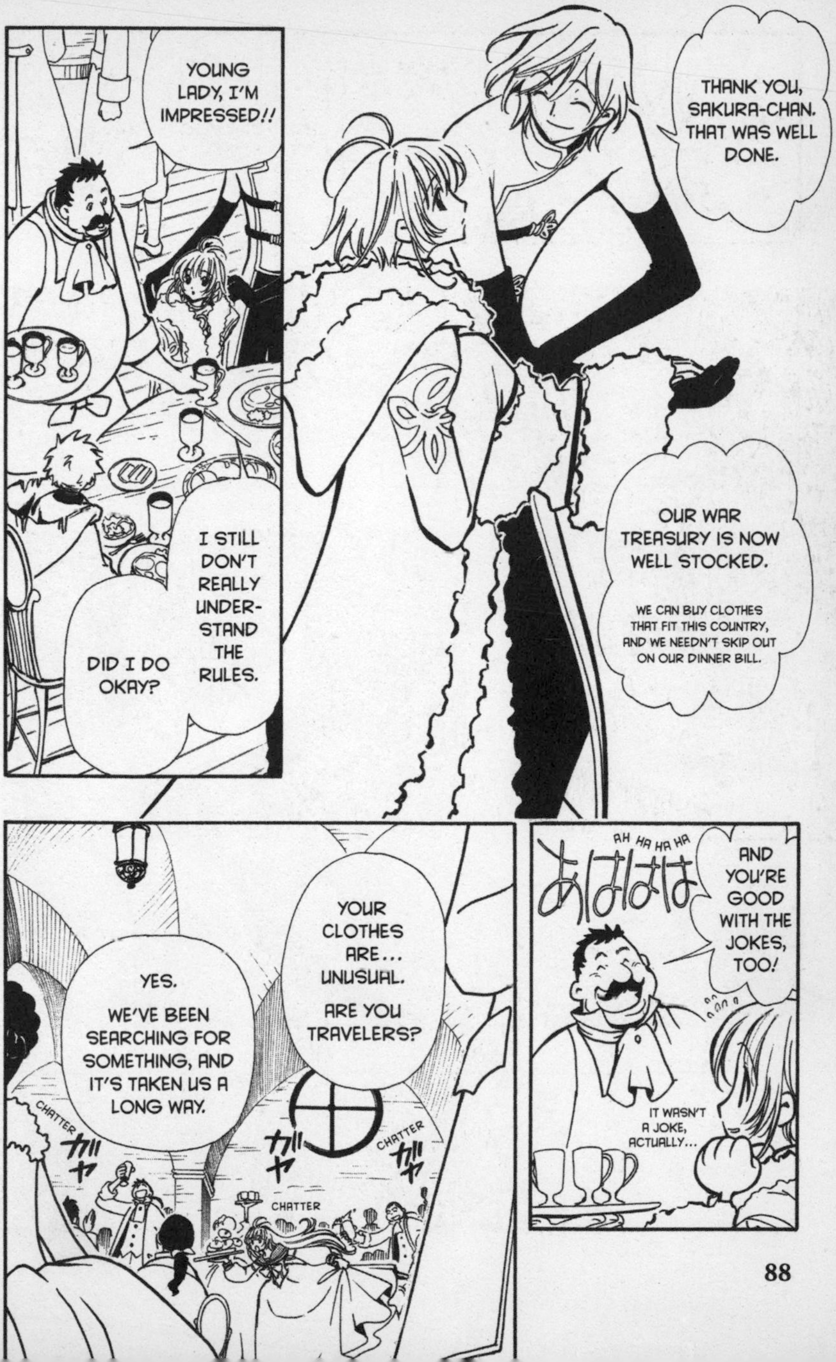
THANK YOU, SAKURA-CHAN. THAT WAS WELL DONE.
OUR WAR TREASURY IS NOW WELL STOCKED.
WE CAN BUY CLOTHES THAT FIT THIS COUNTRY, AND WE NEEDN'T SKIP OUT ON OUR DINNER BILL.
YOUNG LADY, I'M IMPRESSED!!
I STILL DON'T REALLY UNDER-STAND THE RULES.
DID I DO OKAY?
あははは
AH HA HA HA
AND YOU'RE GOOD WITH THE JOKES, TOO!
IT WASN'T A JOKE, ACTUALLY...
YOUR CLOTHES ARE... UNUSUAL.
ARE YOU TRAVELERS?
YES.
WE'VE BEEN SEARCHING FOR SOMETHING, AND IT'S TAKEN US A LONG WAY.
ガヤ
CHATTER
ガヤ
CHATTER
ガヤ
CHATTER

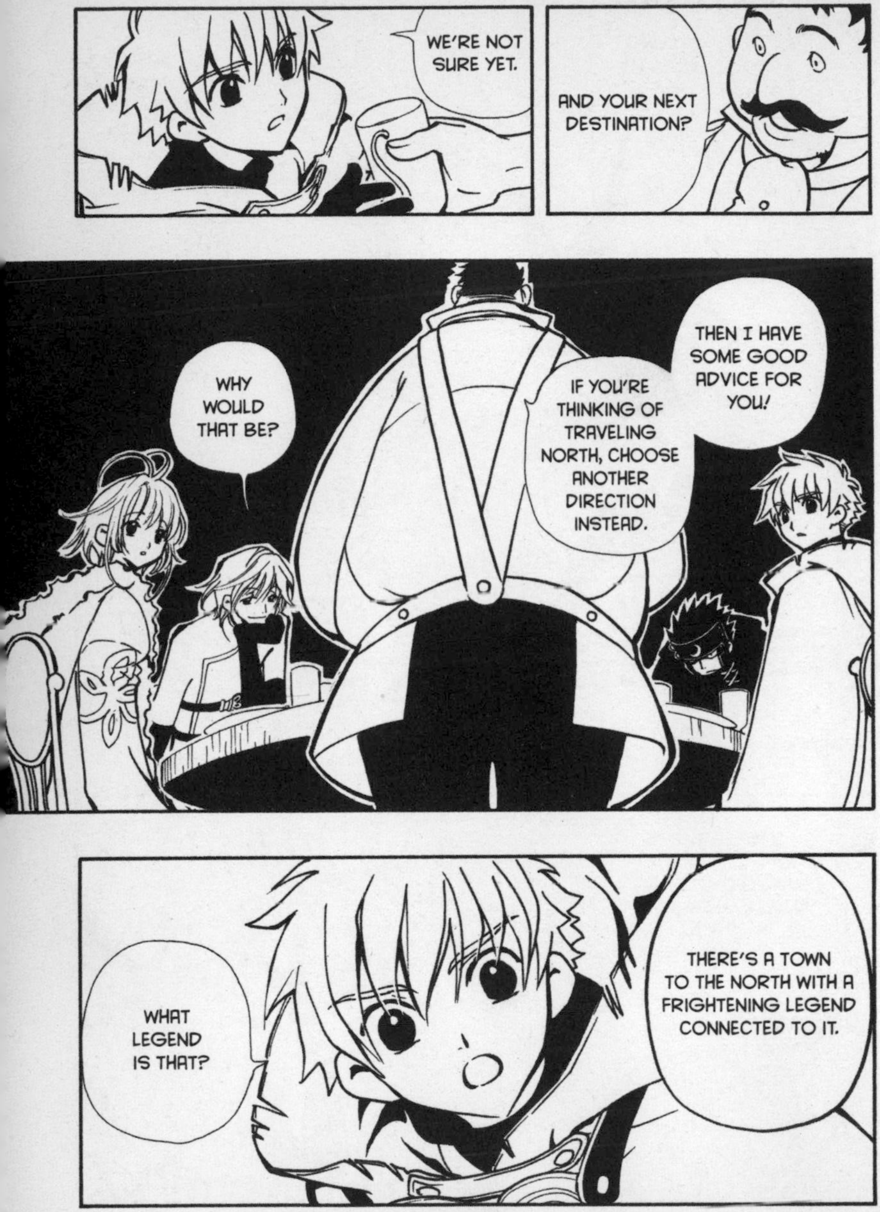
AND YOUR NEXT DESTINATION?
WE'RE NOT SURE YET.
THEN I HAVE SOME GOOD ADVICE FOR YOU!
IF YOU'RE THINKING OF TRAVELING NORTH, CHOOSE ANOTHER DIRECTION INSTEAD.
WHY WOULD THAT BE?
THERE'S A TOWN TO THE NORTH WITH A FRIGHTENING LEGEND CONNECTED TO IT.
WHAT LEGEND IS THAT?

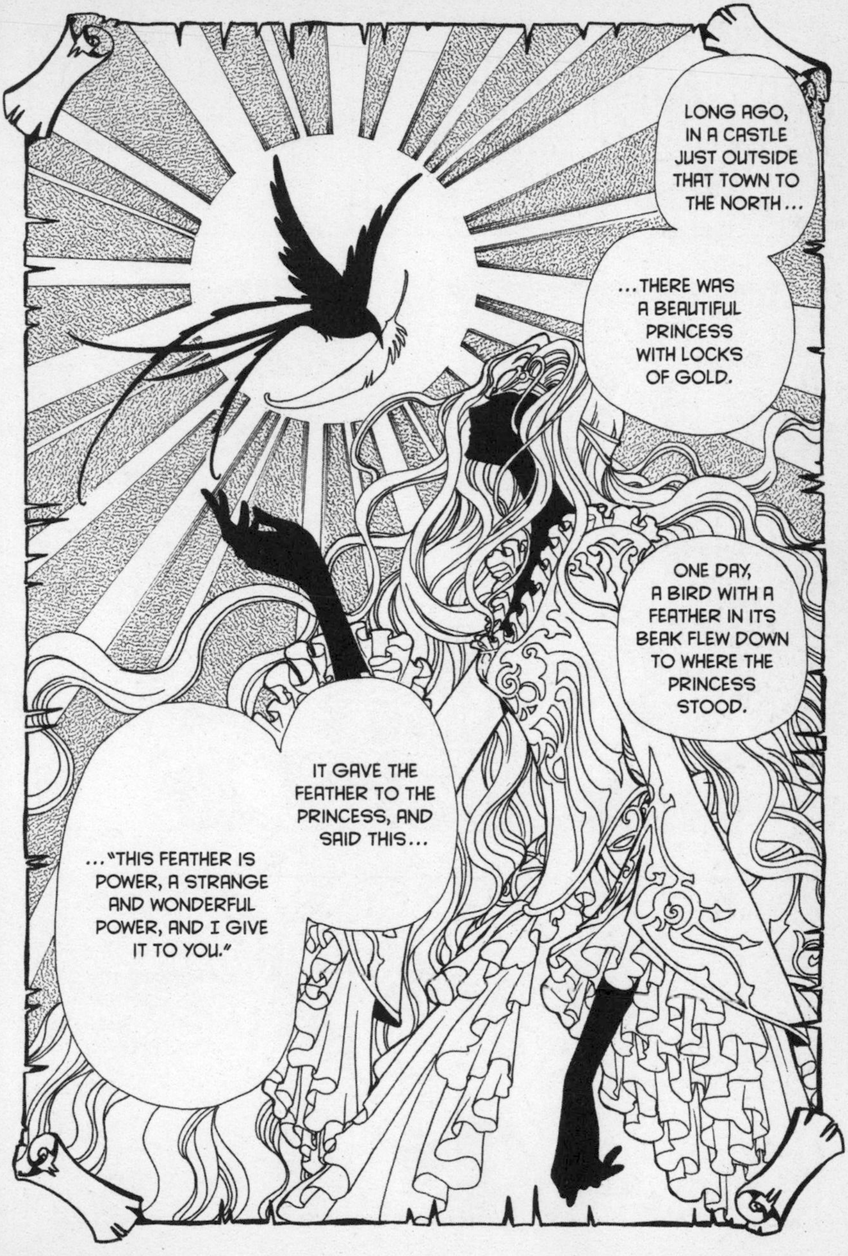
LONG AGO, IN A CASTLE JUST OUTSIDE THAT TOWN TO THE NORTH...
...THERE WAS A BEAUTIFUL PRINCESS WITH LOCKS OF GOLD.
ONE DAY, A BIRD WITH A FEATHER IN ITS BEAK FLEW DOWN TO WHERE THE PRINCESS STOOD.
IT GAVE THE FEATHER TO THE PRINCESS, AND SAID THIS...
..."THIS FEATHER IS POWER, A STRANGE AND WONDERFUL POWER, AND I GIVE IT TO YOU."

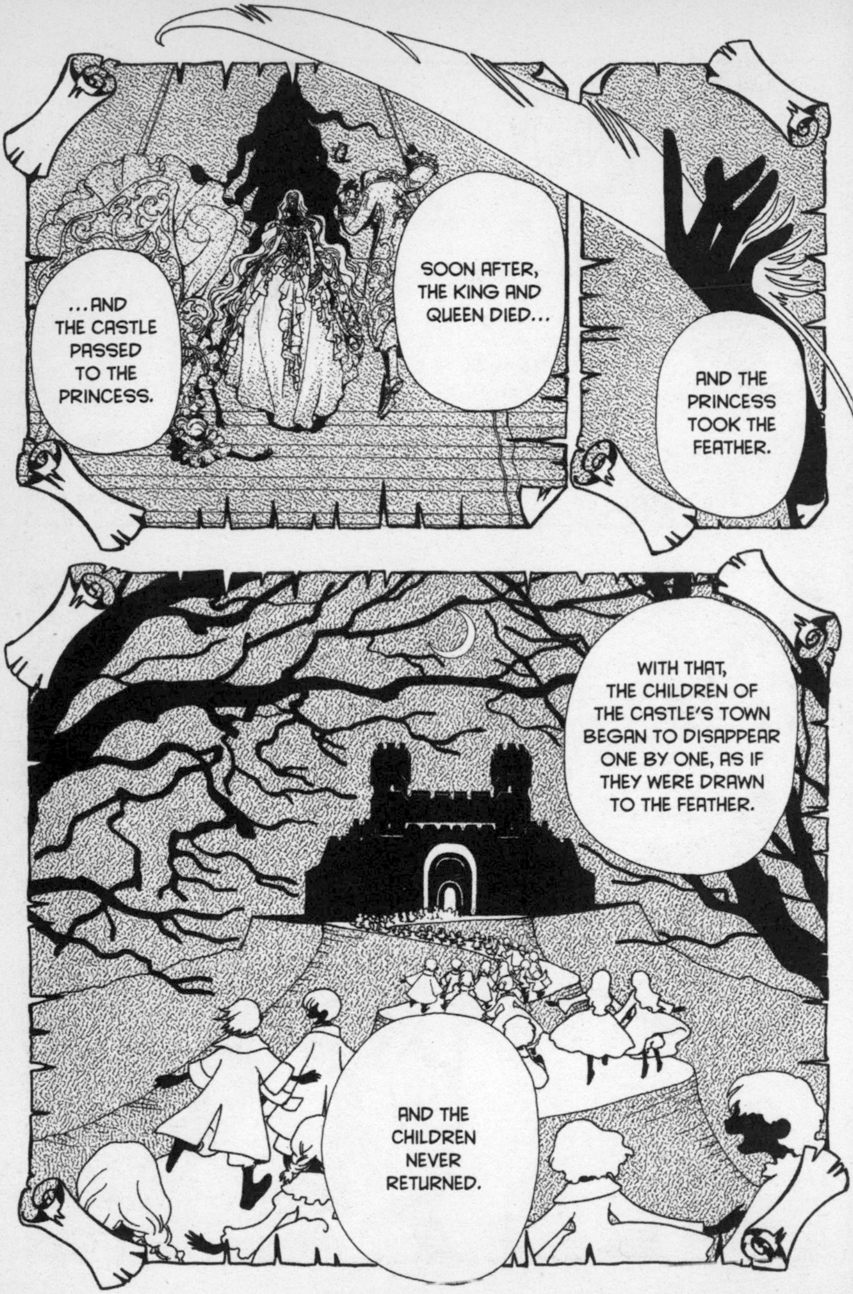
AND THE PRINCESS TOOK THE FEATHER.
SOON AFTER, THE KING AND QUEEN DIED...
...AND THE CASTLE PASSED TO THE PRINCESS.
WITH THAT, THE CHILDREN OF THE CASTLE'S TOWN BEGAN TO DISAPPEAR ONE BY ONE, AS IF THEY WERE DRAWN TO THE FEATHER.
AND THE CHILDREN NEVER RETURNED.

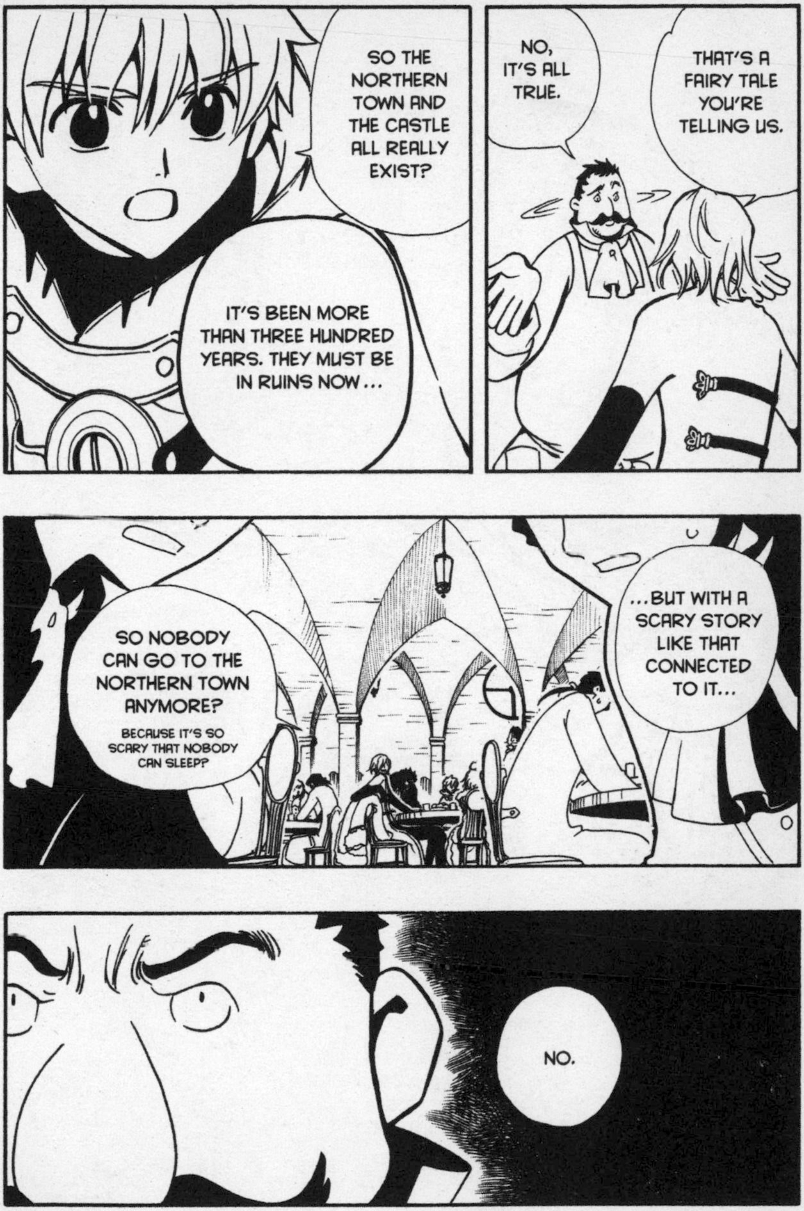
THAT'S A FAIRY TALE YOU'RE TELLING US.
NO, IT'S ALL TRUE.
SO THE NORTHERN TOWN AND THE CASTLE ALL REALLY EXIST?
IT'S BEEN MORE THAN THREE HUNDRED YEARS. THEY MUST BE IN RUINS NOW...
...BUT WITH A SCARY STORY LIKE THAT CONNECTED TO IT...
SO NOBODY CAN GO TO THE NORTHERN TOWN ANYMORE?
BECAUSE IT'S SO SCARY THAT NOBODY CAN SLEEP?
NO.

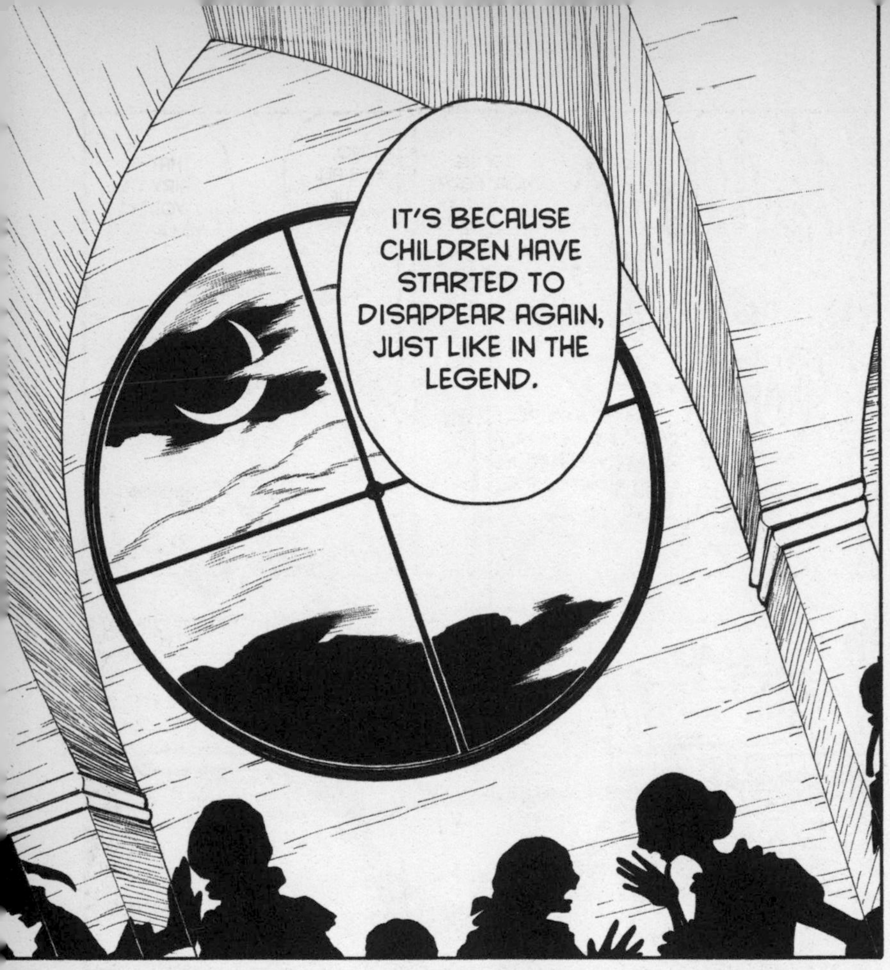
IT'S BECAUSE CHILDREN HAVE STARTED TO DISAPPEAR AGAIN, JUST LIKE IN THE LEGEND.

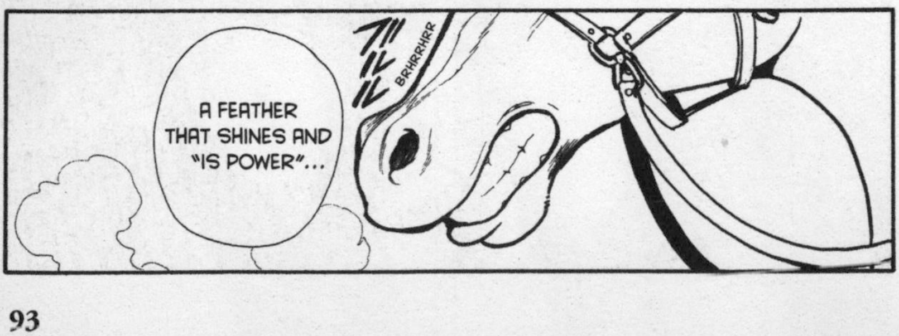
BRHRRHRR
A FEATHER THAT SHINES AND "IS POWER"...

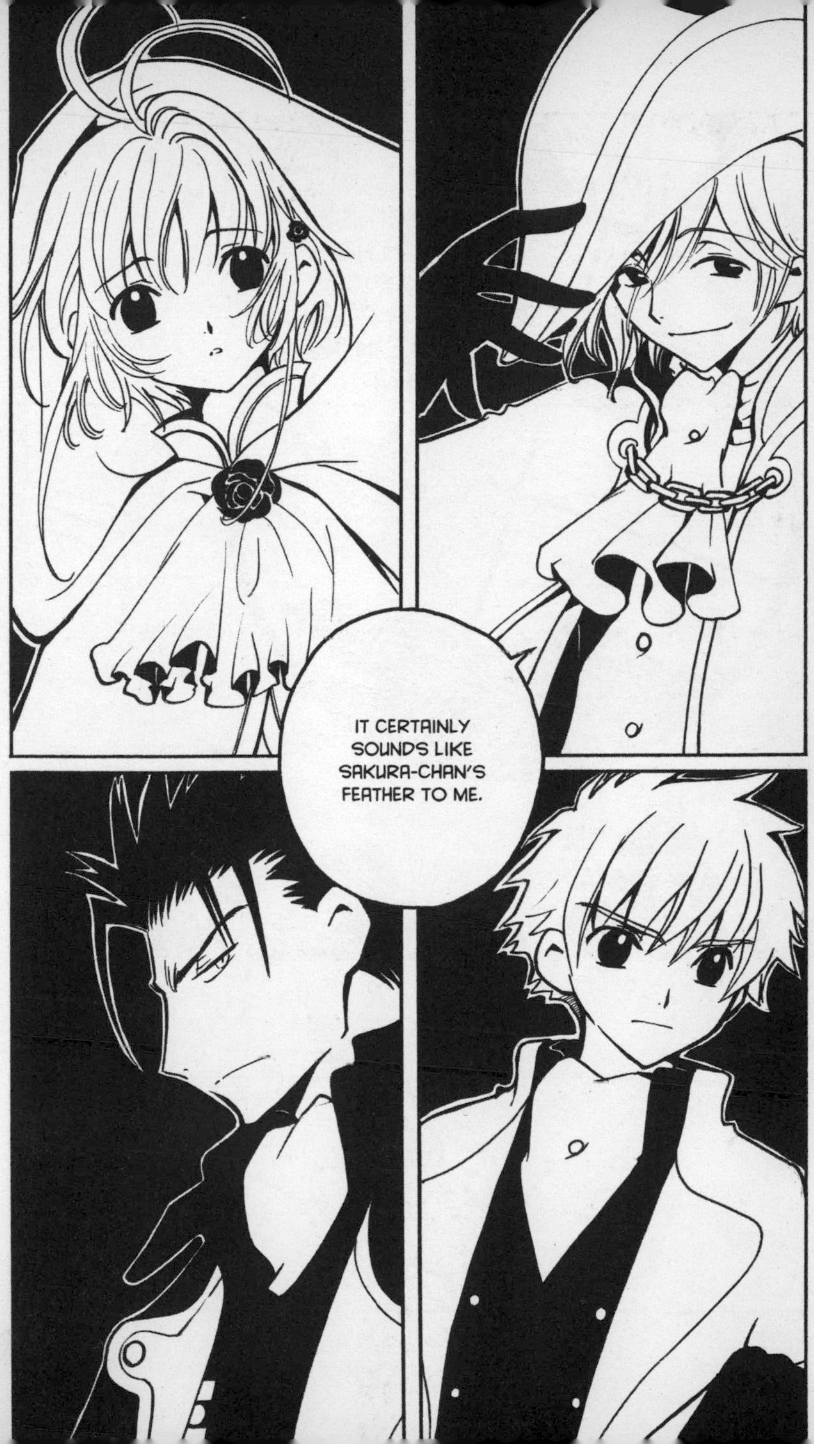
IT CERTAINLY SOUNDS LIKE SAKURA-CHAN'S FEATHER TO ME.

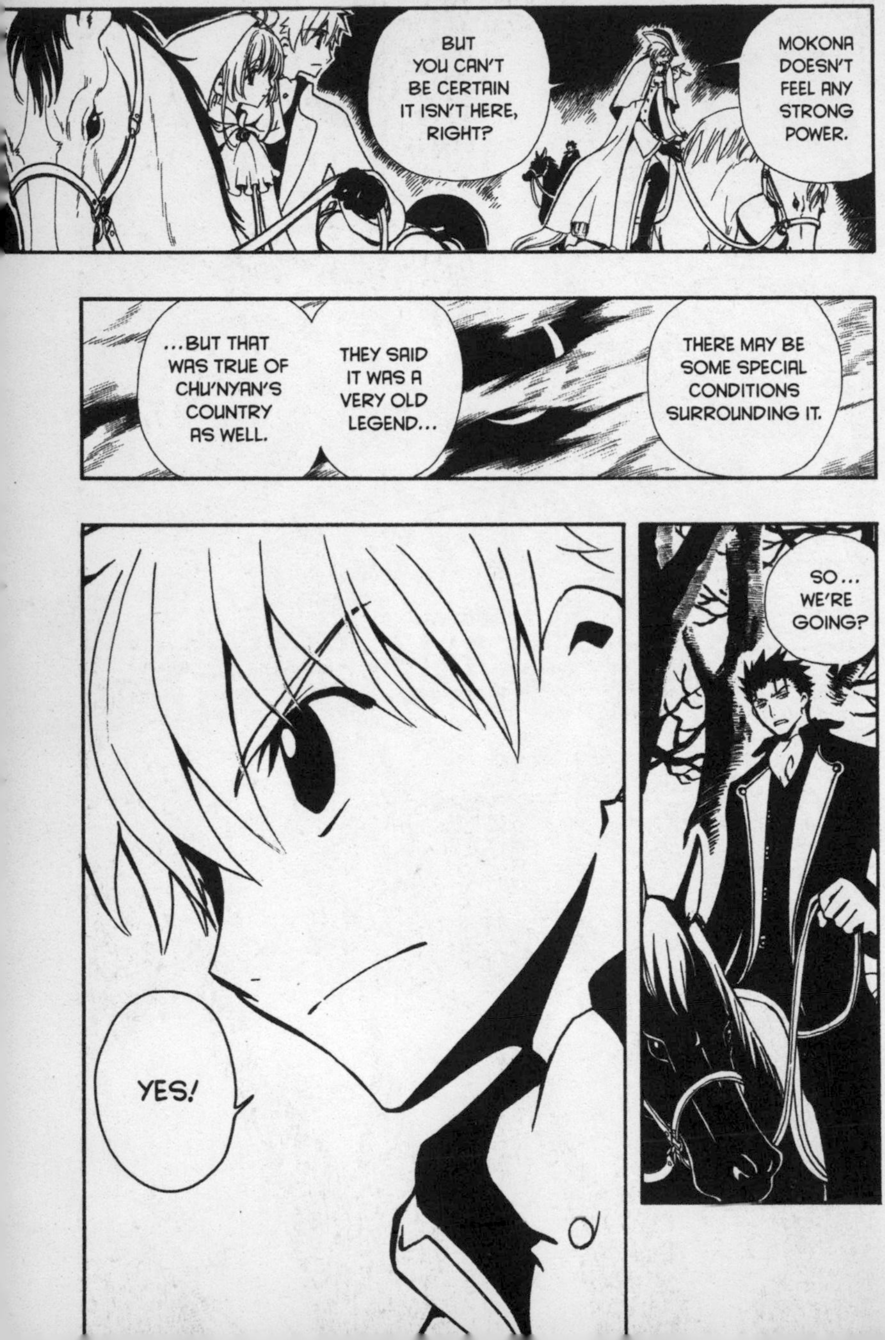
MOKONA DOESN'T FEEL ANY STRONG POWER.
BUT YOU CAN'T BE CERTAIN IT ISN'T HERE, RIGHT?
THERE MAY BE SOME SPECIAL CONDITIONS SURROUNDING IT.
THEY SAID IT WAS A VERY OLD LEGEND...
...BUT THAT WAS TRUE OF CHU'NYAN'S COUNTRY AS WELL.
SO... WE'RE GOING?
YES!

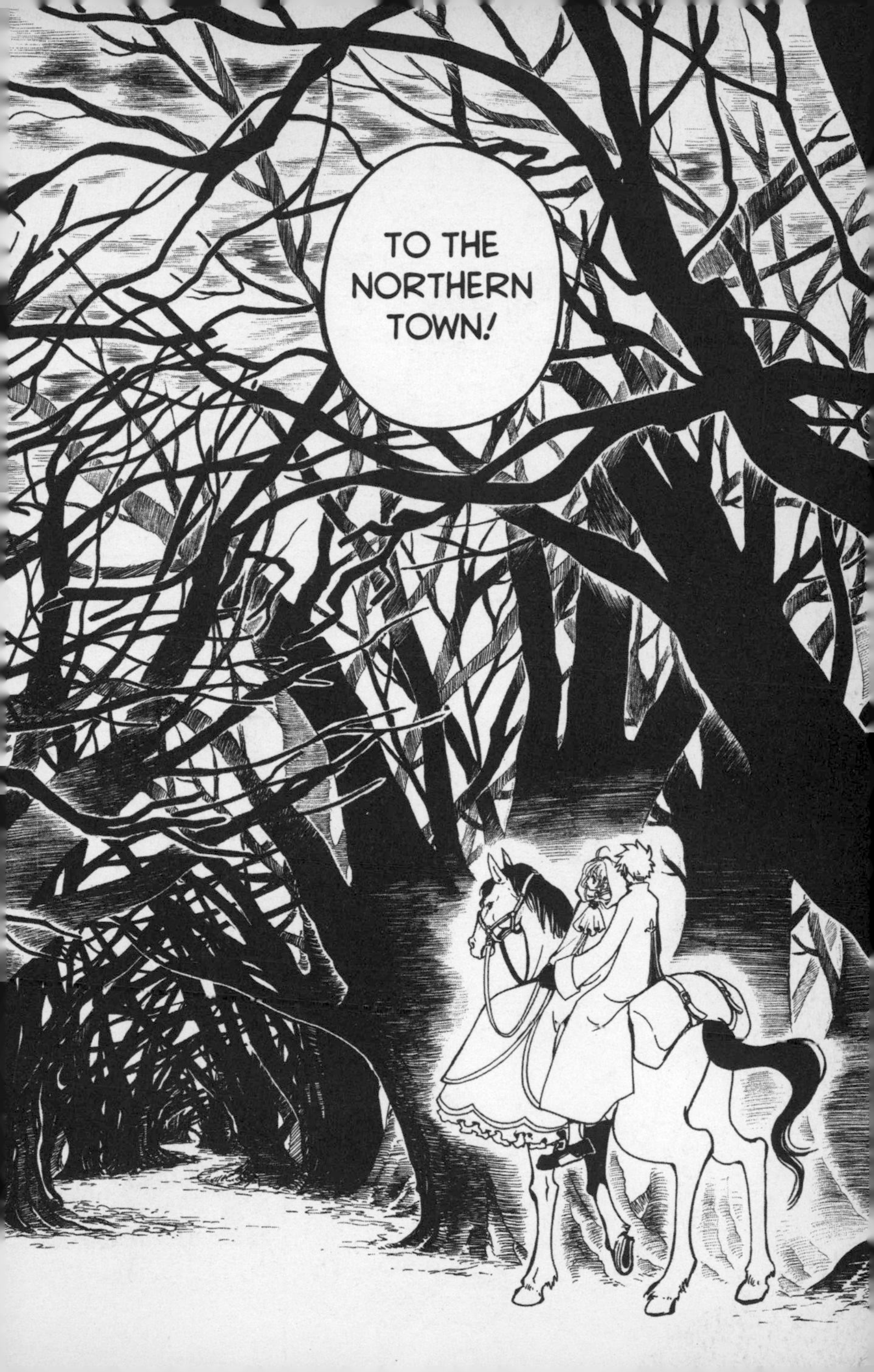
TO THE NORTHERN TOWN!

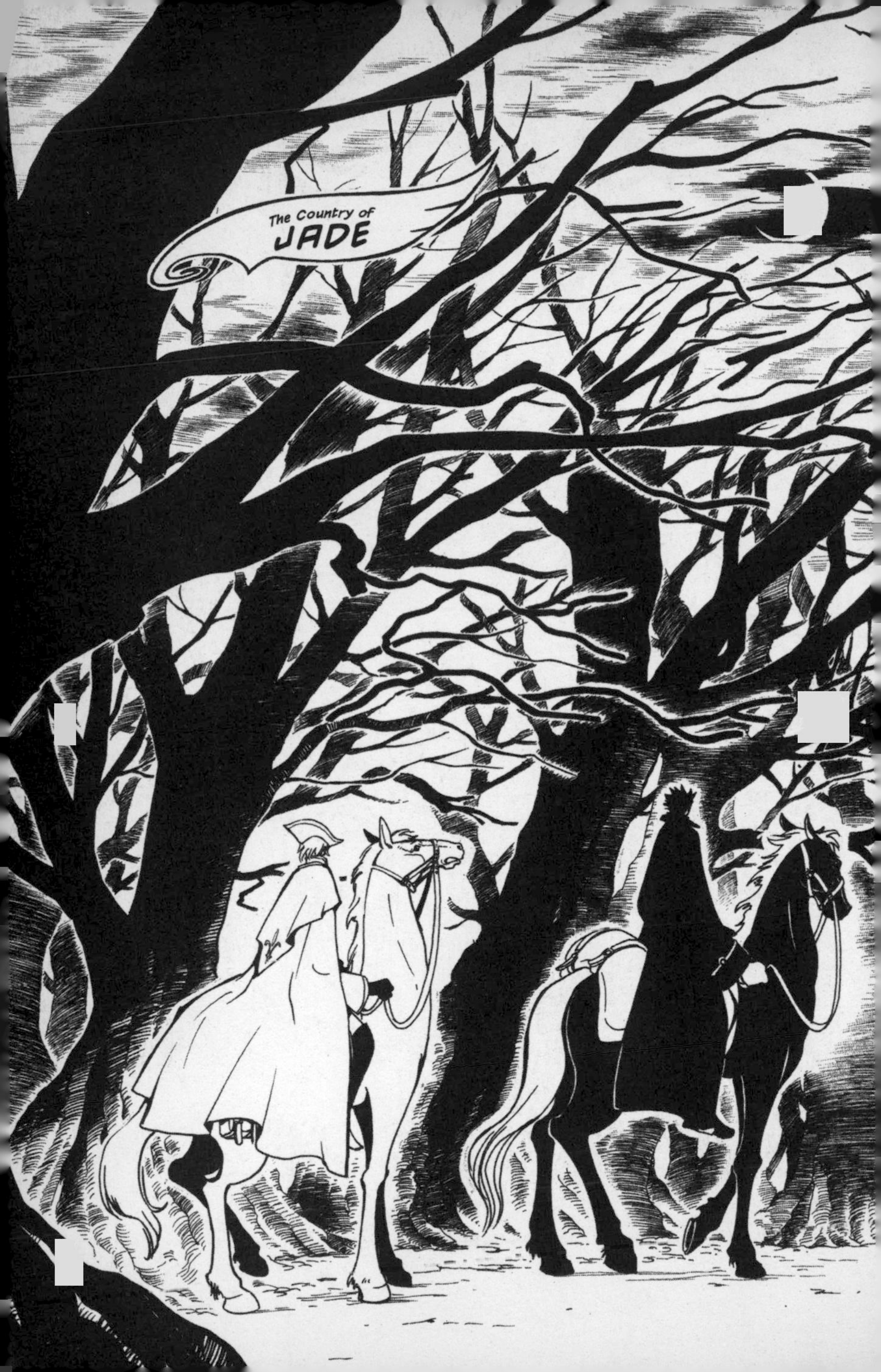
The Country of
JADE

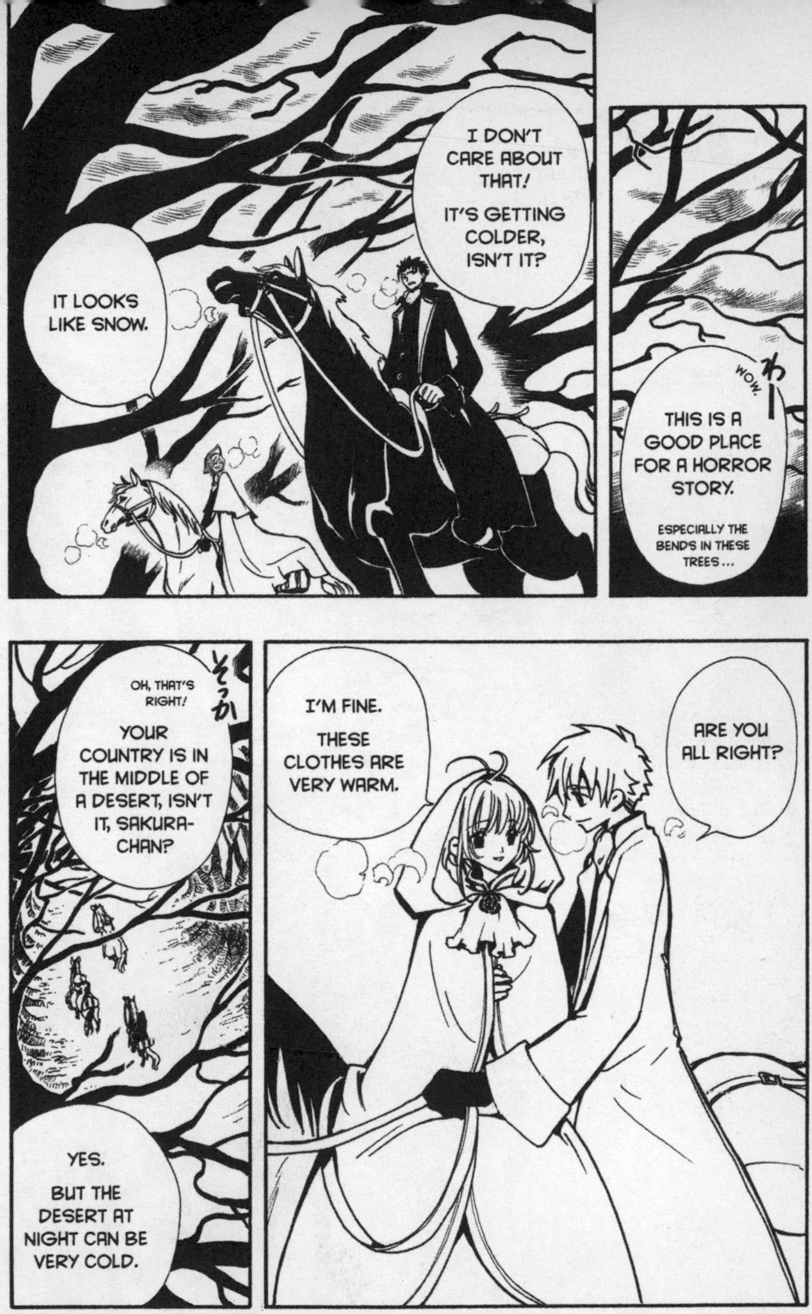
わー
WOW.
THIS IS A GOOD PLACE FOR A HORROR STORY.
ESPECIALLY THE BENDS IN THESE TREES...
I DON'T CARE ABOUT THAT!
IT'S GETTING COLDER, ISN'T IT?
IT LOOKS LIKE SNOW.
ARE YOU ALL RIGHT?
I'M FINE.
THESE CLOTHES ARE VERY WARM.
そっか
OH, THAT'S RIGHT!
YOUR COUNTRY IS IN THE MIDDLE OF A DESERT, ISN'T IT, SAKURA-CHAN?
YES.
BUT THE DESERT AT NIGHT CAN BE VERY COLD.

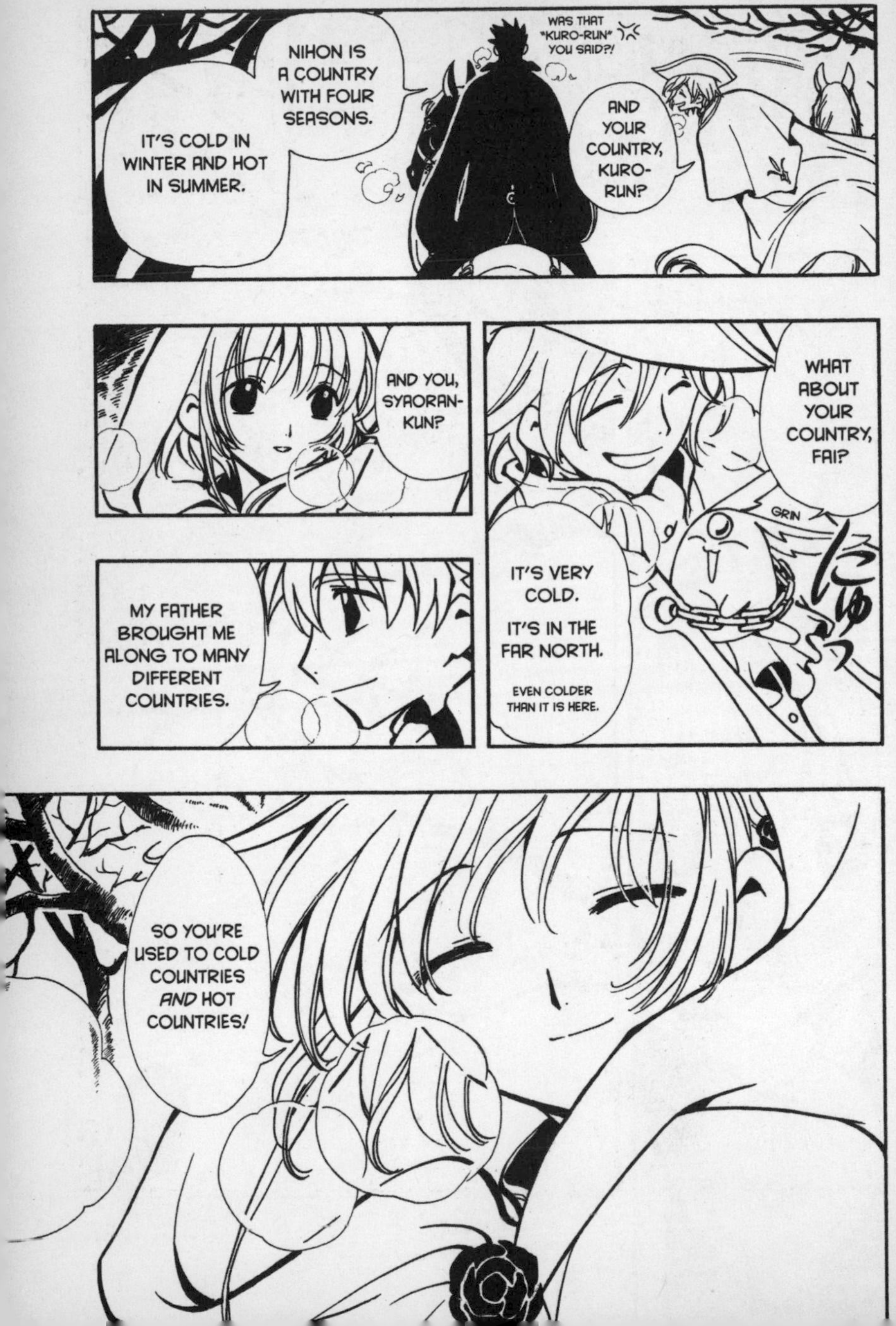
AND YOUR COUNTRY, KURO-RUN?
WAS THAT "KURO-RUN" YOU SAID?!
NIHON IS A COUNTRY WITH FOUR SEASONS.
IT'S COLD IN WINTER AND HOT IN SUMMER.
WHAT ABOUT YOUR COUNTRY, FAI?
GRIN
にゅっ
IT'S VERY COLD.
IT'S IN THE FAR NORTH.
EVEN COLDER THAN IT IS HERE.
AND YOU, SYAORAN-KUN?
MY FATHER BROUGHT ME ALONG TO MANY DIFFERENT COUNTRIES.
SO YOU'RE USED TO COLD COUNTRIES *AND* HOT COUNTRIES!

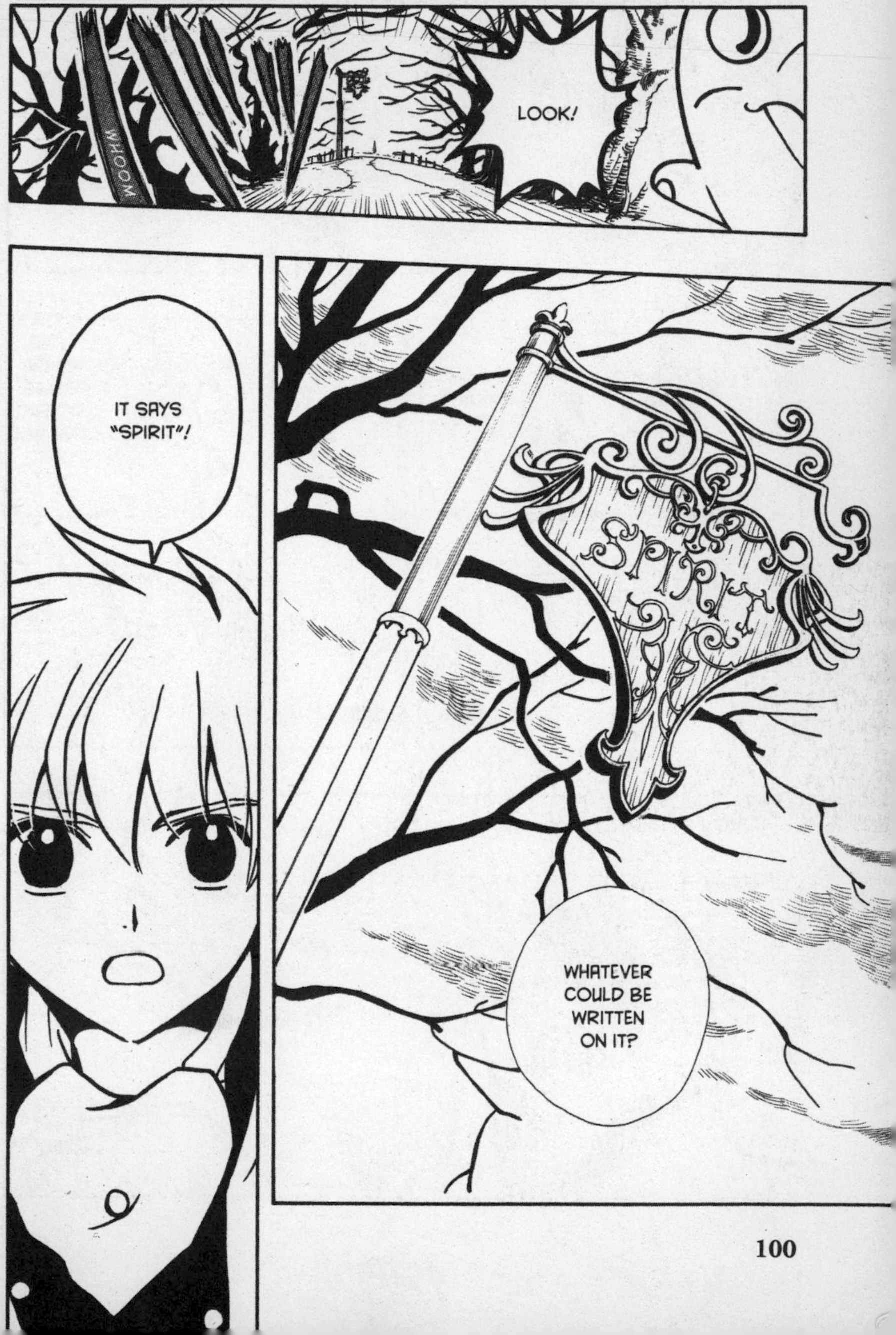
LOOK!
WHOOM
SPIRIT
WHATEVER COULD BE WRITTEN ON IT?
IT SAYS "SPIRIT"!

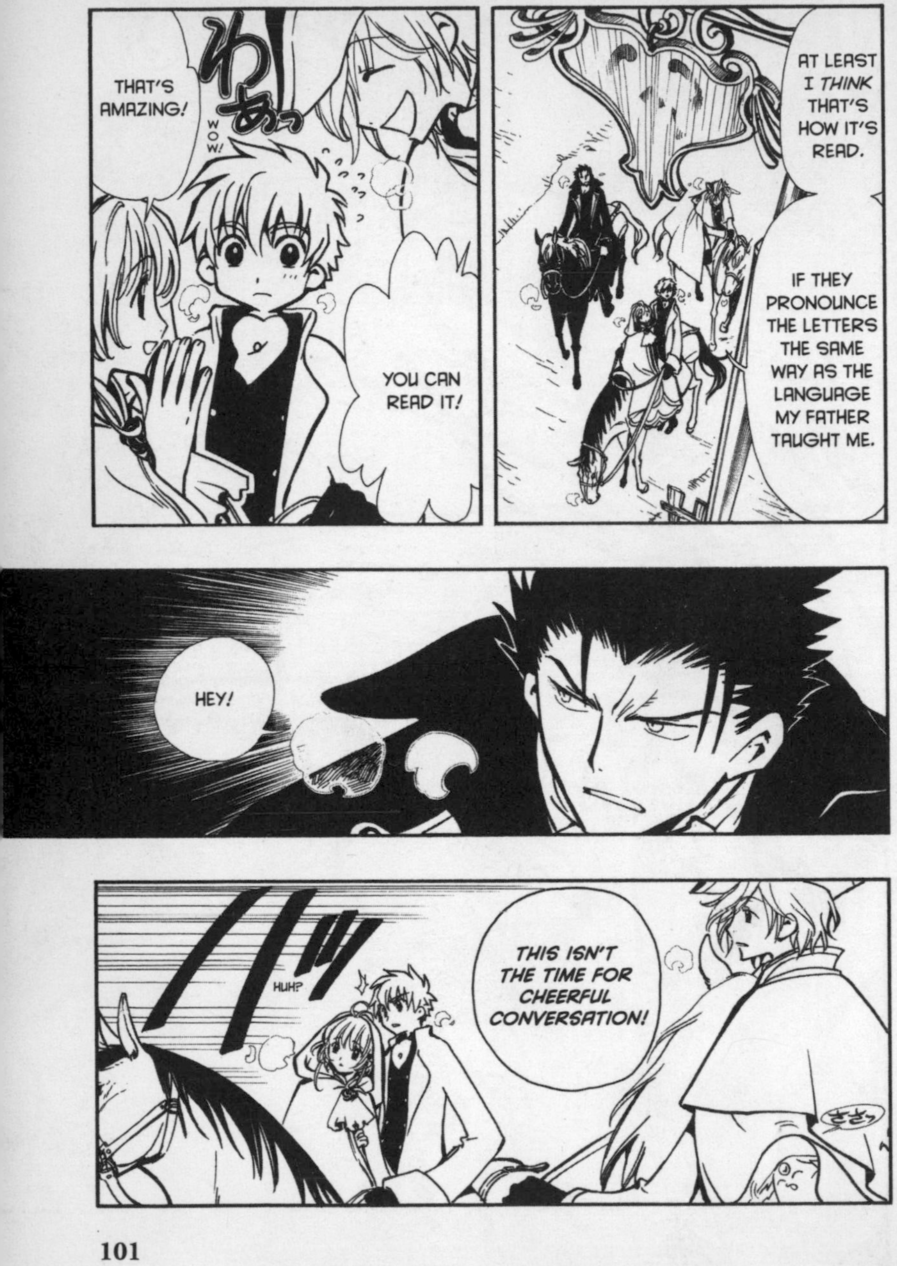
AT LEAST I *THINK* THAT'S HOW IT'S READ.
IF THEY PRONOUNCE THE LETTERS THE SAME WAY AS THE LANGUAGE MY FATHER TAUGHT ME.
わあっ
WOW!
THAT'S AMAZING!
YOU CAN READ IT!
HEY!
THIS ISN'T THE TIME FOR CHEERFUL CONVERSATION!
ハッ
HUH?
ささっ

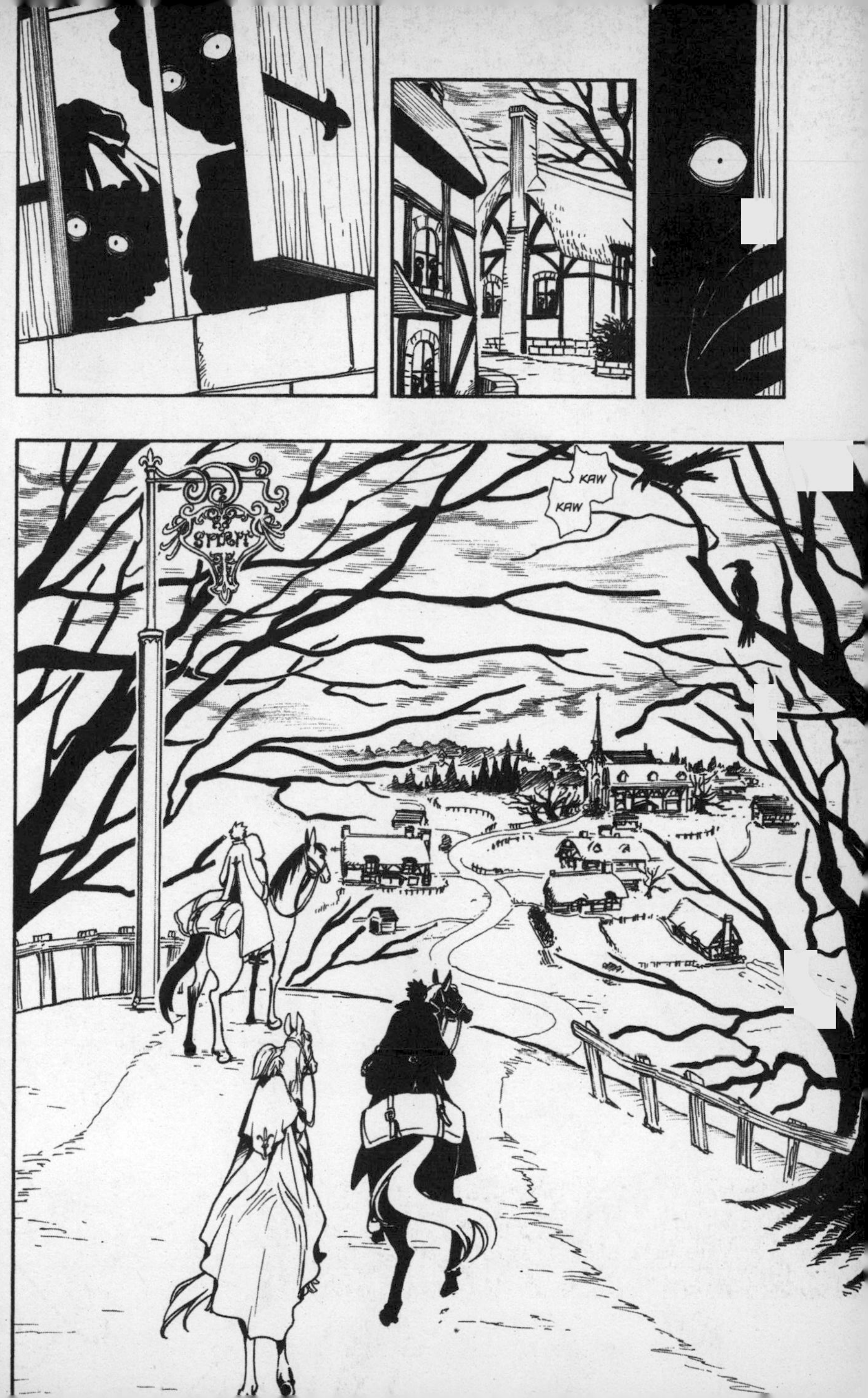
KAW
KAW

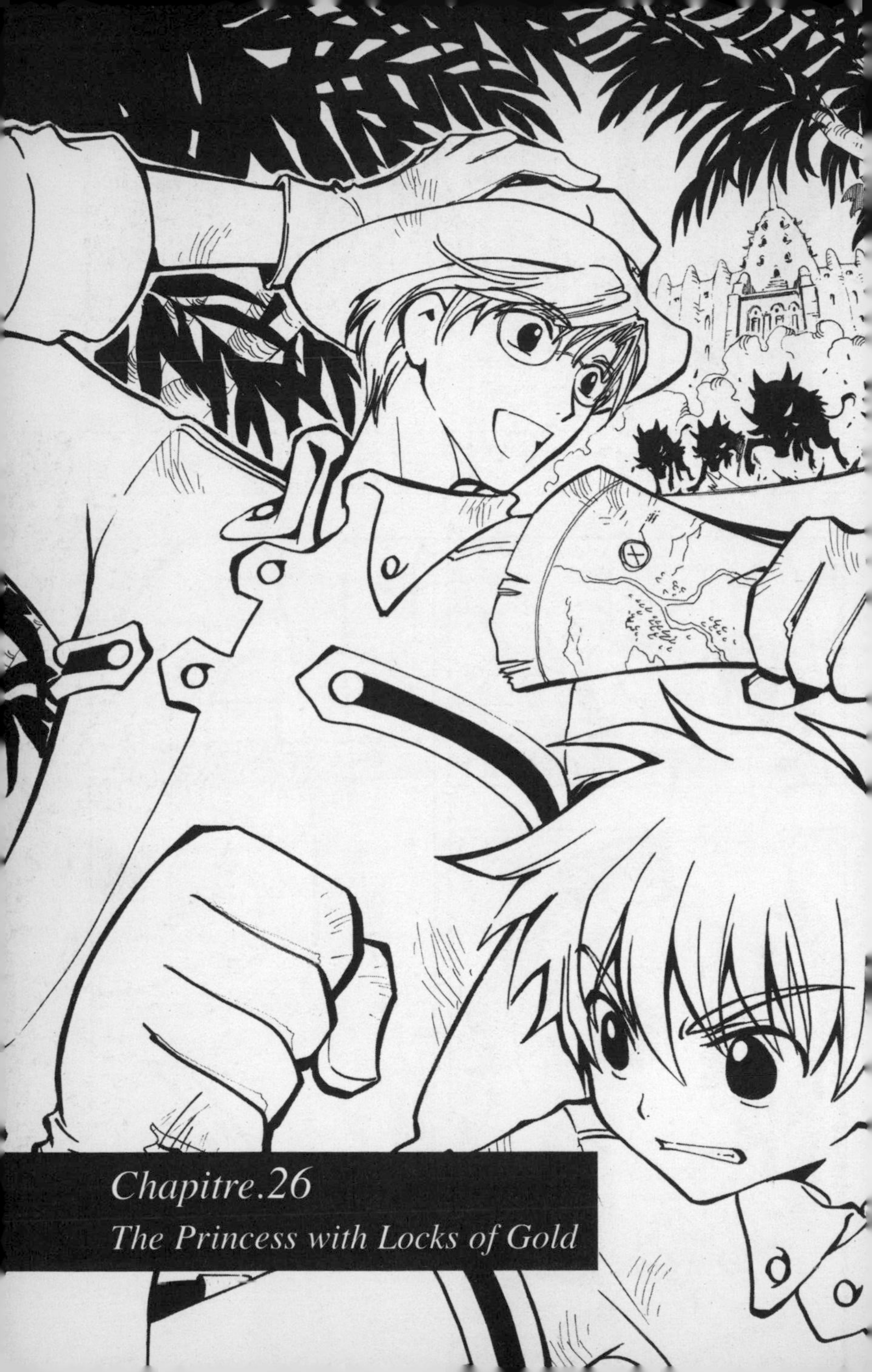

Chapitre.26
The Princess with Locks of Gold

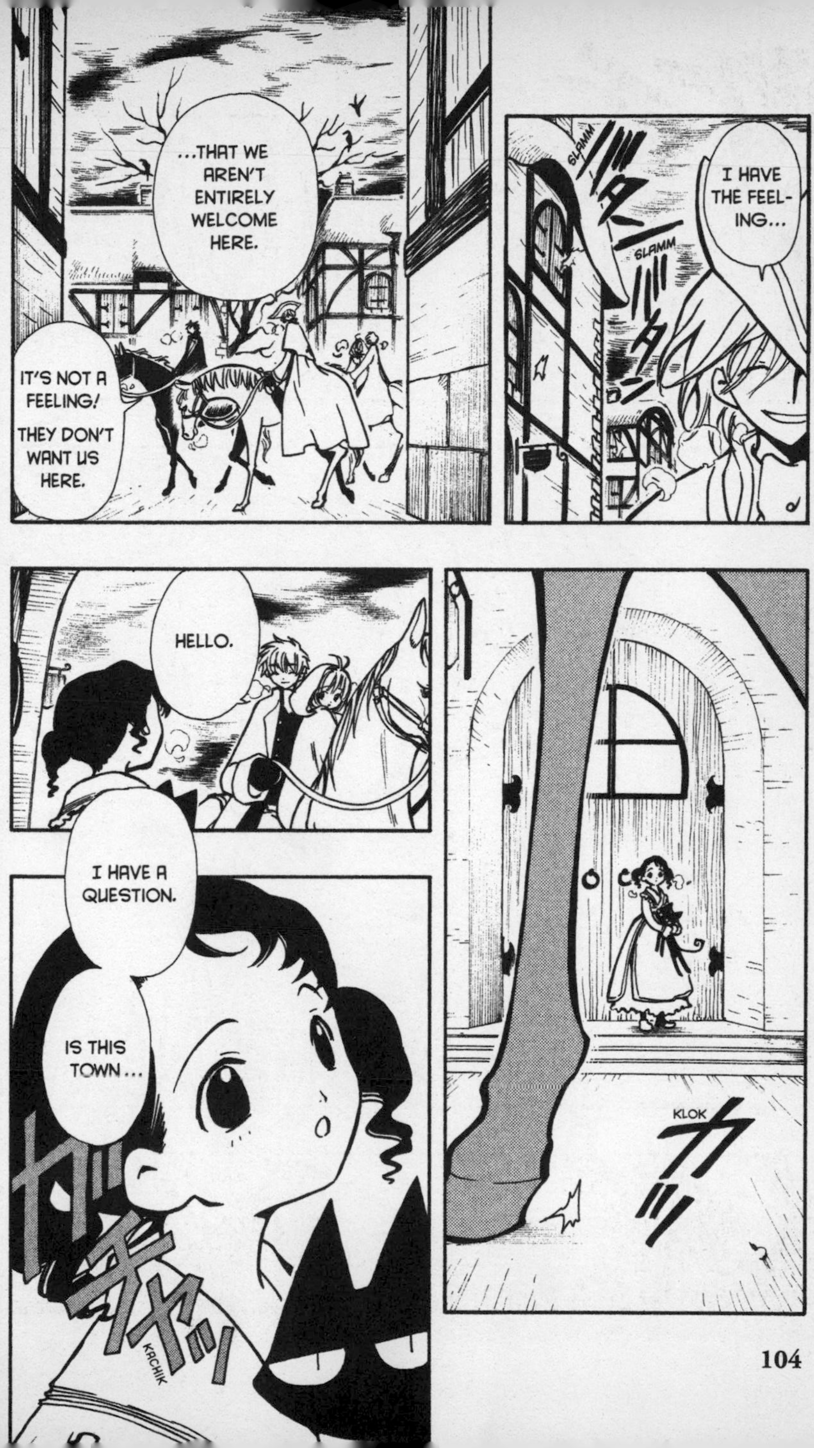
I HAVE THE FEEL- ING...
SLAMM
SLAMM
...THAT WE AREN'T ENTIRELY WELCOME HERE.
IT'S NOT A FEELING!
THEY DON'T WANT US HERE.
KLOK
HELLO.
I HAVE A QUESTION.
IS THIS TOWN...
KACHIK

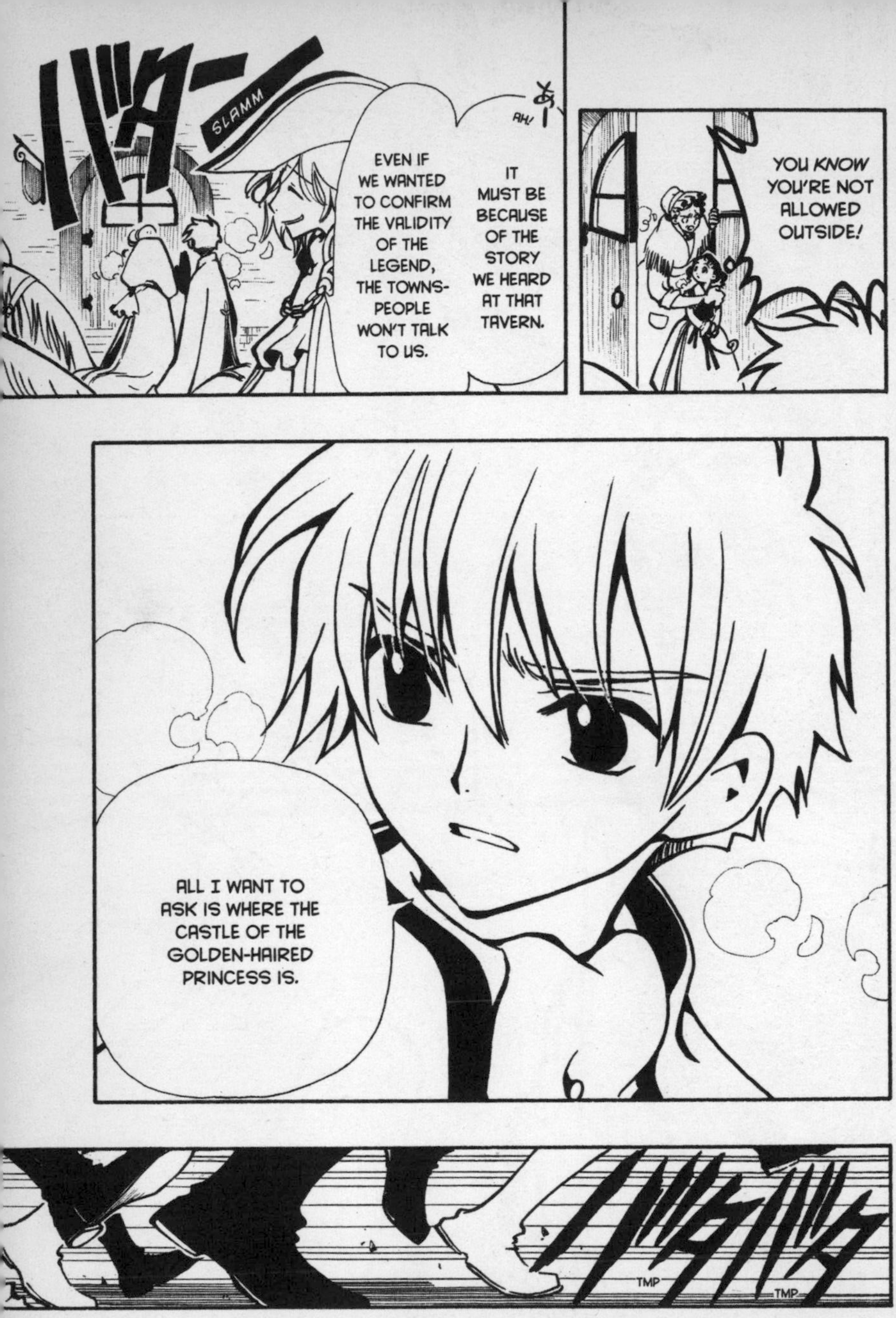
YOU KNOW YOU'RE NOT ALLOWED OUTSIDE!
バターン
SLAMM
あ
AH!
IT MUST BE BECAUSE OF THE STORY WE HEARD AT THAT TAVERN.
EVEN IF WE WANTED TO CONFIRM THE VALIDITY OF THE LEGEND, THE TOWNS-PEOPLE WON'T TALK TO US.
ALL I WANT TO ASK IS WHERE THE CASTLE OF THE GOLDEN-HAIRED PRINCESS IS.
パタパタ
TMP
TMP

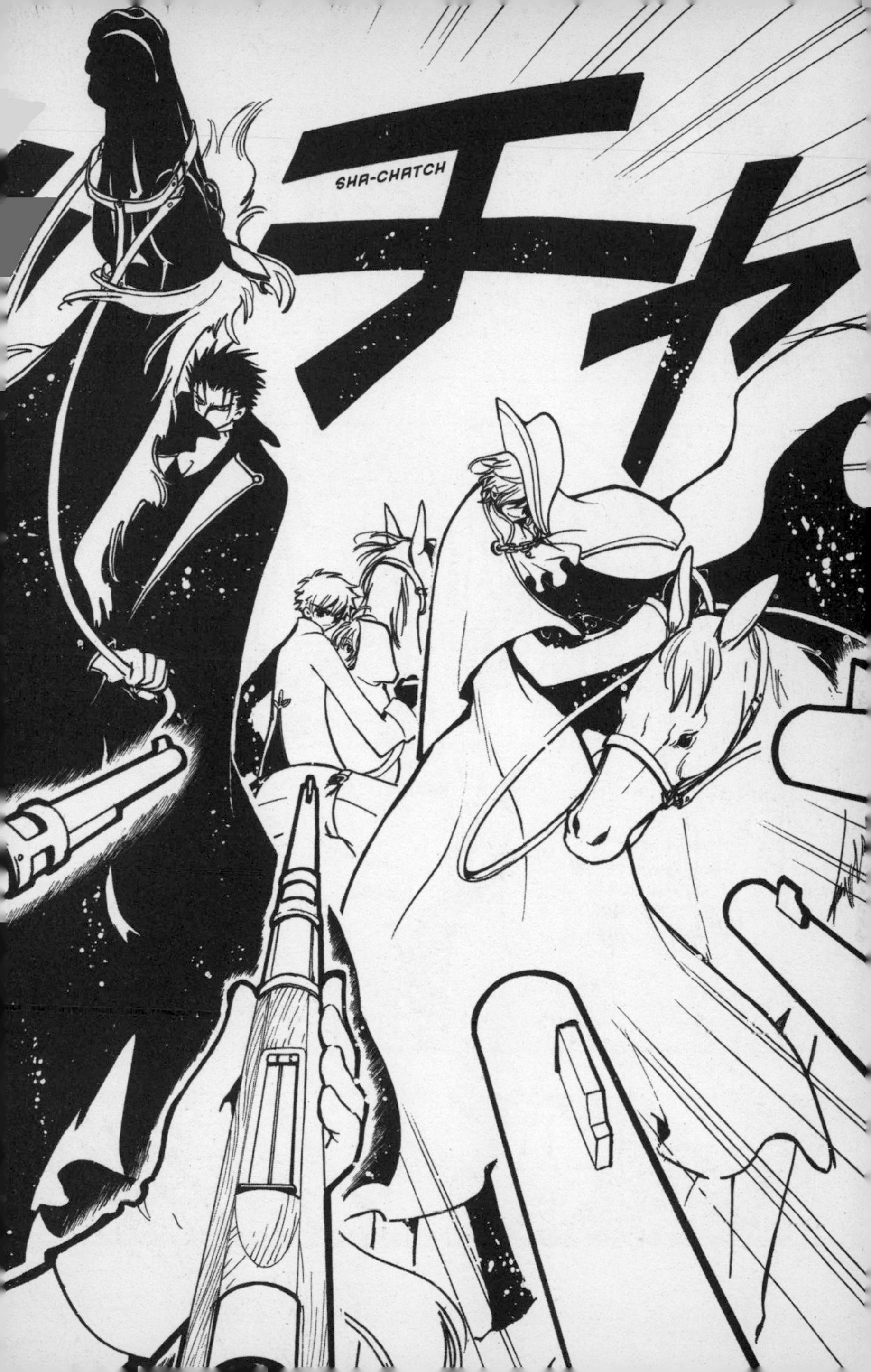
SHA-CHATCH

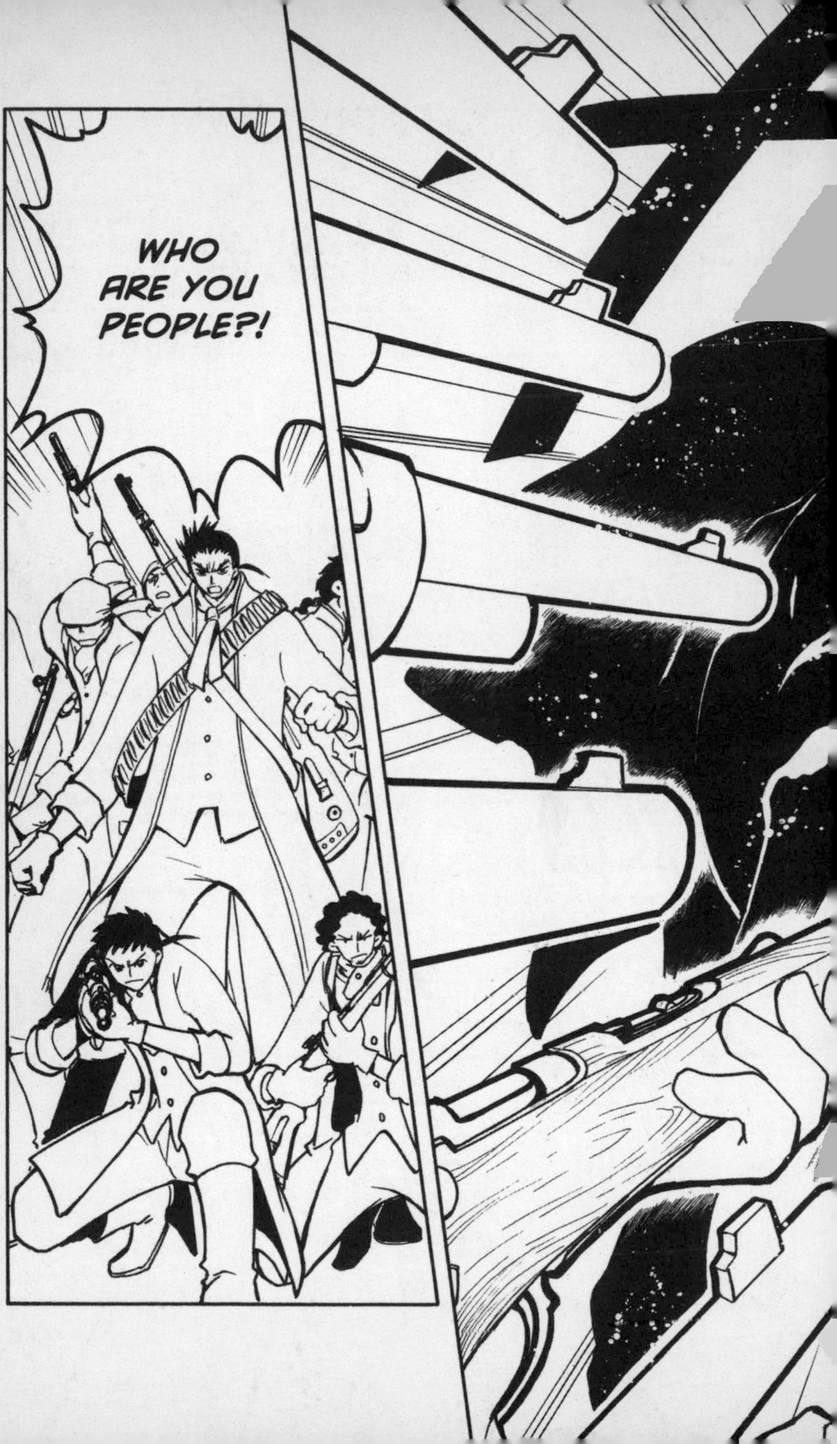
WHO ARE YOU PEOPLE?!

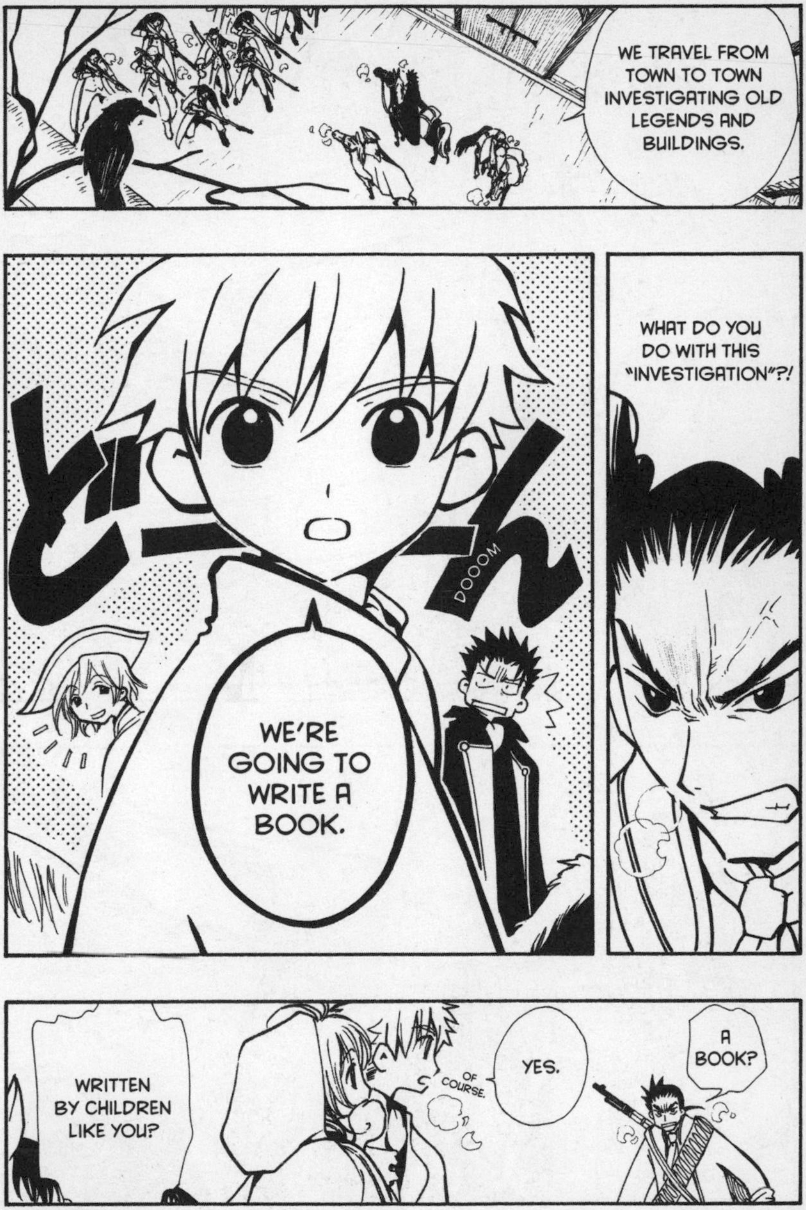
WE TRAVEL FROM TOWN TO TOWN INVESTIGATING OLD LEGENDS AND BUILDINGS.
WHAT DO YOU DO WITH THIS "INVESTIGATION"?!
DOOOM
WE'RE GOING TO WRITE A BOOK.
A BOOK?
YES.
OF COURSE.
WRITTEN BY CHILDREN LIKE YOU?

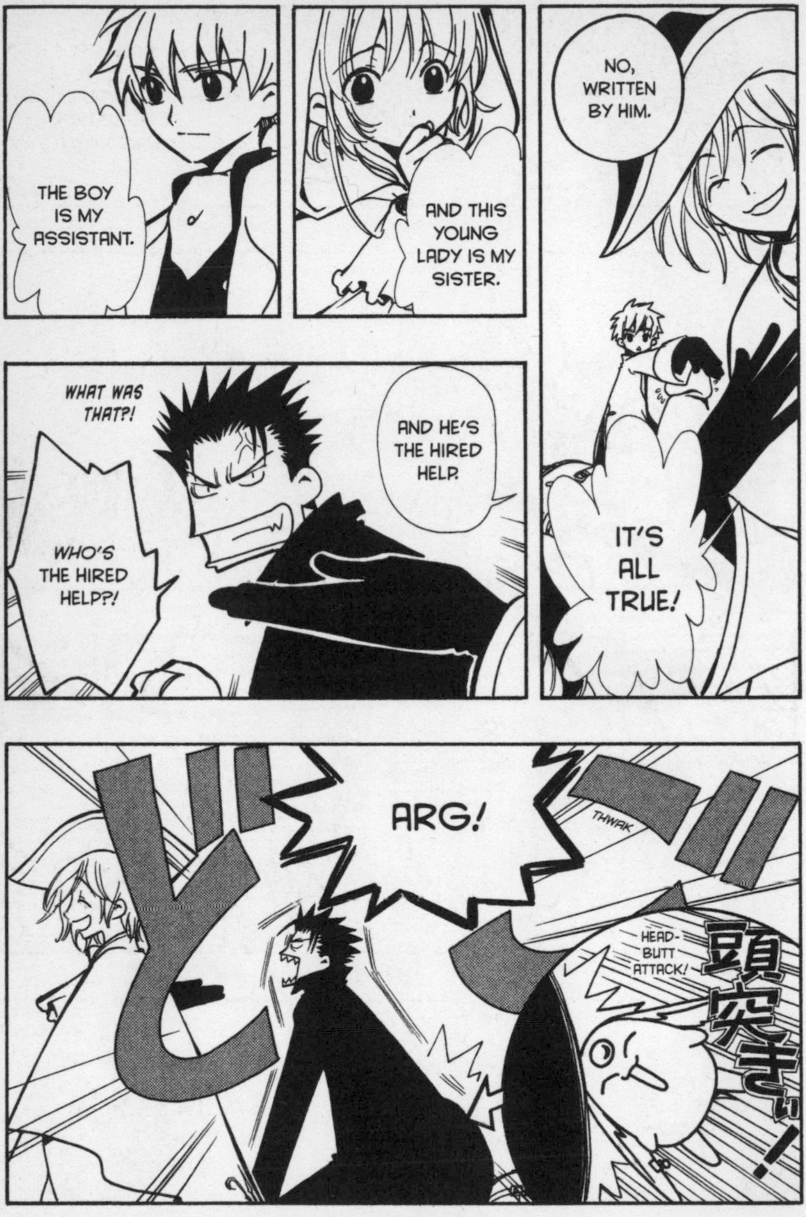
NO, WRITTEN BY HIM.
IT'S ALL TRUE!
AND THIS YOUNG LADY IS MY SISTER.
THE BOY IS MY ASSISTANT.
AND HE'S THE HIRED HELP.
WHAT WAS THAT?!
WHO'S THE HIRED HELP?!
THWAK
ARG!
HEAD-BUTT ATTACK!
頭突きぃ!

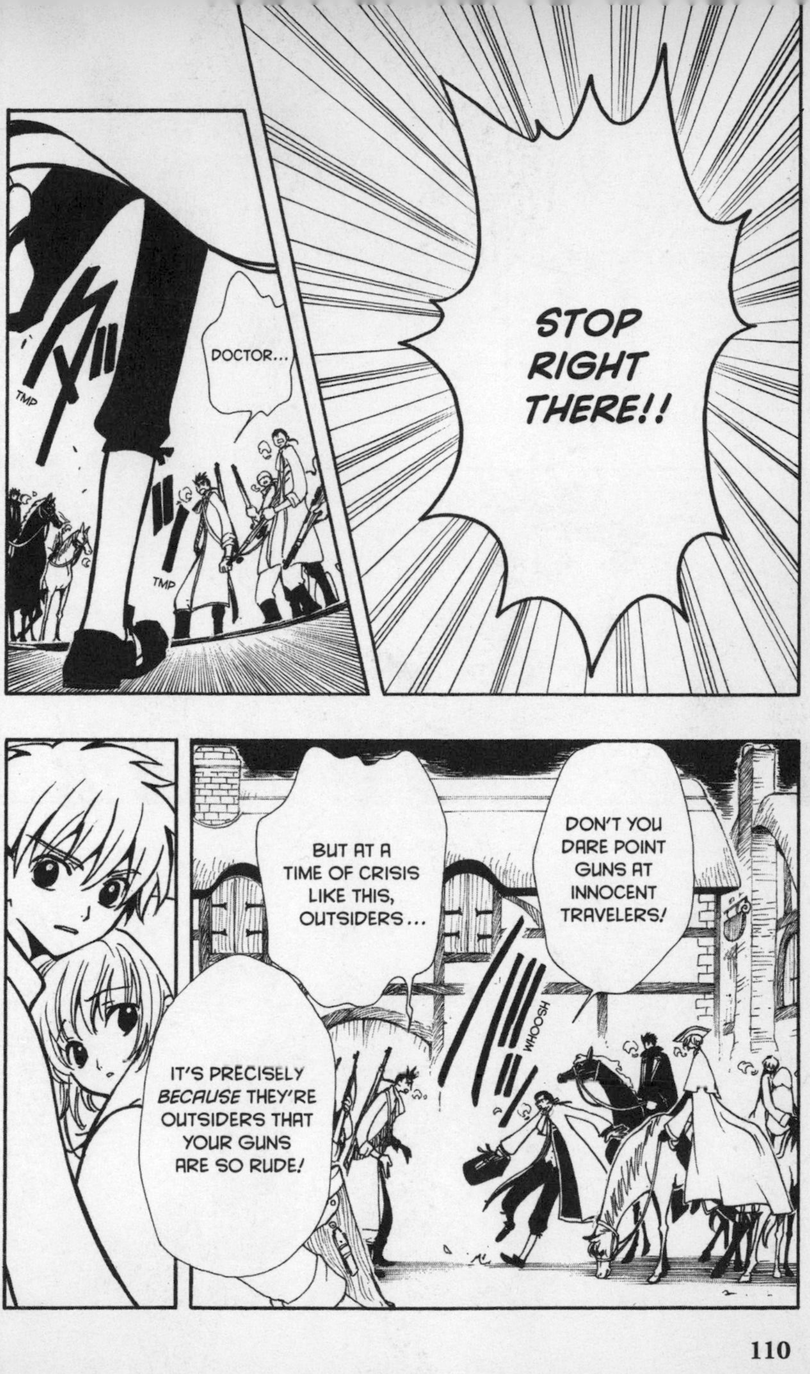
STOP RIGHT THERE!!
DOCTOR...
TMP
TMP
DON'T YOU DARE POINT GUNS AT INNOCENT TRAVELERS!
BUT AT A TIME OF CRISIS LIKE THIS, OUTSIDERS...
WHOOSH
IT'S PRECISELY *BECAUSE* THEY'RE OUTSIDERS THAT YOUR GUNS ARE SO RUDE!

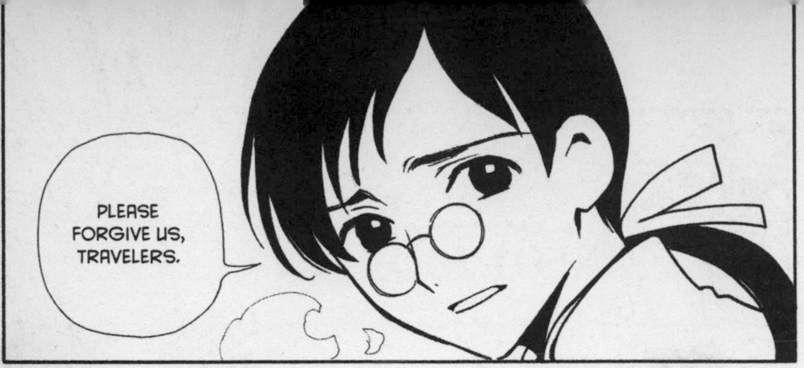
PLEASE FORGIVE US, TRAVELERS.

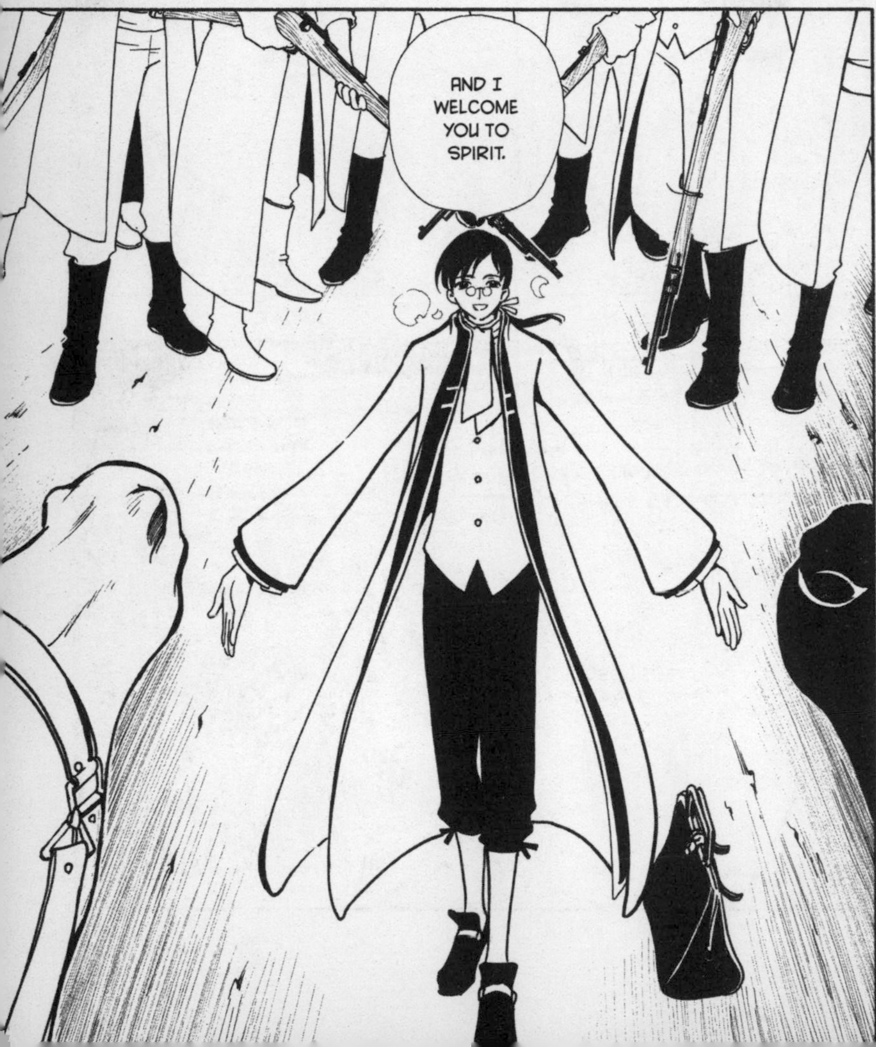
AND I WELCOME YOU TO SPIRIT.

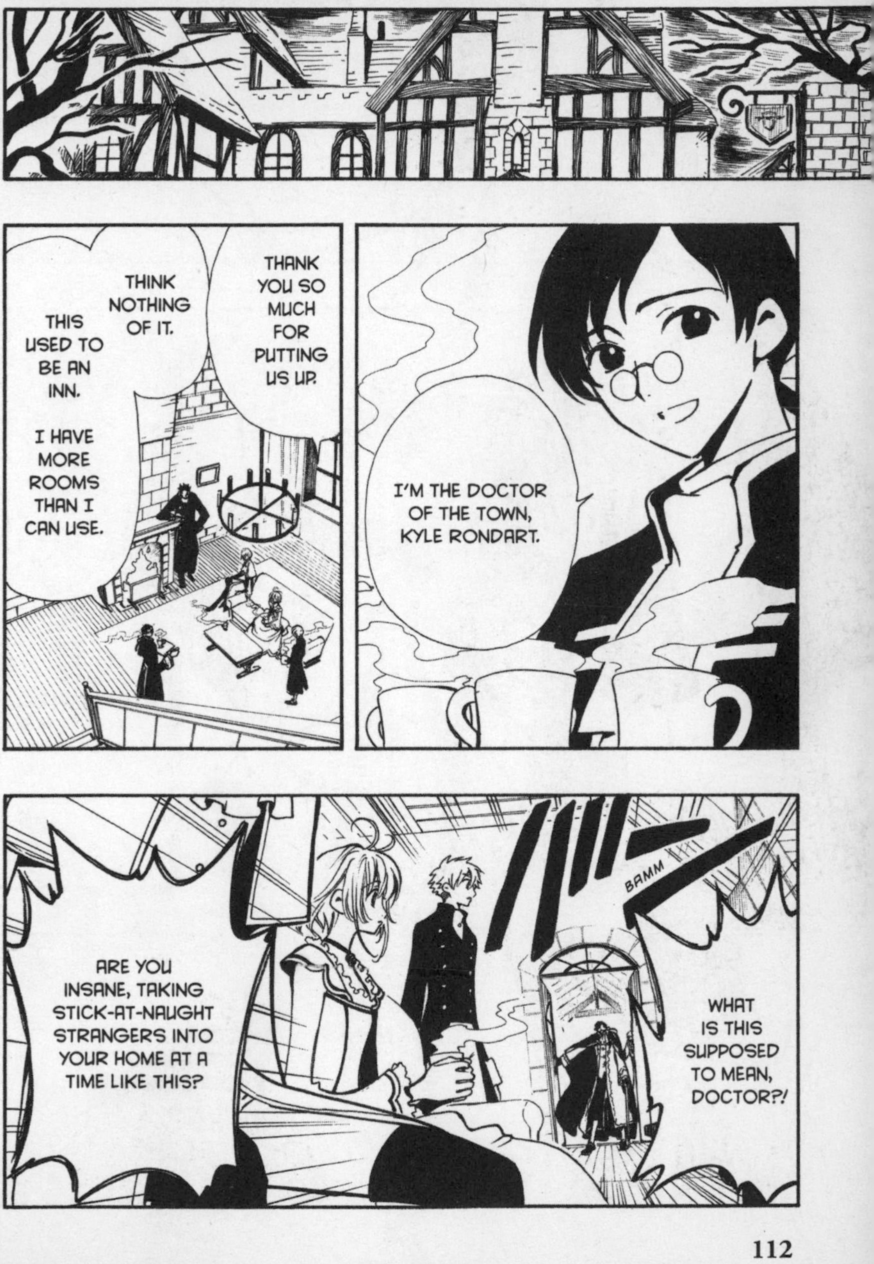
I'M THE DOCTOR OF THE TOWN, KYLE RONDART.
THANK YOU SO MUCH FOR PUTTING US UP.
THINK NOTHING OF IT.
THIS USED TO BE AN INN.
I HAVE MORE ROOMS THAN I CAN USE.
BAMM
WHAT IS THIS SUPPOSED TO MEAN, DOCTOR?!
ARE YOU INSANE, TAKING STICK-AT-NAUGHT STRANGERS INTO YOUR HOME AT A TIME LIKE THIS?

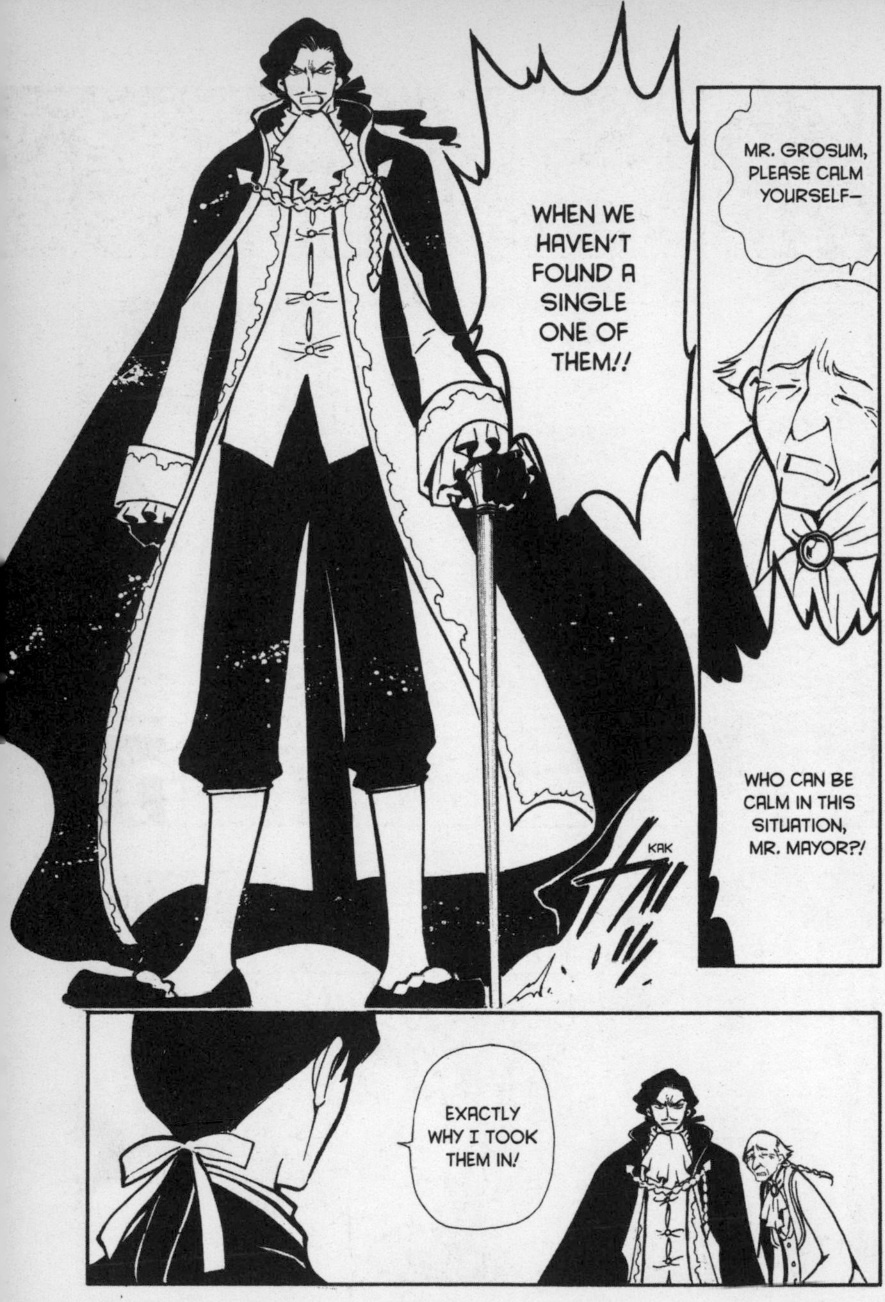
MR. GROSUM, PLEASE CALM YOURSELF—
WHO CAN BE CALM IN THIS SITUATION, MR. MAYOR?!
WHEN WE HAVEN'T FOUND A SINGLE ONE OF THEM!!
KAK
EXACTLY WHY I TOOK THEM IN!

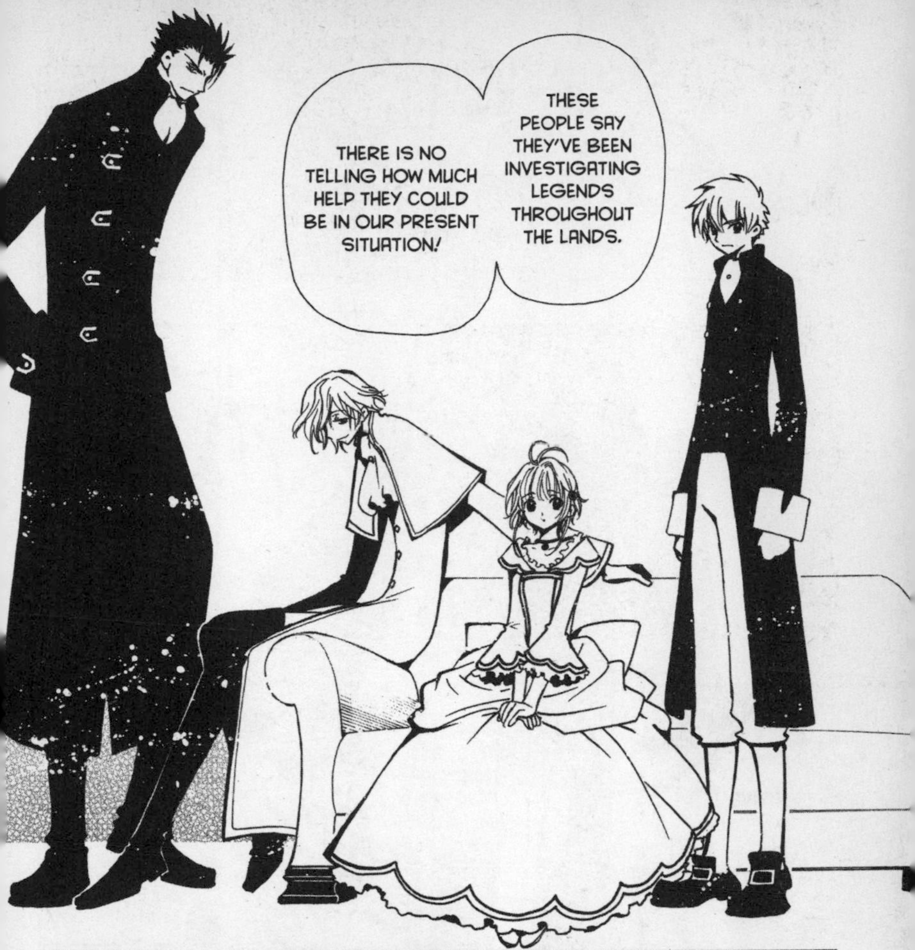
THESE PEOPLE SAY THEY'VE BEEN INVESTIGATING LEGENDS THROUGHOUT THE LANDS.
THERE IS NO TELLING HOW MUCH HELP THEY COULD BE IN OUR PRESENT SITUATION!

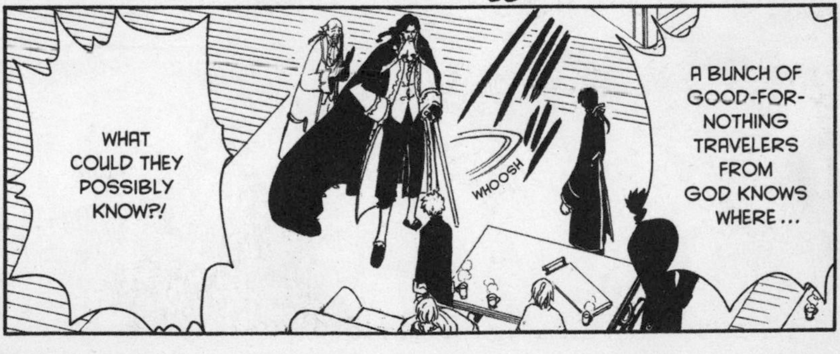
A BUNCH OF GOOD-FOR-NOTHING TRAVELERS FROM GOD KNOWS WHERE...
WHOOSH
WHAT COULD THEY POSSIBLY KNOW?!

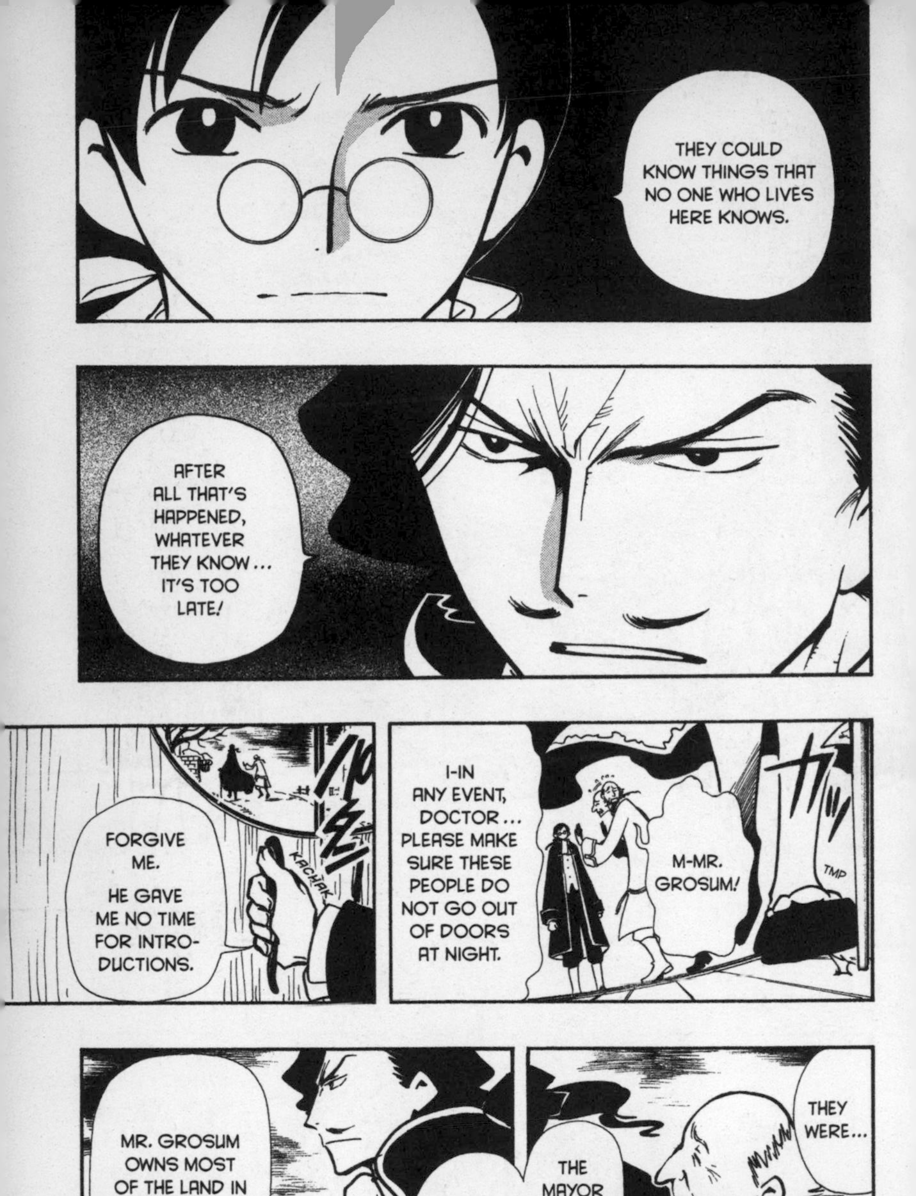
THEY COULD KNOW THINGS THAT NO ONE WHO LIVES HERE KNOWS.
AFTER ALL THAT'S HAPPENED, WHATEVER THEY KNOW... IT'S TOO LATE!
TMP
M-MR. GROSUM!
I-IN ANY EVENT, DOCTOR... PLEASE MAKE SURE THESE PEOPLE DO NOT GO OUT OF DOORS AT NIGHT.
KACHAK
FORGIVE ME.
HE GAVE ME NO TIME FOR INTRO-DUCTIONS.
THEY WERE...
THE MAYOR AND...
...MR. GROSUM.
MR. GROSUM OWNS MOST OF THE LAND IN THE AREA.

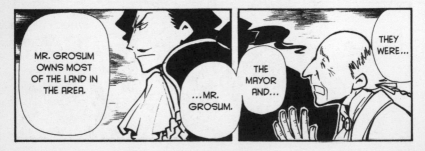

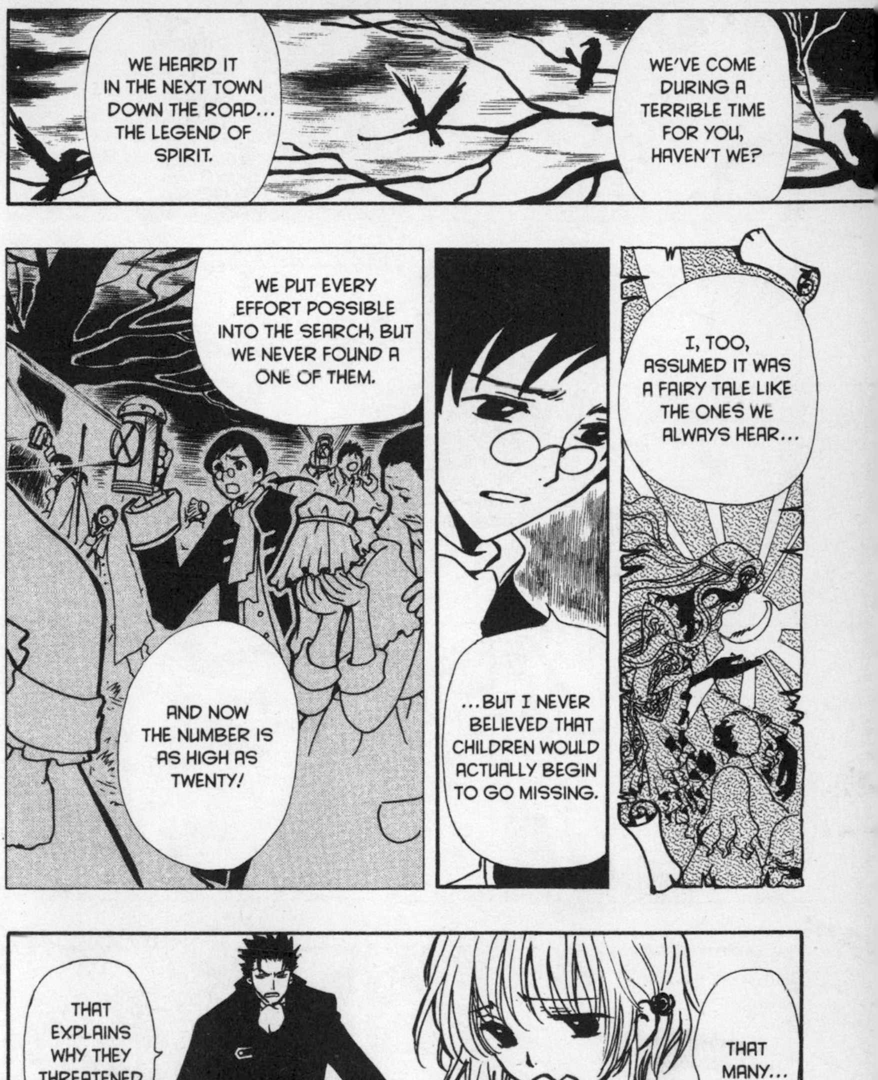
WE'VE COME DURING A TERRIBLE TIME FOR YOU, HAVEN'T WE?
WE HEARD IT IN THE NEXT TOWN DOWN THE ROAD... THE LEGEND OF SPIRIT.
I, TOO, ASSUMED IT WAS A FAIRY TALE LIKE THE ONES WE ALWAYS HEAR...
...BUT I NEVER BELIEVED THAT CHILDREN WOULD ACTUALLY BEGIN TO GO MISSING.
WE PUT EVERY EFFORT POSSIBLE INTO THE SEARCH, BUT WE NEVER FOUND A ONE OF THEM.
AND NOW THE NUMBER IS AS HIGH AS TWENTY!
THAT MANY...
THAT EXPLAINS WHY THEY THREATENED US ON FIRST SIGHT.

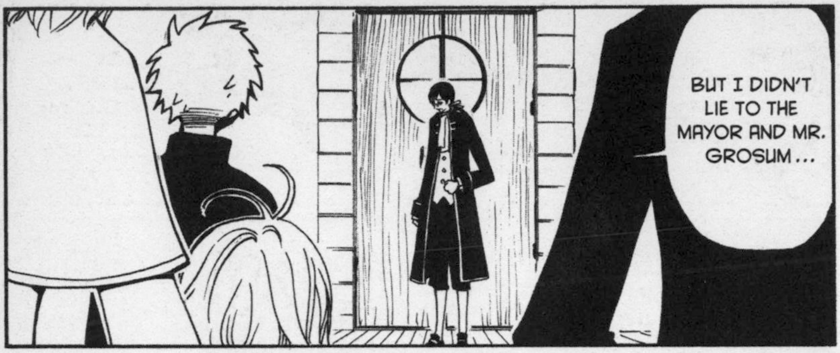
BUT I DIDN'T LIE TO THE MAYOR AND MR. GROSUM...

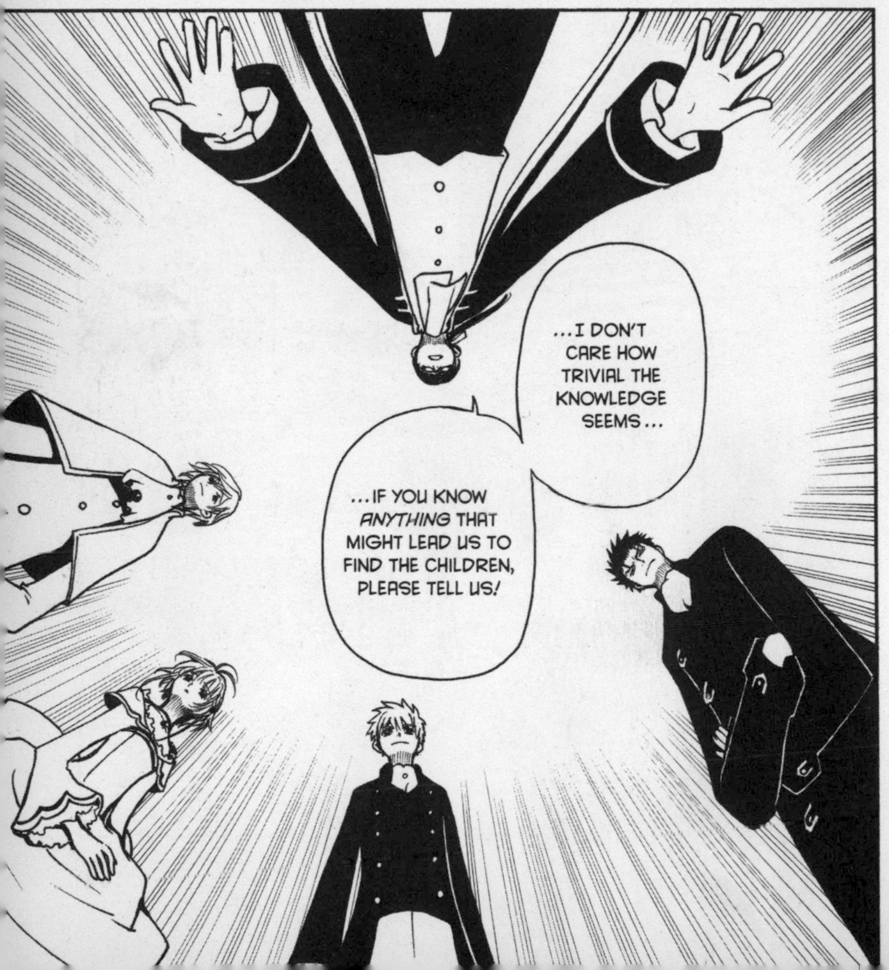
...I DON'T CARE HOW TRIVIAL THE KNOWLEDGE SEEMS...
...IF YOU KNOW *ANYTHING* THAT MIGHT LEAD US TO FIND THE CHILDREN, PLEASE TELL US!

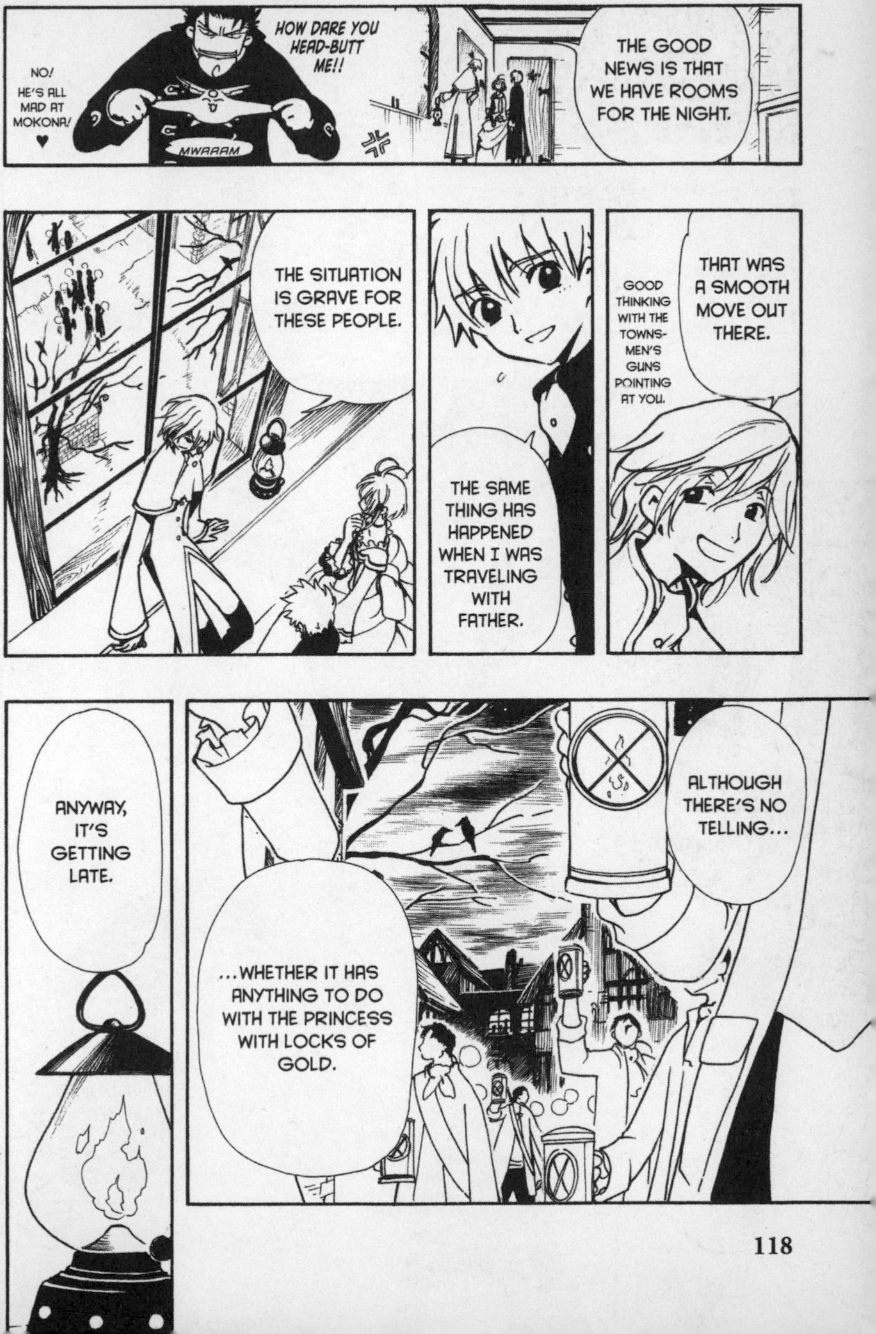
THE GOOD NEWS IS THAT WE HAVE ROOMS FOR THE NIGHT.
HOW DARE YOU HEAD-BUTT ME!!
MWAAAM
NO! HE'S ALL MAD AT MOKONA! ♥
THAT WAS A SMOOTH MOVE OUT THERE.
GOOD THINKING WITH THE TOWNS-MEN'S GUNS POINTING AT YOU.
THE SAME THING HAS HAPPENED WHEN I WAS TRAVELING WITH FATHER.
THE SITUATION IS GRAVE FOR THESE PEOPLE.
ALTHOUGH THERE'S NO TELLING...
...WHETHER IT HAS ANYTHING TO DO WITH THE PRINCESS WITH LOCKS OF GOLD.
ANYWAY, IT'S GETTING LATE.

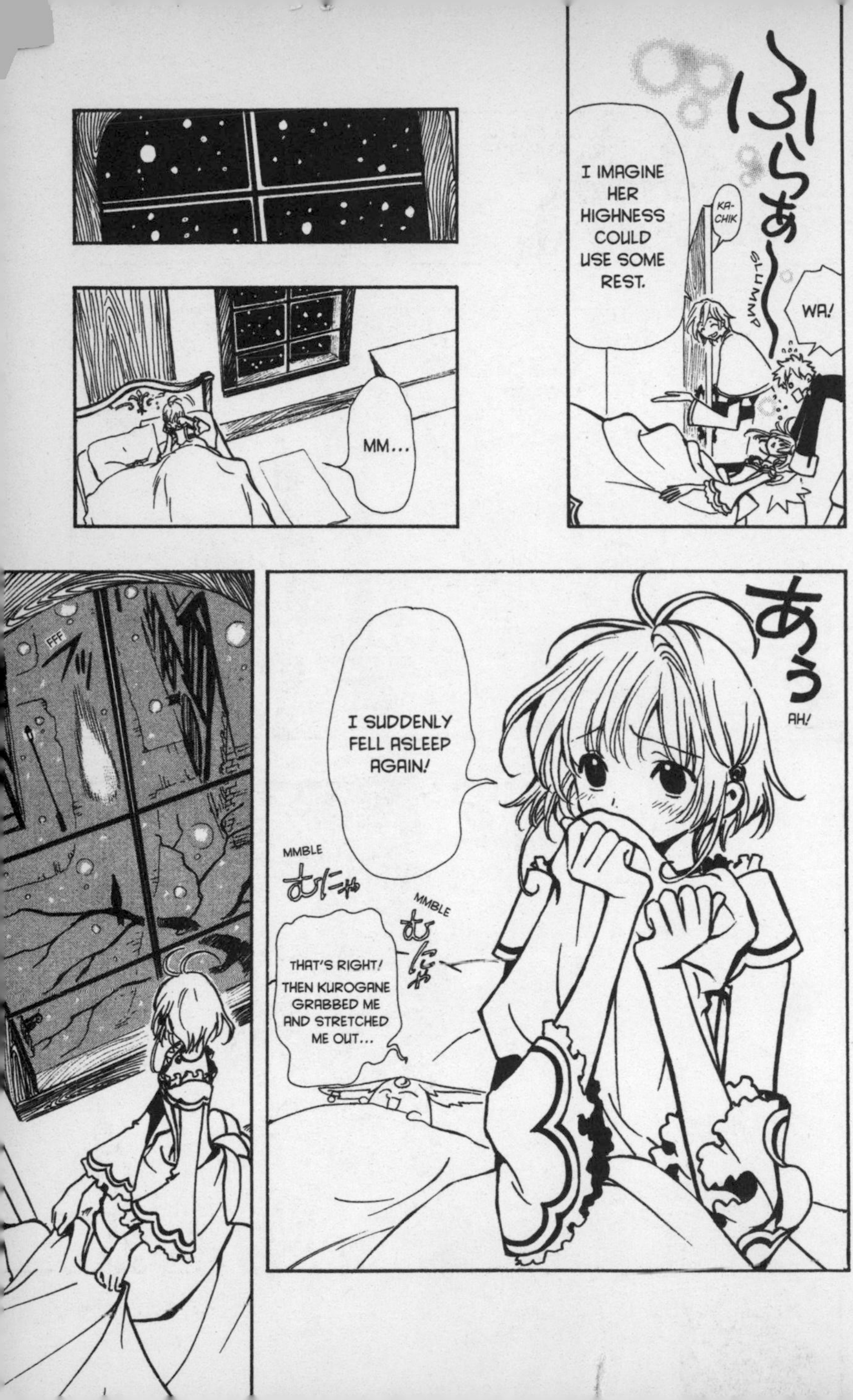
ふらぁ~
I IMAGINE HER HIGHNESS COULD USE SOME REST.
KA-CHIK
SLUMMP
WA!
MM...
あう
AH!
I SUDDENLY FELL ASLEEP AGAIN!
MMBLE
むにゃ
MMBLE
むにゃ
THAT'S RIGHT! THEN KUROGANE GRABBED ME AND STRETCHED ME OUT...
FFF
フッ

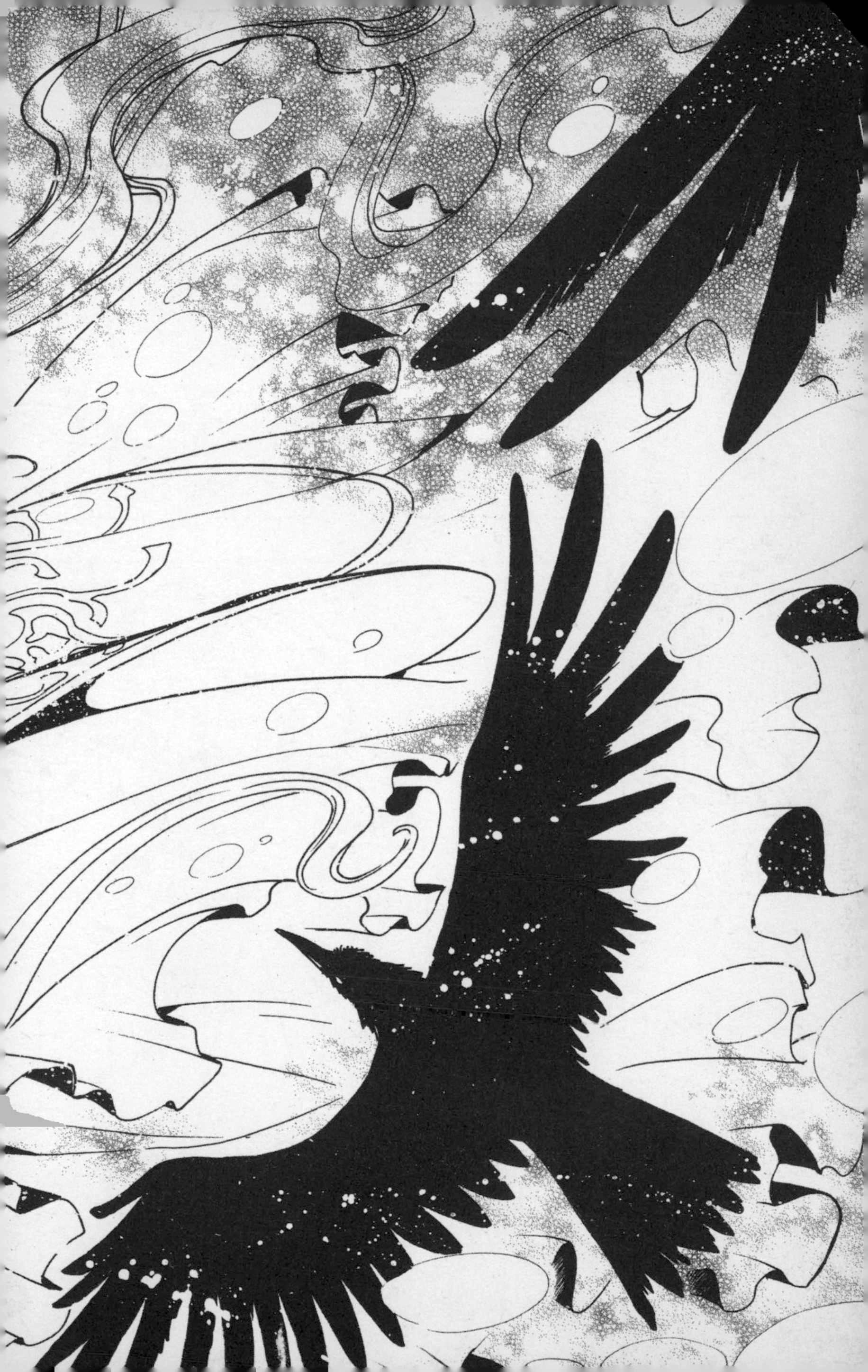

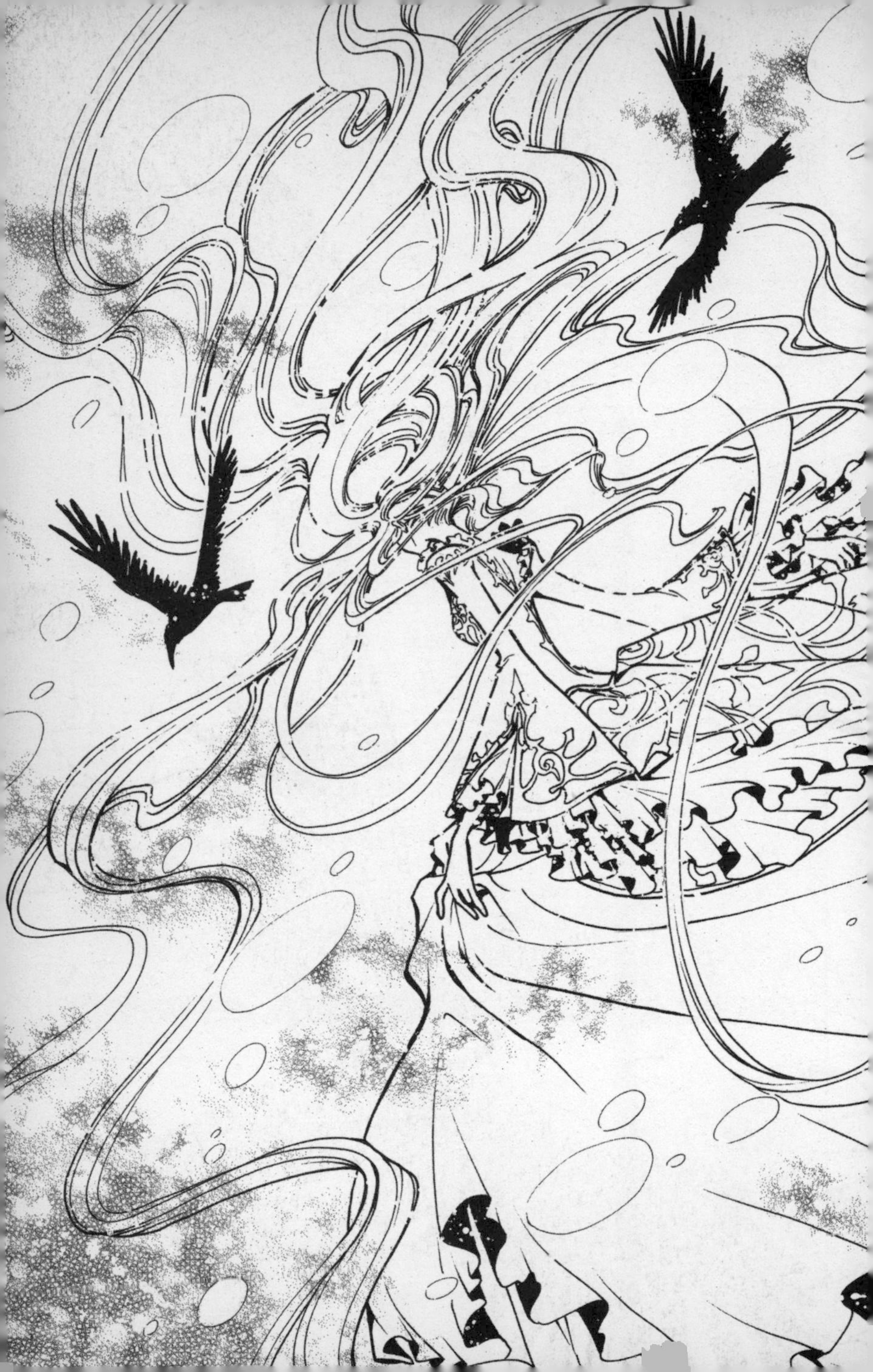

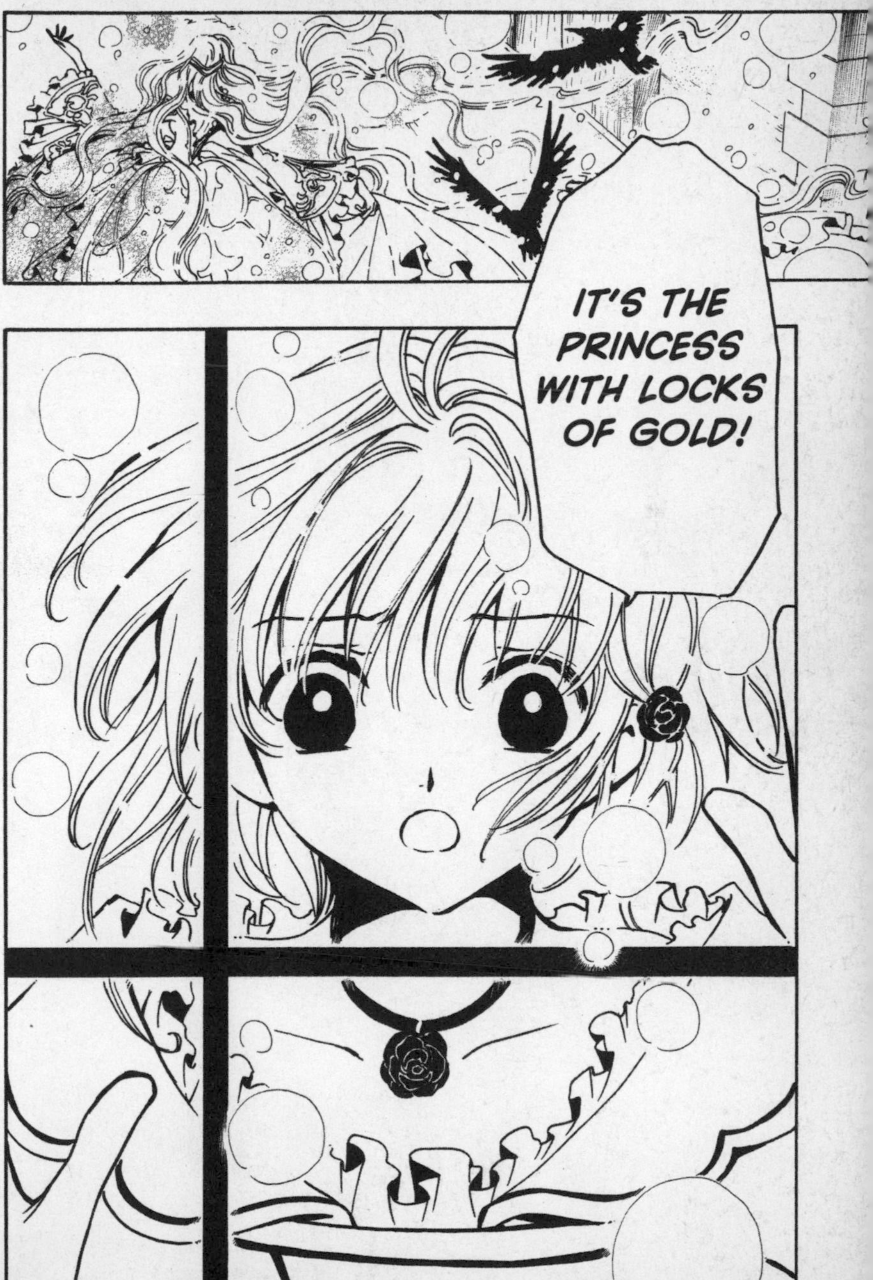
IT'S THE PRINCESS WITH LOCKS OF GOLD!

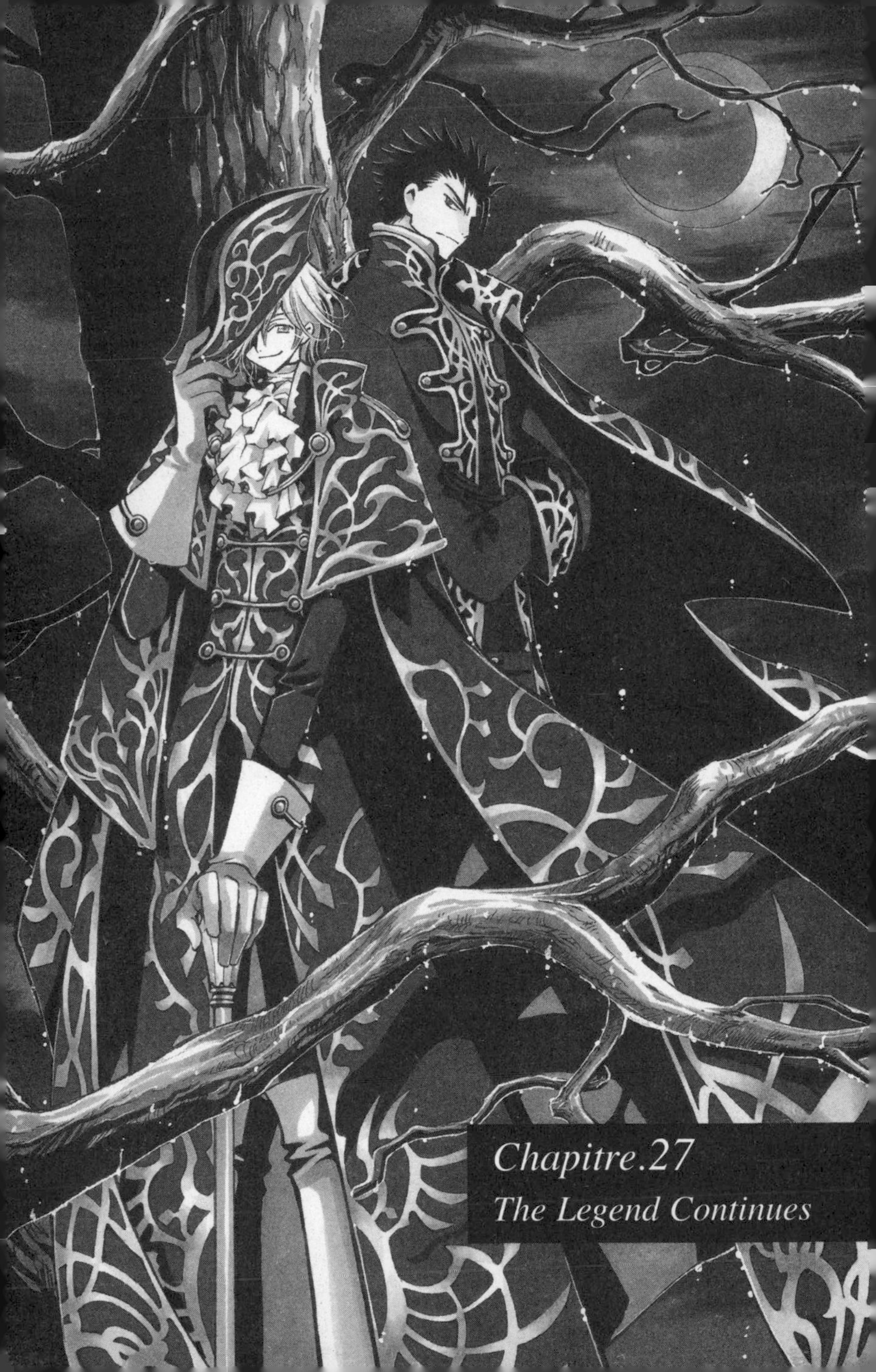

Chapitre.27

The Legend Continues

ツバサ

RESERVoir CHRoNiCLE

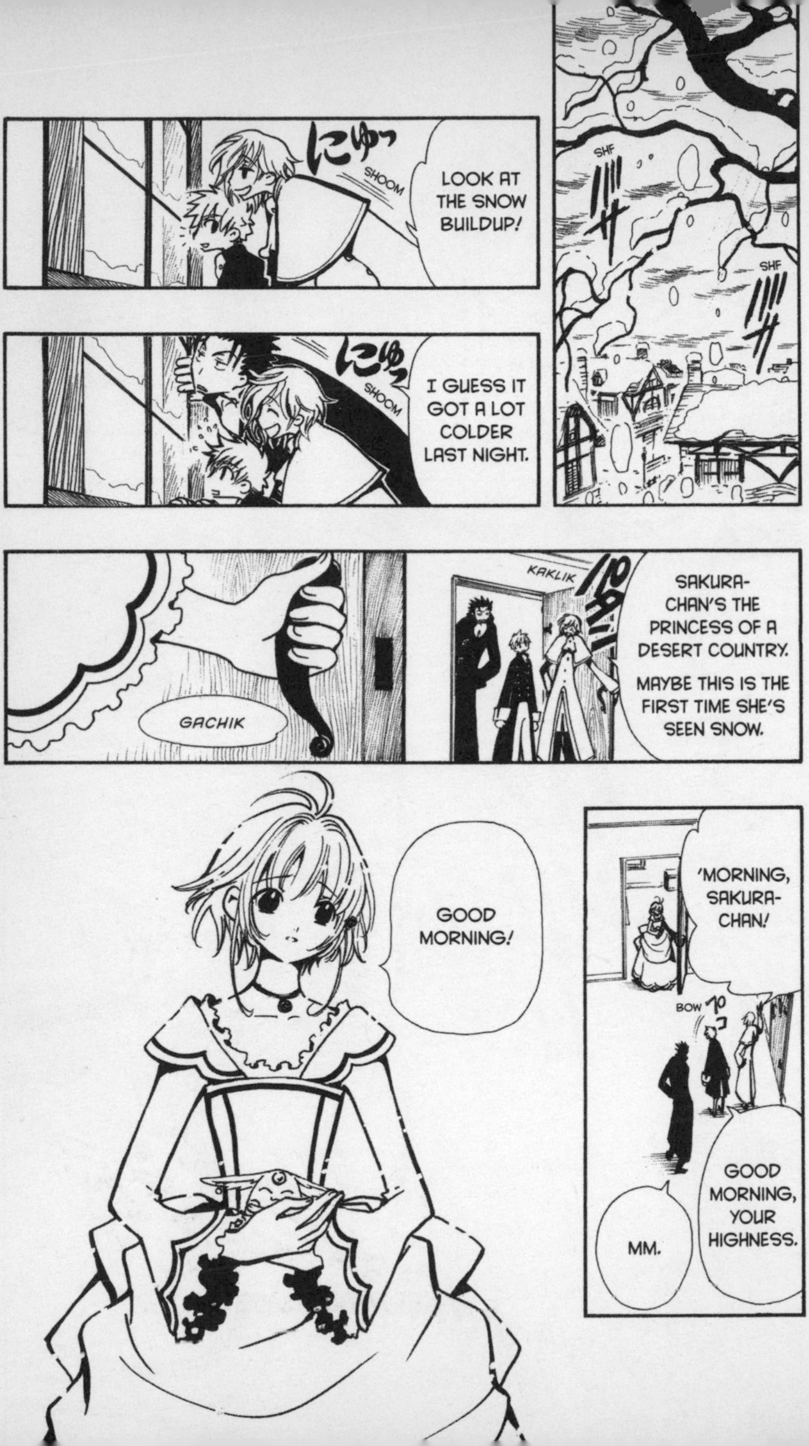
SHF
SHF
にゅっ
SHOOM
LOOK AT THE SNOW BUILDUP!
にゅっ
SHOOM
I GUESS IT GOT A LOT COLDER LAST NIGHT.
KAKLIK
SAKURA-CHAN'S THE PRINCESS OF A DESERT COUNTRY.
MAYBE THIS IS THE FIRST TIME SHE'S SEEN SNOW.
GACHIK
'MORNING, SAKURA-CHAN!
BOW
GOOD MORNING, YOUR HIGHNESS.
MM.
GOOD MORNING!

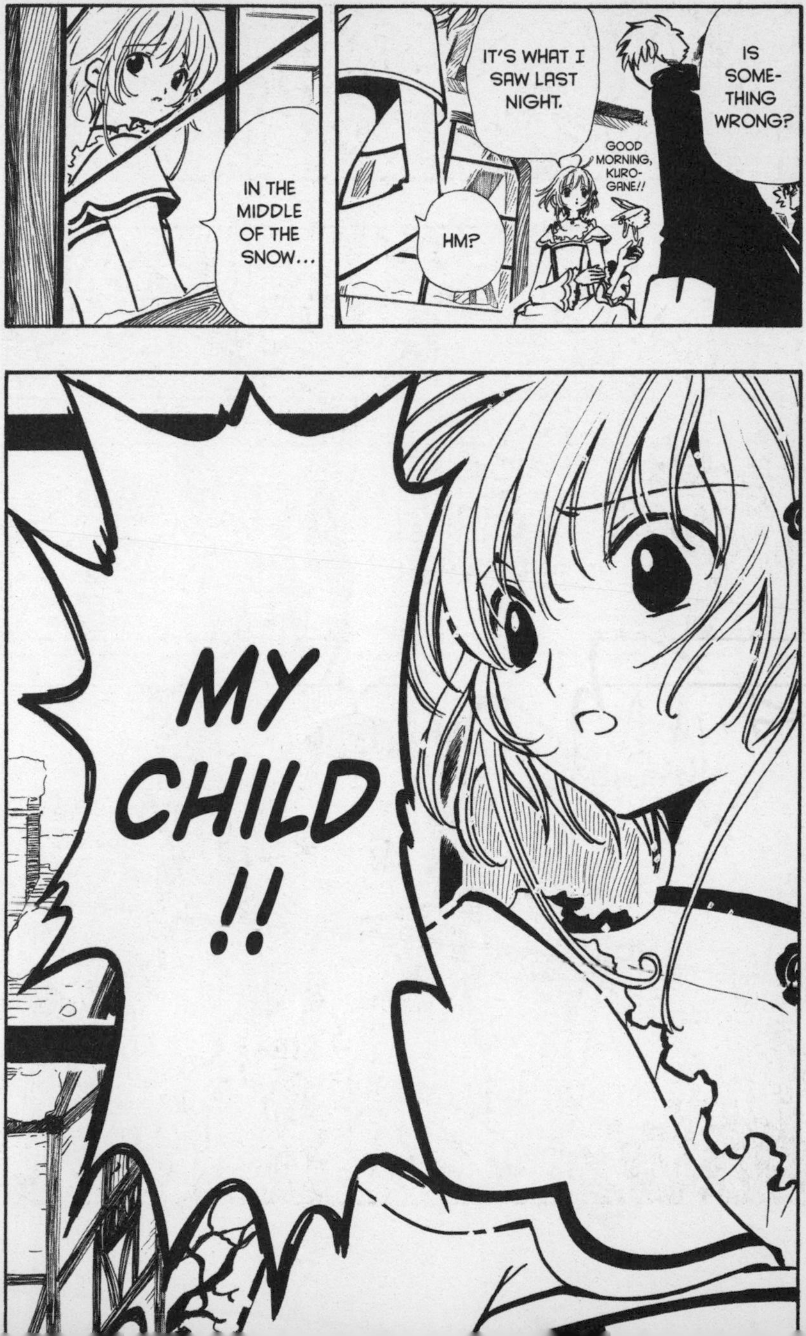
IS SOMETHING WRONG?
IT'S WHAT I SAW LAST NIGHT.
GOOD MORNING, KURO-GANE!!
HM?
IN THE MIDDLE OF THE SNOW...
MY CHILD!!

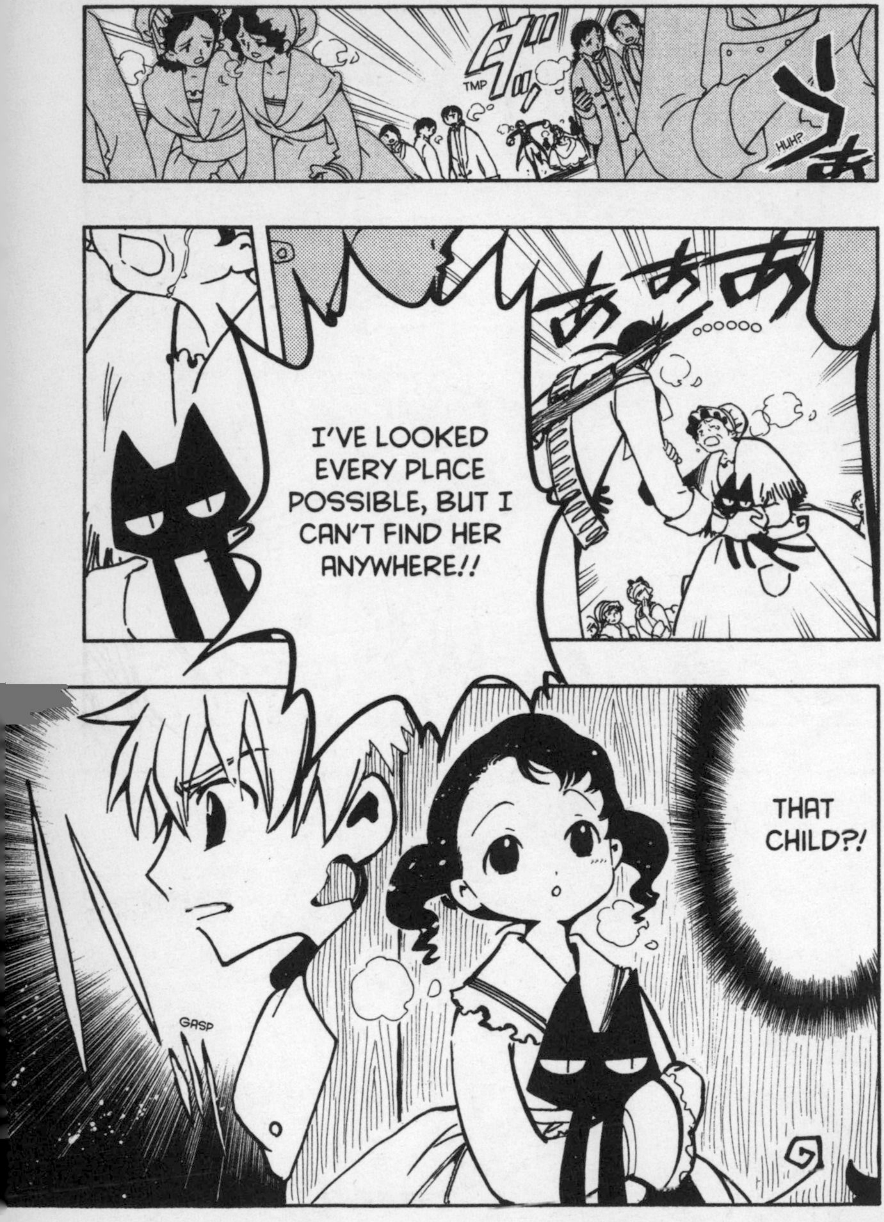
HUH?
TMP
あああ
I'VE LOOKED EVERY PLACE POSSIBLE, BUT I CAN'T FIND HER ANYWHERE!!
THAT CHILD?!
GASP

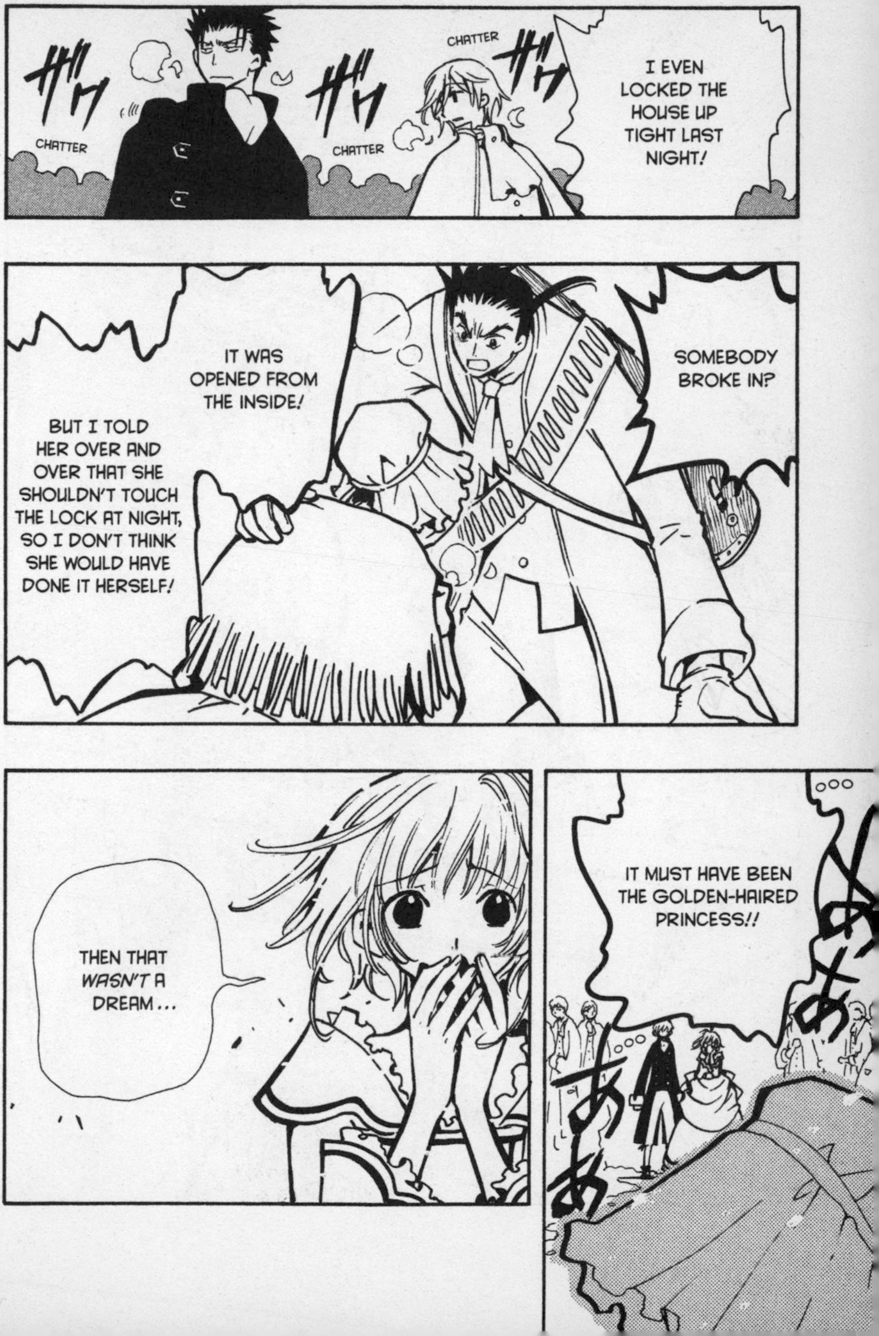
ザワ
I EVEN LOCKED THE HOUSE UP TIGHT LAST NIGHT!
CHATTER
ザワ
CHATTER
ザワ
CHATTER
SOMEBODY BROKE IN?
IT WAS OPENED FROM THE INSIDE!
BUT I TOLD HER OVER AND OVER THAT SHE SHOULDN'T TOUCH THE LOCK AT NIGHT, SO I DON'T THINK SHE WOULD HAVE DONE IT HERSELF!
ooo
IT MUST HAVE BEEN THE GOLDEN-HAIRED PRINCESS!!
THEN THAT *WASN'T* A DREAM...

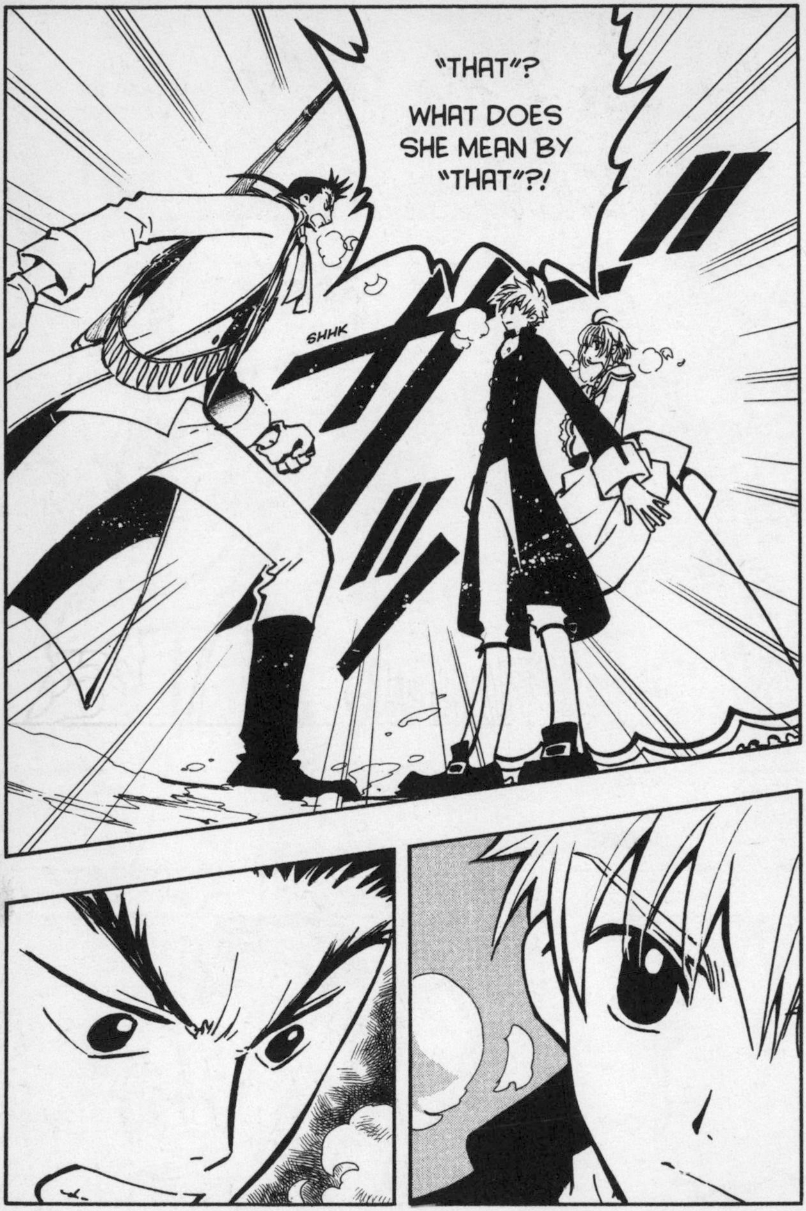
"THAT"?
WHAT DOES SHE MEAN BY "THAT"?!
SHHK

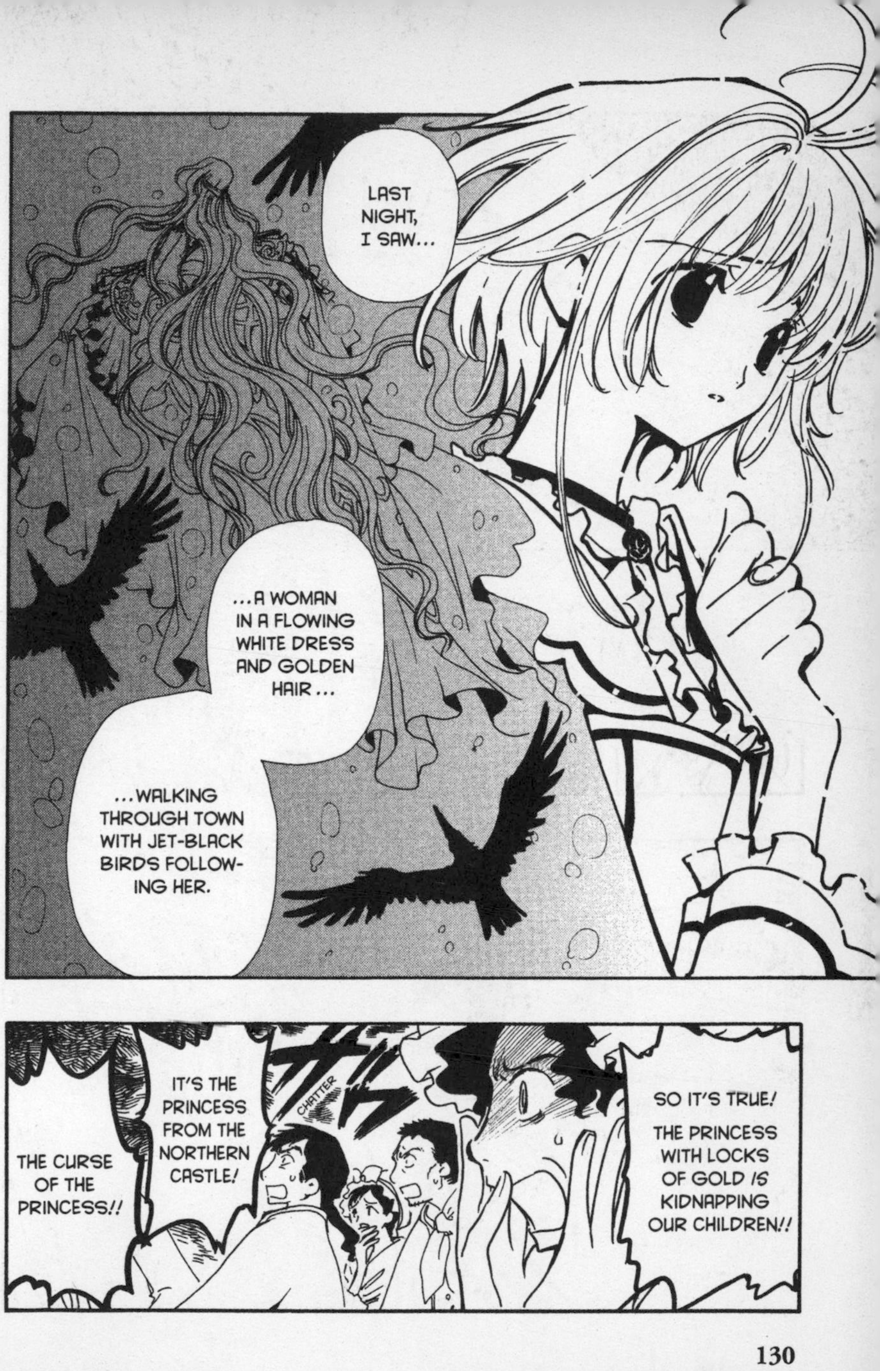
LAST NIGHT, I SAW...
...A WOMAN IN A FLOWING WHITE DRESS AND GOLDEN HAIR...
...WALKING THROUGH TOWN WITH JET-BLACK BIRDS FOLLOWING HER.
SO IT'S TRUE!
THE PRINCESS WITH LOCKS OF GOLD *IS* KIDNAPPING OUR CHILDREN!!
CHATTER
IT'S THE PRINCESS FROM THE NORTHERN CASTLE!
THE CURSE OF THE PRINCESS!!

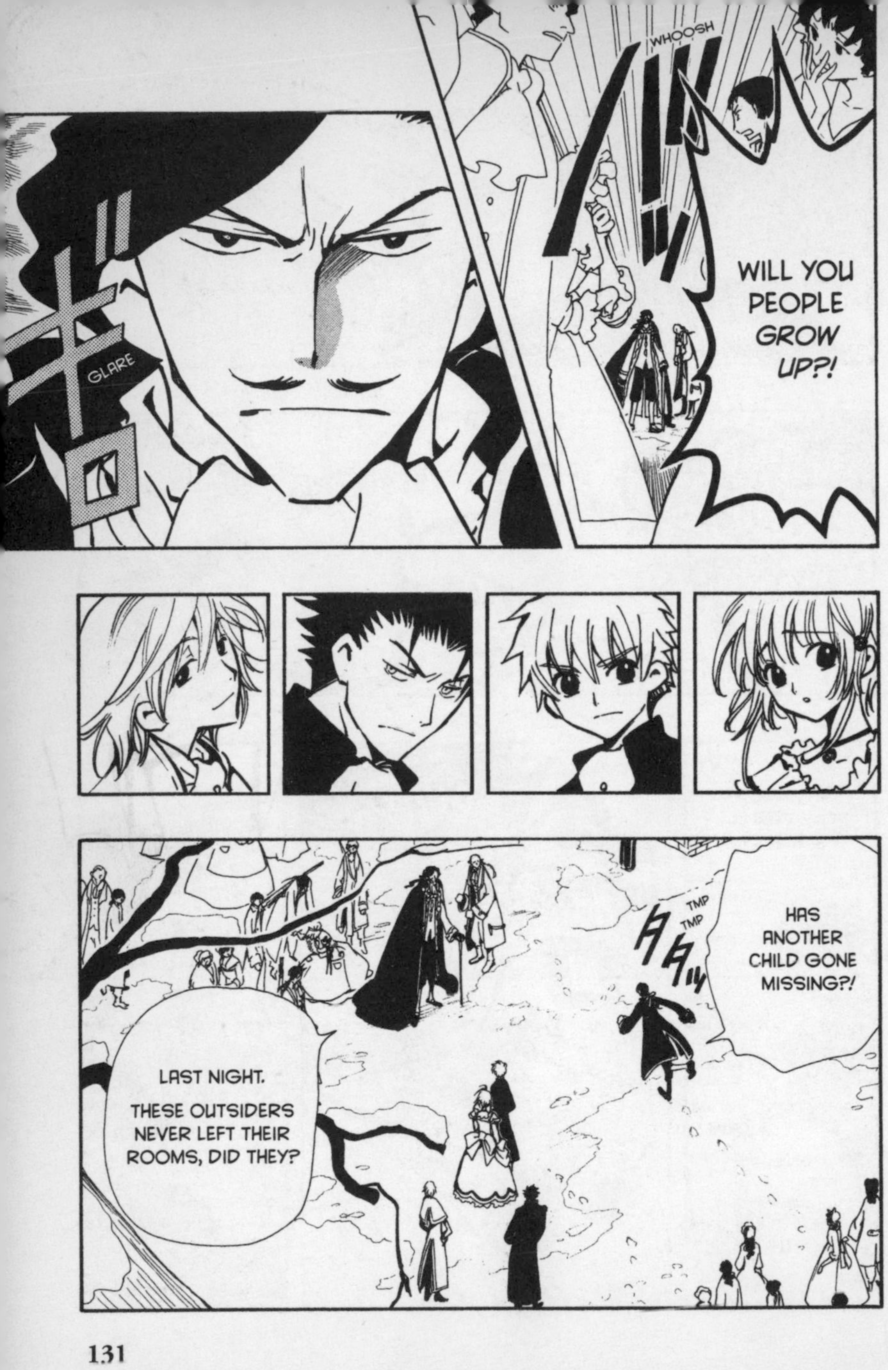
WHOOSH
WILL YOU PEOPLE GROW UP?!
GLARE
TMP TMP
HAS ANOTHER CHILD GONE MISSING?!
LAST NIGHT.
THESE OUTSIDERS NEVER LEFT THEIR ROOMS, DID THEY?

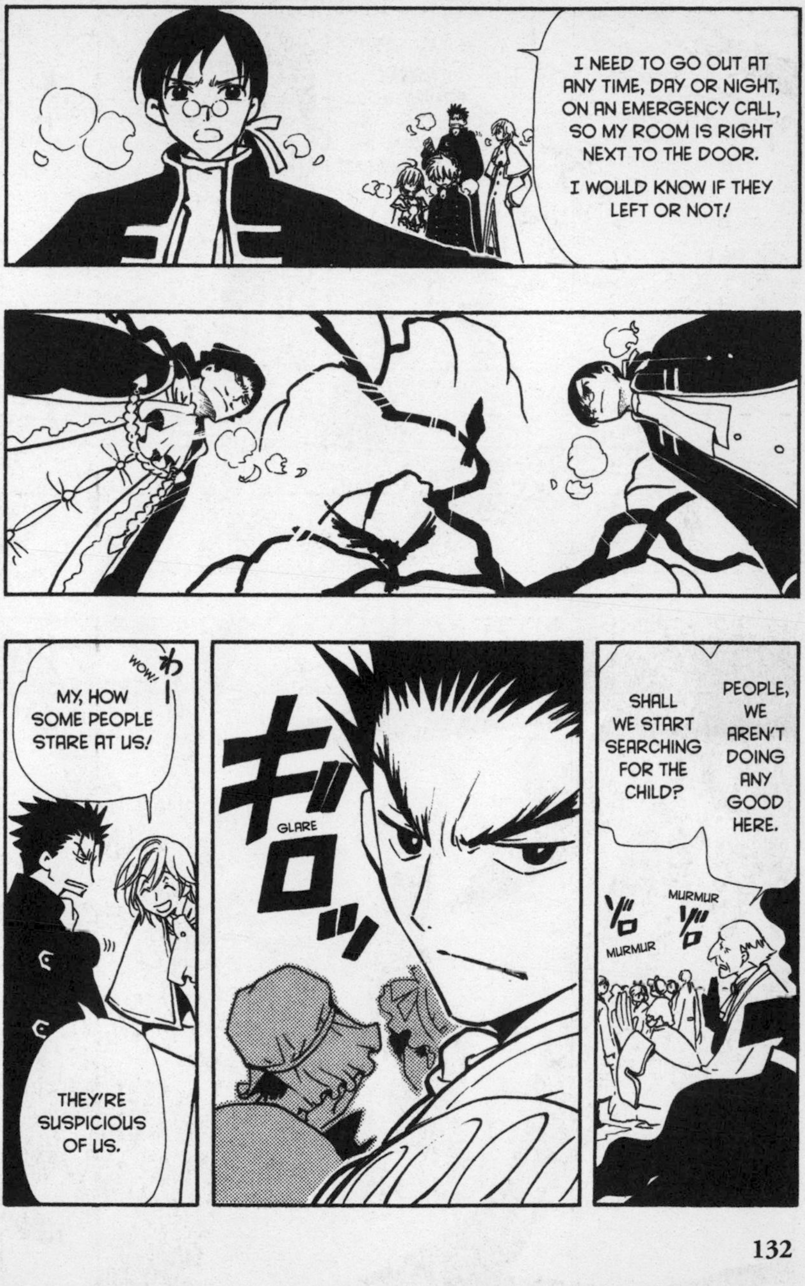
I NEED TO GO OUT AT ANY TIME, DAY OR NIGHT, ON AN EMERGENCY CALL, SO MY ROOM IS RIGHT NEXT TO THE DOOR.
I WOULD KNOW IF THEY LEFT OR NOT!
PEOPLE, WE AREN'T DOING ANY GOOD HERE.
SHALL WE START SEARCHING FOR THE CHILD?
ゾロ
MURMUR
ゾロ
MURMUR
ギロッ
GLARE
わー
WOW!
MY, HOW SOME PEOPLE STARE AT US!
THEY'RE SUSPICIOUS OF US.

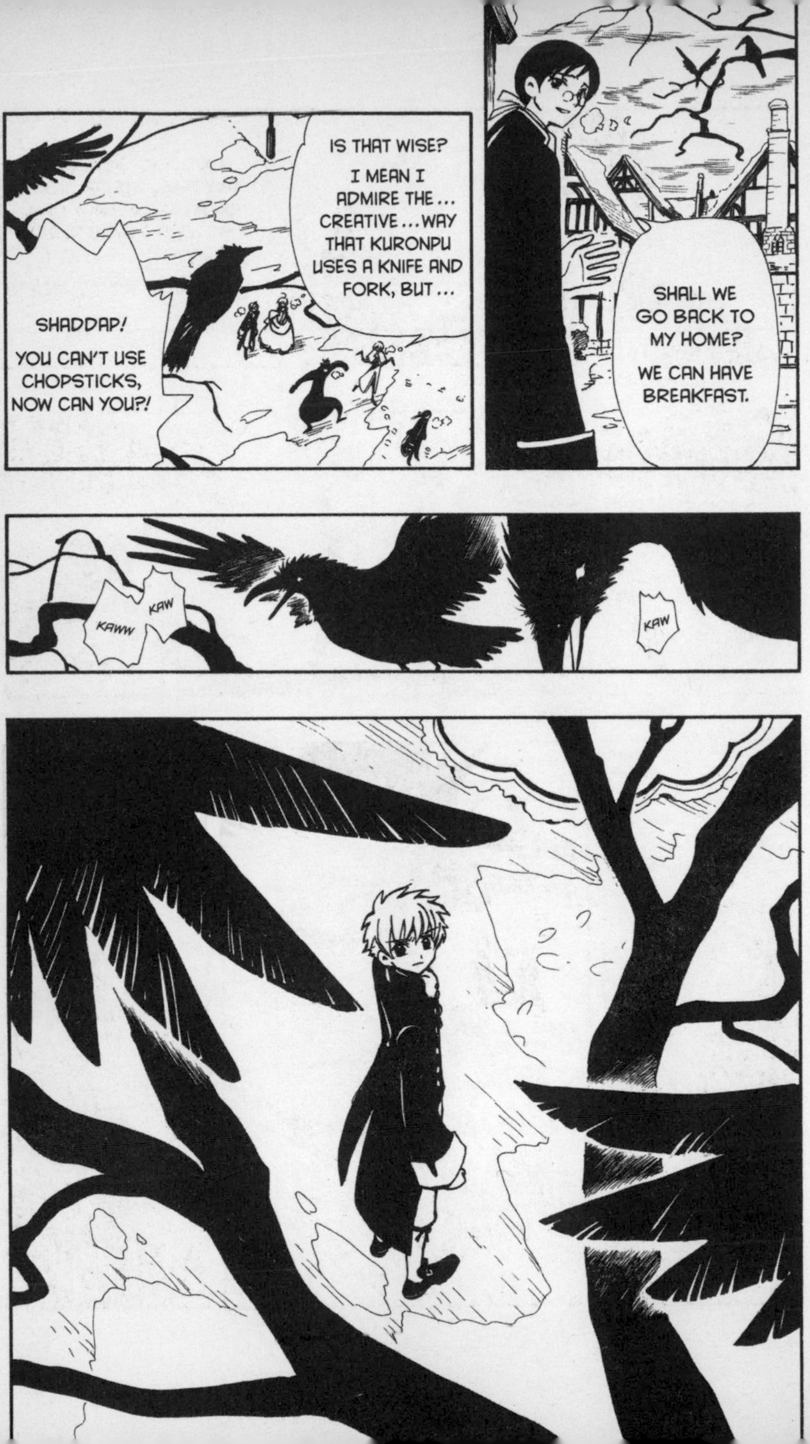
SHALL WE GO BACK TO MY HOME?
WE CAN HAVE BREAKFAST.
IS THAT WISE? I MEAN I ADMIRE THE... CREATIVE... WAY THAT KURONPU USES A KNIFE AND FORK, BUT...
SHADDAP!
YOU CAN'T USE CHOPSTICKS, NOW CAN YOU?!
KAW
KAW
KAWW

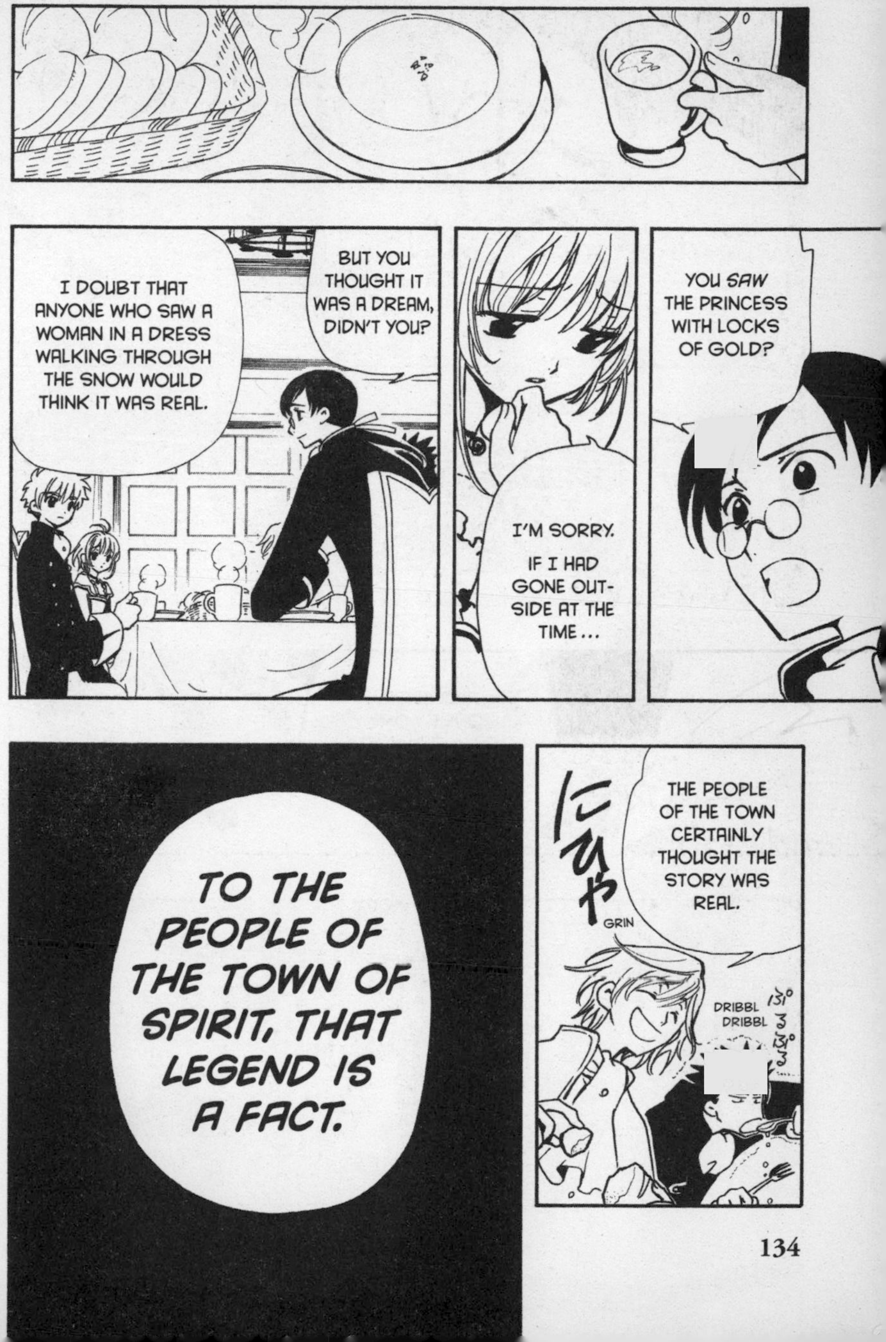
YOU *SAW* THE PRINCESS WITH LOCKS OF GOLD?
I'M SORRY.
IF I HAD GONE OUT-SIDE AT THE TIME...
BUT YOU THOUGHT IT WAS A DREAM, DIDN'T YOU?
I DOUBT THAT ANYONE WHO SAW A WOMAN IN A DRESS WALKING THROUGH THE SNOW WOULD THINK IT WAS REAL.
THE PEOPLE OF THE TOWN CERTAINLY THOUGHT THE STORY WAS REAL.
にひゃ
GRIN
DRIBBL DRIBBL
TO THE PEOPLE OF THE TOWN OF SPIRIT, THAT LEGEND IS A FACT.

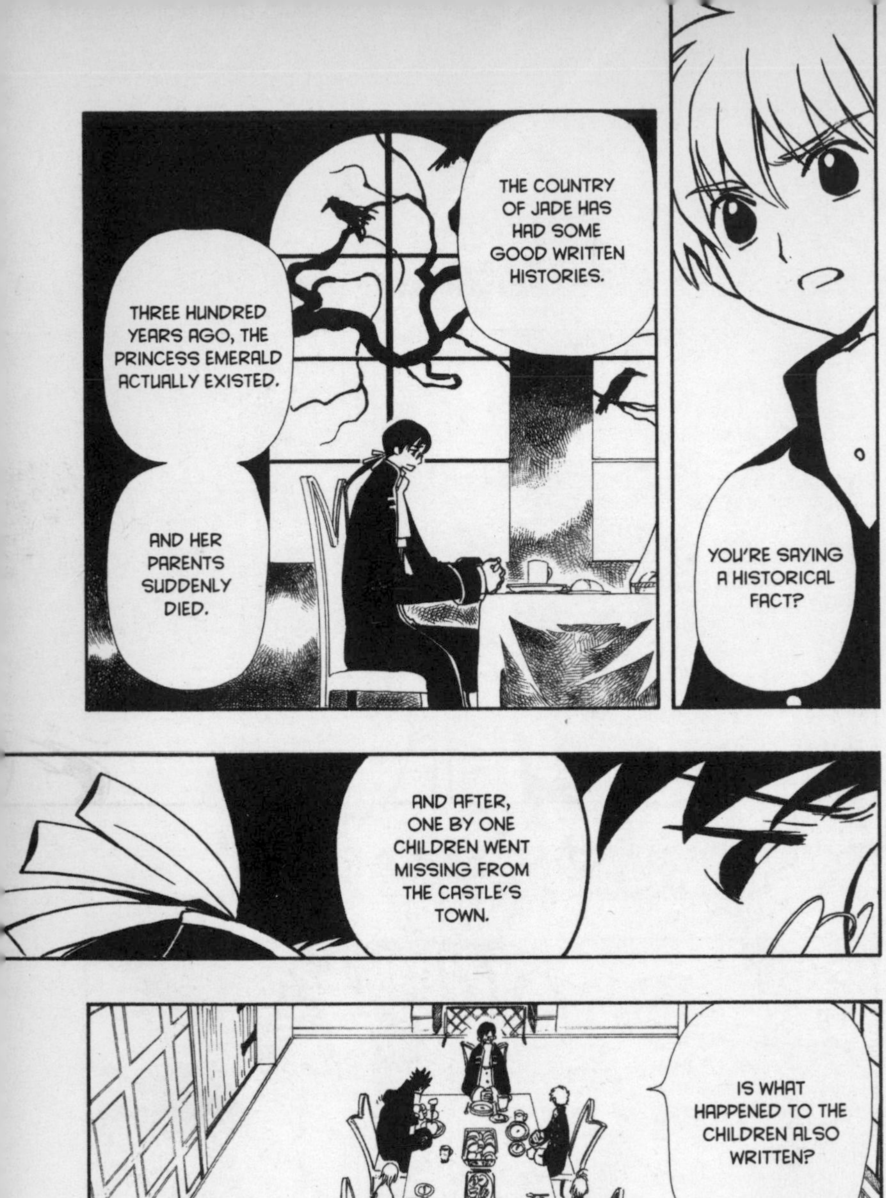
YOU'RE SAYING A HISTORICAL FACT?
THE COUNTRY OF JADE HAS HAD SOME GOOD WRITTEN HISTORIES.
THREE HUNDRED YEARS AGO, THE PRINCESS EMERALD ACTUALLY EXISTED.
AND HER PARENTS SUDDENLY DIED.
AND AFTER, ONE BY ONE CHILDREN WENT MISSING FROM THE CASTLE'S TOWN.
IS WHAT HAPPENED TO THE CHILDREN ALSO WRITTEN?

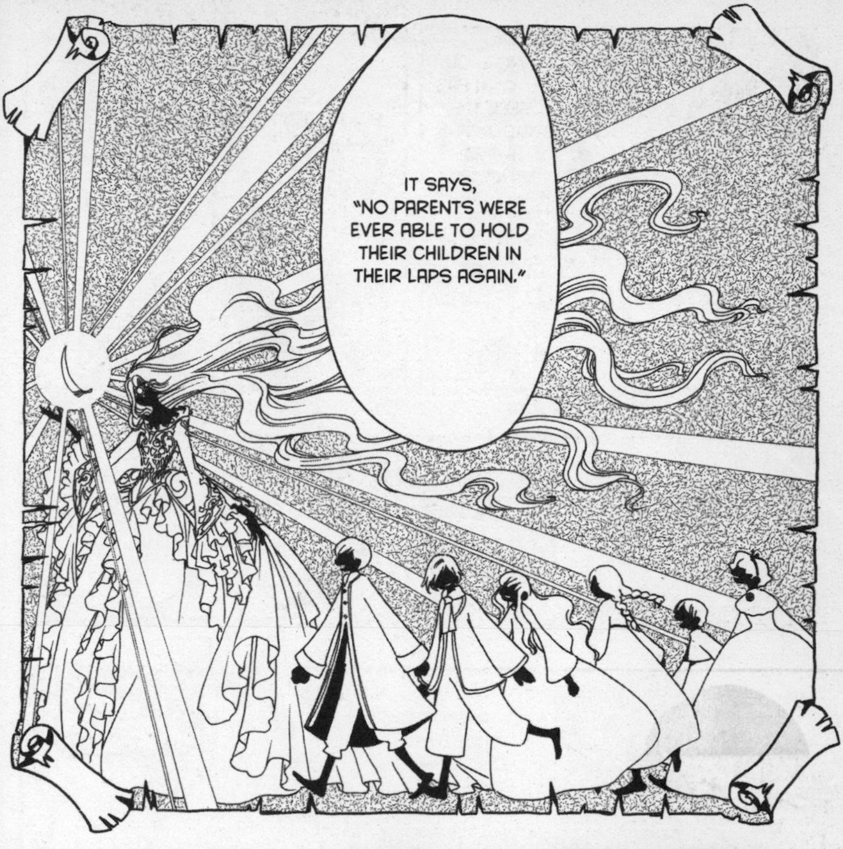
IT SAYS, "NO PARENTS WERE EVER ABLE TO HOLD THEIR CHILDREN IN THEIR LAPS AGAIN."

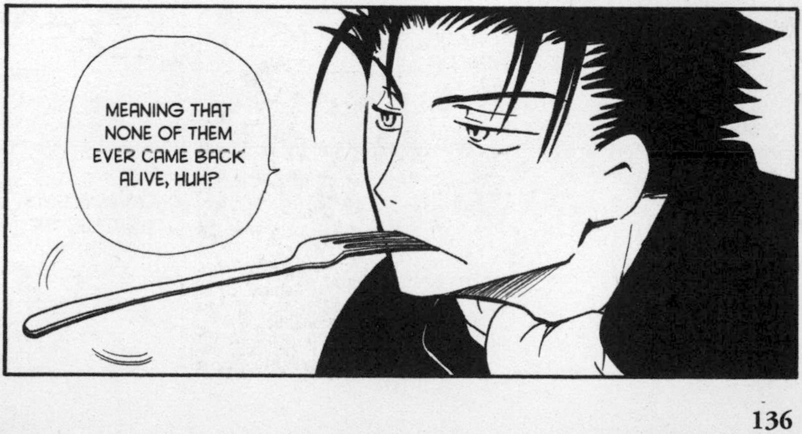
MEANING THAT NONE OF THEM EVER CAME BACK ALIVE, HUH?

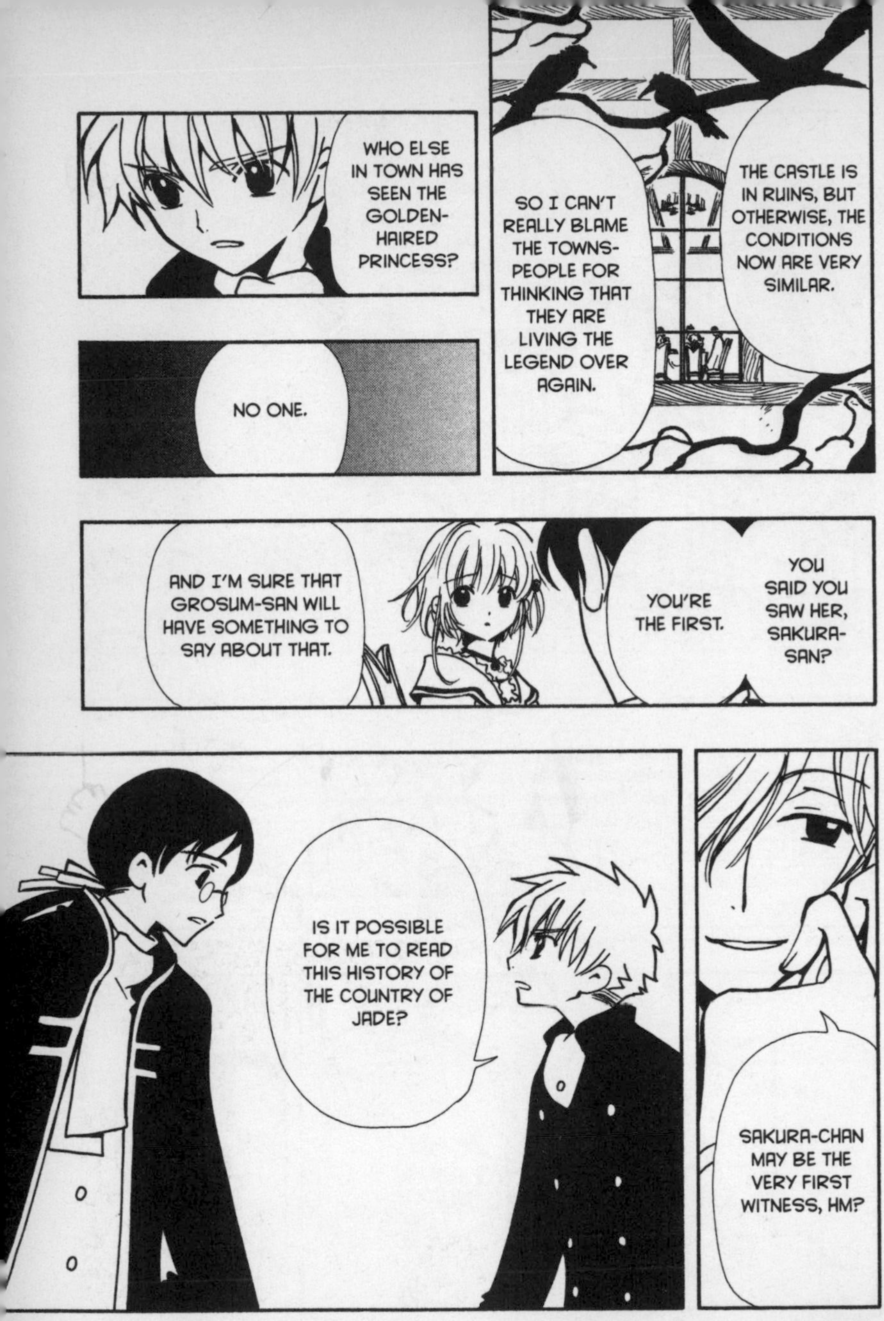
THE CASTLE IS IN RUINS, BUT OTHERWISE, THE CONDITIONS NOW ARE VERY SIMILAR.
SO I CAN'T REALLY BLAME THE TOWNSPEOPLE FOR THINKING THAT THEY ARE LIVING THE LEGEND OVER AGAIN.
WHO ELSE IN TOWN HAS SEEN THE GOLDEN-HAIRED PRINCESS?
NO ONE.
YOU SAID YOU SAW HER, SAKURA-SAN?
YOU'RE THE FIRST.
AND I'M SURE THAT GROSUM-SAN WILL HAVE SOMETHING TO SAY ABOUT THAT.
SAKURA-CHAN MAY BE THE VERY FIRST WITNESS, HM?
IS IT POSSIBLE FOR ME TO READ THIS HISTORY OF THE COUNTRY OF JADE?

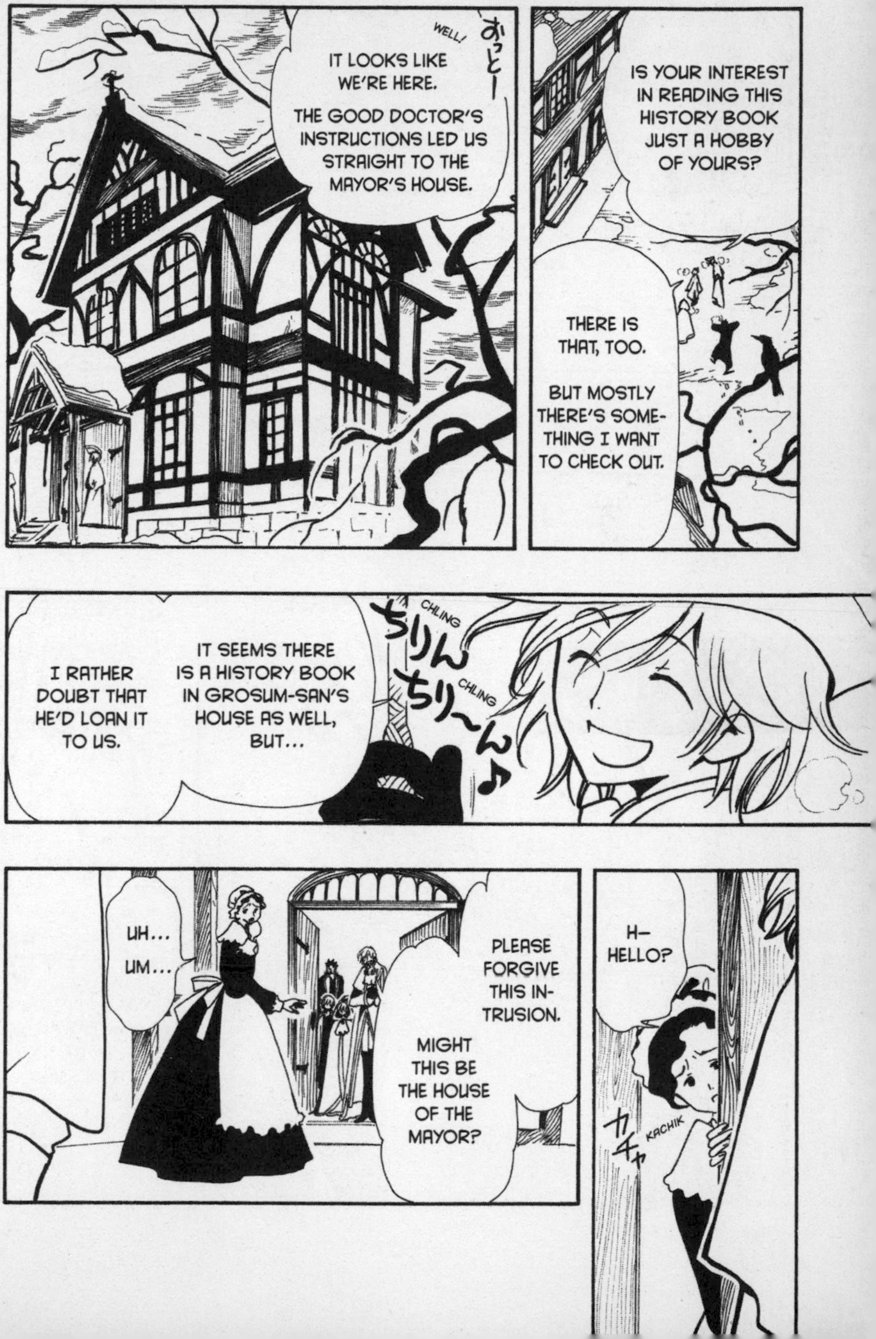
IS YOUR INTEREST IN READING THIS HISTORY BOOK JUST A HOBBY OF YOURS?
THERE IS THAT, TOO.
BUT MOSTLY THERE'S SOME-THING I WANT TO CHECK OUT.
おっとー
WELL!
IT LOOKS LIKE WE'RE HERE.
THE GOOD DOCTOR'S INSTRUCTIONS LED US STRAIGHT TO THE MAYOR'S HOUSE.
ちりんちり～ん♪
CHLING
CHLING
IT SEEMS THERE IS A HISTORY BOOK IN GROSUM-SAN'S HOUSE AS WELL, BUT...
I RATHER DOUBT THAT HE'D LOAN IT TO US.
H— HELLO?
カチャ
KACHIK
PLEASE FORGIVE THIS IN-TRUSION.
MIGHT THIS BE THE HOUSE OF THE MAYOR?
UH... UM...

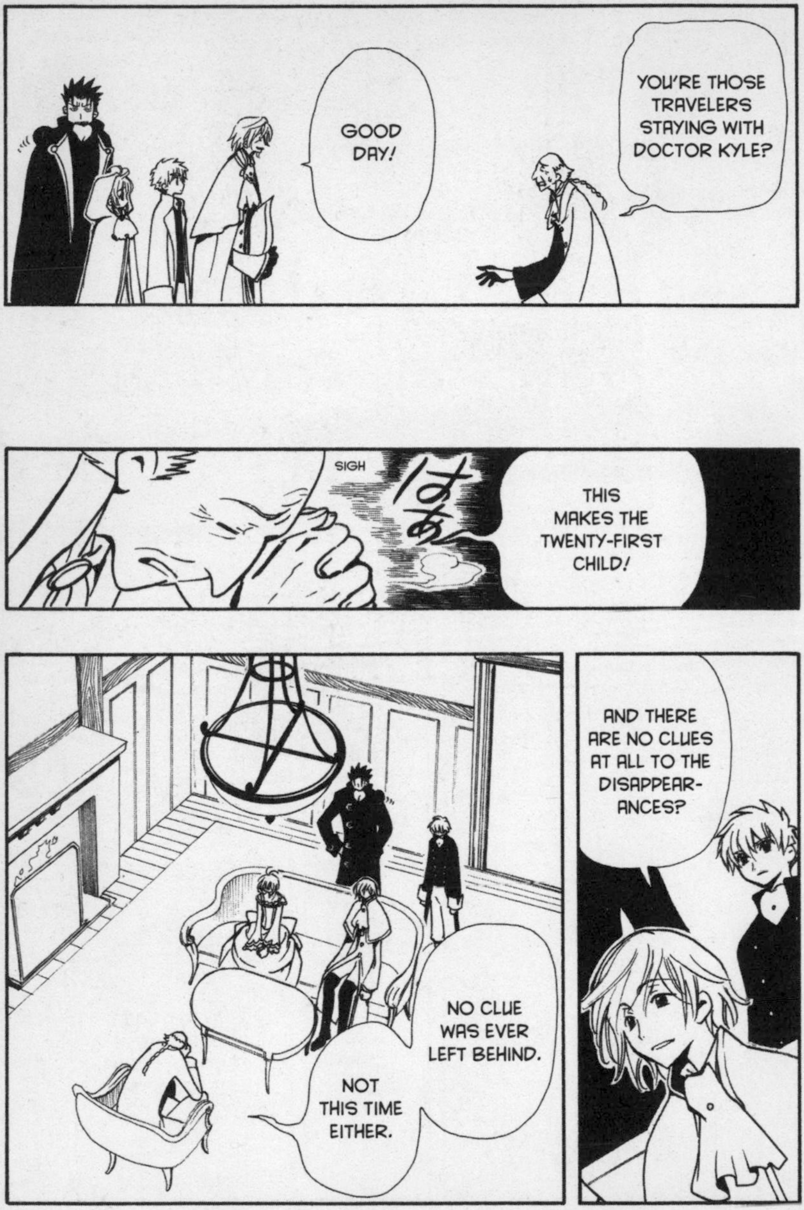
YOU'RE THOSE TRAVELERS STAYING WITH DOCTOR KYLE?
GOOD DAY!
THIS MAKES THE TWENTY-FIRST CHILD!
はあ
SIGH
AND THERE ARE NO CLUES AT ALL TO THE DISAPPEAR-ANCES?
NO CLUE WAS EVER LEFT BEHIND.
NOT THIS TIME EITHER.

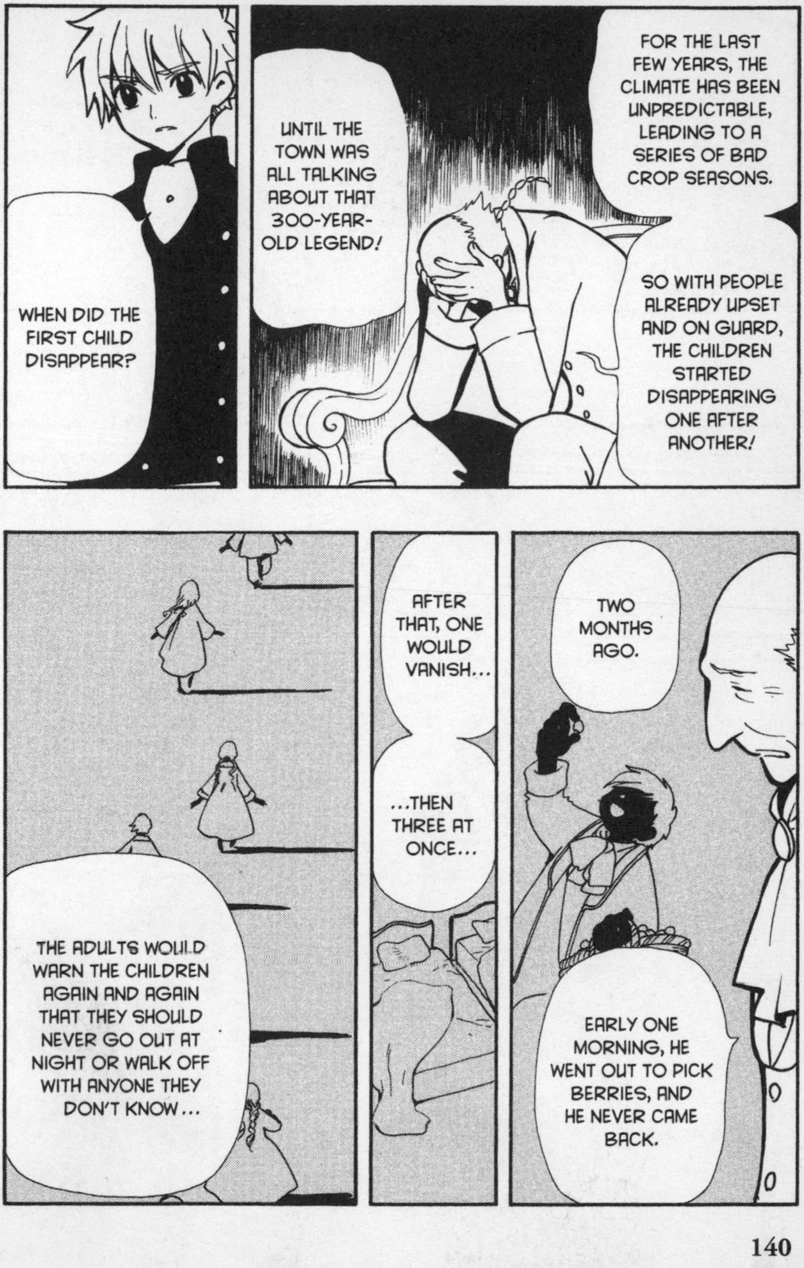
FOR THE LAST FEW YEARS, THE CLIMATE HAS BEEN UNPREDICTABLE, LEADING TO A SERIES OF BAD CROP SEASONS.
SO WITH PEOPLE ALREADY UPSET AND ON GUARD, THE CHILDREN STARTED DISAPPEARING ONE AFTER ANOTHER!
UNTIL THE TOWN WAS ALL TALKING ABOUT THAT 300-YEAR-OLD LEGEND!
WHEN DID THE FIRST CHILD DISAPPEAR?
TWO MONTHS AGO.
EARLY ONE MORNING, HE WENT OUT TO PICK BERRIES, AND HE NEVER CAME BACK.
AFTER THAT, ONE WOULD VANISH...
...THEN THREE AT ONCE...
THE ADULTS WOULD WARN THE CHILDREN AGAIN AND AGAIN THAT THEY SHOULD NEVER GO OUT AT NIGHT OR WALK OFF WITH ANYONE THEY DON'T KNOW...

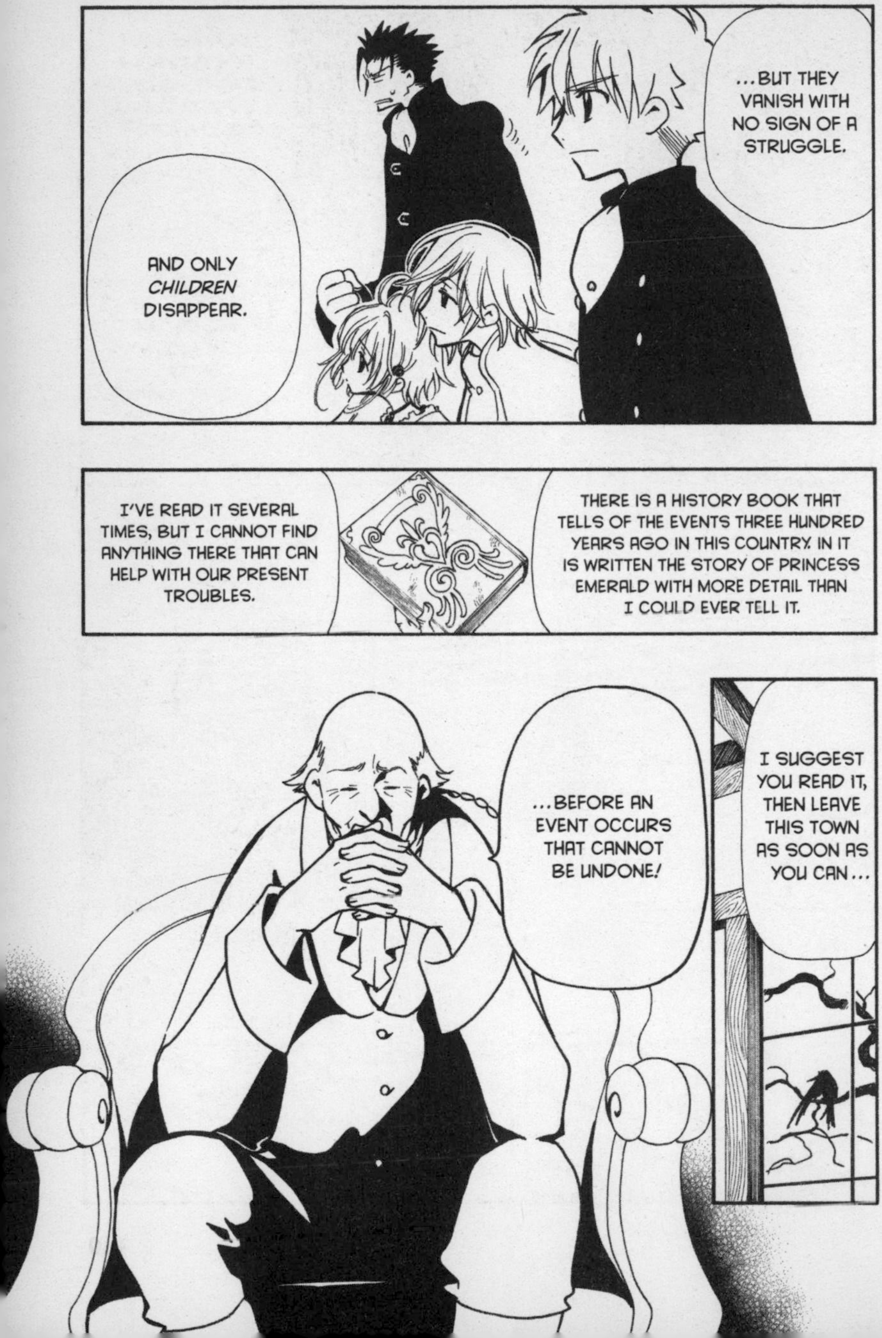
...BUT THEY VANISH WITH NO SIGN OF A STRUGGLE.
AND ONLY *CHILDREN* DISAPPEAR.
THERE IS A HISTORY BOOK THAT TELLS OF THE EVENTS THREE HUNDRED YEARS AGO IN THIS COUNTRY. IN IT IS WRITTEN THE STORY OF PRINCESS EMERALD WITH MORE DETAIL THAN I COULD EVER TELL IT.
I'VE READ IT SEVERAL TIMES, BUT I CANNOT FIND ANYTHING THERE THAT CAN HELP WITH OUR PRESENT TROUBLES.
I SUGGEST YOU READ IT, THEN LEAVE THIS TOWN AS SOON AS YOU CAN...
...BEFORE AN EVENT OCCURS THAT CANNOT BE UNDONE!

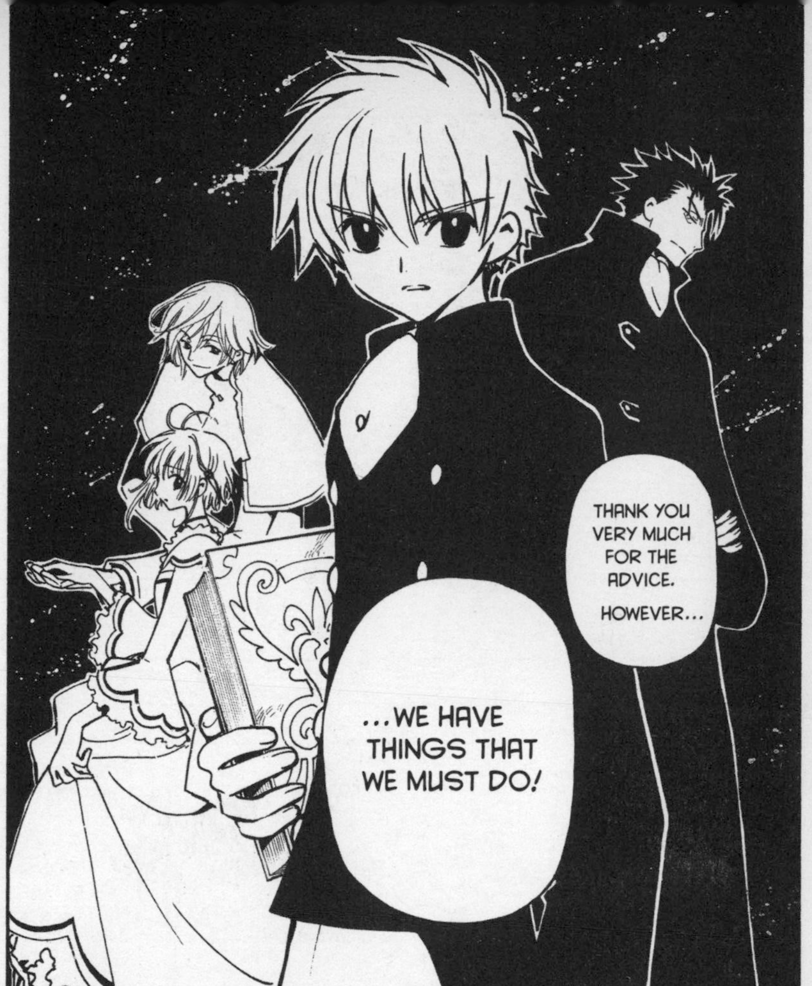
THANK YOU VERY MUCH FOR THE ADVICE.
HOWEVER...
...WE HAVE THINGS THAT WE MUST DO!

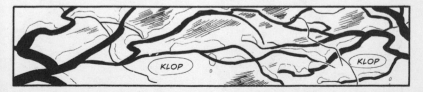

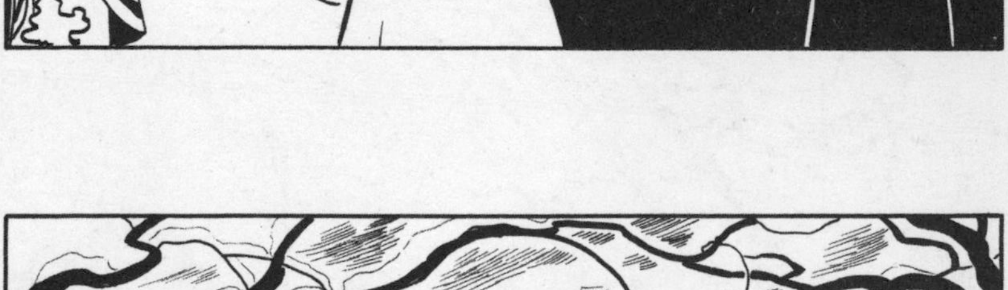
KLOP
KLOP

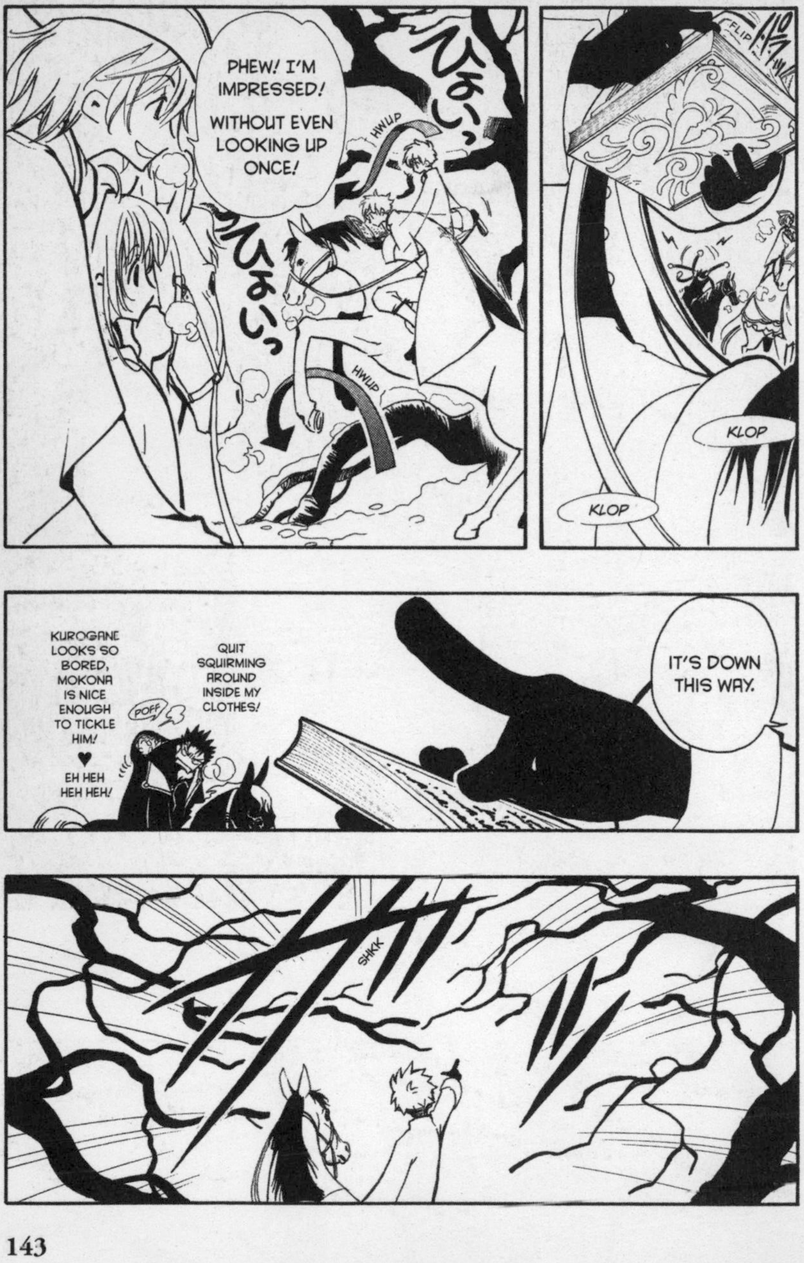
FLIP
KLOP
KLOP
PHEW! I'M IMPRESSED!
WITHOUT EVEN LOOKING UP ONCE!
ひょいっ
HWUP
ひょいっ
HWUP
IT'S DOWN THIS WAY.
QUIT SQUIRMING AROUND INSIDE MY CLOTHES!
POFF
KUROGANE LOOKS SO BORED, MOKONA IS NICE ENOUGH TO TICKLE HIM! ♥
EH HEH HEH HEH!
SHKK

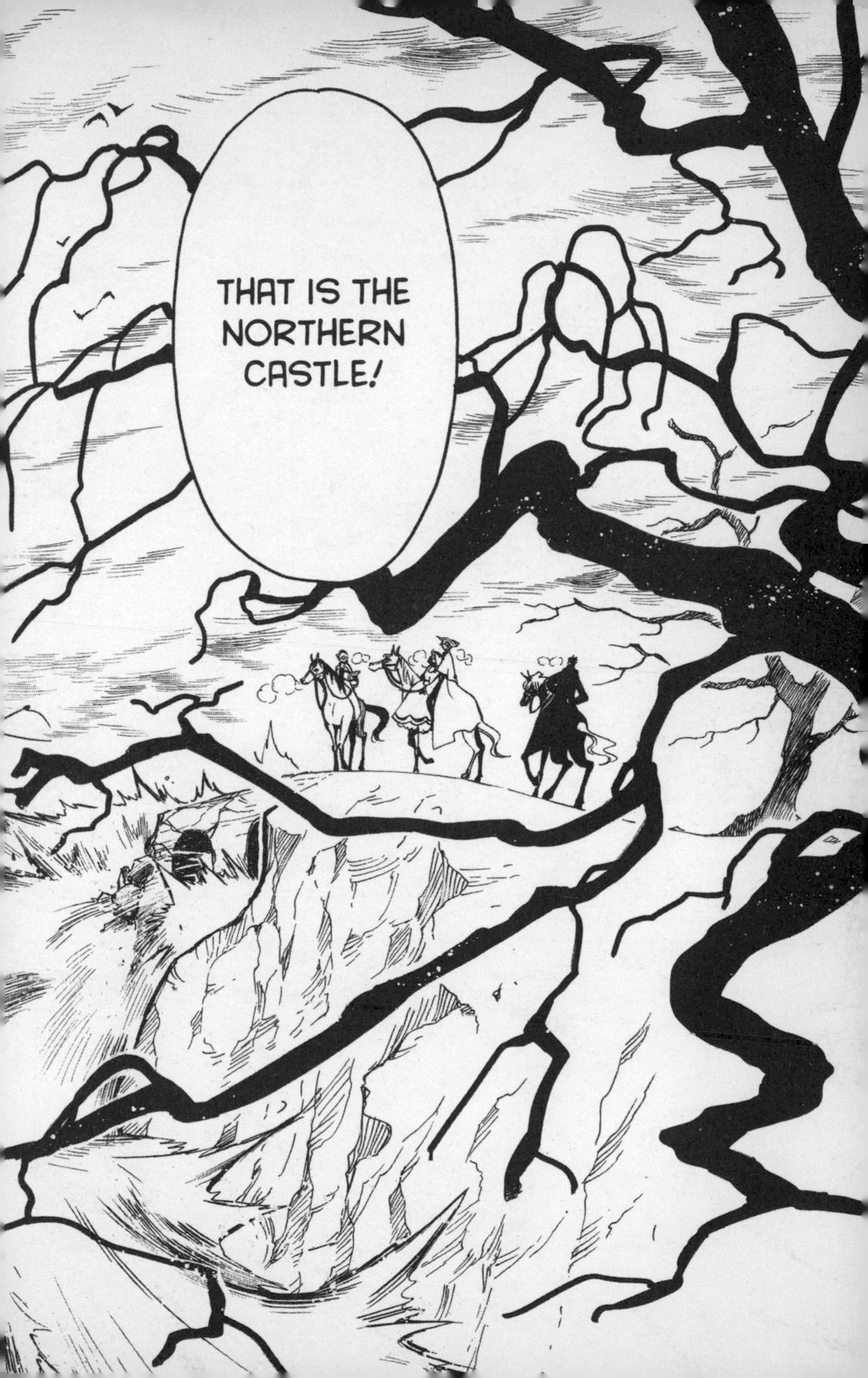
THAT IS THE NORTHERN CASTLE!

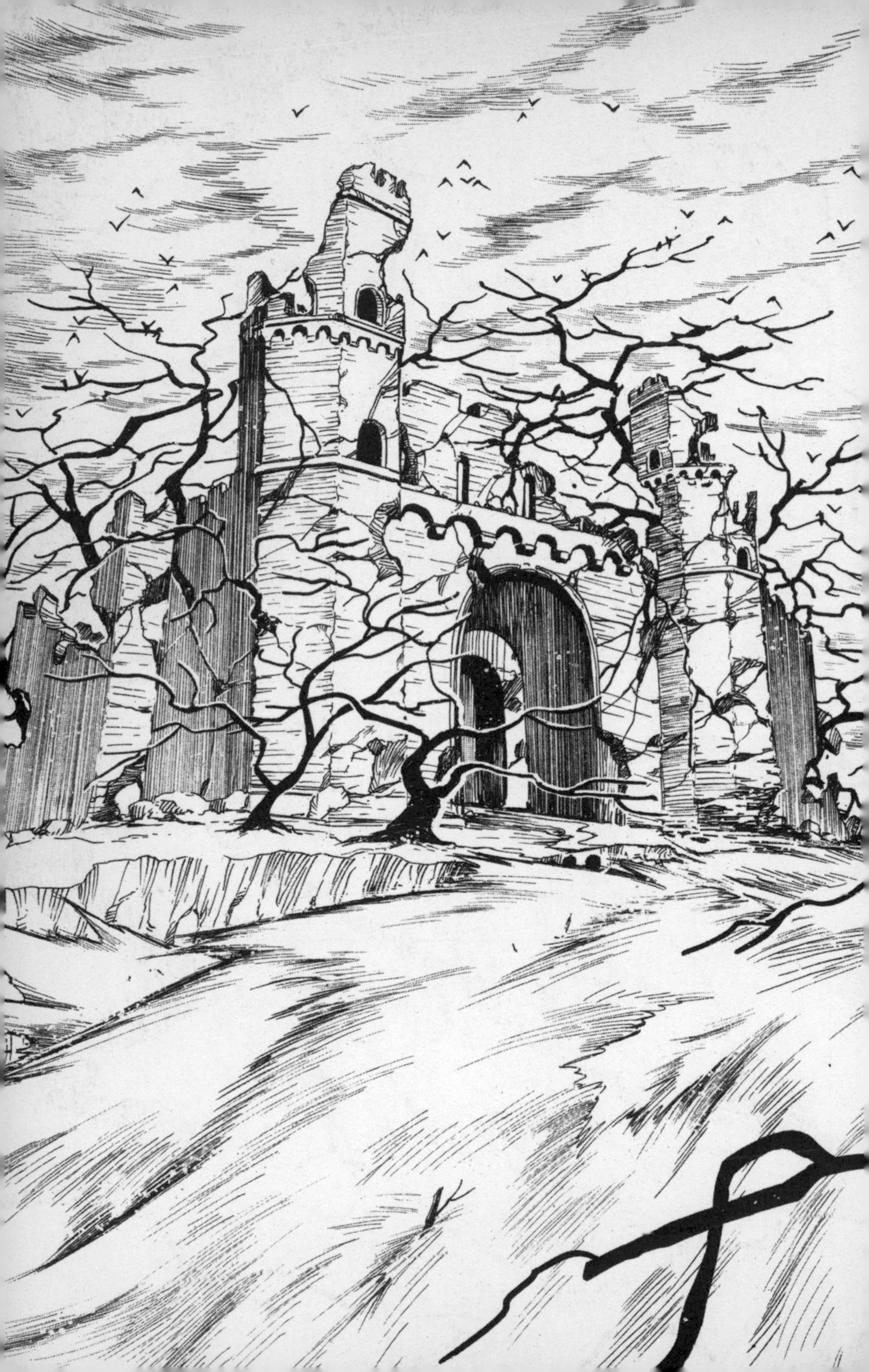

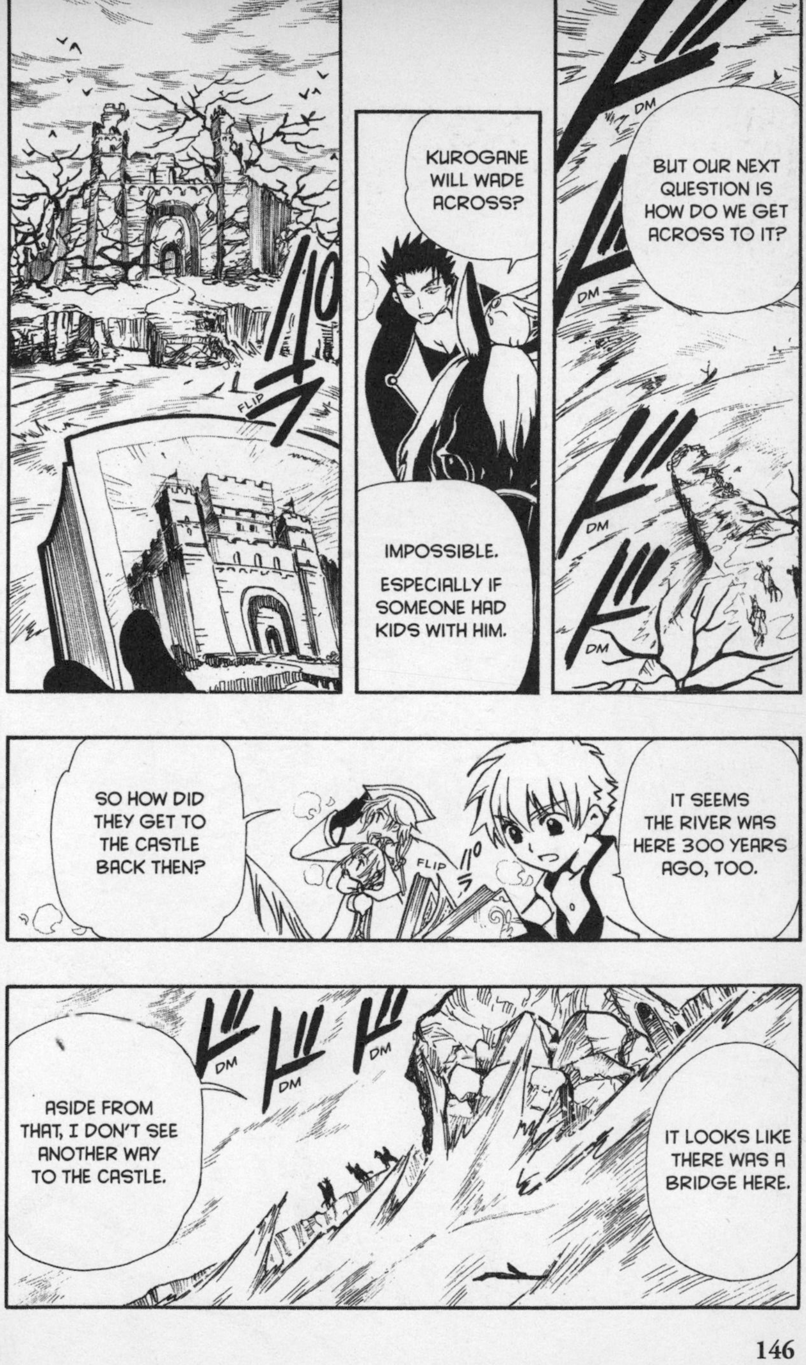
DM
BUT OUR NEXT QUESTION IS HOW DO WE GET ACROSS TO IT?
DM
DM
DM
KUROGANE WILL WADE ACROSS?
IMPOSSIBLE.
ESPECIALLY IF SOMEONE HAD KIDS WITH HIM.
FLIP
IT SEEMS THE RIVER WAS HERE 300 YEARS AGO, TOO.
FLIP
SO HOW DID THEY GET TO THE CASTLE BACK THEN?
IT LOOKS LIKE THERE WAS A BRIDGE HERE.
DM
DM
DM
ASIDE FROM THAT, I DON'T SEE ANOTHER WAY TO THE CASTLE.

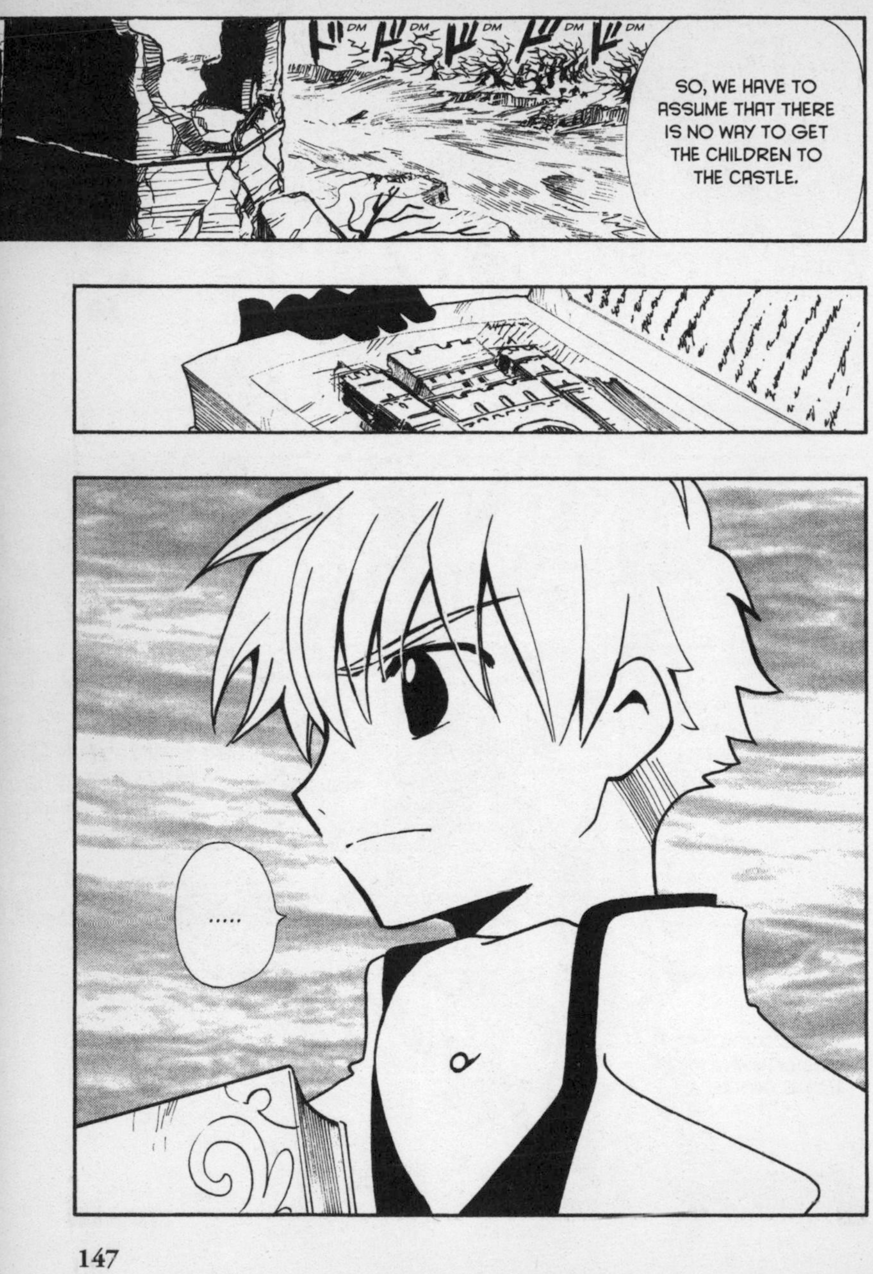
SO, WE HAVE TO ASSUME THAT THERE IS NO WAY TO GET THE CHILDREN TO THE CASTLE.
DM
DM
DM
DM
DM
......

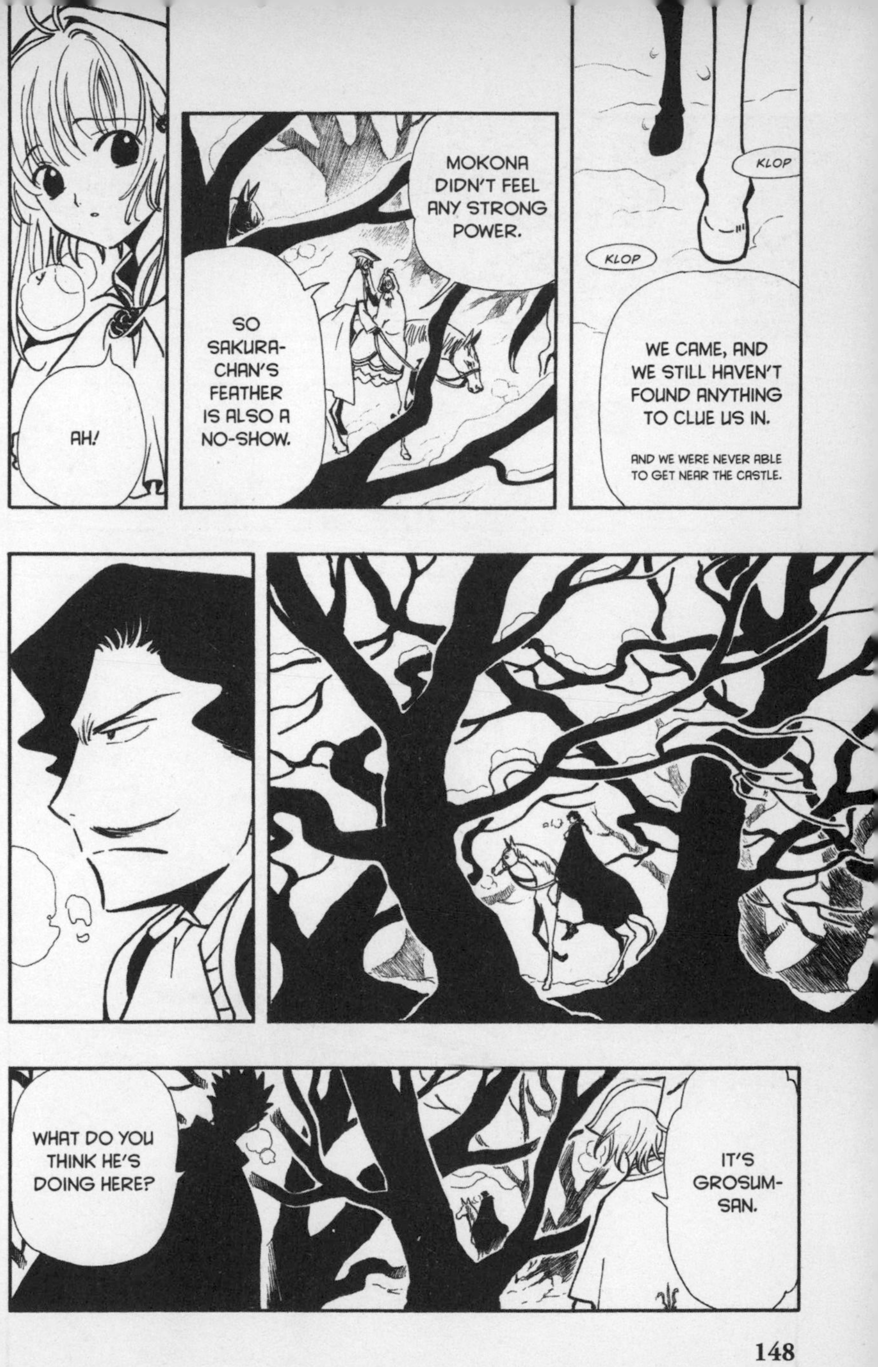
KLOP
KLOP
WE CAME, AND WE STILL HAVEN'T FOUND ANYTHING TO CLUE US IN.
AND WE WERE NEVER ABLE TO GET NEAR THE CASTLE.
MOKONA DIDN'T FEEL ANY STRONG POWER.
SO SAKURA-CHAN'S FEATHER IS ALSO A NO-SHOW.
AH!
IT'S GROSUM-SAN.
WHAT DO YOU THINK HE'S DOING HERE?

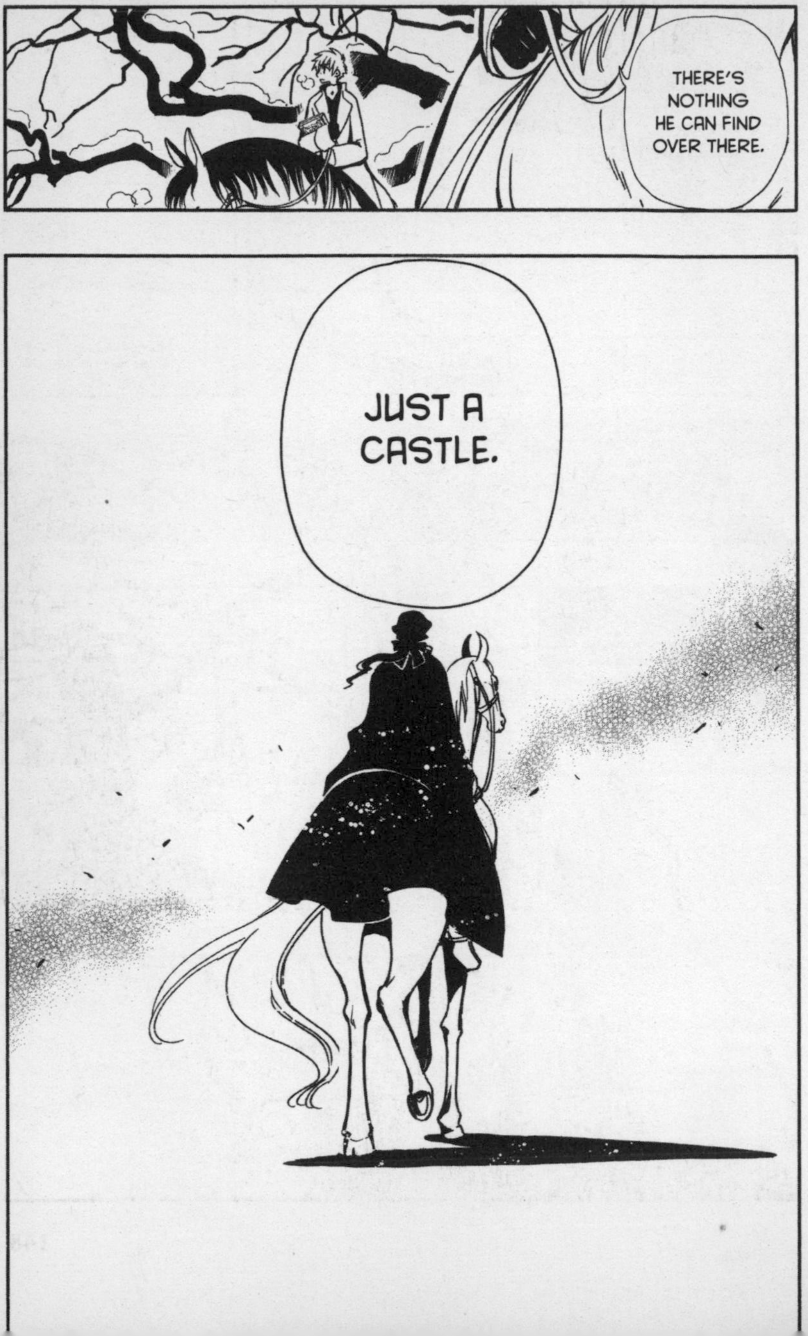
THERE'S NOTHING HE CAN FIND OVER THERE.
JUST A CASTLE.

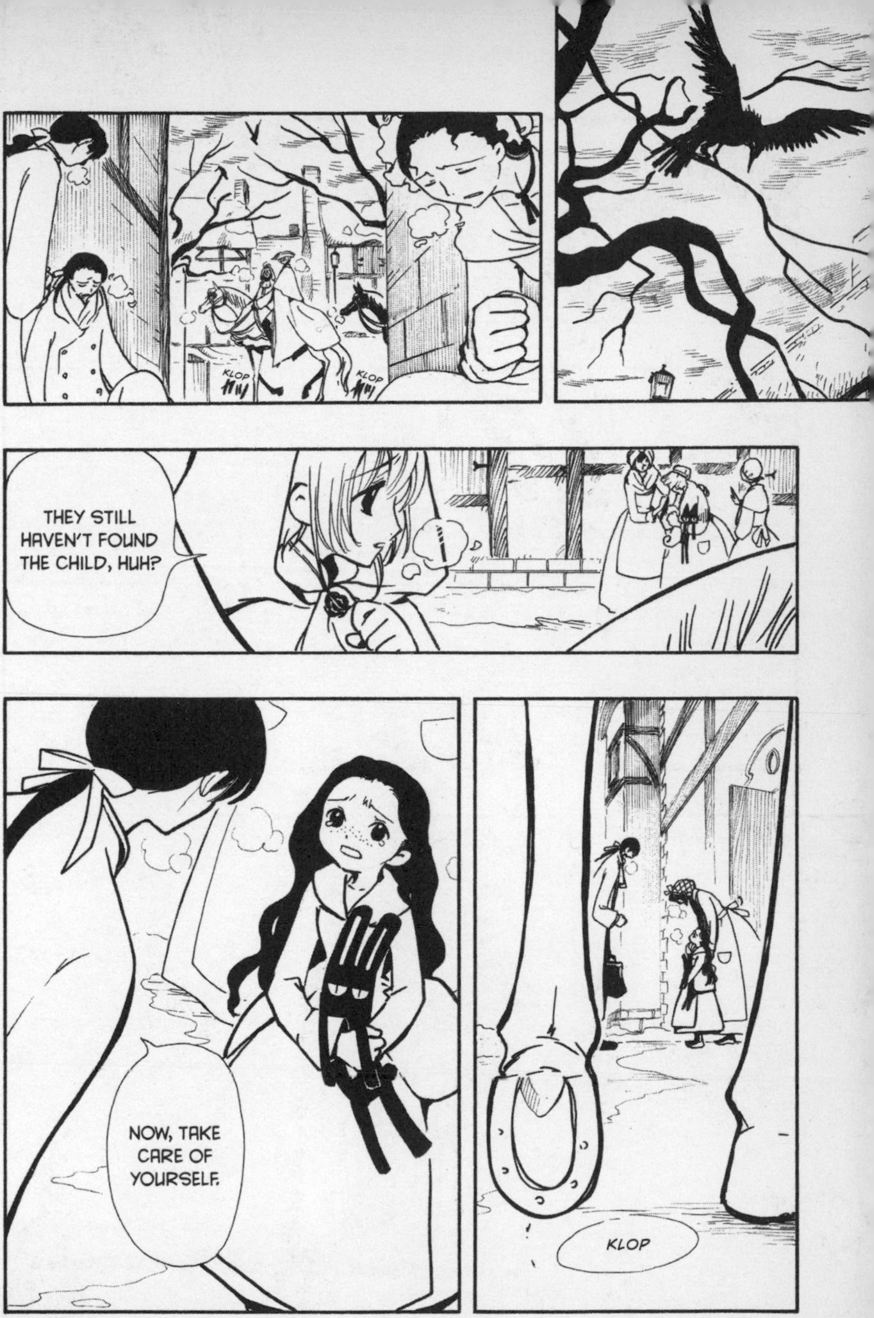
KLOP
KLOP
THEY STILL HAVEN'T FOUND THE CHILD, HUH?
KLOP
NOW, TAKE CARE OF YOURSELF.

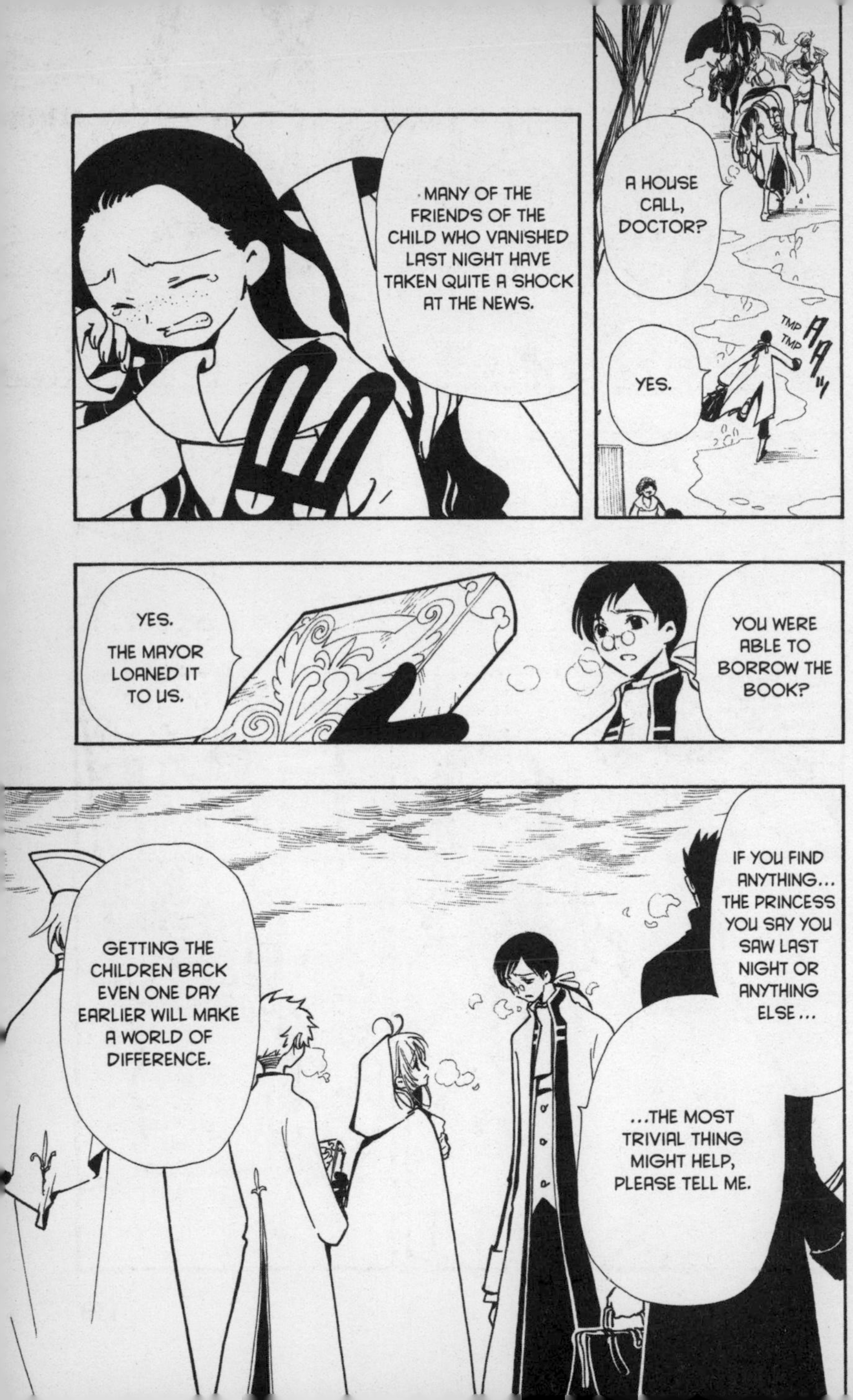
A HOUSE CALL, DOCTOR?
YES.
TMP TMP
MANY OF THE FRIENDS OF THE CHILD WHO VANISHED LAST NIGHT HAVE TAKEN QUITE A SHOCK AT THE NEWS.
YOU WERE ABLE TO BORROW THE BOOK?
YES.
THE MAYOR LOANED IT TO US.
IF YOU FIND ANYTHING... THE PRINCESS YOU SAY YOU SAW LAST NIGHT OR ANYTHING ELSE...
...THE MOST TRIVIAL THING MIGHT HELP, PLEASE TELL ME.
GETTING THE CHILDREN BACK EVEN ONE DAY EARLIER WILL MAKE A WORLD OF DIFFERENCE.

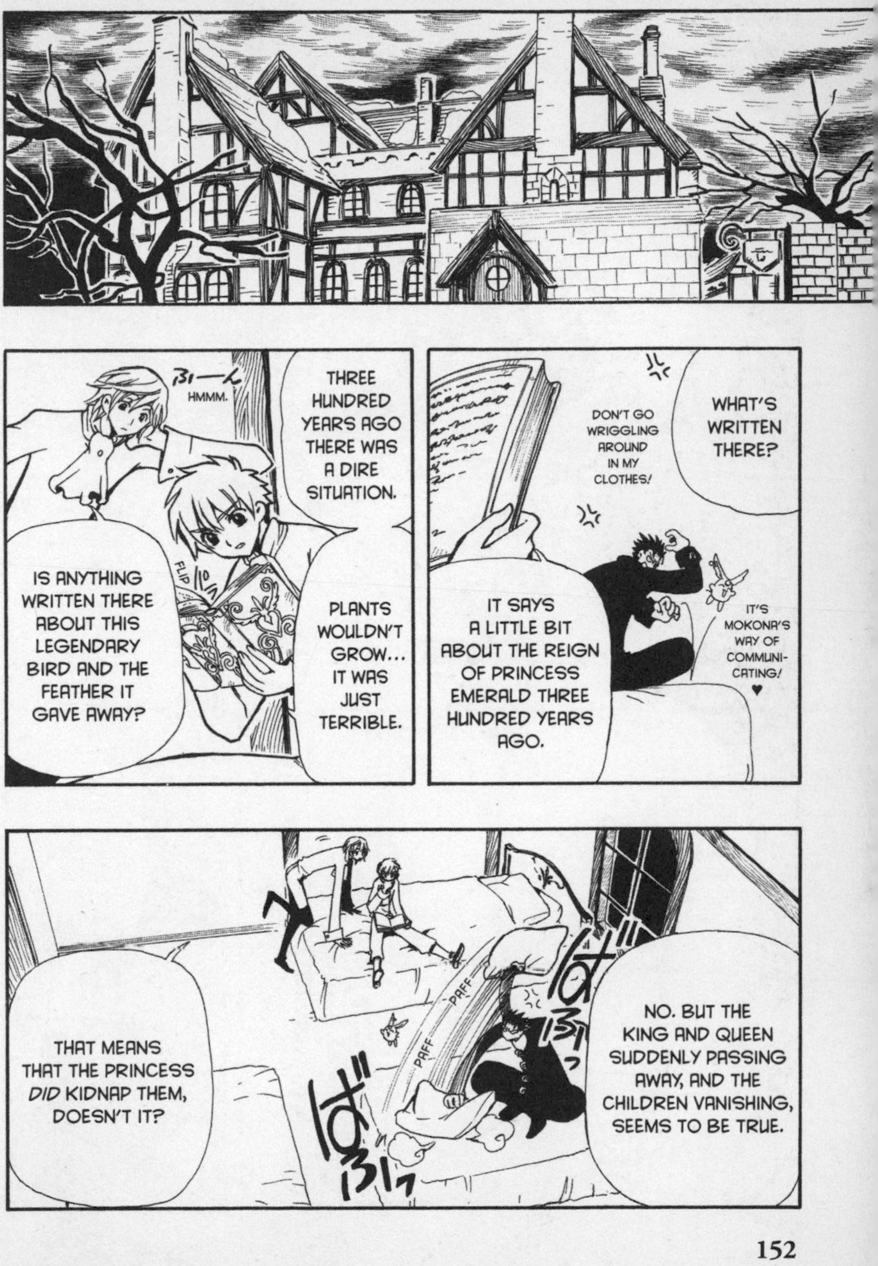
WHAT'S WRITTEN THERE?
DON'T GO WRIGGLING AROUND IN MY CLOTHES!
IT'S MOKONA'S WAY OF COMMUNICATING! ♥
IT SAYS A LITTLE BIT ABOUT THE REIGN OF PRINCESS EMERALD THREE HUNDRED YEARS AGO.
THREE HUNDRED YEARS AGO THERE WAS A DIRE SITUATION.
HMMM.
PLANTS WOULDN'T GROW... IT WAS JUST TERRIBLE.
FLIP
IS ANYTHING WRITTEN THERE ABOUT THIS LEGENDARY BIRD AND THE FEATHER IT GAVE AWAY?
NO. BUT THE KING AND QUEEN SUDDENLY PASSING AWAY, AND THE CHILDREN VANISHING, SEEMS TO BE TRUE.
PAFF
PAFF
PAFF
THAT MEANS THAT THE PRINCESS *DID* KIDNAP THEM, DOESN'T IT?

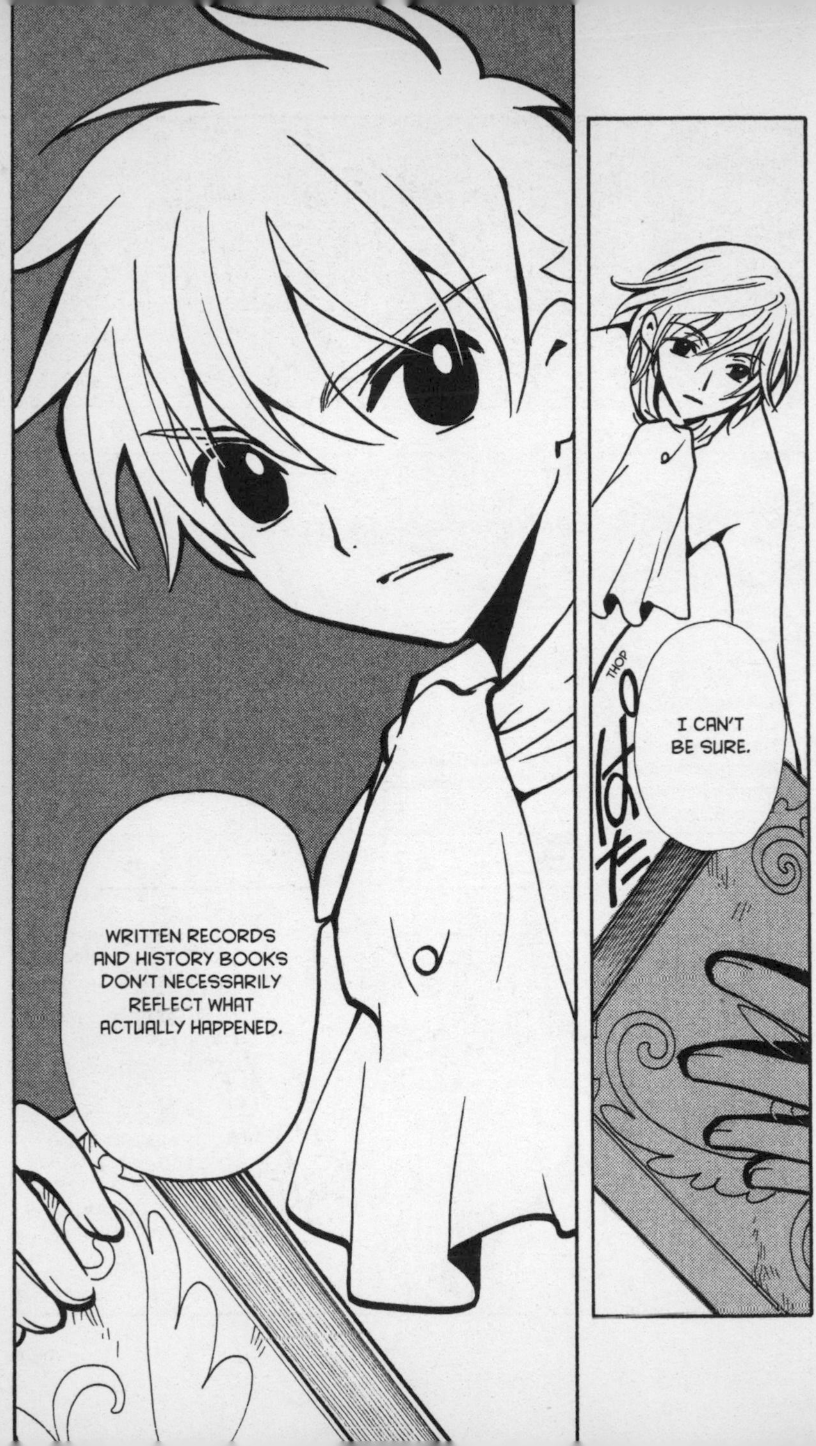
THOP
I CAN'T BE SURE.
WRITTEN RECORDS AND HISTORY BOOKS DON'T NECESSARILY REFLECT WHAT ACTUALLY HAPPENED.

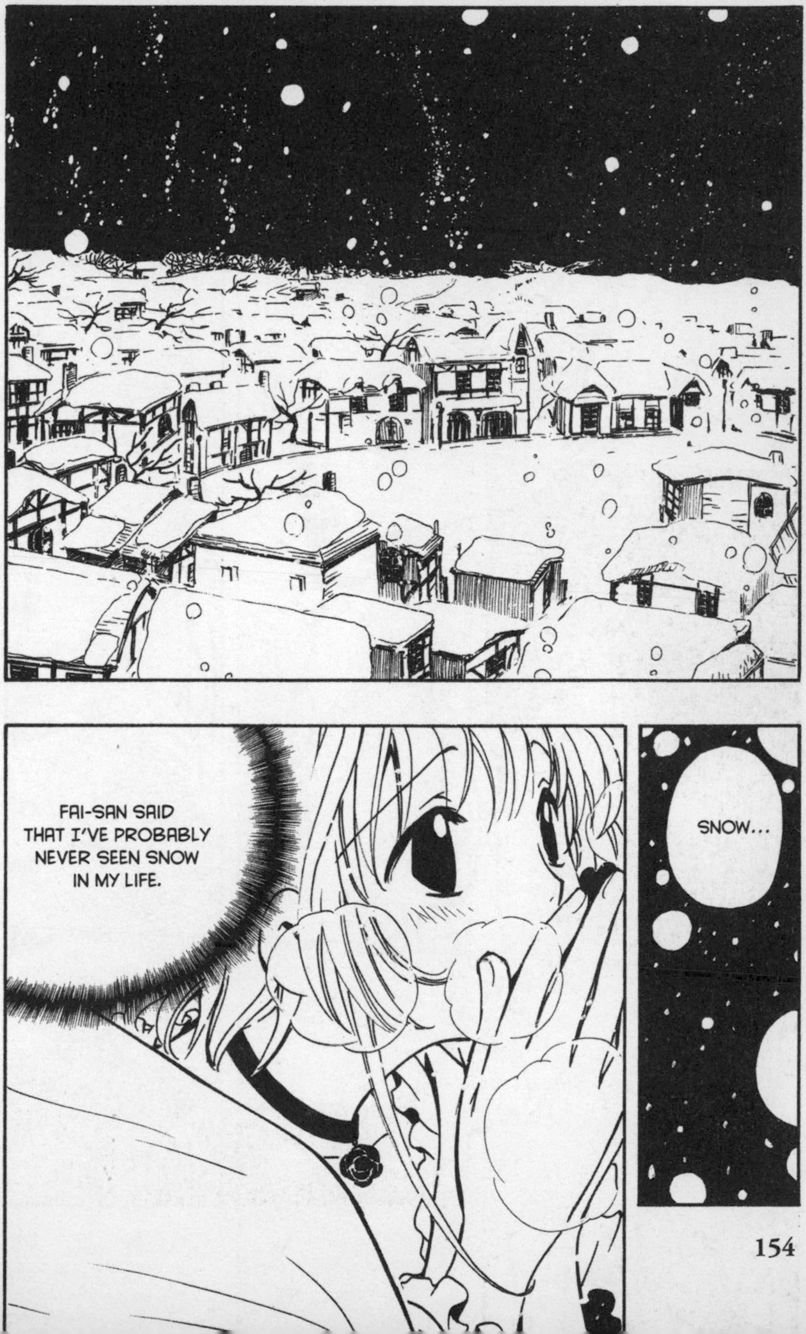
SNOW...
FAI-SAN SAID THAT I'VE PROBABLY NEVER SEEN SNOW IN MY LIFE.

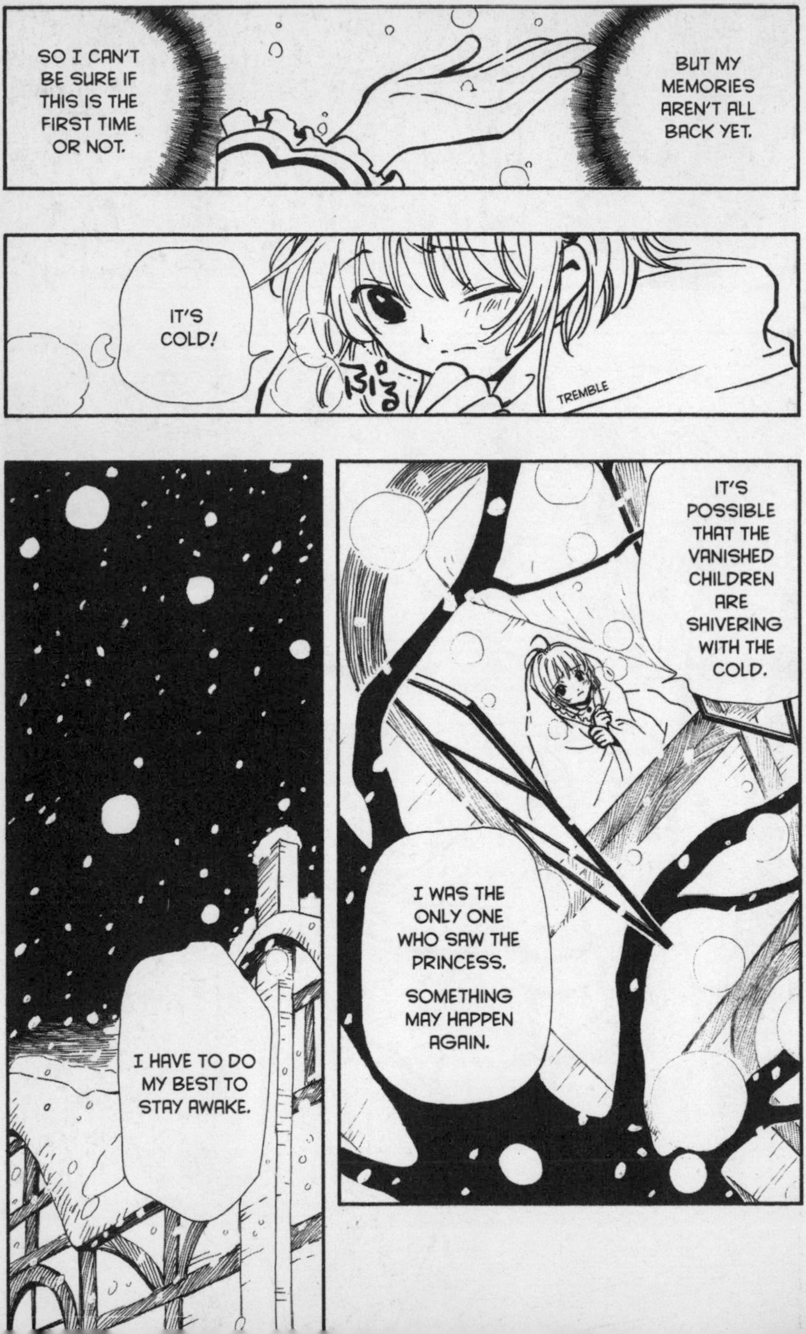
BUT MY MEMORIES AREN'T ALL BACK YET.
SO I CAN'T BE SURE IF THIS IS THE FIRST TIME OR NOT.
IT'S COLD!
TREMBLE
IT'S POSSIBLE THAT THE VANISHED CHILDREN ARE SHIVERING WITH THE COLD.
I WAS THE ONLY ONE WHO SAW THE PRINCESS.
SOMETHING MAY HAPPEN AGAIN.
I HAVE TO DO MY BEST TO STAY AWAKE.

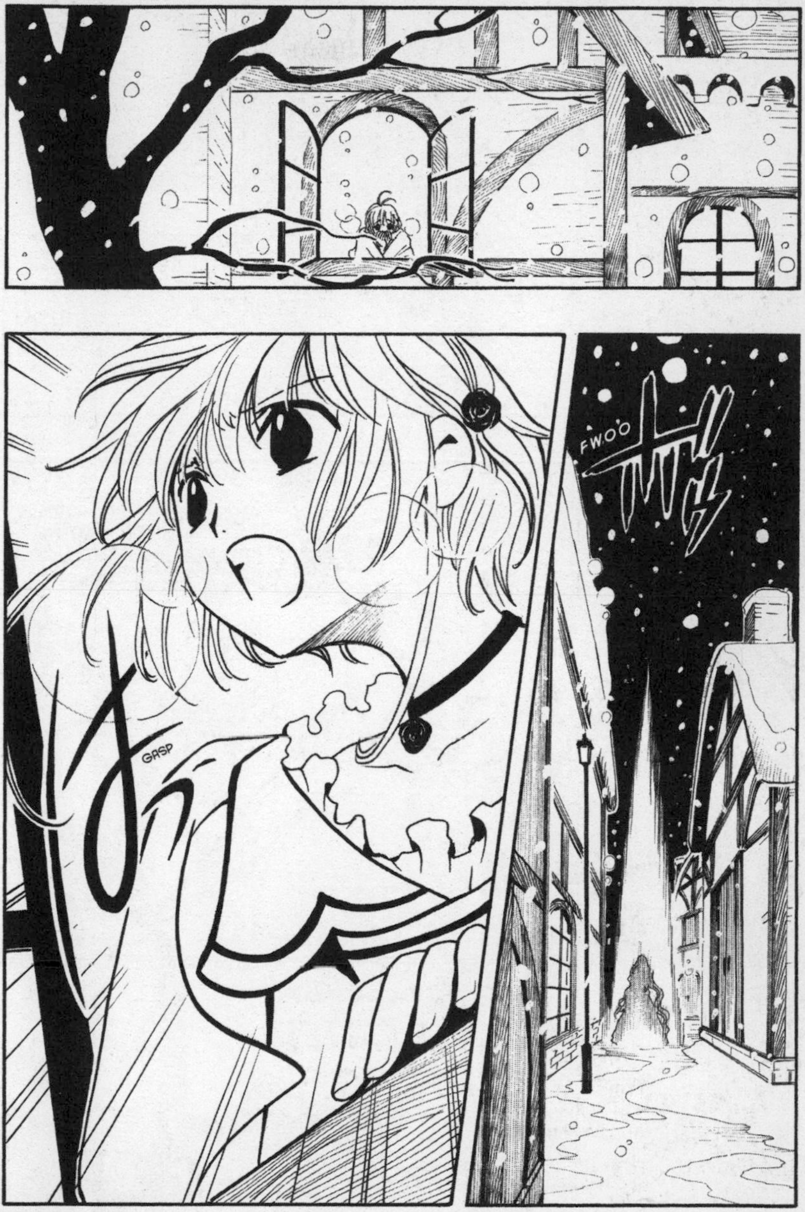
FWOO
GASP

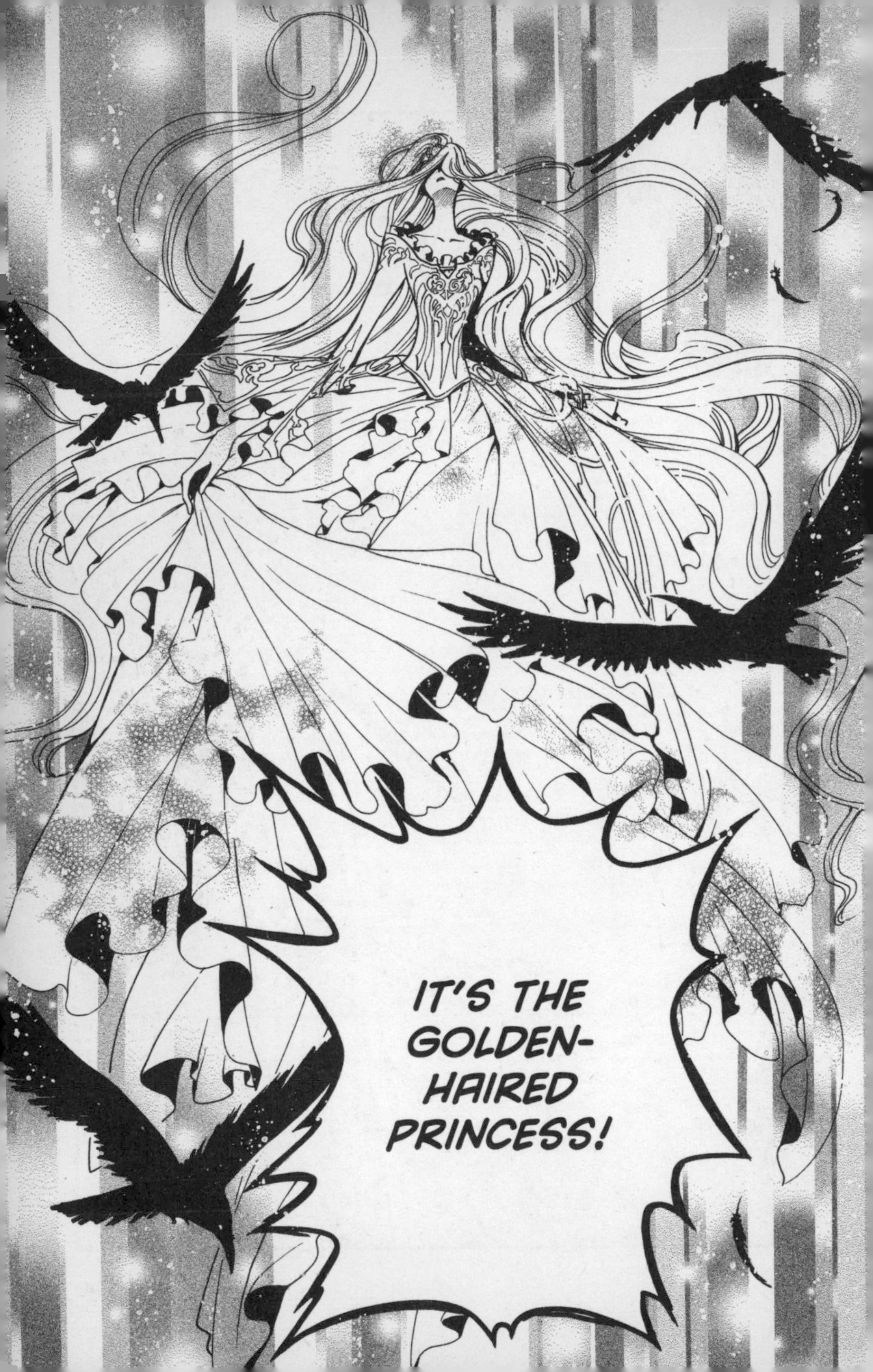
IT'S THE GOLDEN-HAIRED PRINCESS!

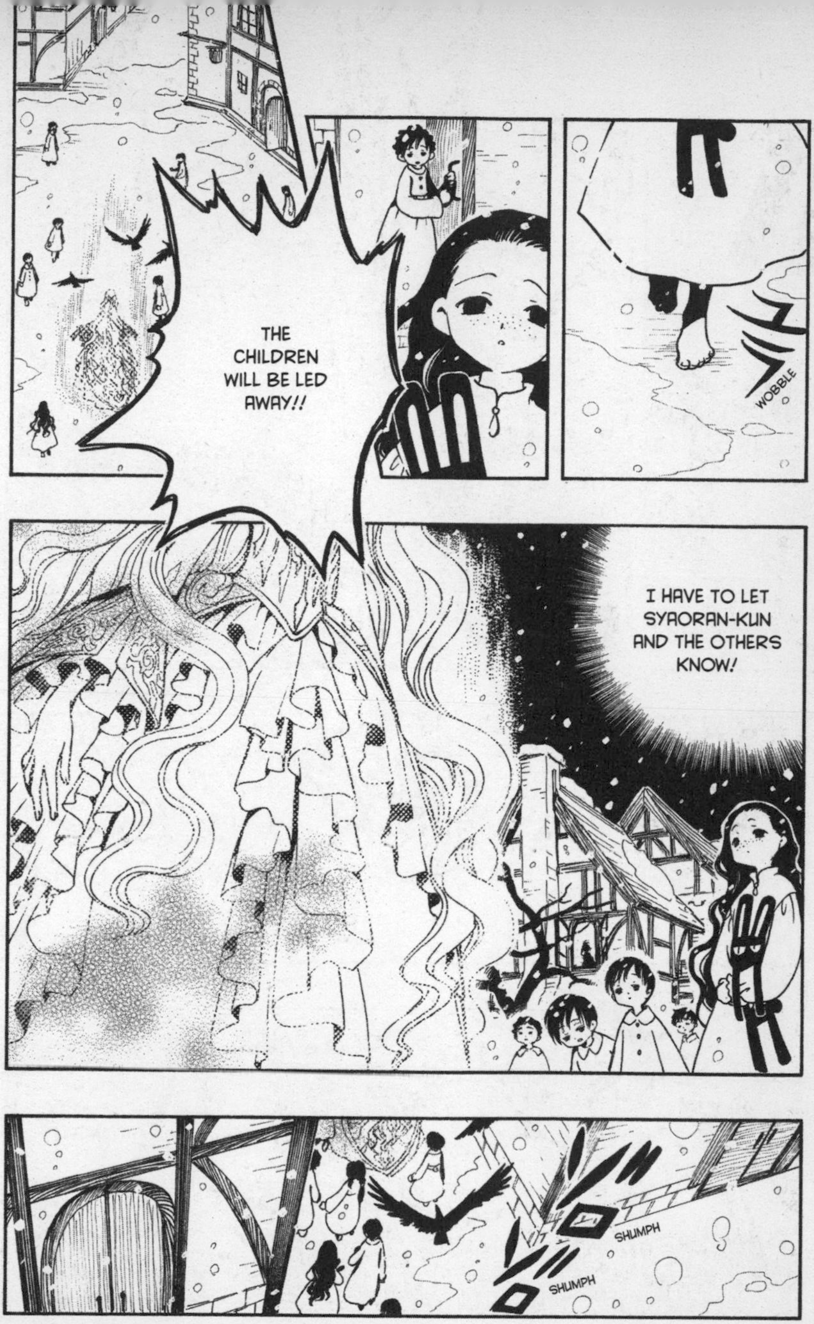
WOBBLE
THE CHILDREN WILL BE LED AWAY!!
I HAVE TO LET SYAORAN-KUN AND THE OTHERS KNOW!
SHUMPH
SHUMPH

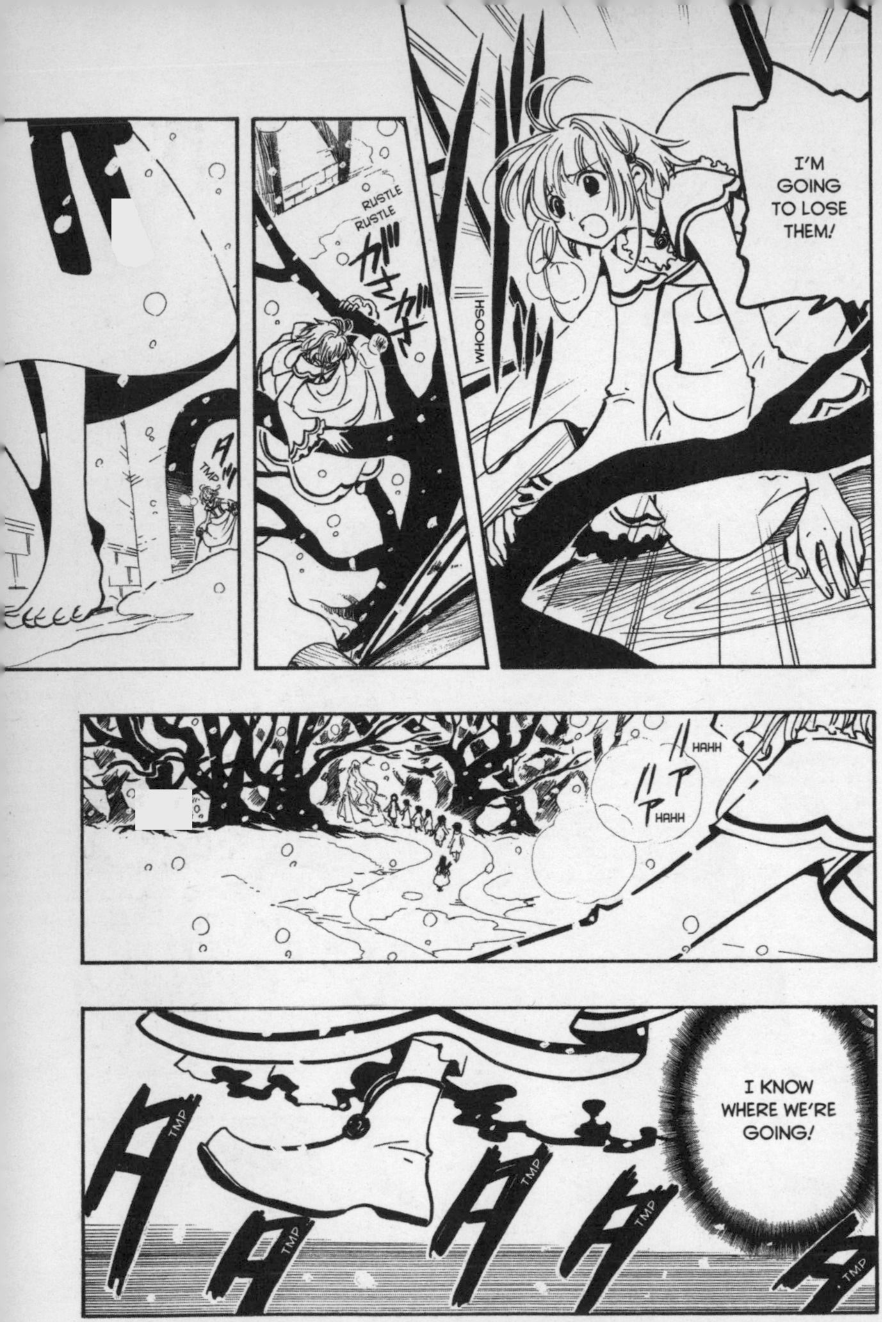
I'M GOING TO LOSE THEM!
WHOOSH
RUSTLE RUSTLE
TMP
HAHH
HAHH
I KNOW WHERE WE'RE GOING!
TMP
TMP
TMP
TMP
TMP

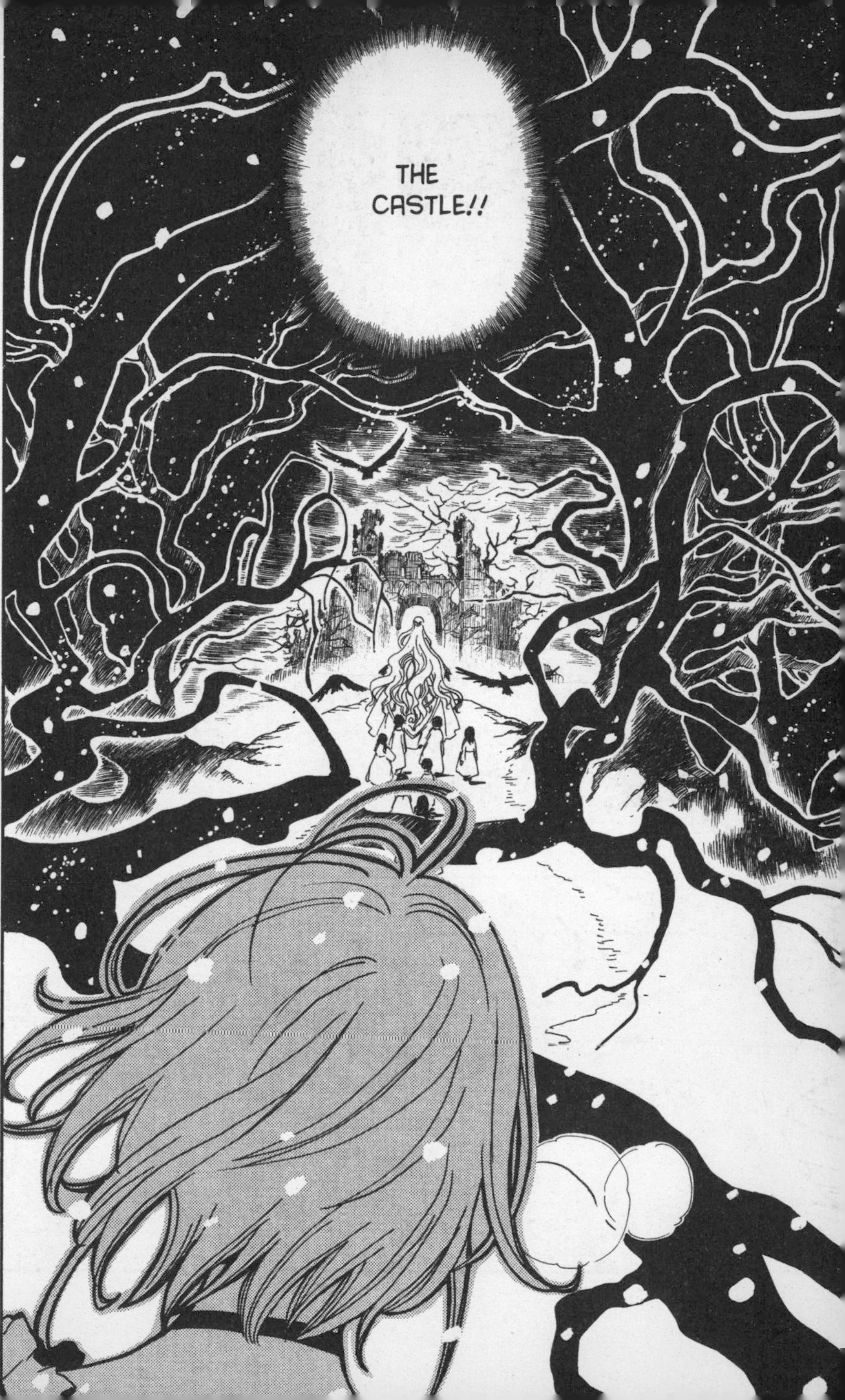
THE CASTLE!!

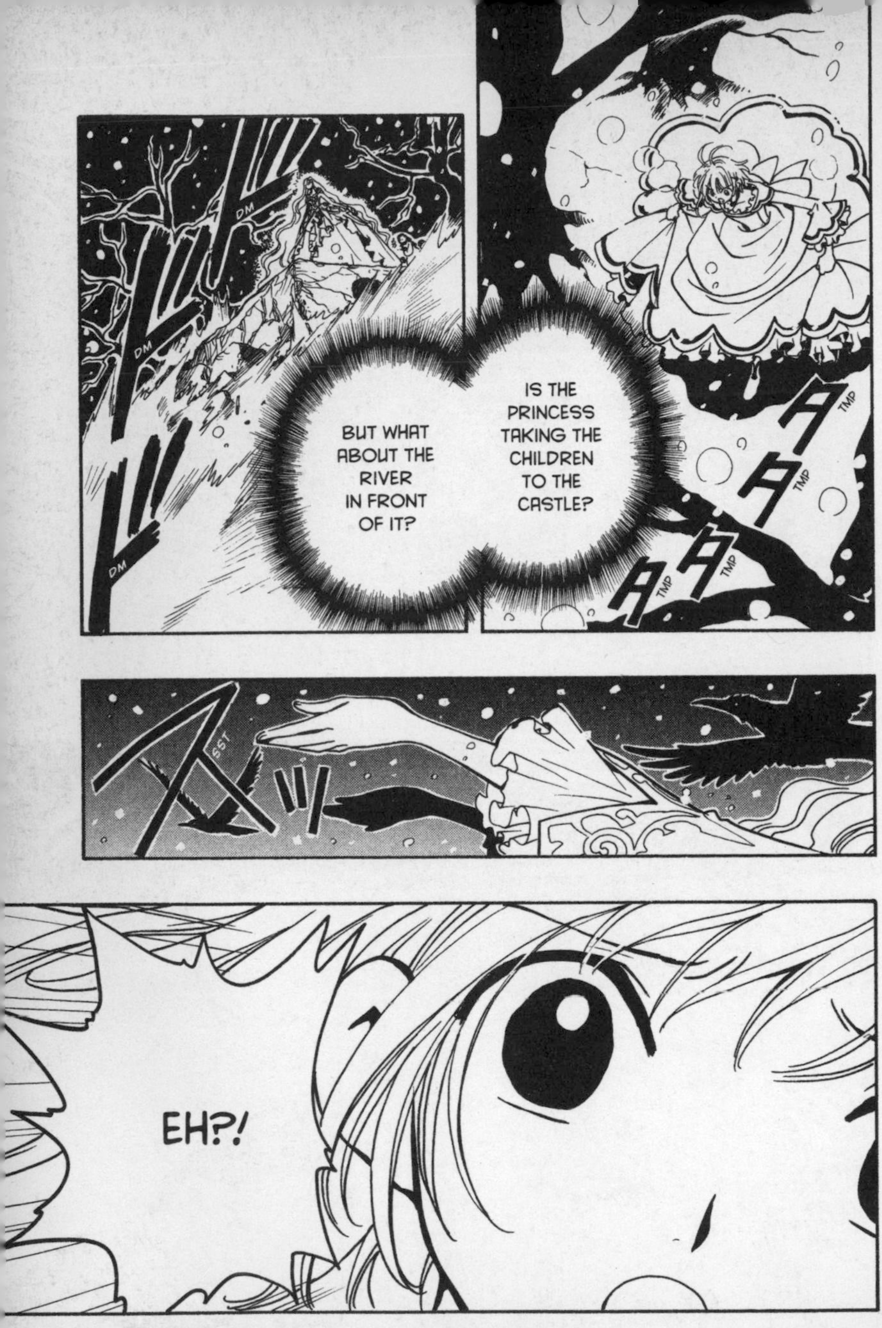
TMP
TMP
TMP
TMP
IS THE PRINCESS TAKING THE CHILDREN TO THE CASTLE?
DM
DM
DM
BUT WHAT ABOUT THE RIVER IN FRONT OF IT?
SST
EH?!

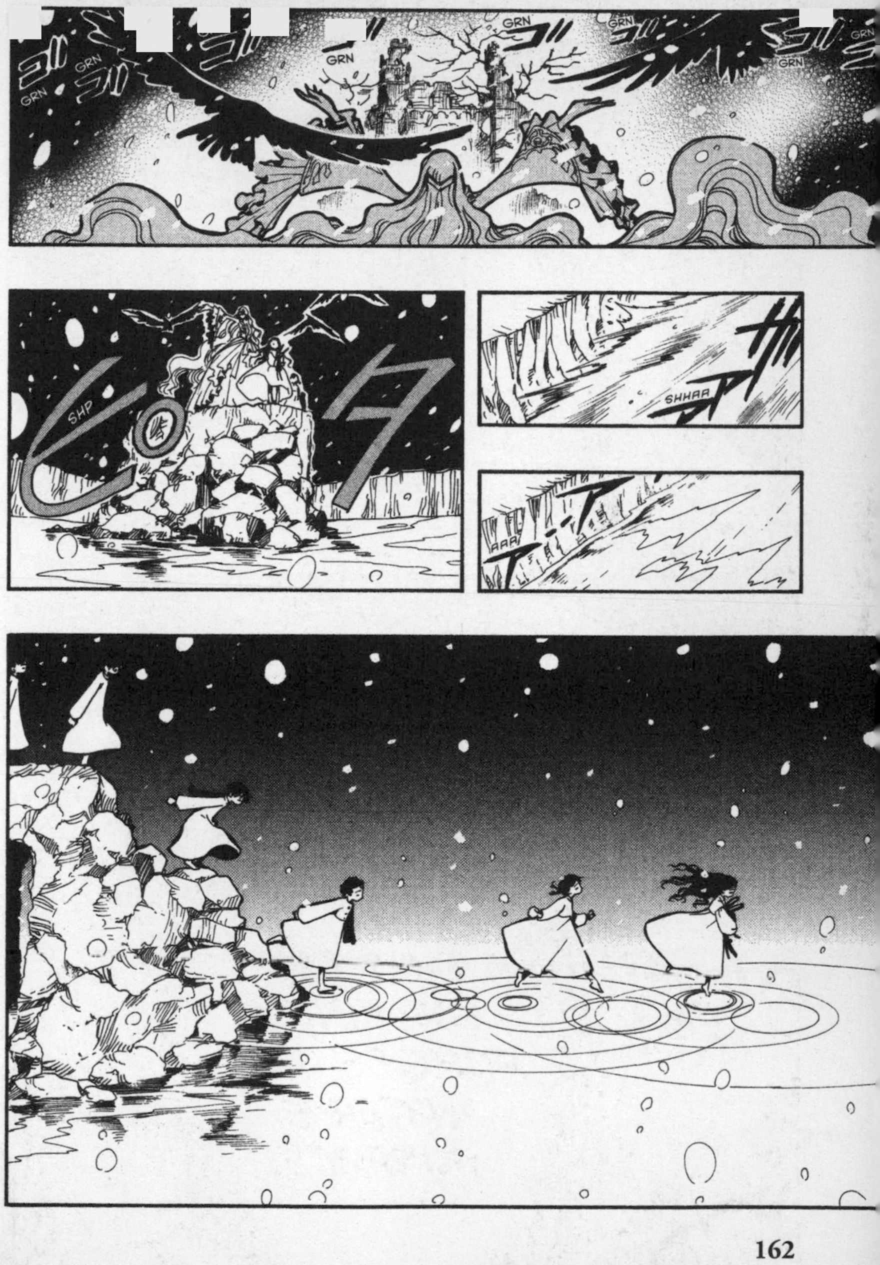
GRN
GRN
GRN
GRN
GRN
GRN
GRN
SHHAA
AAA
SHP

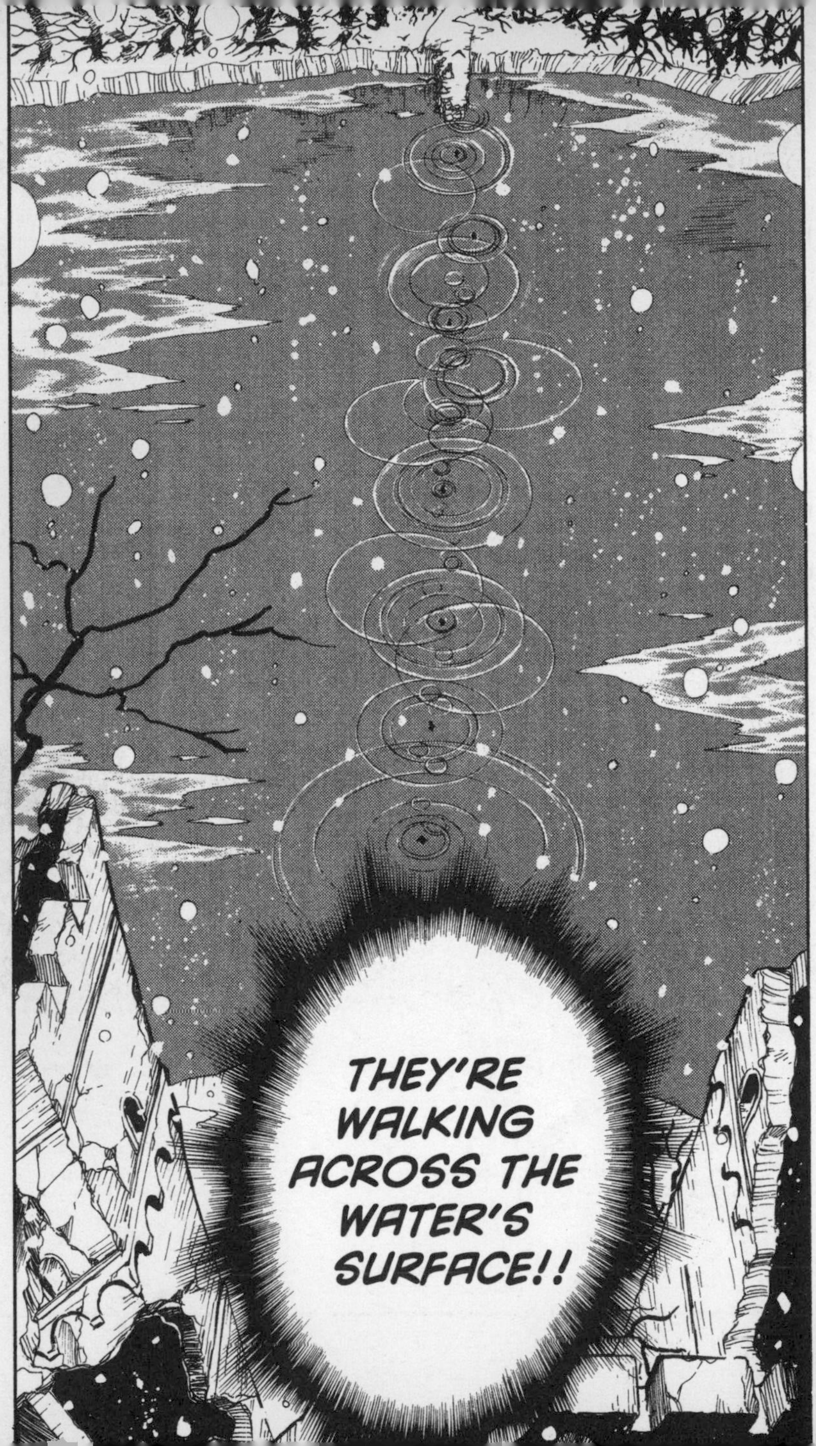
THEY'RE WALKING ACROSS THE WATER'S SURFACE!!

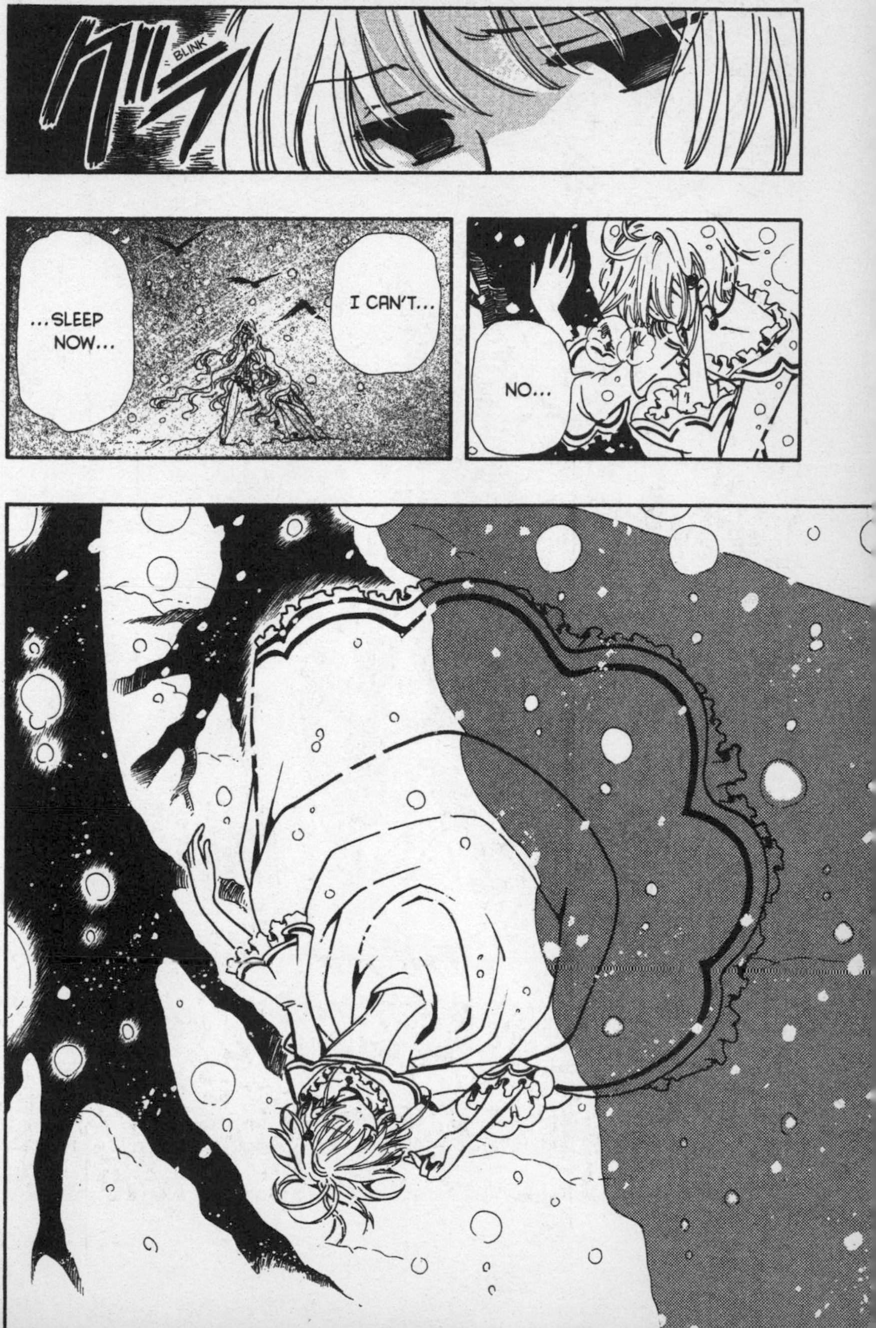
BLINK
NO...
I CAN'T...
...SLEEP NOW...

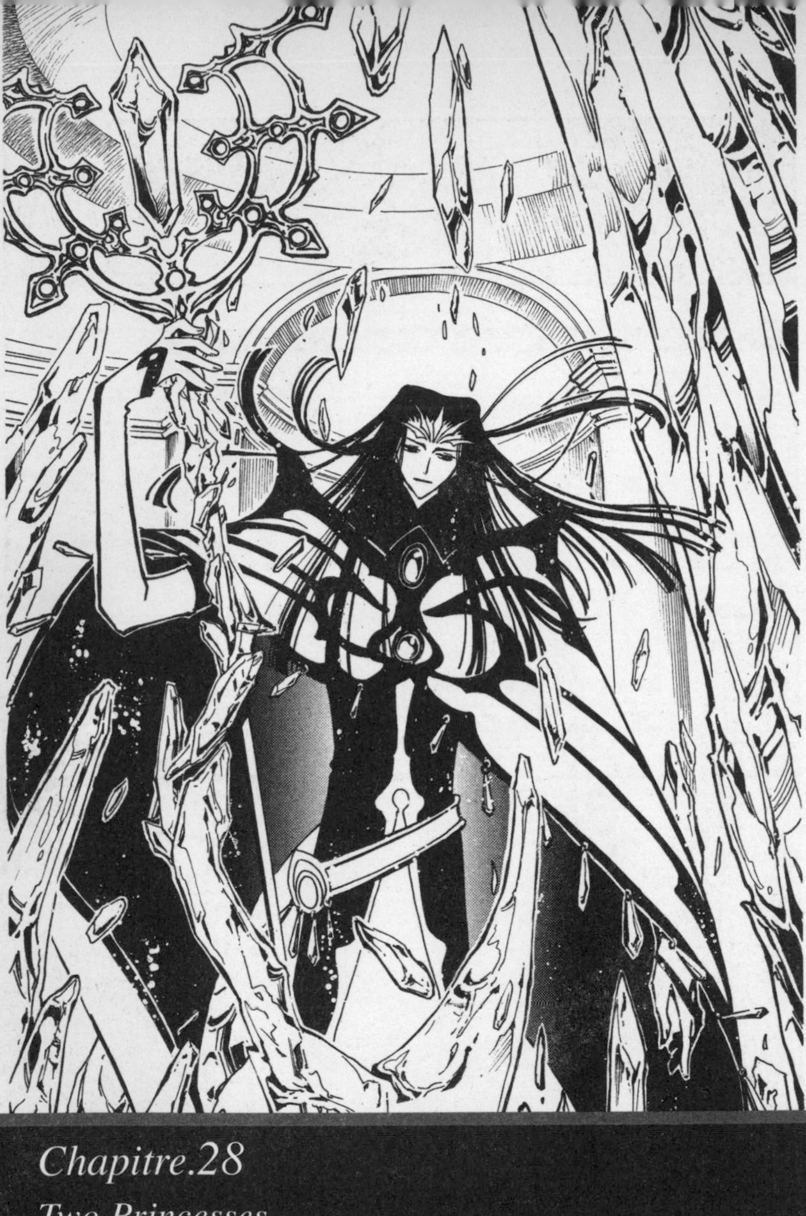

Chapitre.28
Two Princesses

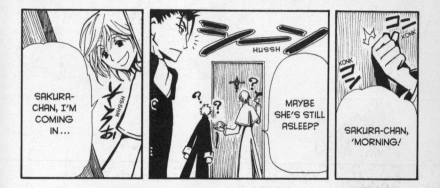

KONK
KONK
SAKURA-CHAN, 'MORNING!
HUSSH
MAYBE SHE'S STILL ASLEEP?
WHSSH
SAKURA-CHAN, I'M COMING IN...

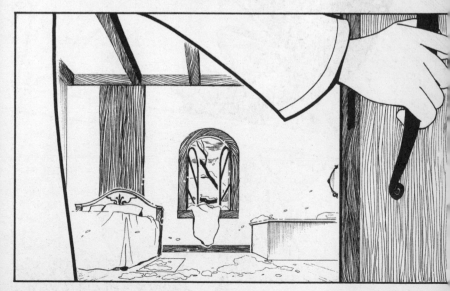

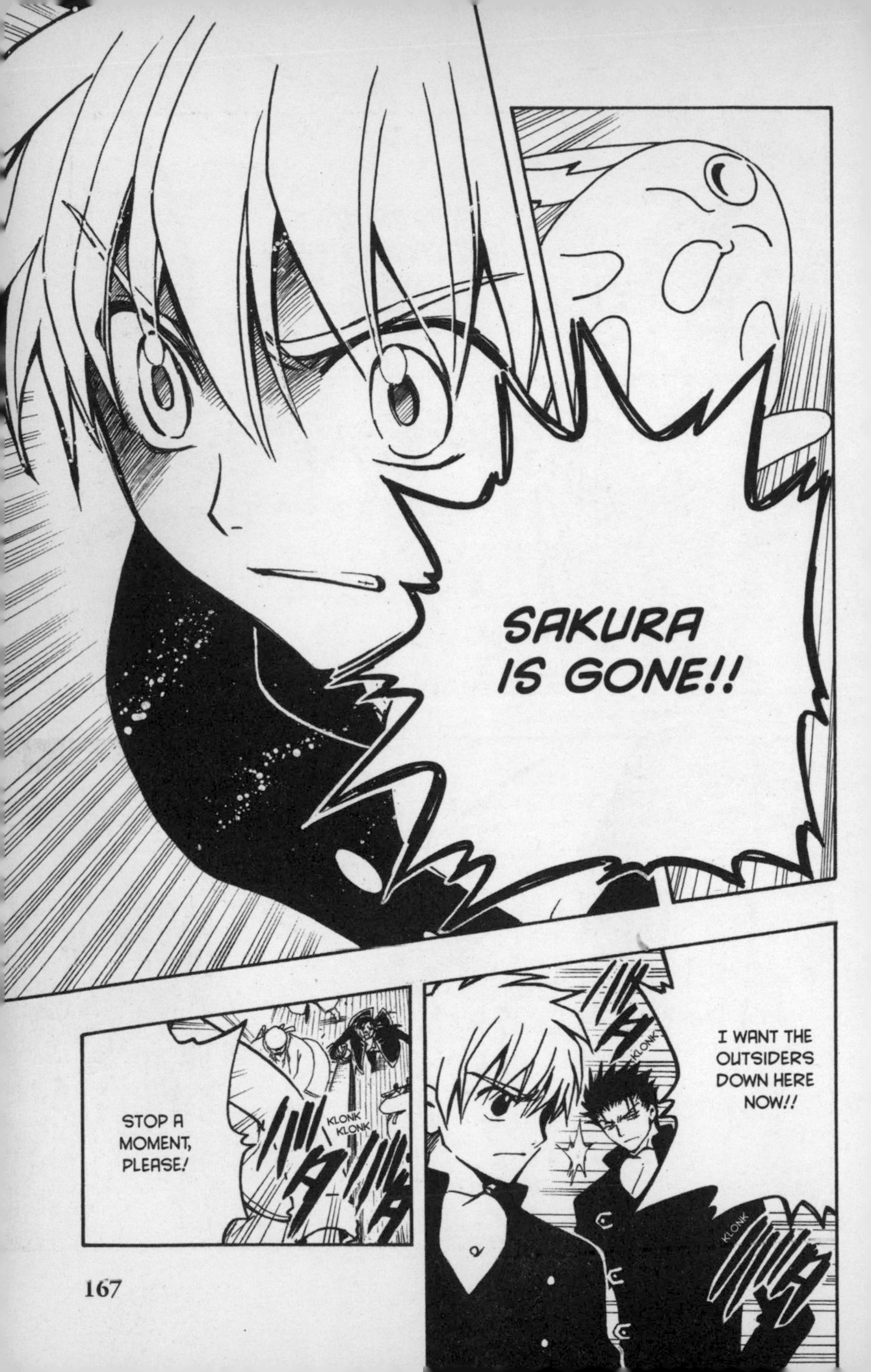
SAKURA IS GONE!!
I WANT THE OUTSIDERS DOWN HERE NOW!!
KLONK
KLONK
STOP A MOMENT, PLEASE!
KLONK KLONK

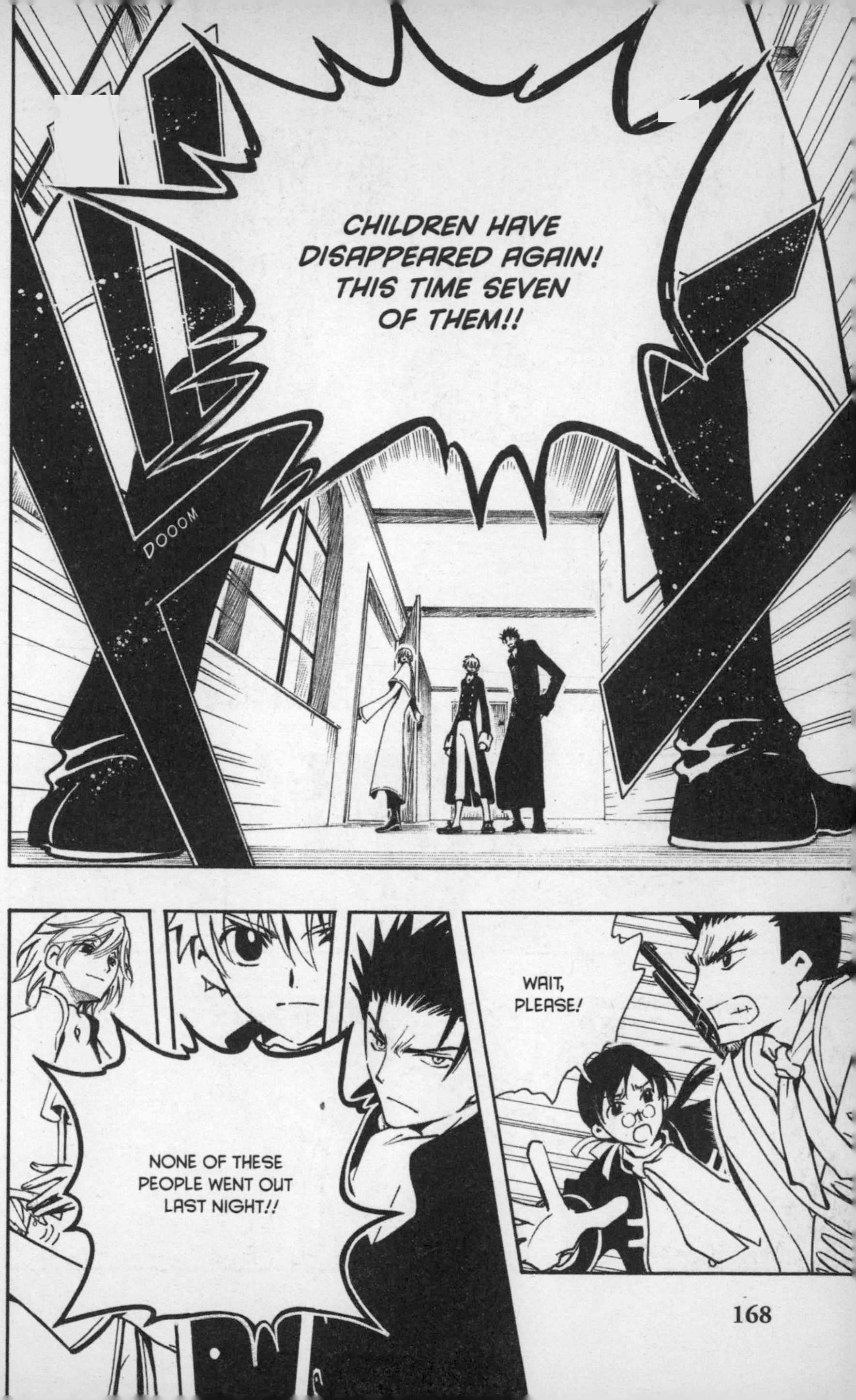
CHILDREN HAVE DISAPPEARED AGAIN! THIS TIME SEVEN OF THEM!!
DOOOM
WAIT, PLEASE!
NONE OF THESE PEOPLE WENT OUT LAST NIGHT!!

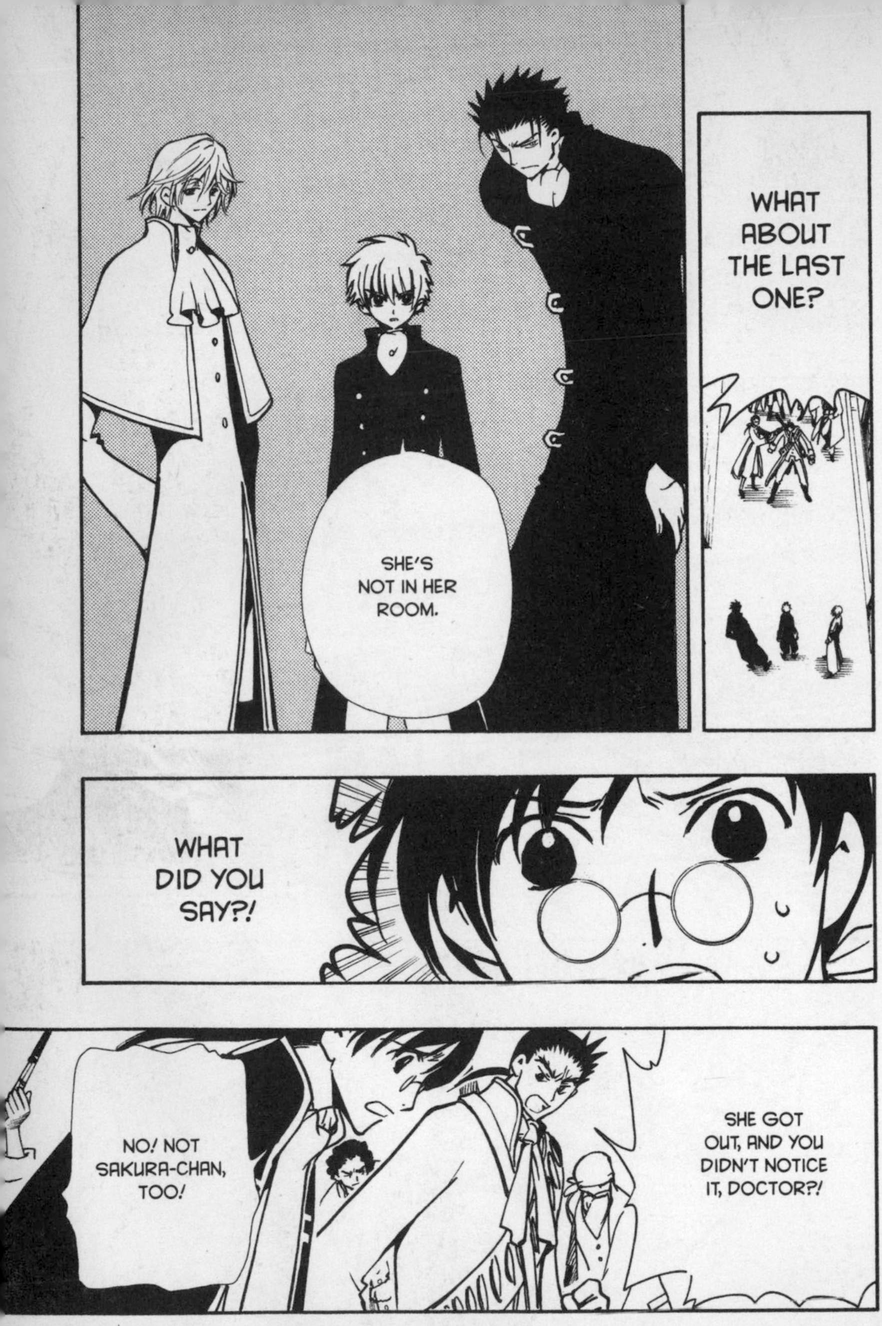
WHAT ABOUT THE LAST ONE?
SHE'S NOT IN HER ROOM.
WHAT DID YOU SAY?!
SHE GOT OUT, AND YOU DIDN'T NOTICE IT, DOCTOR?!
NO! NOT SAKURA-CHAN, TOO!

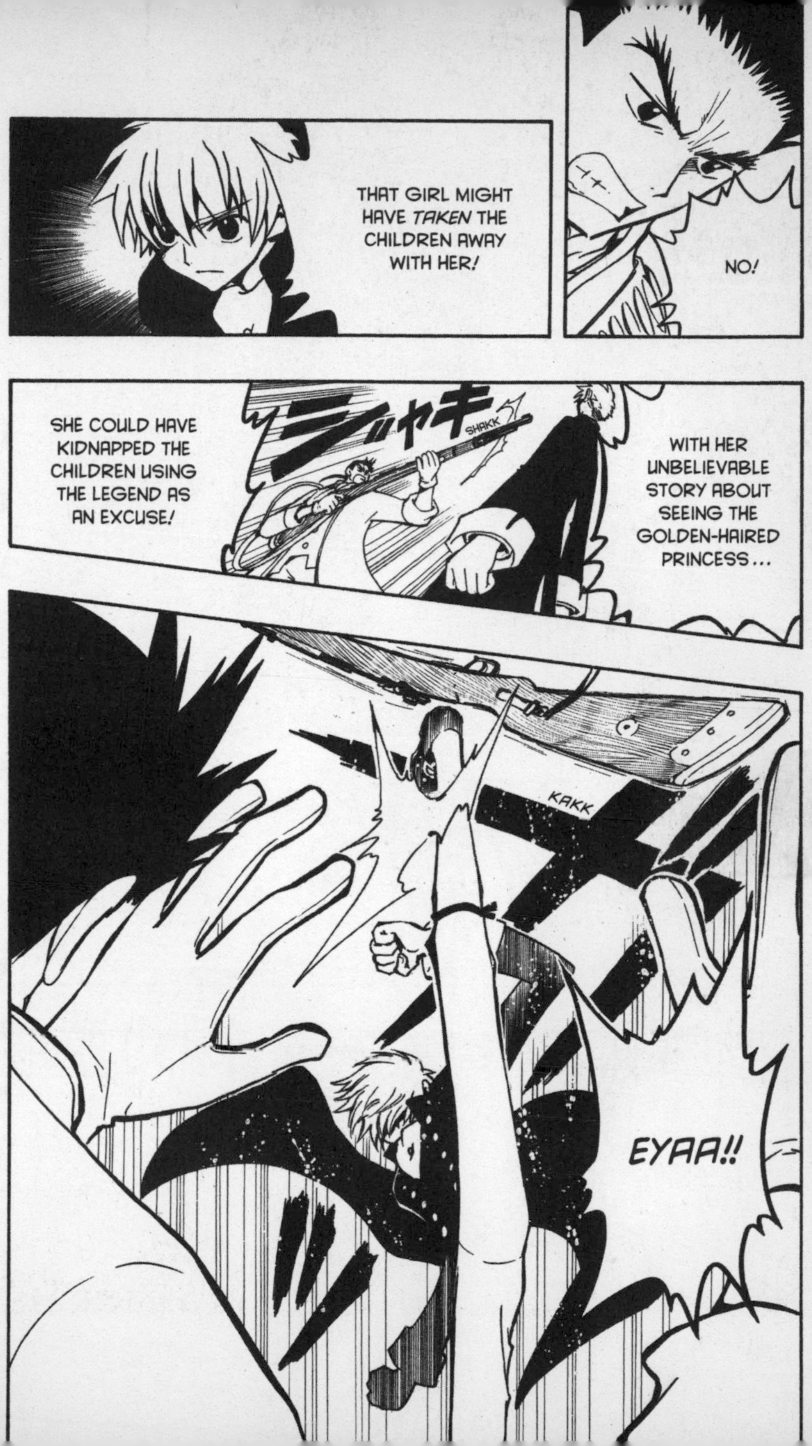
NO!
THAT GIRL MIGHT HAVE *TAKEN* THE CHILDREN AWAY WITH HER!
WITH HER UNBELIEVABLE STORY ABOUT SEEING THE GOLDEN-HAIRED PRINCESS...
SHAKK
SHE COULD HAVE KIDNAPPED THE CHILDREN USING THE LEGEND AS AN EXCUSE!
KAKK
EYAA!!

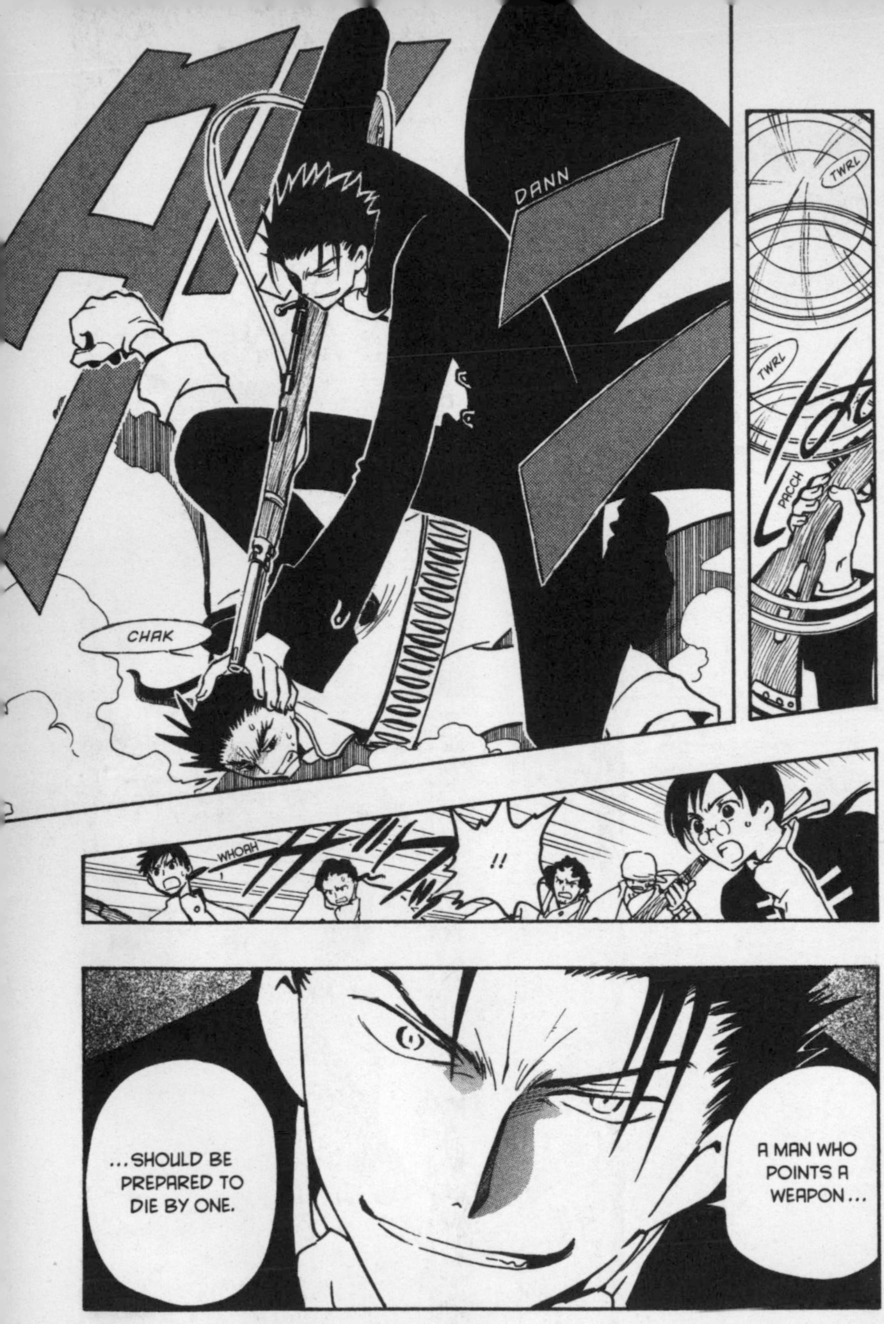
TWRL
TWRL
PACCH
DANN
CHAK
!!
WHOAH
A MAN WHO POINTS A WEAPON...
...SHOULD BE PREPARED TO DIE BY ONE.

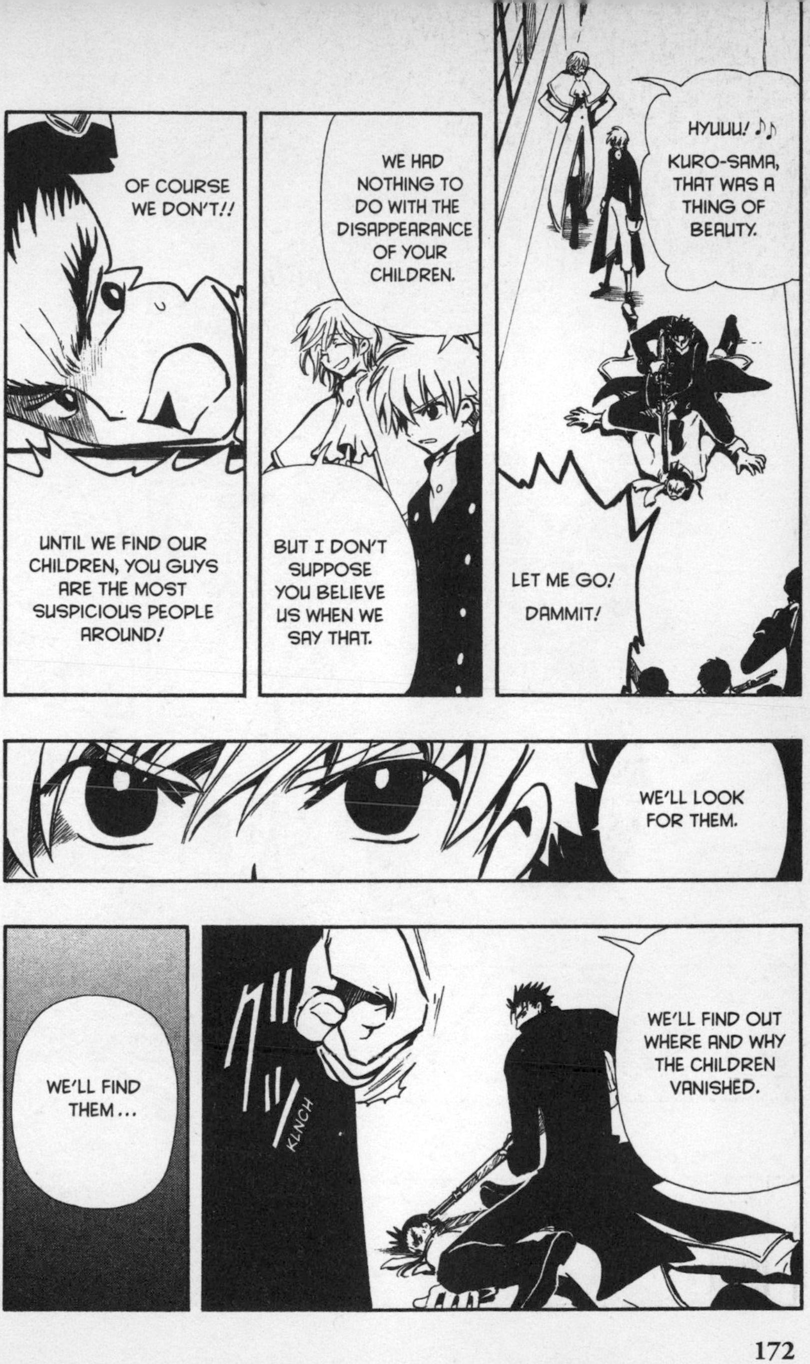
HYUUU! ♪♪
KURO-SAMA, THAT WAS A THING OF BEAUTY.
LET ME GO! DAMMIT!
WE HAD NOTHING TO DO WITH THE DISAPPEARANCE OF YOUR CHILDREN.
BUT I DON'T SUPPOSE YOU BELIEVE US WHEN WE SAY THAT.
OF COURSE WE DON'T!!
UNTIL WE FIND OUR CHILDREN, YOU GUYS ARE THE MOST SUSPICIOUS PEOPLE AROUND!
WE'LL LOOK FOR THEM.
WE'LL FIND OUT WHERE AND WHY THE CHILDREN VANISHED.
KLNCH
WE'LL FIND THEM...

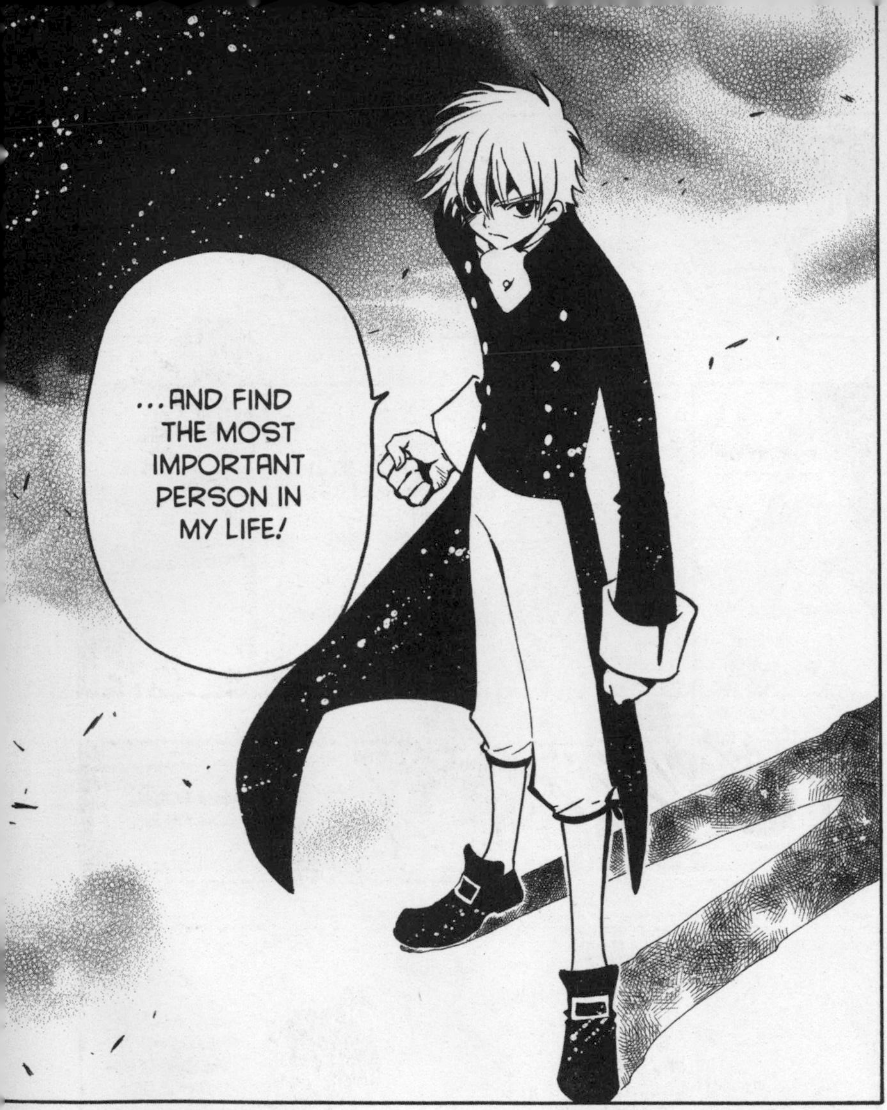
...AND FIND THE MOST IMPORTANT PERSON IN MY LIFE!

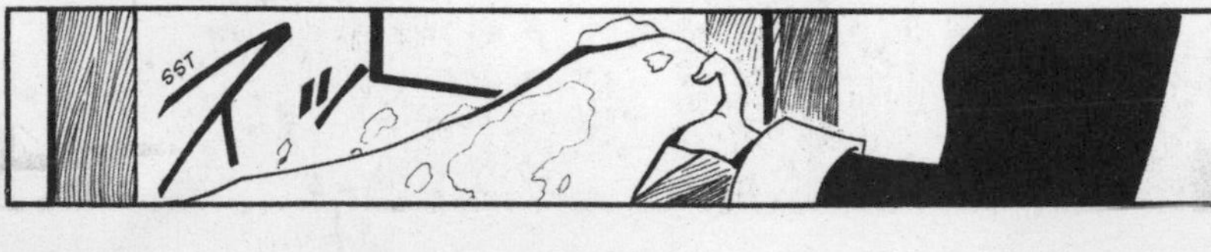
SST

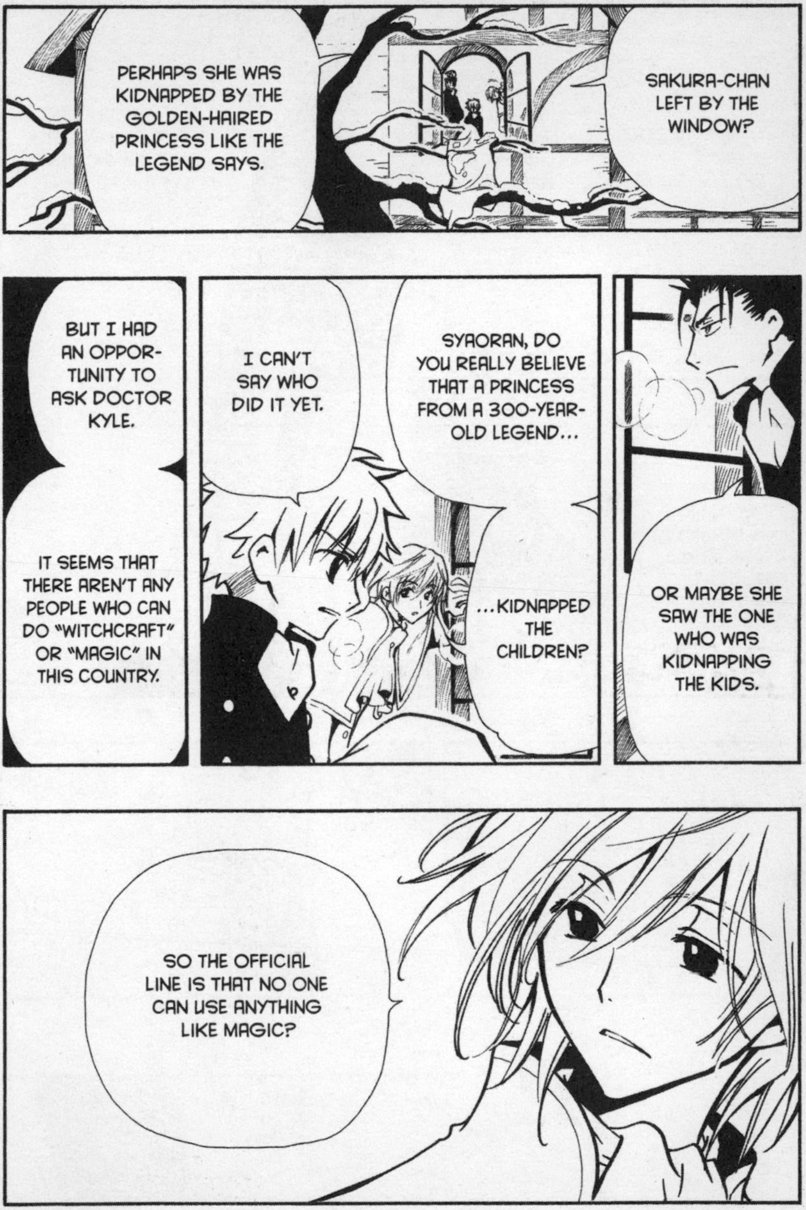
SAKURA-CHAN LEFT BY THE WINDOW?
PERHAPS SHE WAS KIDNAPPED BY THE GOLDEN-HAIRED PRINCESS LIKE THE LEGEND SAYS.
OR MAYBE SHE SAW THE ONE WHO WAS KIDNAPPING THE KIDS.
SYAORAN, DO YOU REALLY BELIEVE THAT A PRINCESS FROM A 300-YEAR-OLD LEGEND...
...KIDNAPPED THE CHILDREN?
I CAN'T SAY WHO DID IT YET.
BUT I HAD AN OPPOR-TUNITY TO ASK DOCTOR KYLE.
IT SEEMS THAT THERE AREN'T ANY PEOPLE WHO CAN DO "WITCHCRAFT" OR "MAGIC" IN THIS COUNTRY.
SO THE OFFICIAL LINE IS THAT NO ONE CAN USE ANYTHING LIKE MAGIC?

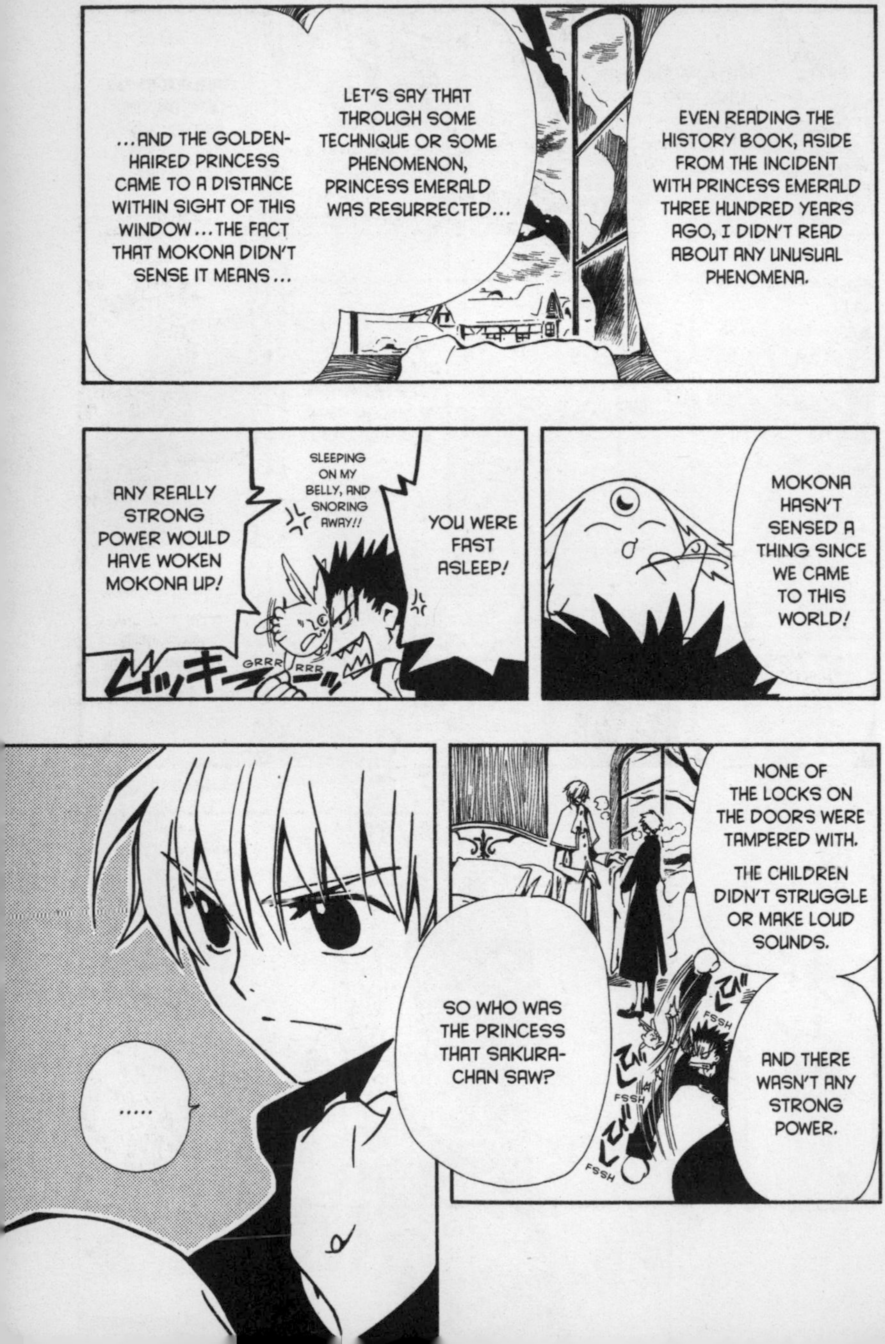
EVEN READING THE HISTORY BOOK, ASIDE FROM THE INCIDENT WITH PRINCESS EMERALD THREE HUNDRED YEARS AGO, I DIDN'T READ ABOUT ANY UNUSUAL PHENOMENA.
LET'S SAY THAT THROUGH SOME TECHNIQUE OR SOME PHENOMENON, PRINCESS EMERALD WAS RESURRECTED...
...AND THE GOLDEN-HAIRED PRINCESS CAME TO A DISTANCE WITHIN SIGHT OF THIS WINDOW... THE FACT THAT MOKONA DIDN'T SENSE IT MEANS...
MOKONA HASN'T SENSED A THING SINCE WE CAME TO THIS WORLD!
YOU WERE FAST ASLEEP!
SLEEPING ON MY BELLY, AND SNORING AWAY!!
ANY REALLY STRONG POWER WOULD HAVE WOKEN MOKONA UP!
GRRR RRR
NONE OF THE LOCKS ON THE DOORS WERE TAMPERED WITH.
THE CHILDREN DIDN'T STRUGGLE OR MAKE LOUD SOUNDS.
AND THERE WASN'T ANY STRONG POWER.
FSSH
FSSH
FSSH
SO WHO WAS THE PRINCESS THAT SAKURA-CHAN SAW?
.....

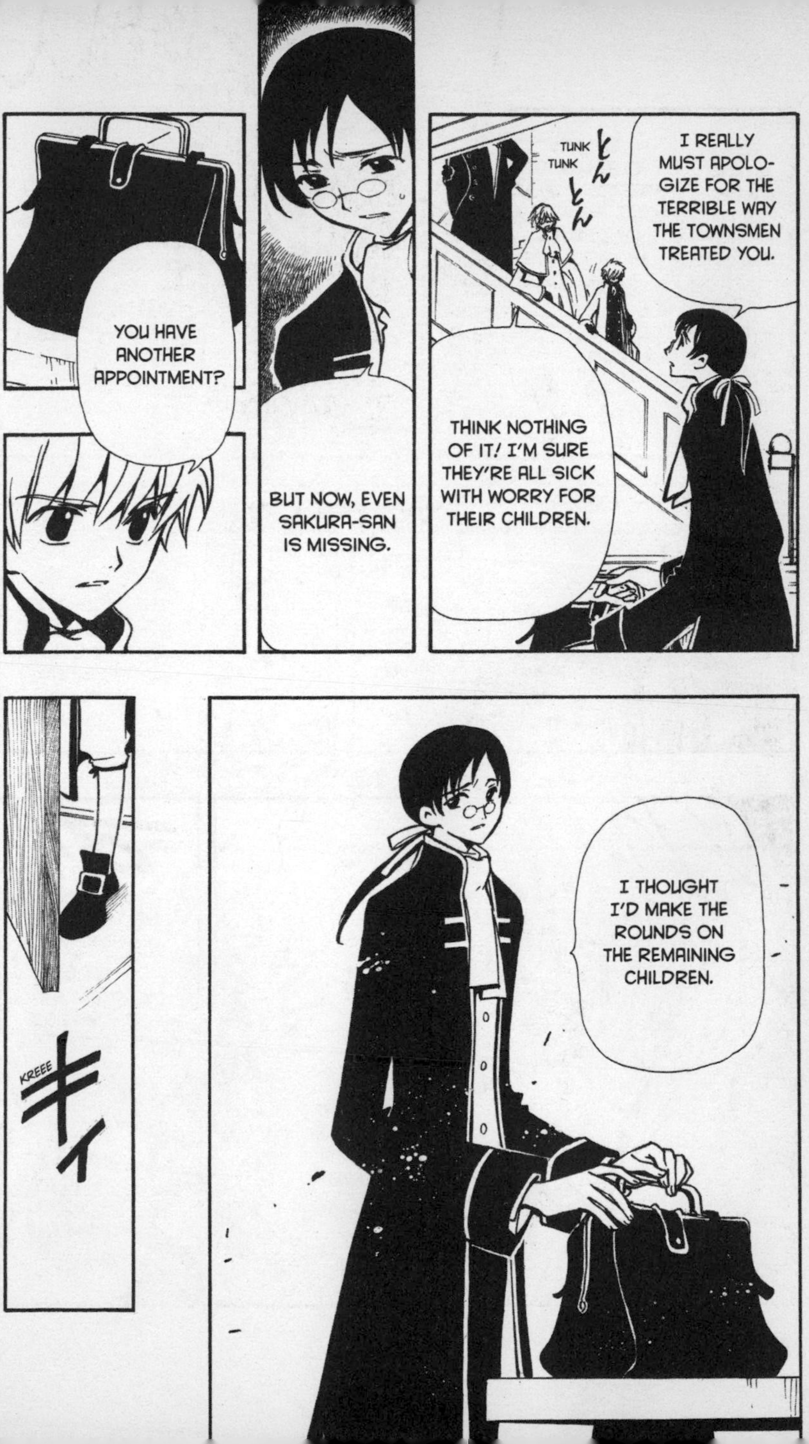
TUNK TUNK
I REALLY MUST APOLOGIZE FOR THE TERRIBLE WAY THE TOWNSMEN TREATED YOU.
THINK NOTHING OF IT! I'M SURE THEY'RE ALL SICK WITH WORRY FOR THEIR CHILDREN.
BUT NOW, EVEN SAKURA-SAN IS MISSING.
YOU HAVE ANOTHER APPOINTMENT?
I THOUGHT I'D MAKE THE ROUNDS ON THE REMAINING CHILDREN.
KREEE

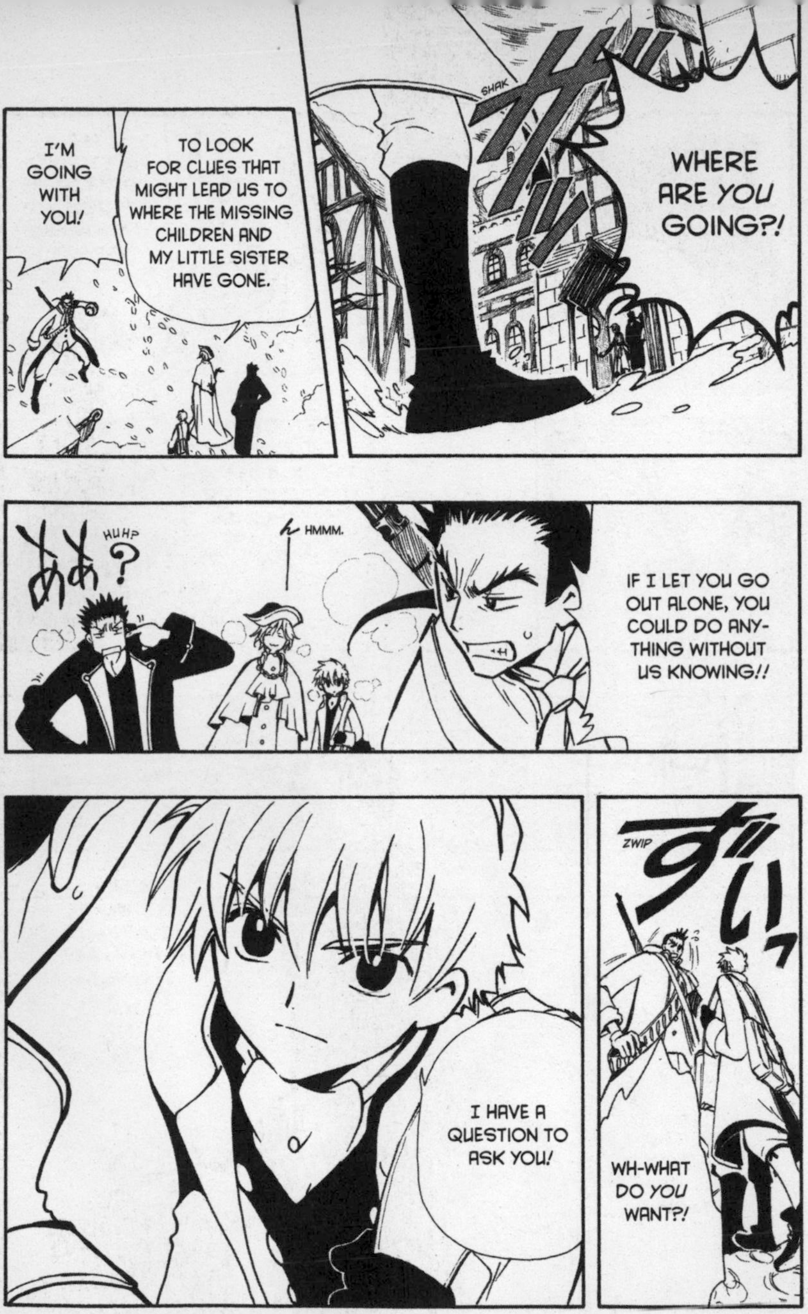

ガッ
SHAK
WHERE ARE *YOU* GOING?!
TO LOOK FOR CLUES THAT MIGHT LEAD US TO WHERE THE MISSING CHILDREN AND MY LITTLE SISTER HAVE GONE.
I'M GOING WITH YOU!
IF I LET YOU GO OUT ALONE, YOU COULD DO ANYTHING WITHOUT US KNOWING!!
HMMM.
ああ?
HUH?
ずいっ
ZWIP
WH-WHAT DO *YOU* WANT?!
I HAVE A QUESTION TO ASK YOU!

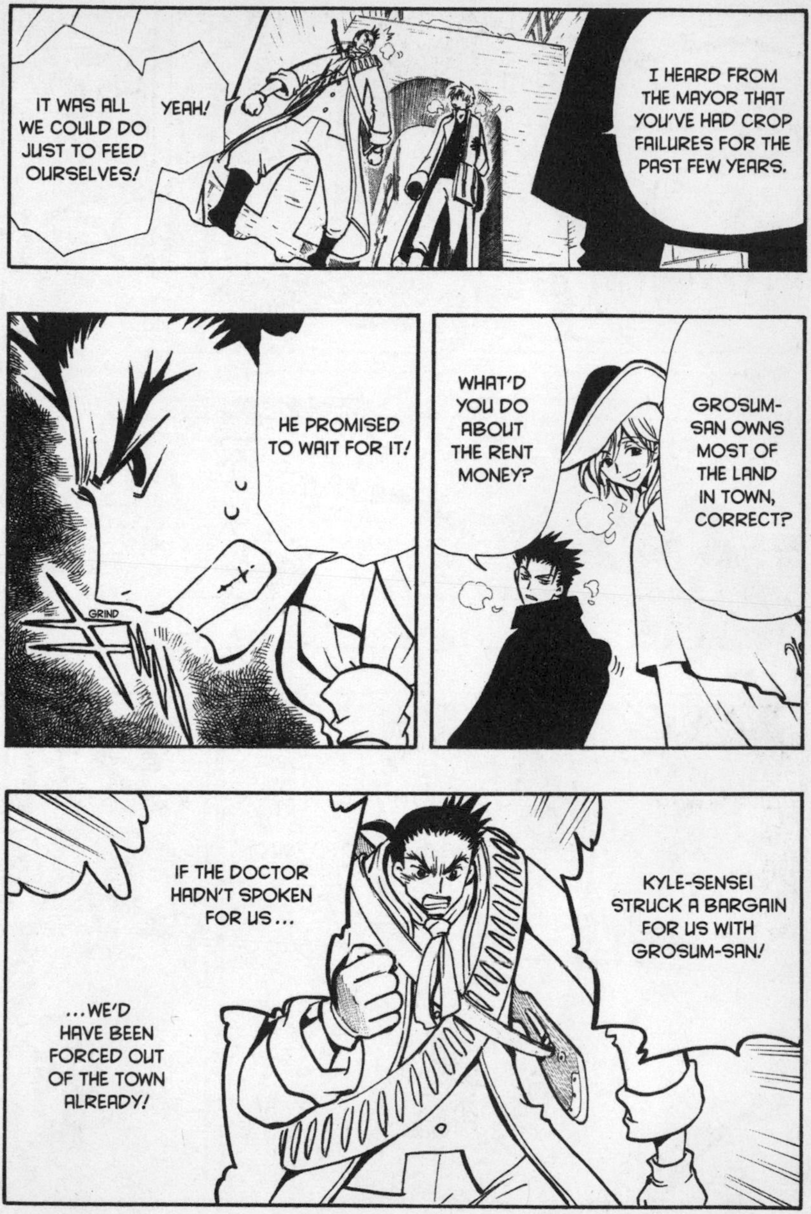
I HEARD FROM THE MAYOR THAT YOU'VE HAD CROP FAILURES FOR THE PAST FEW YEARS.
YEAH!
IT WAS ALL WE COULD DO JUST TO FEED OURSELVES!
GROSUM-SAN OWNS MOST OF THE LAND IN TOWN, CORRECT?
WHAT'D YOU DO ABOUT THE RENT MONEY?
HE PROMISED TO WAIT FOR IT!
GRIND
KYLE-SENSEI STRUCK A BARGAIN FOR US WITH GROSUM-SAN!
IF THE DOCTOR HADN'T SPOKEN FOR US...
...WE'D HAVE BEEN FORCED OUT OF THE TOWN ALREADY!

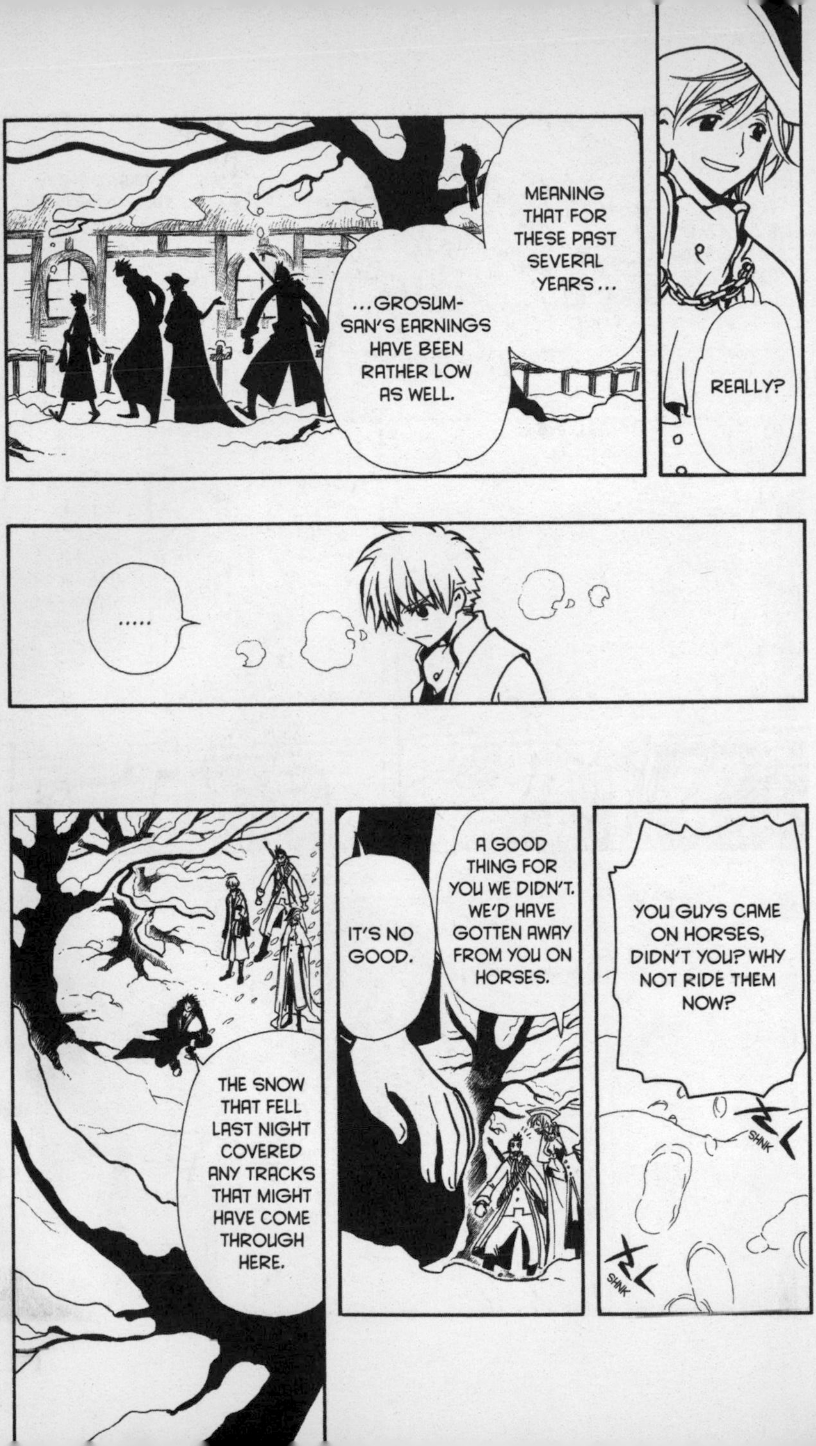
REALLY?
MEANING THAT FOR THESE PAST SEVERAL YEARS...
...GROSUM-SAN'S EARNINGS HAVE BEEN RATHER LOW AS WELL.
......
YOU GUYS CAME ON HORSES, DIDN'T YOU? WHY NOT RIDE THEM NOW?
SHNK
SHNK
A GOOD THING FOR YOU WE DIDN'T. WE'D HAVE GOTTEN AWAY FROM YOU ON HORSES.
IT'S NO GOOD.
THE SNOW THAT FELL LAST NIGHT COVERED ANY TRACKS THAT MIGHT HAVE COME THROUGH HERE.

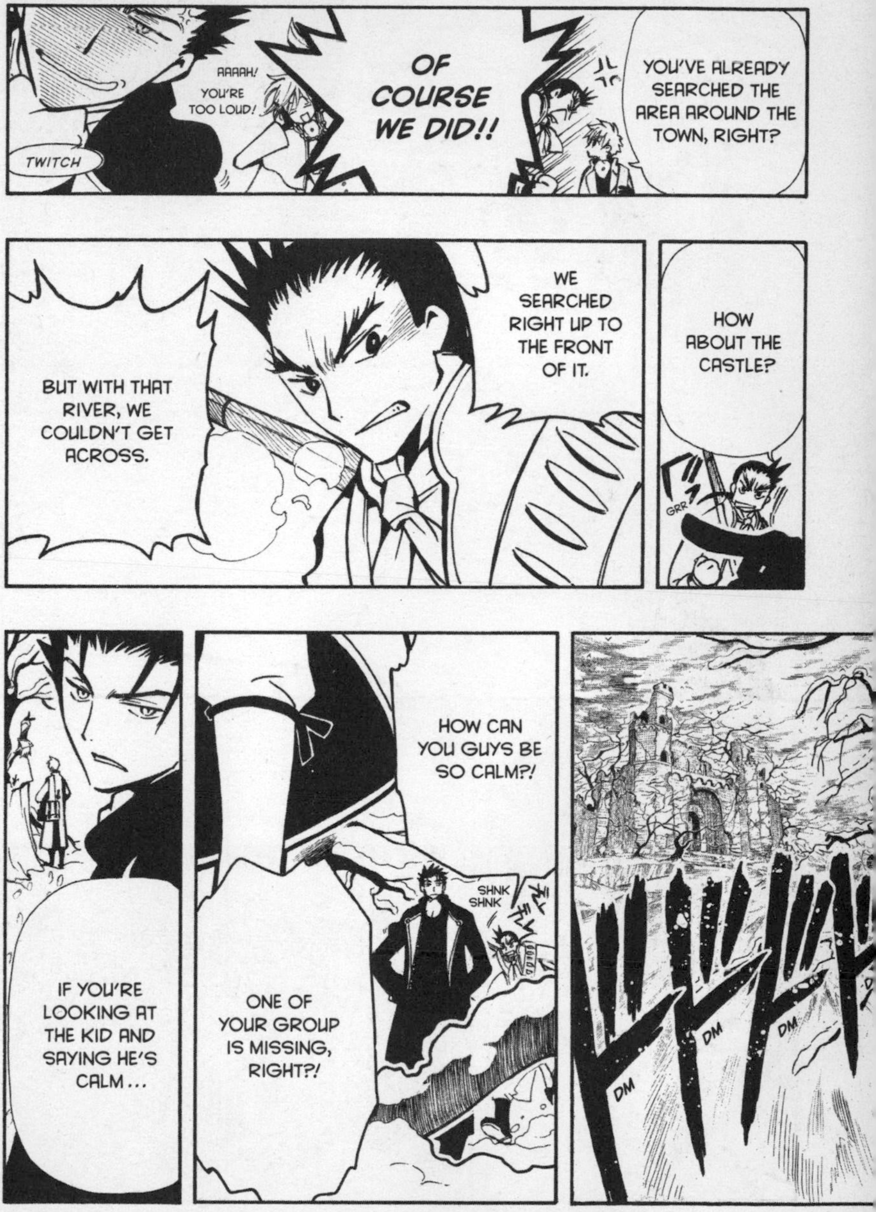
YOU'VE ALREADY SEARCHED THE AREA AROUND THE TOWN, RIGHT?
OF COURSE WE DID!!
AAAAH! YOU'RE TOO LOUD!
TWITCH
HOW ABOUT THE CASTLE?
GRR
WE SEARCHED RIGHT UP TO THE FRONT OF IT.
BUT WITH THAT RIVER, WE COULDN'T GET ACROSS.
DM
DM
DM
HOW CAN YOU GUYS BE SO CALM?!
SHNK SHNK
ONE OF YOUR GROUP IS MISSING, RIGHT?!
IF YOU'RE LOOKING AT THE KID AND SAYING HE'S CALM...

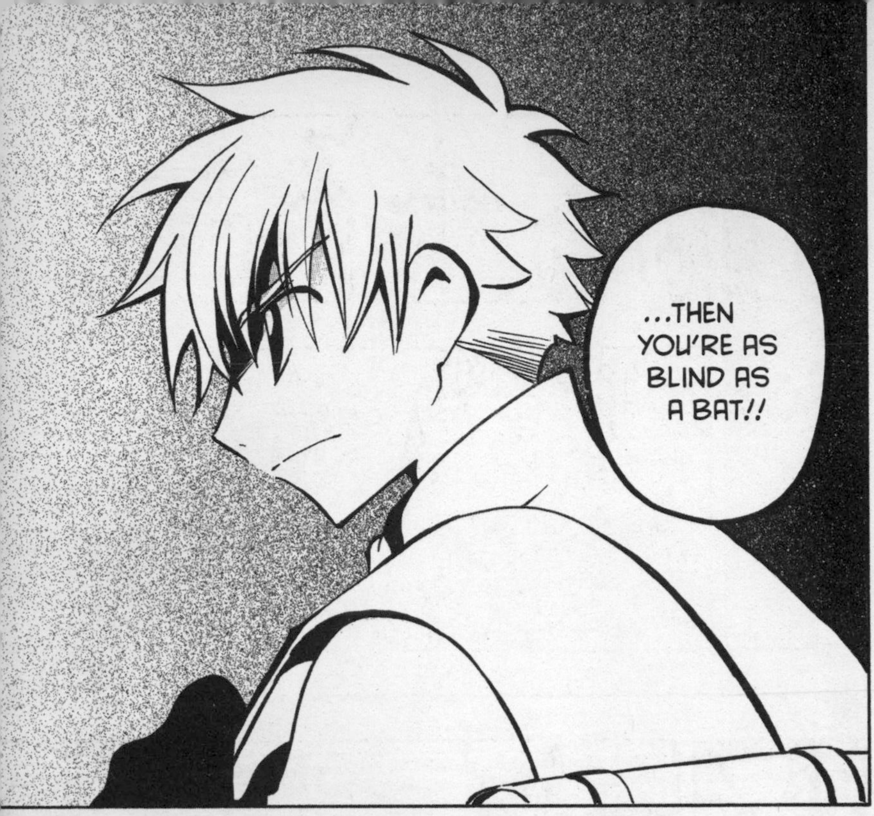
...THEN YOU'RE AS BLIND AS A BAT!!

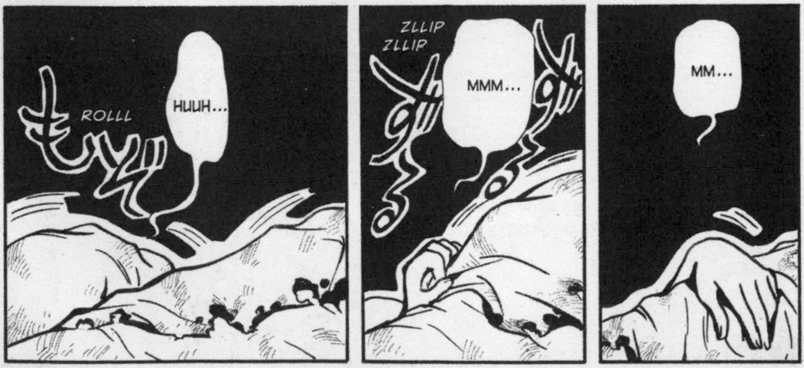
MM...
ZLLIP ZLLIP
MMM...
HUUH...
ROLLL

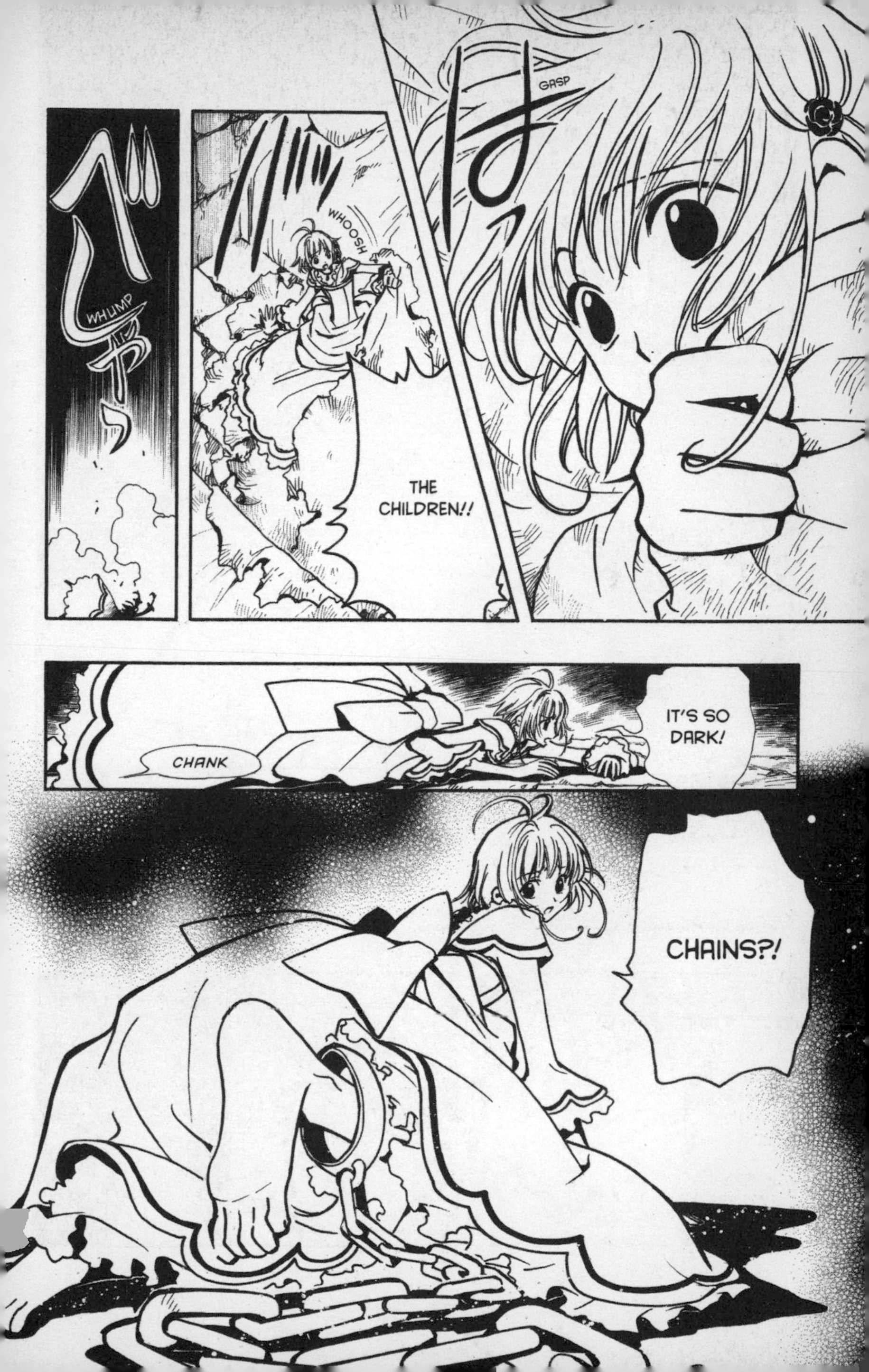
GASP
WHOOSH
THE CHILDREN!!
WHUMP
IT'S SO DARK!
CHANK
CHAINS?!

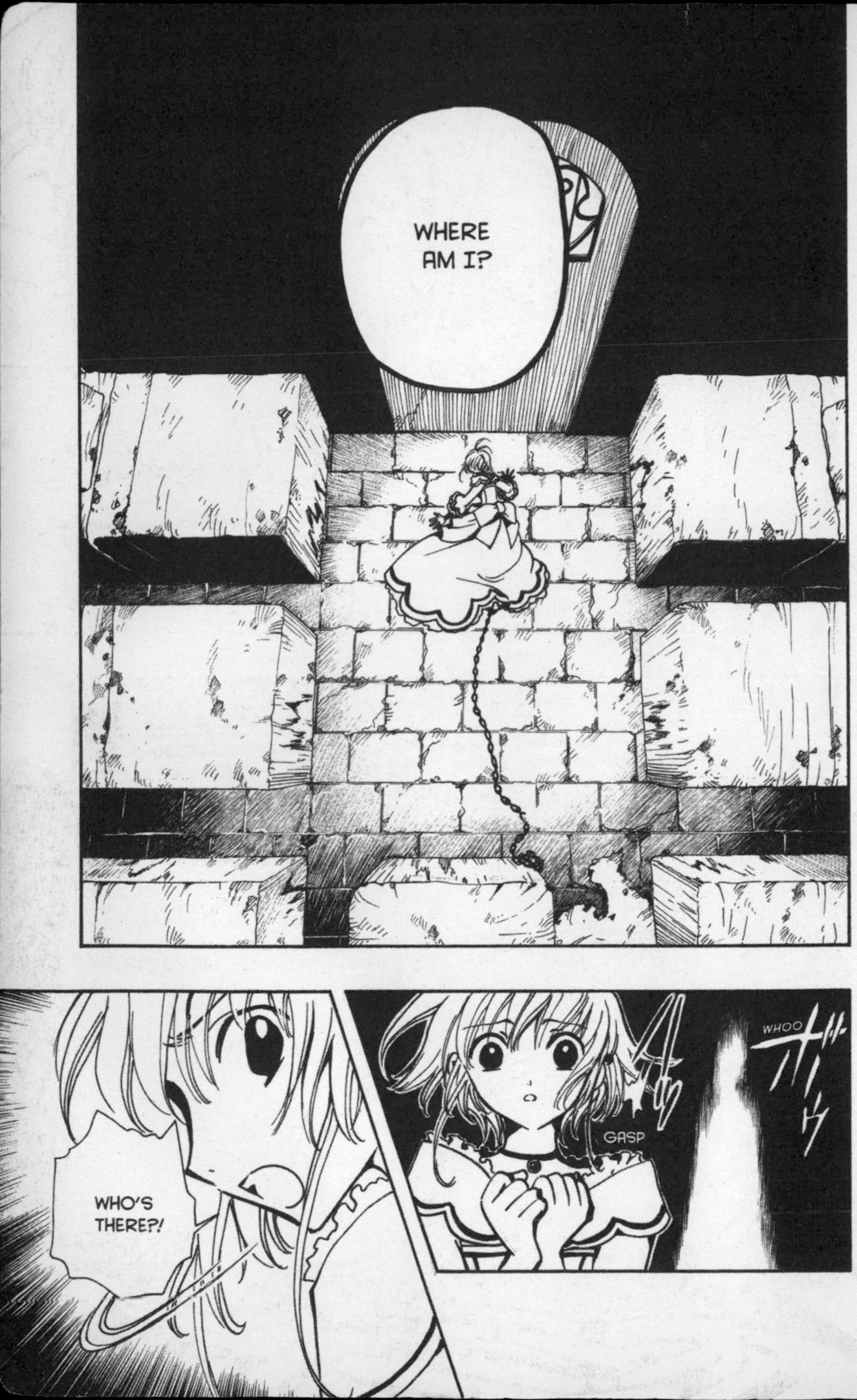
WHERE AM I?
WHOO
GASP
WHO'S THERE?!

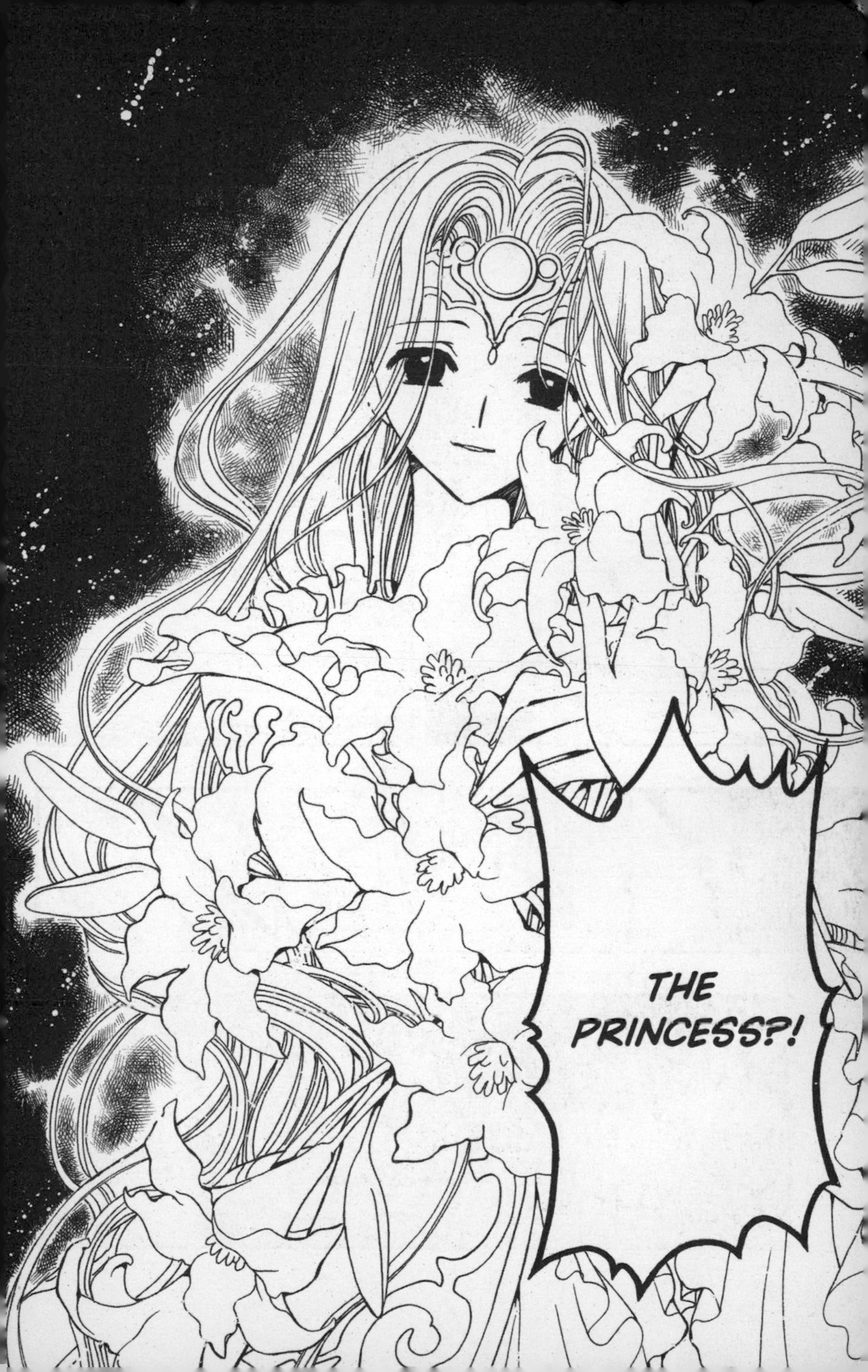
THE PRINCESS?!

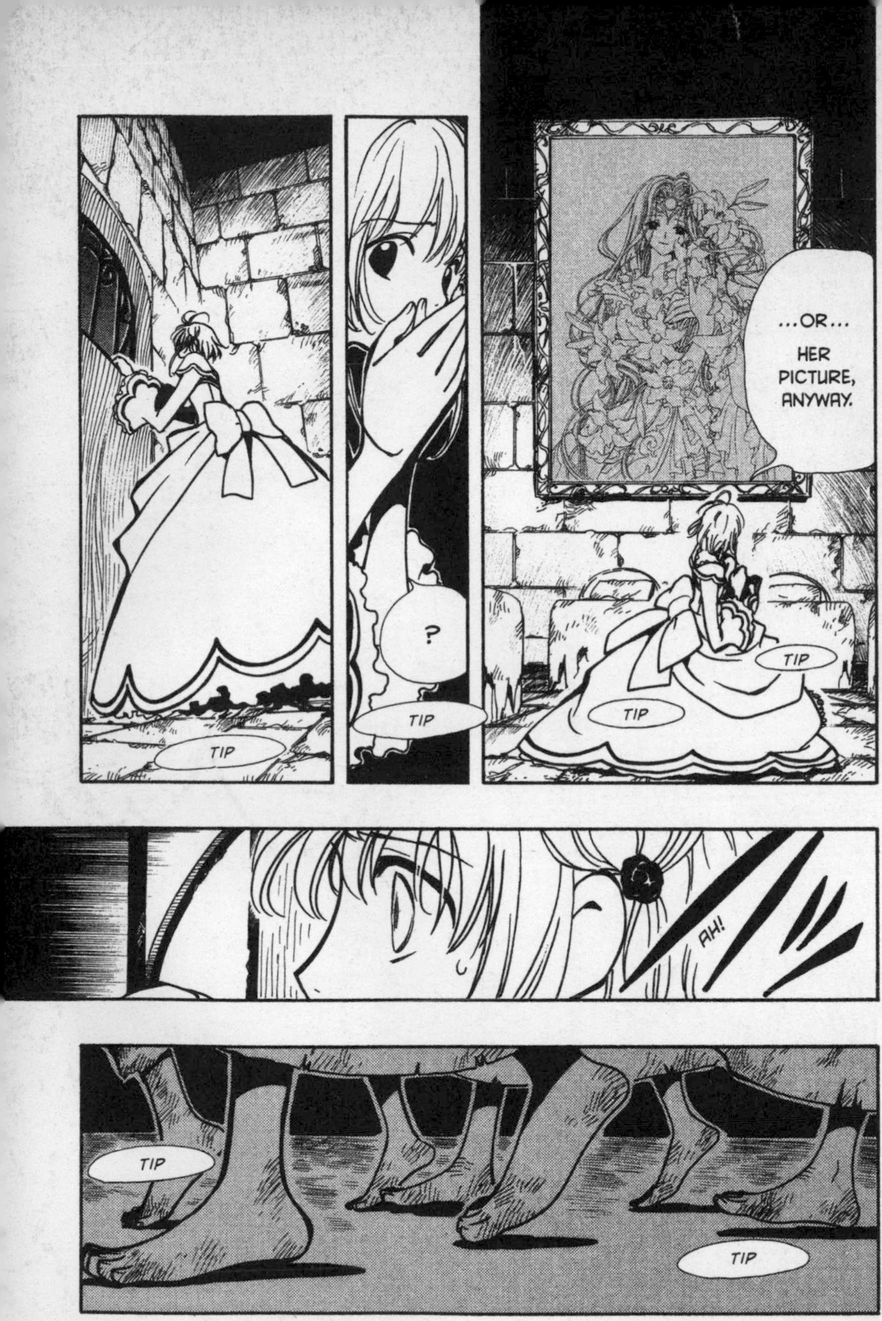
...OR...
HER PICTURE, ANYWAY.
TIP
TIP
?
TIP
TIP
AH!
TIP
TIP

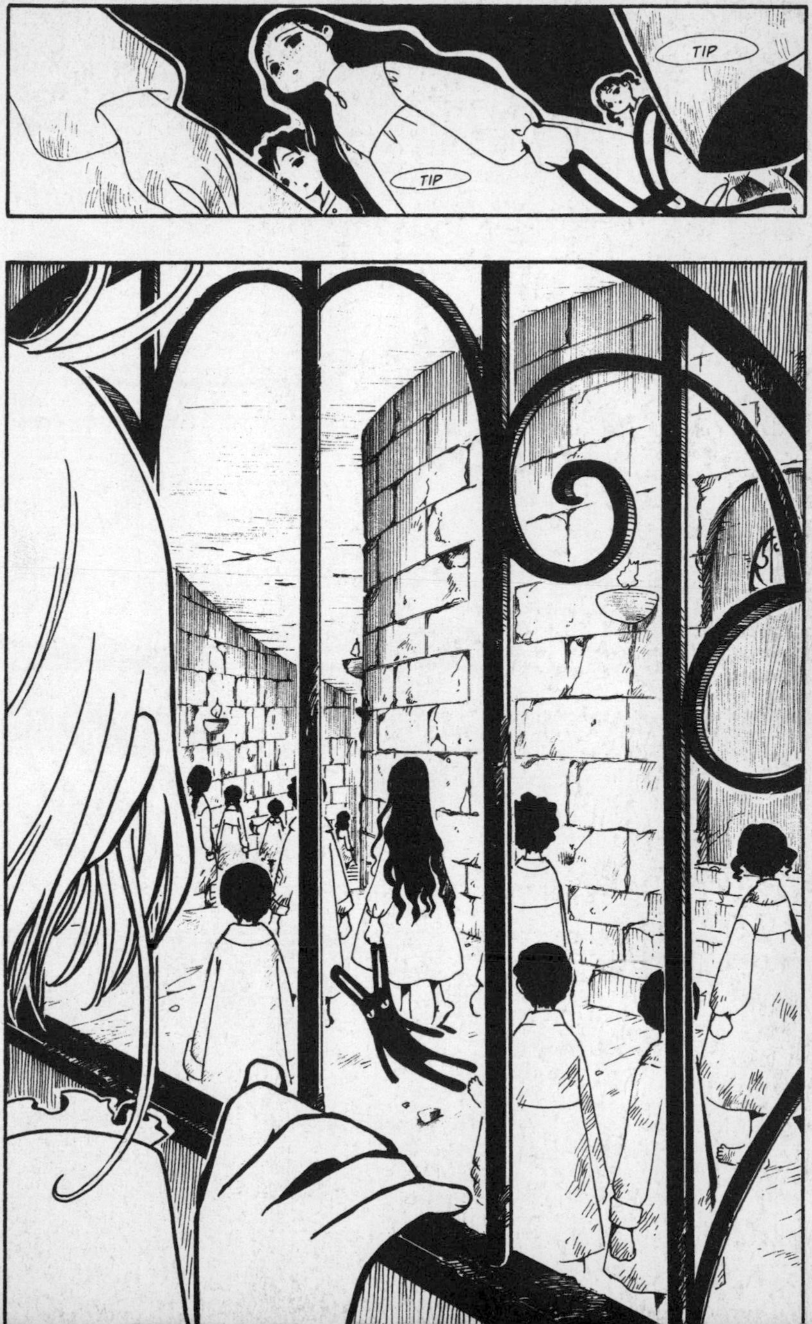
TIP
TIP

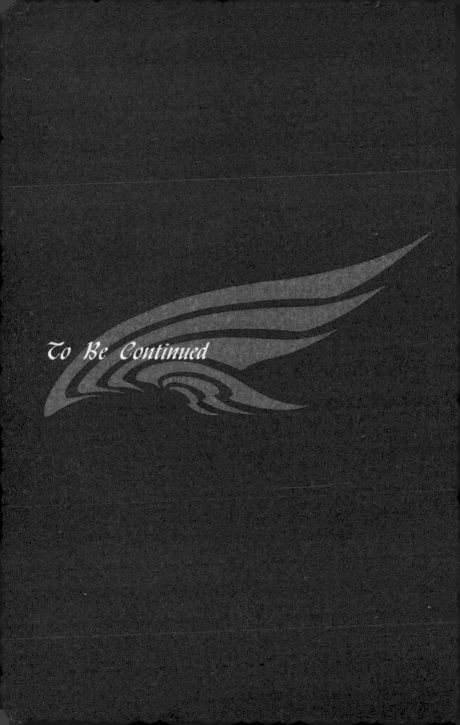

To Be Continued

About the Creators

CLAMP is a group of four women who have become the most popular manga artists in America—Satsuki Igarashi, Tsubaki Nekoi, Mokona, and Ageha Ohkawa. They started out as doujinshi (fan comics) creators, but their skill and craft brought them to the attention of publishers very quickly. Their first work from a major publisher was *RG Veda*, but their first mass success was with *Magic Knight Rayearth*. From there, they went on to write many series, including *Cardcaptor Sakura* and *Chobits*, two of the most popular manga in the United States. Like many Japanese manga artists, they prefer to avoid the spotlight, and little is known about them personally.

CLAMP is currently publishing three series in Japan: *Tsubasa* and *xxxHOLiC* with Kodansha and *Gohou Drug* with Kadokawa.

Translation Notes

Japanese is a tricky language for most Westerners, and translation is often more art than science. For your edification and reading pleasure, here are notes on some of the places where we could have gone in a different direction in our translation of the work, or where a Japanese cultural reference is used.

A glossary of terms from the country of Koryo

Ryanban:	Feudal Lord
Shinban:	Magician/practitioner of the secret arts
Omoni:	Mother
Kiishim:	A magic-using creature that can be summoned by a strong Shinban

Polishing skills, page 5

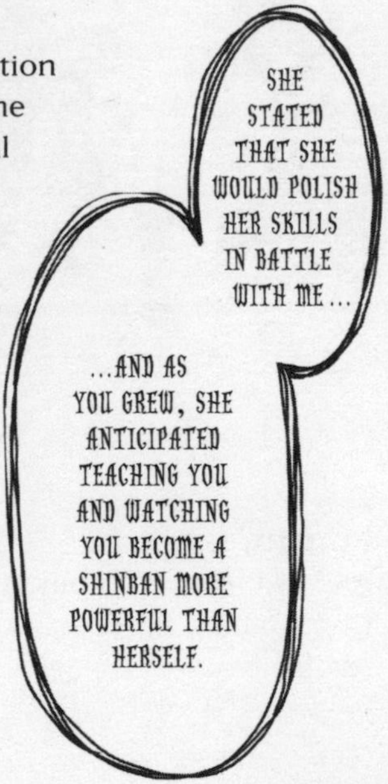
SHE STATED THAT SHE WOULD POLISH HER SKILLS IN BATTLE WITH ME...
...AND AS YOU GREW, SHE ANTICIPATED TEACHING YOU AND WATCHING YOU BECOME A SHINBAN MORE POWERFUL THAN HERSELF.

Polishing one's skills by going into competition against an opponent is fully engrained in the Japanese popular culture. It was an integral part of swordsmanship during the time of the Tokugawa Shogunate, when swordsmen in training would go to swordsmanship schools and challenge the master of each school to a duel. And the tradition continued with martial arts training after the Shogunate fell. Perhaps the biggest book to popularize this phenomenon was *Musashi* by Eiji Yoshikawa, the fictionalized story of Musashi Miyamoto, the accomplished samurai and author of *The Book of Five Rings*. Yoshikawa's book was made into a trilogy of movies known in the west as the Samurai Trilogy.

Maganyan, page 18

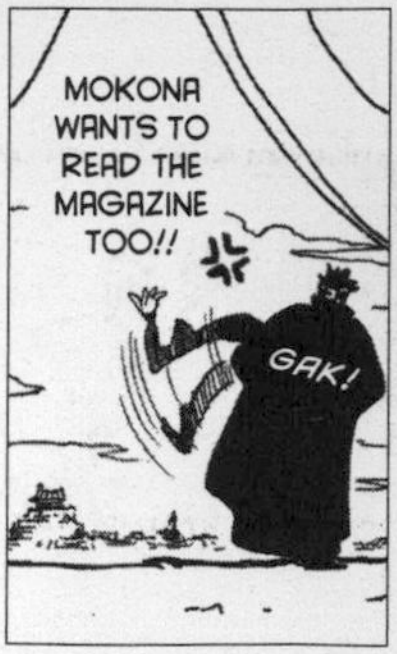
MOKONA WANTS TO READ THE MAGAZINE TOO!!
GAK!

Remember the manga magazine, *Shonen Maganyan,* that Kurogane picked up from Primela's legion of fans in Volume 2? He kept it all through the adventure in Koryo, and he still has it. By the way, *Tsubasa* was originally published in *Shonen Magazine*.

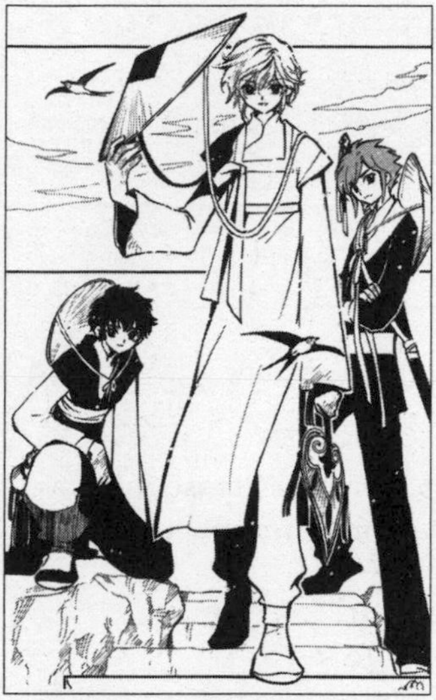

Amen'osa, page 23

Here is another set of characters that have alternate selves in the dimensions of other CLAMP titles. They are Nokoru, Suoh, and Akira, the main characters in CLAMP's light, comic *CLAMP School (Campus) Detectives* manga and anime series. They also make cameos in other CLAMP titles such as *X (X/1999)*. Here, a little older than their appearance in *CLAMP School Detectives,* they are the unnamed members of Amen'osa.

Manju, page 24

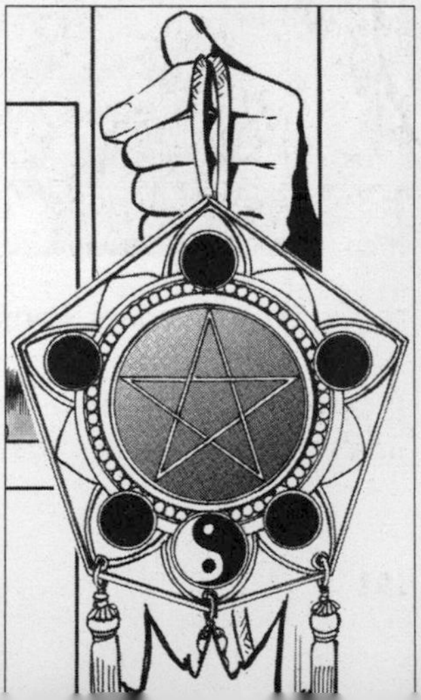

And just like Mito Kômon (see the notes from Volume 3), Amen'osa pulls out the seal!

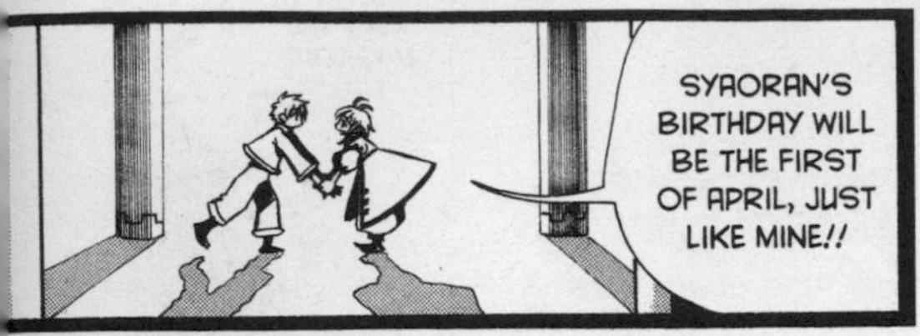
SYAORAN'S BIRTHDAY WILL BE THE FIRST OF APRIL, JUST LIKE MINE!!

The first of April, page 40

xxxHOLiC fans may recognize Sakura's birthday as the same day on which Kimihiro Watanuki was born.

I'll give it all I have, page 75

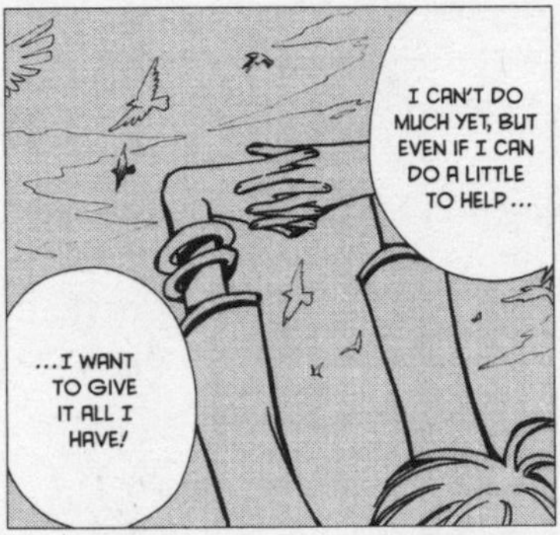
I CAN'T DO MUCH YET, BUT EVEN IF I CAN DO A LITTLE TO HELP...
...I WANT TO GIVE IT ALL I HAVE!

Of course Sakura is sincere in her statement, but what you see in this scene is very common when a new member joins a group. First there is the modest statement saying that one may turn out to be a hindrance, followed with one's commitment to the goals of the group and finally the required *yoroshiku onegaishimasu*, which means literally, "Please think well of me," but can be translated different ways in different contexts.

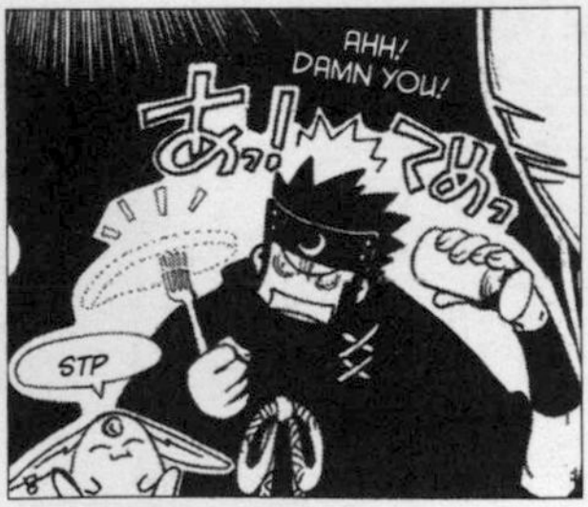
AHH! DAMN YOU!
STP

Kurogane and Western utensils, page 85

Whenever a Westerner goes to Japan and is able to use chopsticks with any effectiveness, someone (usually a waitress) is bound to come over and comment on how *jôzu* ("skillful") the Westerner is. After a while of living in Japan, these compliments can be a little trying for foreigners, considering how necessary the skill of using chopsticks is to daily life. However, for that stereotype to continue for so long, there must be millions of tourists who come to Japan unable to use Japan's basic dining utensils. So for someone who

was an ex-pat in Japan, to see Kurogane's inability to use a knife and fork is a delightful reversal.

Country with four seasons, page 99

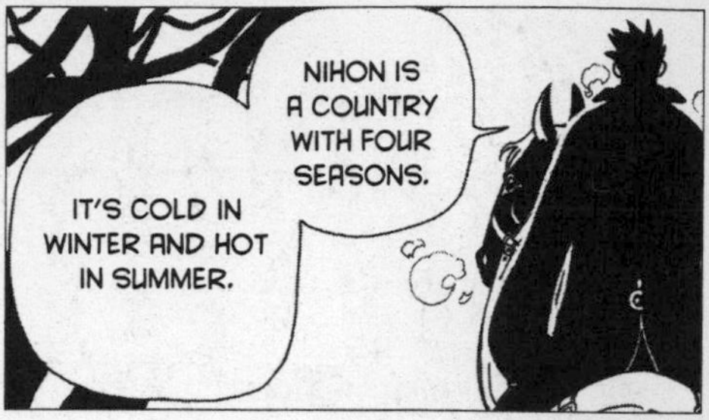
NIHON IS A COUNTRY WITH FOUR SEASONS.
IT'S COLD IN WINTER AND HOT IN SUMMER.

If you remember in Volume 1, Sorata characterized the Hanshin Republic as being a land with four seasons as well. As anyone who has spent more than one season in Japan can attest, the turn of the seasons is immensely important to the Japanese people, and there are a great many traditions attached to each season. Perhaps only the characterization of "island nation" is more important to Japan's image of itself.

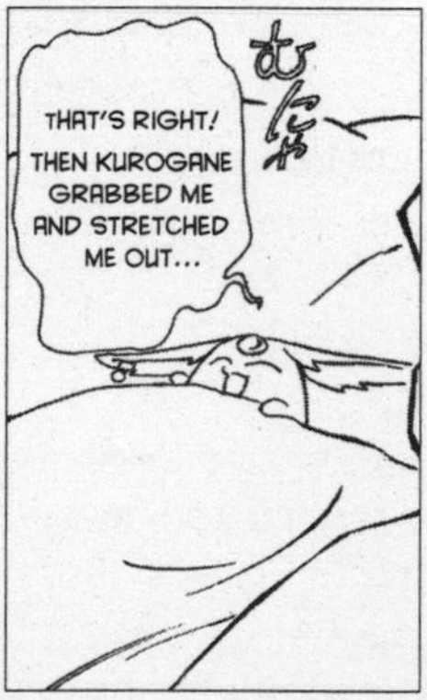
THAT'S RIGHT! THEN KUROGANE GRABBED ME AND STRETCHED ME OUT...

White Mokona, page 119

Mokona is, of course, talking to the Black Mokona character of *xxxHOLiC*.

Preview of Volume 5

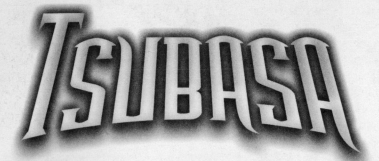

CLAMP

Here is an excerpt from Volume 5, on sale now in English.

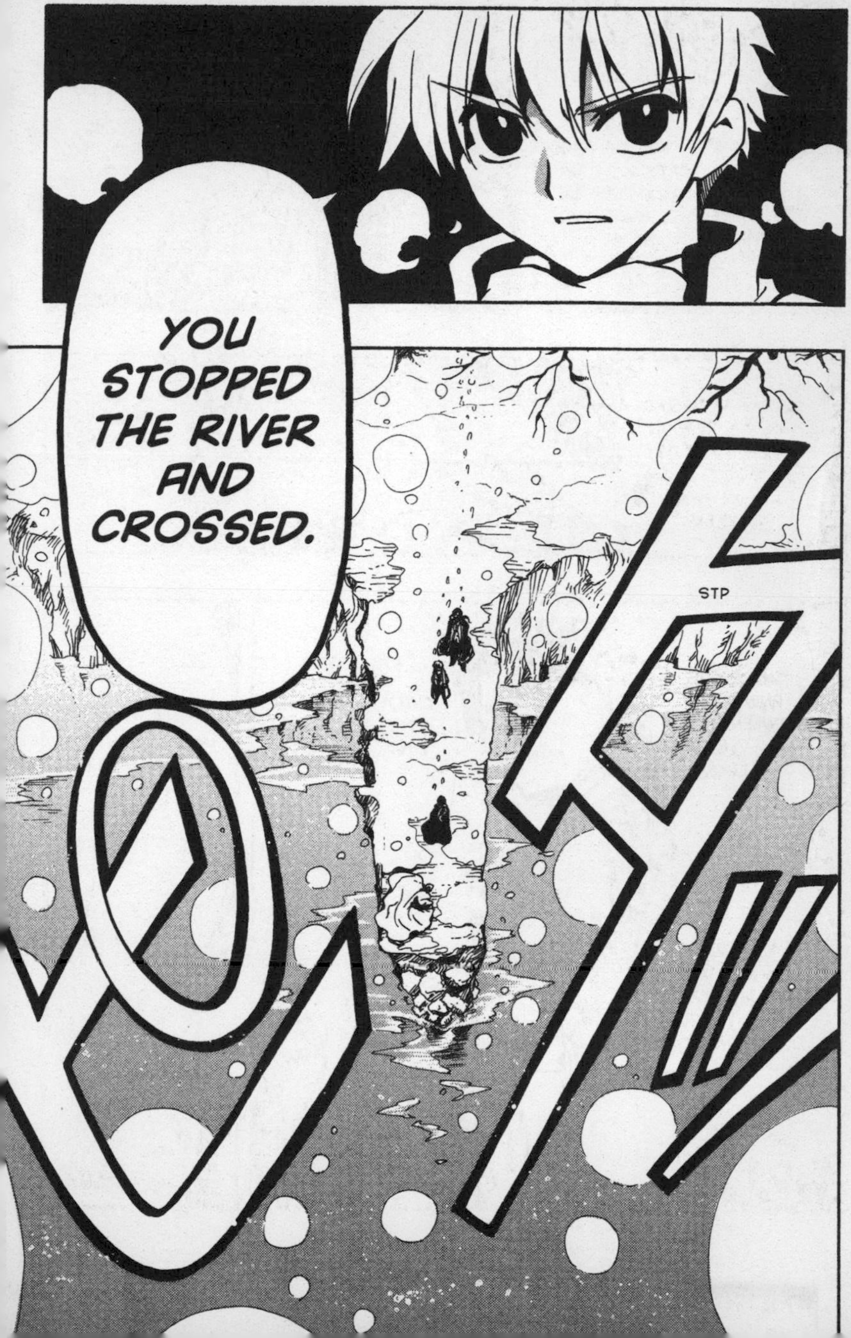
YOU STOPPED THE RIVER AND CROSSED.
STP

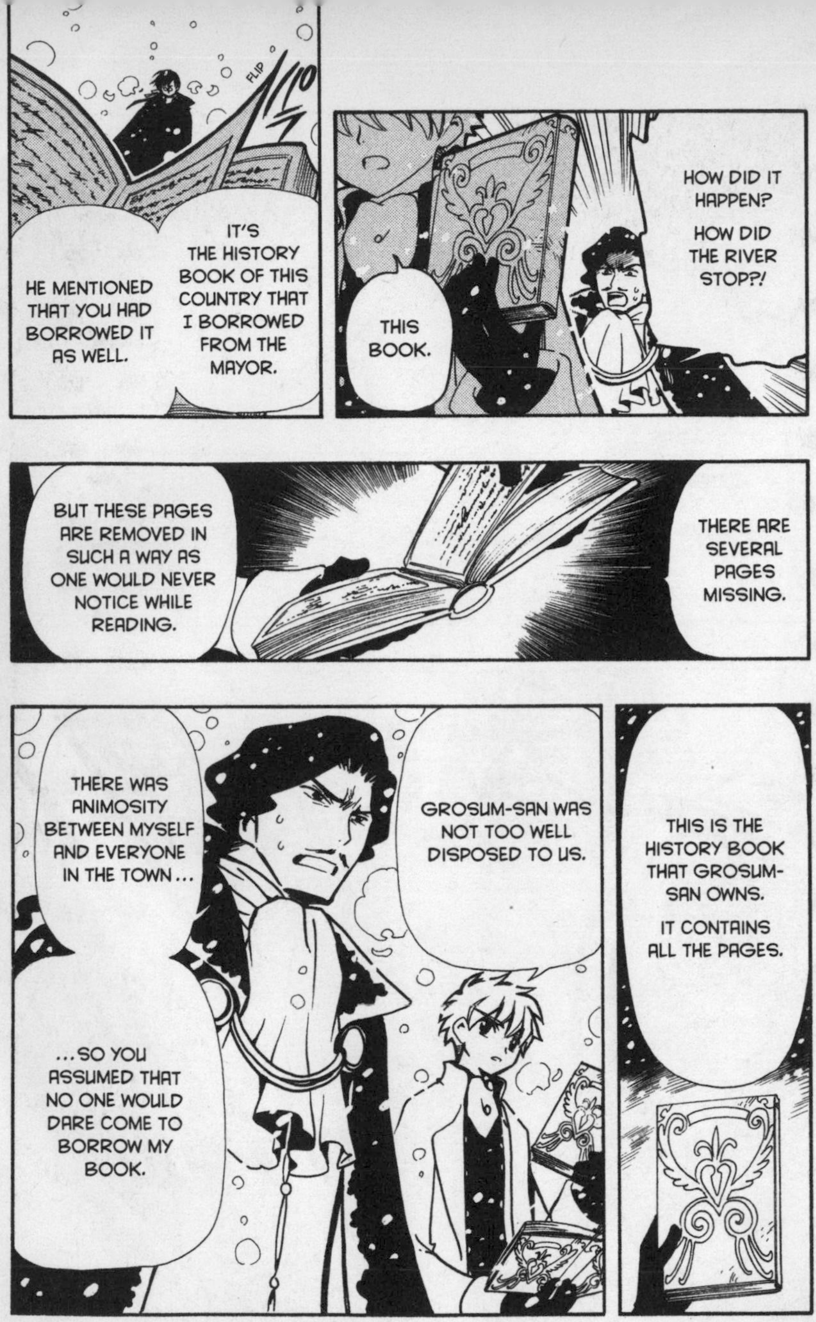
HOW DID IT HAPPEN?
HOW DID THE RIVER STOP?!
THIS BOOK.
FLIP
IT'S THE HISTORY BOOK OF THIS COUNTRY THAT I BORROWED FROM THE MAYOR.
HE MENTIONED THAT YOU HAD BORROWED IT AS WELL.
THERE ARE SEVERAL PAGES MISSING.
BUT THESE PAGES ARE REMOVED IN SUCH A WAY AS ONE WOULD NEVER NOTICE WHILE READING.
THIS IS THE HISTORY BOOK THAT GROSUM-SAN OWNS.
IT CONTAINS ALL THE PAGES.
GROSUM-SAN WAS NOT TOO WELL DISPOSED TO US.
THERE WAS ANIMOSITY BETWEEN MYSELF AND EVERYONE IN THE TOWN...
...SO YOU ASSUMED THAT NO ONE WOULD DARE COME TO BORROW MY BOOK.

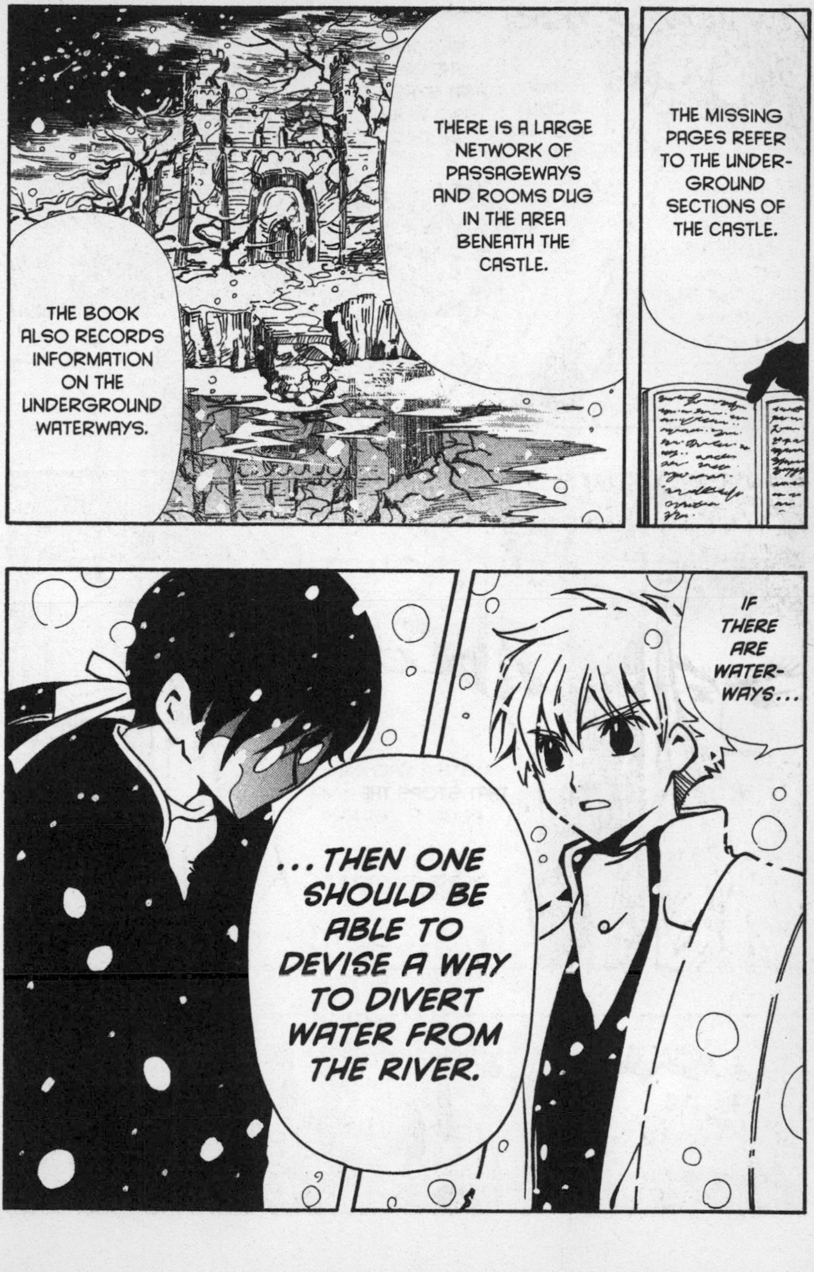
THE MISSING PAGES REFER TO THE UNDER-GROUND SECTIONS OF THE CASTLE.
THERE IS A LARGE NETWORK OF PASSAGEWAYS AND ROOMS DUG IN THE AREA BENEATH THE CASTLE.
THE BOOK ALSO RECORDS INFORMATION ON THE UNDERGROUND WATERWAYS.
IF THERE ARE WATER-WAYS...
...THEN ONE SHOULD BE ABLE TO DEVISE A WAY TO DIVERT WATER FROM THE RIVER.

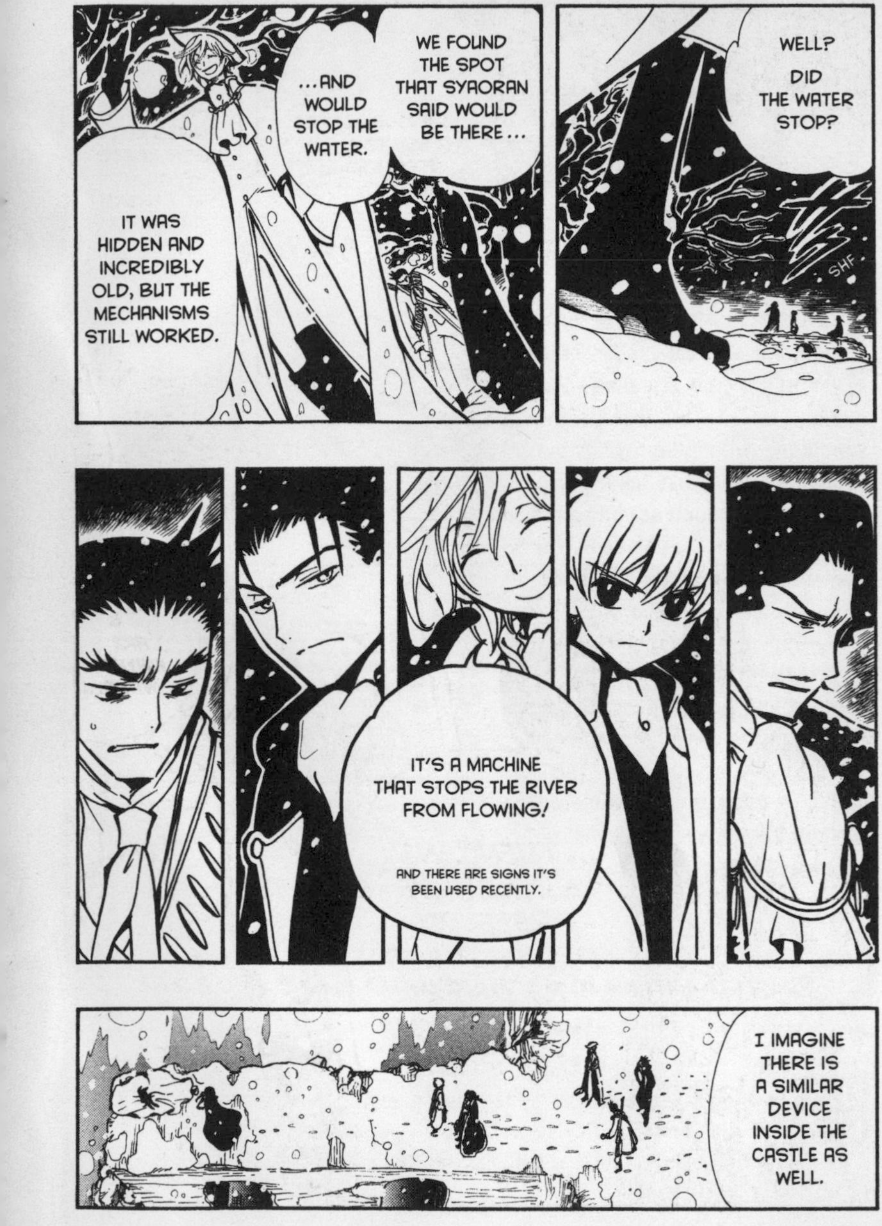
WELL? DID THE WATER STOP?
SHF
WE FOUND THE SPOT THAT SYAORAN SAID WOULD BE THERE...
...AND WOULD STOP THE WATER.
IT WAS HIDDEN AND INCREDIBLY OLD, BUT THE MECHANISMS STILL WORKED.
IT'S A MACHINE THAT STOPS THE RIVER FROM FLOWING!
AND THERE ARE SIGNS IT'S BEEN USED RECENTLY.
I IMAGINE THERE IS A SIMILAR DEVICE INSIDE THE CASTLE AS WELL.

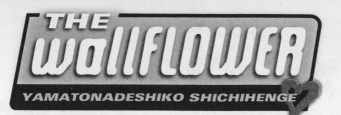

THE WALLFLOWER
YAMATONADESHIKO SHICHIHENGE

BY TOMOKO HAYAKAWA

It's a beautiful, expansive mansion, and four handsome, fifteen-year-old friends are allowed to live in it for free! But there is one condition—within three years the young men must take the owner's niece and transform her into a proper lady befitting the palace in which they all live! How hard can it be?

Enter Sunako Nakahara, the horror-movie-loving, pock-faced, frizzy-haired, fashion-illiterate hermit who has a tendency to break into explosive nosebleeds whenever she sees anyone attractive. This project is going to take far more than our four heroes ever expected; it needs a miracle!

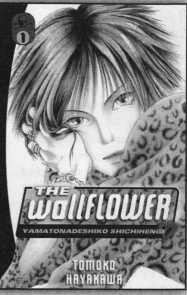

Ages: 16+

Special extras in each volume! Read them all!

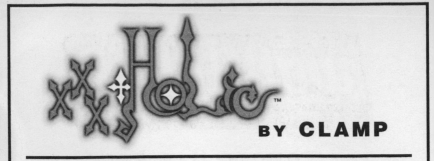

BY CLAMP

Watanuki Kimihiro is haunted by visions. When he finds himself irresistibly drawn into a shop owned by Yûko, a mysterious witch, he is offered the chance to rid himself of the spirits that plague him. He accepts, but soon realizes that he's just been tricked into working for the shop to pay off the cost of Yûko's services! But this isn't any ordinary kind of shop . . . In this shop, Yûko grants wishes to those in need. But they must have the strength of will not only to truly understand their need, but to give up something incredibly precious in return.

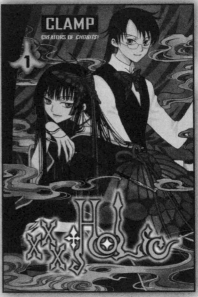

Ages: 13+

Special extras in each volume! Read them all!

VISIT WWW.DELREYMANGA.COM TO:
- View release date calendars for upcoming volumes
- Sign up for Del Rey's free manga e-newsletter
- Find out the latest about new Del Rey Manga series

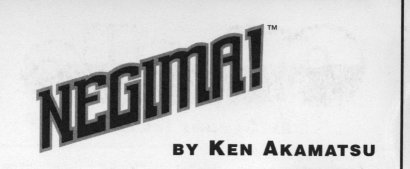

NEGIMA!™

BY KEN AKAMATSU

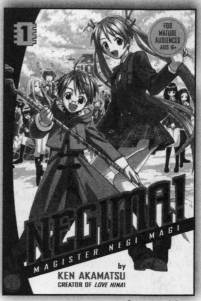

Negi Springfield is a ten-year-old wizard teaching English at an all-girls Japanese school. He dreams of becoming a master wizard like his legendary father, the Thousand Master. At first his biggest concern was concealing his magic powers, because if he's ever caught using them publicly, he thinks he'll be turned into an ermine! But in a world that gets stranger every day, it turns out that the strangest people of all are Negi's students! From a librarian with a magic book to a centuries-old vampire, from a robot to a ninja, Negi will risk his own life to protect the girls in his care!

Ages: 16+

Special extras in each volume! Read them all!

Othello

BY SATOMI IKEZAWA

satomi ikezawa
Othello

Yaya Higuchi has a rough life. Constantly teased and tormented by her classmates, she takes her solace in dressing up as a member of her favorite rock band, Juliet, on the weekends. Things begin to look up for Yaya when a cute classmate befriends her. Her devotion to Juliet, however, eventually just brings her more of the teasing and harassment she gets at school. Unable to cope, Yaya . . . changes. Suddenly, Yaya is gone—and in the blink of an eye, a new personality emerges. She is now Nana and she is tough, confident, and in charge. Nana can do things that Yaya could never do—like beating up the boys and taking care of all of Yaya's problems. How will Yaya live with this new, super-confident alternate personality? Who will be the dominant one, and who is the REAL Yaya?

Ages: 16+

Special extras in each volume! Read them all!

DEL REY

VISIT WWW.DELREYMANGA.COM TO:

- View release date calendars for upcoming volumes
- Sign up for Del Rey's free manga e-newsletter
- Find out the latest about new Del Rey Manga series

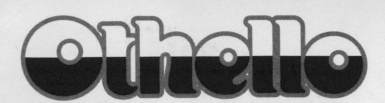

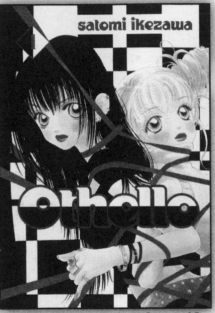

TOMARE!

[STOP!]

You're going the wrong way!

Manga is a completely
different type of reading
experience.

To start at the *beginning*,
go to the *end*!

That's right! Authentic manga is read the traditional Japanese way—from right to left. Exactly the *opposite* of how American books are read. It's easy to follow: Just go to the other end of the book, and read each page—and each panel—from right side to left side, starting at the top right. Now you're experiencing manga as it was meant to be.